THE
RELUCTANT
EMPRESS

BRIGITTE
HAMANN

TRANSLATED FROM THE GERMAN
BY RUTH HEIN

ULLSTEIN

Biography
Ullstein Buchverlage GmbH,
Berlin

Originally published in Germany and Austria
under the title:
Elisabeth: Kaiserin wider Willen
by Amalthea Verlag Vienna; Munich
Copyright © 1982 by Amalthea Verlag,
Vienna and Munich
Translated from the German by Ruth Hein
Translation copyright
© Alfred A. Knopf, Inc. 1986
First published by Alfred A. Knopf,
Inc. New York 1986
This Ullstein ip edition is published by
arrangement with Alfred A. Knopf, Inc.
Published in Germany by Ullstein ip,
a Division of
Verlag Ullstein GmbH, Berlin
All rights reserved
With 69 black-and-white illustrations
Jacket Painting:
Kaiserin Elisabeth in Hofgala mit
Diamantsternen by Franz Xaver Winterhalter.
Courtesy of Archiv für Kunst und Geschichte, Berlin
Jacket Design: HildenDesign, München (according to Theodor Bayer-Eynck)
Printed in Germany by CPI books GmbH, Leck
ISBN 978-3-548-35479-8

15th edition 2022

Die Deutsche Bibliothek – CIP-Einheitsaufnahme
Hamann, Brigittte:
The reluctant empress / Brigitte Hamann.
Transl. from the German by Ruth Hein. –
Berlin : Ullstein, 1998
(Ullstein-Buch ; No. 35479 : Ullstein-IP : Biography)
Einheitssacht.: Elisabeth <engl.>
ISBN 978-3-548-35479-8
NE: GT

CONTENTS

Illustrations follow pages 114 and 210.

PREFACE

This book is the life story of a woman who refused to behave according to her rank. Drawing on remarkable self-confidence, she strove for and achieved the goal that it took the twentieth-century feminist movement to name "self-realization."

She played none of the roles assigned to her by tradition and her surroundings: not the role of loving and devoted wife, not the role of mother, not the role of principal figurehead in a gigantic empire. She insisted on her rights as an individual—and she prevailed. That her self-realization did not make her happy is the tragedy of her life—aside from the tragedies that befell her most immediate family, set in motion by her refusal to be co-opted. Elisabeth, Empress of Austria, Queen of Hungary and Bohemia (to list only her most important titles), was at heart a republican, calling the venerable monarchy the "skeleton of former splendor" and an oak tree that was bound to fall, since it had "outlived its usefulness" (see page 297). She excoriated the excesses of the aristocratic system, and she flouted kings and princes, as she had learned to do from her revered model and "master," Heinrich Heine.

Class consciousness was not in her nature, foreign to her to such a degree that in the end the Empress-Queen seemed an alien outsider at the court of Vienna, an irritant to the court society living by the traditional rules. This effect Elisabeth deliberately cultivated.

On the one hand, as a proponent of democratic ideals, Elisabeth represents an anomaly (even a curiosity); on the other, her example above all illustrates the power of the antimonarchist ideas current in the late nineteenth century. These ideas did not stop short of princes, who were beginning to question the legitimacy of their (inherited rather than earned) elite positions. The remark Count Alexander Hübner entered in his diary on November 18, 1884, was surely true: "It is a fact that no one any longer believes in kings, and I do not know if they believe in themselves." And Elisabeth's friend, the poet Carmen Sylva (Queen Elisabeth of Romania), expressed the same belief even more bluntly: "The republican form of government is the only rational one; I can never understand the foolish people, the fact that they continue to tolerate us" (see page 291).

This attitude gave rise to considerable conflicts in the area of class consciousness. For though the awareness of his "individuality" made the aristocrat who was touched by modern ideas willing to present himself as merely one among many equals (distinguished primarily by the middle-class virtues of "accomplishment" and "culture"), only too often he would have to recognize that he could not hold his own in the competition (at least not to an extent due his noble origins)—that his individual worth did not, therefore, coincide with his special social standing; these nobles understood that in the last resort they would leave nothing behind but a title they had not earned and a function whose value they did not acknowledge. This was the tragedy of Empress Elisabeth, as it was of her son, Rudolf.

Elisabeth's life is full of grim, even desperate efforts to gain recognition as an individual. Her first and most successful struggle was to be beautiful. The legendary beauty of Empress Elisabeth was in no way merely a gift of nature; it was also the result of rigorous self-control and lifelong discipline, which in the end became physical torment. In similar fashion she earned her reputation as an outstanding sportswoman, the top woman rider in hunts all over Europe during the 1870s. This was a form of fame that, like the fame of her beauty, could not but wane with increasing age, in spite of all her self-discipline. Her highest hopes for wresting renown from posterity lay in another direction: she would be known as an inspired poet. The evidence of her efforts—poems, hitherto unknown, covering more than five hundred pages, all written in the 1880s—forms the basis of the present study. These lines provide Elisabeth's most intimate and personal statements about herself, about the world around her, and about her times. But they also clearly show her failure; for the poems in no way justify Elisabeth's hope for posthumous fame. The lines are interesting not for their literary worth (the dilettantism of the Heine imitation is hard to ignore or gloss over); rather, as the work of an empress and queen, they furnish us with source material for the history of the Habsburg monarchy as well as the intellectual history of an enlightened aristocrat, a cultured woman of the nineteenth century. Finally, Elisabeth's poetry serves to illustrate the "nervous century," with an emotional life often transcending the limits of reality.

I am deeply grateful to the Swiss federal government and the directors of the Swiss Federal Archives in Bern for granting me permission for the first perusal of these sources, which were kept under strictest secrecy until now. Our friend Dr. Prof. Jean-Rudolf von Salis graciously used his good offices to secure this permission. The circumstance that the Empress entrusted what she believed to be her most valuable possession, her literary bequest, to a republic (though the one she considered the prototype and ideal) best characterizes her attitude to the Austro-Hungarian monarchy as well as to the House of Habsburg.

Besides the Empress's literary estate, I worked through still other new sources, such as the documents referring to Elisabeth in the archives of Archduke Albrecht (Hungarian State Archives, Budapest); Privy Councillor Baron Adolf von Braun (Imperial Haus- , Hof- und Staatsarchiv, Vienna); the Imperial Adjutant General Count Karl Grünne (in private hands).

Additional sources include the diaries of Archduchess Sophie (with kind permission of Dr. Otto von Habsburg) and of Prince Karl Khevenhüller (with kind permission of Prince Max von Khevenhüller-Metsch).

I am also indebted to the estate of the archivist and historian Richard Sexau of Munich for a vast amount of new material. Sexau made detailed and reliable copies of sources in private hands which were unfortunately not available to me in the original. The most valuable among these are the diary of the Emperor's younger daughter, Archduchess Marie Valerie, and the diary of Elisabeth's niece, Duchess Amélie von Urach, as well as the extensive correspondence of the Empress's mother, mother-in-law, and aunts to and from each other.

Valuable notes on conversations with Countess Marie Festetics, one of Elisabeth's ladies-in-waiting, were made available to me in the papers of the historian Heinrich Friedjung (State Library, Vienna, Manuscript Division).

I found several though widely scattered source copies (especially of Elisabeth's letters to her husband, to her daughter Marie Valerie, and to her mother, Duchess Ludovika) among the papers of Egon Caesar Conte Corti (Haus-, Hof- und Staatsarchiv, Vienna). However, whenever I worked with sources earlier cited by Corti, I made use of the originals. Without exception, my opinion of what passages were worth quoting differed from Corti's—though I do not mean even by implication to diminish his merits in interpreting primary sources. It is precisely to this renewed perusal of the following original sources that I owe many new insights: diary of Countess Marie Festetics (Széchenyi Library, Budapest); diary of Count Alexander Hübner (Historical Institute of the University of Padua); estate of the Imperial Adjutant General Count Franz Folliot de Crenneville (Haus-, Hof- und Staatsarchiv, Vienna); estate of Landgravine Therese Fürstenberg (Fürstenberg Family Archives, Veitra, with kind permission of Prince and Landgrave Johannes von und zu Fürstenberg).

Of course I made use of the diplomatic correspondence, insofar as it concerns the Empress, in the Haus-, Hof- und Staatsarchiv, Vienna; in the Swiss Federal Archives, Bern; and in the Federal Archives, Bonn. Another rich lode was furnished by the contemporary newspapers preserved in the Periodicals Division of the Austrian National Library.

The days of the Court Circular are gone—every bit as much as are the days of disparaging the Old Monarchy. I feel committed to the scholarly quest for truth, and in this search I consider the figure of the Empress Elisabeth—with all her problems, but also with her surprisingly modern, never ordinary peculiarities—typical of the final days of the Austro-Hungarian monarchy. The levelheaded and dutiful "official," Emperor Franz Joseph, and the unorthodox, highly intelligent, dreamy Empress Elisabeth—these two were like plus and minus, like day and night: opposites that nevertheless affected each other, each one the other's misfortune. A private tragedy at the end of a dying empire at the close of a century.

BRIGITTE HAMANN

CHRONOLOGY

So as to be able to develop the most important themes, I have occasionally abandoned strict chronological order, preferring to summarize the ample available material by subject. The most significant dates are therefore placed at the beginning to make it easier for readers to get their bearings.

August 18, 1830	Franz Joseph born in Vienna
December 24, 1837	Elisabeth born in Munich
December 2, 1848	Emperor Franz Joseph's accession to the throne
1849	Subjugation of Hungary with Russian military aid
July 1853 to	Crimean War. Consequences: Russia loses her
March 18, 1853	preeminence in Europe to France; enmity between Austria and Russia
August 18, 1853	Engagement in Bad Ischl
April 24, 1854	Wedding in the Augustinerkirche, Vienna
March 5, 1855	Birth of Archduchess Sophie (d. 1857)
July 15, 1856	Birth of Archduchess Gisela
August 21, 1858	Birth of Crown Prince Rudolf
June 1859	Austria wages war against Sardinia and France; Austria is defeated at Magenta and retreats from Solferino
November 1859	Peace of Zurich; Austria loses Lombardy
February 1861	The King and Queen of the Two Sicilies flee from Naples to Rome
March 1861	Victor Emmanuel assumes the title of King of Italy
September 1862	Bismarck becomes Prussian Minister-President
August 1863	Congress of German Princes, Frankfurt
April 1864	Archduke Ferdinand Maximilian accepts the imperial crown of Mexico
1864	The Danish War over Schleswig-Holstein, with Austria and Prussia fighting together
June–July 1866	War between Austria and Prussia; defeat of

	Königgrätz on July 3, 1866. War between Austria and Italy; victories of Custozza and Lissa
August 1866	Peace of Prague; dissolution of the German Confederation. No territorial losses of Austria to Prussia; loss of Venetia to Italy.
1867–1871	Beust serves as prime minister and chancellor
June 8, 1867	Franz Joseph crowned King of Hungary
June 19, 1867	Emperor Ferdinand Maximilian of Mexico executed
August 1867	Franz Joseph and Napoleon III meet in Salzburg
April 22, 1868	Birth of Archduchess Marie Valerie
1870–1871	Franco-Prussian War; France becomes a republic; the German Empire is created
1871–1879	Andrássy serves as imperial and royal foreign minister
May 27, 1872	Death of Archduchess Sophie
1873	World Exhibition, Vienna
1875	Death of Emperor Ferdinand I; Franz Joseph is his principal heir
1878	Occupation of the Turkish provinces of Bosnia and Hercegovina
October 1879	Conclusion of the Dual Alliance between Germany and Austria
1879–1893	Eduard Taaffe serves as prime minister
1881	Marriage of Crown Prince Rudolf and Stephanie of Belgium
May 1882	Triple Alliance among Germany, Austria, and Italy
June 13, 1886	Death of Ludwig II of Bavaria
June 1888	Wilhelm II succeeds to the German throne
January 30, 1889	Suicide of the Crown Prince at Mayerling
February 18, 1890	Death of Gyula Andrássy
July 1890	Wedding of Marie Valerie and Archduke Franz Salvator of Tuscany
1897	Badeni crisis, with dangerous ethnic riots
September 10, 1898	Assassination of Empress Elisabeth in Geneva
November 21, 1916	Death of Emperor Franz Joseph in Vienna

THE RELUCTANT EMPRESS

CHAPTER ONE

ENGAGEMENT IN BAD ISCHL

On Thursday, August 18, 1853—the twenty-third birthday of Emperor Franz Joseph I—a fifteen-year-old girl from provincial Possenhofen in Bavaria took her place in Austrian history. It was on that day that the Emperor asked for the hand of his cousin, Duchess Elisabeth of Bavaria. To no one's surprise, he was accepted.

Until that moment nothing had occurred to call the bride to anyone's notice. She was a shy young thing, only just past childhood, a long way from being fully developed. She was remarkably slender, with long dark-blond braids and light-brown eyes with a melancholy cast. She had grown up a child of nature, among seven high-spirited brothers and sisters, far from all the pressures of court life. She excelled at horseback riding, swimming, fishing, mountain climbing. She loved her home, especially the

Bavarian hills and Lake Starnberg, on whose shores stood the small castle of Possenhofen, the family summer residence. Elisabeth spoke Bavarian dialect, and her playmates were the children of the local peasantry. Her upbringing and manners left a good deal to be desired. Like her father and her brothers and sisters, she set little store by ceremony and protocol—which did not matter much at the Munich court. Since the ducal branch of the Wittelsbachs had no official function at court in any case, the family could afford to indulge in a colorful private life.

Elisabeth's mother, Duchess Ludovika, had for some time been searching for a suitable match for Elisabeth, her second daughter. She had already made cautious and not very confident inquiries in Saxony. "I would certainly consider it a great happiness to think of Sisi as one of you . . . but alas, it is not likely to happen—for the only one who could be hoped for [presumably Prince Georg, second son of Johann, King of Saxony] is unlikely to consider her; first, I seriously question whether he would find her attractive, and then, he is surely looking for a fortune . . . true, she's pretty because she is very young and animated, but she has no single pretty feature."[1] When Sisi returned from Dresden in the spring of 1853, it was without a groom.

She stood completely in the shadow of her older sister, Helene, who was much more beautiful, better educated, more serious, and more widely admired; Helene was intended for a higher destiny—marriage to the Emperor of Austria. Compared to the older daughter, Sisi was the family ugly duckling. The fact that it was little Elisabeth who made the most brilliant match of the nineteenth century surprised no one more than herself.

The groom, Emperor Franz Joseph, was an exceptionally good-looking young man, with blond hair, soft features, and a very delicate, slender figure, flatteringly emphasized by the close-fitting general's uniform he habitually wore. No wonder that he was the idol of all the Viennese countesses, all the more as he proved himself a passionate and spirited dancer at the balls of the high nobility.

This charming youngster with the exceptional good manners was one of the most powerful men of his day. His complete title was: Franz Joseph I, by the grace of God Emperor of Austria; King of Hungary and Bohemia; King of Lombardy and Venice, of Dalmatia, Croatia, Slavonia, Galicia, Lodomeria, and Illyria; King of Jerusalem, etc.; Archduke of Austria; Grand Duke of Tuscany and Cracow; Duke of Lorraine, of Salzburg, Styria, Carinthia, Carniola, and Bukovina; Grand Duke of Transylvania,

Margrave of Moravia; Duke of Upper and Lower Silesia, of Modena, Parma, Piacenza, and Guastalla, of Auschwitz and Zator, of Teschen, Friuli, Ragusa, and Zara; Count with Princely Rank of Habsburg and Tyrol, of Kyburg, Gorizia, and Gradiska; Prince of Trent and Bressanone; Margrave of Upper and Lower Lusatia and in Istria; Count of Hohenembs, Feldkirch, Bregenz, Sonnenberg, etc.; Lord of Trieste, of Cattaro, and in the Wendic Mark; Grand Voivode of the Voivodeship of Serbia, etc., etc.

In 1848, the year of the Revolution, the eighteen-year-old Franz Joseph ascended to the throne after his feebleminded uncle, Emperor Ferdinand I, abdicated and his father, the weak-willed Archduke Franz Karl, renounced the succession. After the pitiful figure cut by his predecessor, the young Emperor very quickly won popular favor.

Franz Joseph was an absolute monarch: He was commander in chief, and he governed without parliament or constitution, even without a prime minister. His ministers were no more than advisers to their ruler, who alone was responsible for policy. It is probably not wrong to call the young Emperor head of a military monarchy—"by the grace of God," of course.

Franz Joseph governed his lands by wielding the power of the army and the police, suppressing the democratic and nationalist forces. The old joke of the Metternich period was also applicable to the years of Franz Joseph's reign: The government was reinforced by a standing army of soldiers, a sitting army of bureaucrats, a kneeling army of priests, and a creeping army of informers.

In 1853, Austria was the largest state in Europe with the exception of Russia. It had roughly 40 million inhabitants, not including the 600,000 soldiers. The multiethnic state consisted of 8.5 million Germans, 16 million Slavs, 6 million Italians, 5 million Magyars, 2.7 million Romanians, about a million Jews, and around 100,000 gypsies. The northernmost point of the empire was Hilgersdorf in northern Bohemia (today's Czechoslovakia); the southernmost, Mount Ostrawizza in Dalmatia (today's Yugoslavia); the westernmost, near Rocca d'Angera on Lake Maggiore in Lombardy (now Italy); and the farthest east, near Chilischeny in the Bukovina (now in the Soviet Union).[2]

Most of the monarchy's subjects (29 million) made their living from agriculture, the country's primary source of income. Austria was a world leader in the cultivation of flax and hemp and second only to France in wine growing. Farming and cattle raising were still carried on in conformity with centuries-old customs. Technical progress lagged far behind that of Western nations.

Thanks to brilliant generals, Austria came through the Revolution of

1848 without territorial losses. The Constituent Assembly at Kremsier, a gathering of the intellectual elite of "Forty-Eighters," was dispersed by force of arms. Many of the delegates were able to escape abroad, many others crowded the prisons. The young Emperor broke his own solemn promise to give the country a constitution at long last.

But in spite of the continuing state of siege and strong military force, signal fires flickered on the political horizon as late as 1853, first and foremost in Hungary and Northern Italy. At the beginning of February, the Italian revolutionary leader Giuseppe Mazzini tried to instigate a popular uprising in Milan. During Carnival, Italian nationalists, armed with daggers, attacked Austrian soldiers. Ten Austrians were killed, fifty-nine were wounded. Some were skewered alive to house doors with long nails—a warning to the central government in Vienna. The rebellion was suppressed within a few hours, sixteen Italians were executed, and another forty-eight were given harsh prison sentences "in irons."

Equally deceptive was the calm that reigned in Vienna: At the time of the Milanese troubles, a serious attempt was made on the life of the young Emperor. While Franz Joseph was walking on the Bastei—the original city fortifications—one Johann Libényi, a Hungarian journeyman tailor, stabbed him through the neck with a daggerlike knife; the Emperor was seriously wounded. Even in this situation Franz Joseph showed his unusual coolheadedness and bravery. His first words to his mother were "Now I am wounded along with my soldiers, I like that."[3]

Libényi considered his crime a principled political act; when he was apprehended, he shouted, "*Eljen* Kossuth!" He thus saluted the Habsburgs' archenemy, the Hungarian revolutionary who had proclaimed the Hungarian Republic in 1849 and who was now, in exile, urging the secession of Hungary from Austria.

Libényi was executed. But his deed could not but serve as a warning to the young Emperor that his throne was not founded as firmly as it seemed.

While the Emperor's awareness of his position kept him remote from most people, he had an extremely close and intimate relationship with the one person whose authority he respected: his mother, Archduchess Sophie.

Sophie, a nineteen-year-old Bavarian princess, had arrived at the court in Vienna in 1824, at a time when Metternich ruled the nation. Emperor Franz was old; Ferdinand, his first son and successor, was sickly and feebleminded. The young ambitious Princess with a flair for politics found a vacuum at the Viennese court; it was not long before her strong personality filled it completely. Even Metternich soon learned that she was a factor to be reckoned with. Sophie was said to be the only man at this court swarming with weaklings. It was she who energetically contributed to Metternich's fall in 1848. It was her accusation "that he wanted an impossible thing: to rule the monarchy without an emperor and with a numbskull as the representative of the crown,"[4] by which she meant her feebleminded and epileptic brother-in-law, Emperor Ferdinand "the Kindly." Sophie also deterred her husband from assuming the succession—thus relinquishing her chance to become empress and to govern through her husband, who was wholly devoted to her. She was the guiding force behind the accession to the throne of her "Franzi" in December 1848 at Olmütz. Her maternal pride was boundless.

For the rest of his life Franz Joseph was grateful to his mother for her services. He let himself be guided by her sure hand, even if Sophie earnestly declared that "at my son's accession to the throne, I firmly resolved not to interfere in any matters of state; I felt I had no right, and I also know them to be in such good hands after a thirteen-year period without a ruler —that I am happy with all my heart, after the hard-fought year '48, to be able to sit by and observe current policy calmly and with confidence!"[5]

Sophie did not keep her good resolutions. The merciless and bloody sentences handed out to the revolutionaries, the wrongful abrogation of the promised (and, briefly, realized) constitution, the close ties Austria maintained with the church, culminating in the Concordat of 1855—all these were seen by the people, not as the decisions of the diffident young Emperor, but as the work of Archduchess Sophie, who was Austria's covert empress during the 1850s.

That Sophie would give serious thought to her son's future consort— and by no means solely out of concern for the young Emperor's heart, but more particularly with an eye to political considerations—was only natural. After the Revolution of 1848, Austria's policies clearly had Germany in view: The nation strove to remain the leading power in the German Confederation—or, more precisely, to recover and assert its diminishing power against Prussia. It was Sophie's idea to move closer to achieving this major objective—which was in direct conflict with Prussia's notion—by means of a political marriage.

There was much talk at court of an alliance between the Emperor and Archduchess Elisabeth from the Hungarian line of the House of Habsburg.[6] This plan, however, had no chance of succeeding in the face of Sophie's strong aversion to anything that came from Hungary. She definitely preferred a German connection. First she set her sights on the House of Hohenzollern as a way to improve the problematic relations between Austria and Prussia and to secure again Austria's dominance in Germany. To gain this political end, she would even have put up with a Protestant daughter-in-law, provided only that she convert before the marriage.

So, in the winter of 1852, the young Emperor—naturally under the pretext of political and family occasions—traveled to Berlin and promptly fell in love with a niece of the Prussian King, Princess Anna, who was his own age. Of course, the young woman was already engaged; but Sophie was not one to give up easily. She asked her sister Queen Elise of Prussia "whether there is any hope that this sad marriage, which they are imposing on this charming Anna and which leaves her with no prospect of happiness whatsoever, could be prevented." Sophie wrote frankly how much the young Emperor was already smitten. She mentioned the

> happiness that showed itself to him like a fleeting dream and made an impression on his heart—hélas—much stronger and deeper than I had at first thought. . . . You know him well enough [to know] that it is not so easy to satisfy his taste and that he is not content with the first pretty face that comes his way, that he must be able to love the creature who is to become his companion, that she please him, that he have a liking for her. Your dear little girl seems to fulfill all these requirements, judge for yourself, then, how greatly I wish to have her for a son who is so much in need of happiness after having had to renounce so soon the freedom from care and the illusions of youth.[7]

Queen Elise could not win against the Prussian statesmen. An alliance by marriage with Austria had no place in the Prussian calculations. The young Emperor had to swallow a personal defeat; in addition, his visit to Berlin was interpreted in terms that were far from flattering, as illustrated in the remark by Prince Wilhelm, the subsequent Emperor Wilhelm I: "We in Prussia congratulate ourselves on the fact that Austria has testified to its submission in our capital without our having surrendered so much as a foot of political ground."[8]

Sophie's preliminary efforts to achieve a suitable marriage for the Emperor that would at the same time strengthen Austrian influence in Germany next turned to Dresden. This time the object was young Princess Sidonie of Saxony, even though she was sickly and did not appeal to the Emperor.

The tenacity with which Sophie clung to her intention to pluck a German princess for the Viennese court is evident in her third plan, hatched with her sister, Duchess Ludovika of Bavaria. Ludovika's oldest daughter, Helene, was the right age for the Emperor, even if she constituted a far less distinguished match than the first two young ladies. After all, she was descended merely from a collateral Bavarian line—not, like Sophie, directly from the Bavarian royal house. Nevertheless, next to Saxony, Bavaria was Austria's most loyal partner in the German Confederation; an additional connection between Austria and Bavaria had clear political advantages.

In the past, there had been no fewer than twenty-one alliances between the Bavarian and the Austrian families. The most prominent marriage in recent years had been that of Emperor Franz to Karoline Auguste, Sophie's oldest sister. (By her marriage to Archduke Franz Karl, Emperor Franz's son from his first marriage, Sophie became her sister's daughter-in-law.)

Duchess Ludovika was something like her powerful sister's poor relation. She was the only one of the nine daughters of the Bavarian King Max I to have made merely a modest match, marrying her second cousin, Duke Maximilian of Bavaria, who did not receive the title of Royal Highness until 1845. The marriage was an unhappy one, but it resulted in eight beautiful though extremely demanding children.

Ludovika loved her sister Sophie—older by three years—in a submissive, even servile way, holding her up constantly to her children as a model, following her advice anxiously, all in order to remain in Sophie's good graces. The prospect of marrying off her daughter to the most eligible bachelor of the day was the final touch, turning her into the unquestioning and compliant handmaiden of her forceful sister.

The two women had little in common. By the time of the engagement in Bad Ischl, she had been completely "countrified," Ludovika reported later. She loved the countryside and unspoiled nature, paying little heed to the dress and society proper to her rank. Ludovika was frightened of the Viennese court. Nor did she have many dealings with the court in Munich, where her nephew, Max II, ruled and where the ducal line of the Wittelsbachs had no official function. Thus Ludovika was a purely private person. She lived for her children, whom she raised herself—an extraordinary practice among the aristocracy of the time.

In contrast to the devoutly Catholic—even sanctimonious—Sophie, Ludovika was not very religious. She proudly boasted of her liberal upbringing in the Bavarian royal household: "When we were young—how we were Protestantized!" To pass the time, Ludovika collected clocks and occupied herself with studying geography—although, as her husband scoffed, most of her learning came from missionary almanacs. She did not know the first thing about politics.[9]

The father of the prospective bride, Duke Maximilian of Bavaria, was not at all to Sophie's taste. True, he was the most popular Wittelsbach of his time; but popularity was hardly a quality with which to win the respect of Sophie, who thought in strictly dynastic terms. Max was a man who had traveled widely and read a vast amount. (His library comprised about 27,000 volumes, history being a predominant subject.) He had enjoyed a wholly unaristocratic education. For seven years he attended an academy in Munich, so that his schooling took place in the company of young men of his own age (and not alone with a private tutor, as was customary among the aristocracy). He then took courses at the University of Munich, especially in history and natural history.[10]

For the rest of his life, Max remained true to the predilections of his student days; he cared nothing at all for conventional decorum, surrounding himself instead with a group of middle-class scholars and artists—his famous "Artusrunde," or Round Table. Max's companions were given to considerable drinking, versifying, singing, and composing, but they also enjoyed deep intellectual discussions.

Max's new palace in the Ludwigstrasse, where Elisabeth was born, had as one of its attractions a *café chantant* on the Parisian model and a ballroom with an oversize "Bacchus frieze" by Ludwig Schwanthaler; the forty-four-meters-long painting took a liberal view of its subject. The courtyard boasted a circus, with boxes and orchestra seats from which Munich society could admire Max at his riding feats, which he performed proudly, surrounded by pantomimes, crude clown acts, and military spectacles.

Another hobby was playing the zither. Max took the instrument along when he traveled abroad; he insisted on playing his favorite melodies, Bavarian Schnadahüpfel—comic songs in three-four time—even on the pyramid of Cheops, to the openmouthed astonishment of his Egyptian attendants. In 1846, Duke Max published a collection of Bavarian folk tunes.

Duke Max was not a man to turn up his nose at a pretty face, and he did not hold home life in very high regard. He was, however, a stickler for routine: Noontime was invariably sacrosanct; he was available to no one, especially not to his wife or his legitimate children. That was when he dined in his rooms with his two illegitimate daughters, whom he loved dearly.[11]

Max openly expressed democratic views, if only to annoy those around him. "But if he thought that someone was stepping on his toes, there was hell to pay," one of his relatives noted.

The spirit of the household came to the fore in 1848, during the Revolution. The royal family fled the disturbances and street riots in Munich by taking refuge in Duke Max's palace, because here, thanks to the popularity of the master of the house, there was the least likelihood of the doors being battered down.

Max also paraded his liberal views in numerous articles on history that appeared anonymously in various periodicals. His book *Wanderungen nach dem Orient* (Travels to the East; Munich, 1839) gave proof of his wit; throughout he inserted sections of several blank lines, declaring them to be censorship gaps. Such antics were not designed to make him popular with his sister-in-law Sophie. The existence of Duke Max was all but ignored during the early phases of the marriage plot. He would too easily have compromised the bride's family, with his odd brainstorms and with his anticourt attitude, which might have brought the whole project tumbling down.

The prospective couple—Franz Joseph and Helene—were to meet and get to know each other at the imperial summer resort of Bad Ischl, where the engagement would then take place; such was both their mothers' wish. The relaxed, somewhat familial atmosphere of Bad Ischl would ease the undertaking. Setting out for the momentous trip to the Salzkammergut, Ludovika took along her second daughter, fifteen-year-old Elisabeth, who was causing her much worry at that time. Elisabeth had fallen in love with a totally unsuitable man, a Count Richard S——, who was in the duke's service. The idyll was brought to a rapid end; the young man was sent away under some pretext. Though he did return, he was ill and died shortly thereafter.

Sisi was inconsolable. Her broken heart grew heavier to the point of depression. She locked herself in her room for hours to weep and write poetry. (The slim volume with many love poems dating from the winter of 1852–1853 is preserved among the family papers.) Duchess Ludovika hoped that the trip to Bad Ischl would pull the fifteen-year-old out of her doldrums. She also secretly thought that the trip could serve to bring together Sisi and Franz Joseph's younger brother Archduke Karl Ludwig. Her hope was far from idle. The two young people had been corresponding for years. They exchanged gifts, even simple rings. Karl Ludwig was obviously in love with his cousin. Ludovika reckoned that she had a good chance of succeeding.

The political situation in August 1853, on the other hand, was extremely critical, hardly conducive to romantic engagements. The Crimean War had broken out, muddling international relations. What was at stake were concrete political and economic interests in Turkey, which was facing dissolution. In July 1853, Russian troops occupied the Danube principalities (the nucleus of what was to become Romania). Czar Nicholas was counting on support from Austria—reciprocating for Russia's help against the Hungarian insurgents of 1849. As an added incentive, the Czar offered Austria the Turkish provinces of Bosnia and Hercegovina, in addition to a promise of his protection should revolution break out anew in Austria —that is, military intervention in support of the monarchy, as he had extended in 1849 in Hungary.

The Emperor's advisers could not agree among themselves. Count Joseph Radetzky, the old general, favored fighting on the Russian side, but he was not opposed to strict neutrality on the part of Austria. Count Karl Buol-Schauenstein, the foreign minister, and some of the business leaders wanted to move against Russia, siding with England and France. The young, indecisive Emperor was unable to rise to the difficult occasion. He complained to Sophie "[a]bout the ever more complicated Eastern complications."[12] Even during the journey to Bad Ischl he kept himself informed on developments; but once arrived, he hardly allowed higher politics to worry him further. The hesitations and months-long vacillations of the inexperienced Emperor—further distracted by his engagement— had calamitous consequences for Austria.

Duchess Ludovika had other matters on her mind when she and her daughters arrived in Bad Ischl on August 16, 1853. A migraine had forced her to interrupt the journey, so that her party arrived in Bad Ischl with some delay, upsetting all of Sophie's carefully laid plans for the first day. Furthermore, while her daughters were with her on her arrival, Ludovika was accompanied by neither baggage nor ladies-in-waiting. All three women wore mourning for the death of an aunt. Since the carriage with the light-colored dresses had not yet arrived, they could not change before the crucial meeting. Archduchess Sophie sent one of her own ladies-in-waiting to their hotel.

Care went to providing the designated bride at least with an exquisite coiffure, even though she would have to appear before the Emperor in her dusty black traveling dress. Sisi looked after her own hair—simple long braids. She never noticed that Archduchess Sophie had a watchful eye, not only for Helene, but for Elisabeth as well. At any rate, Sophie later described this hairdressing scene at great length to her sister Marie of

Saxony, stressing the "charm and grace" of the younger girl's movements, "all the more so as she was so completely unaware of having produced such a pleasing effect. In spite of the mourning . . . Sissy [sic] was adorable in her very plain, high-necked black dress."[13] Next to her completely artless, childlike sister, Helene seemed all at once very austere. The black dress was not flattering to her—and perhaps really did determine the course of her life, as some people later claimed.

Sophie invited Duchess Ludovika and the two young women to tea. Here they met the Emperor. Queen Elise of Prussia was also present at this first meeting, as were two of the Emperor's younger brothers and other family members. None of those present had the gift of easy small talk. The stiff, embarrassed mood was unrelieved; all of them knew what was at stake.

It was love at first sight, at least as far as Franz Joseph was concerned. His younger brother, Archduke Karl Ludwig, a sharp and jealous observer, later told their mother "that at the moment when the Emperor caught sight of Sisi, an expression of such great pleasure appeared on his face that there was no longer any doubt whom he would choose."

Sophie wrote to Marie of Saxony, "He beamed, and you know how his face can beam when he is happy. The dear little one did not suspect the deep impression she had made on Franzi. Until the moment her mother spoke to her about it, she was filled by nothing but the shyness and timidity inspired in her by the many people around her." She was so excited that she could not eat, and she explained to the lady-in-waiting, "Néné [Helene] is lucky, because she has already seen so many people, but I haven't. I am so scared that I can't even eat." In her confusion, Elisabeth did not notice how intently the Emperor concerned himself with her, rather than with Helene.

The following morning, August 17, the Emperor appeared very early at his mother's; the Archduchess had only just arisen. Sophie to Marie of Saxony: "He told me, his expression beaming, that he found Sisi charming. I begged him not to act rashly, to think the matter over carefully, but he felt that it would not be right to delay."

In her diary Archduchess Sophie described that morning at greater length. The Emperor raved, "Oh, but how sweet Sisi is, she's as fresh as a budding almond, and what a magnificent crown of hair frames her face! What lovely, soft eyes she has, and lips like strawberries." His mother tried to point him in the direction of the bride of her choosing: "Don't you think that Helene is clever, that she has a beautiful, slender figure?" "Well, yes, a little grave and quiet, certainly pleasant and nice, yes, but Sisi—Sisi—such loveliness, such exuberance, like a little girl's, and yet so sweet!"[14]

Everything was settled. That day Franz Joseph even refused to go hunting, a pleasure he did not usually let slip by. Elise of Prussia, when she heard of this, immediately made a sign to her sister Sophie which meant, "He is smitten."[15] Queen Elise was thoroughly satisfied with the way things were turning out; little Elisabeth was her goddaughter. There was confusion all around. The two young ladies were distressed. Only the Emperor was radiant.

A ball marked the eve of Franz Joseph's birthday. Helene appeared in a splendid gown of white silk. Ivy tendrils wreathed her forehead, lending her tall, slightly austere appearance a touch of simple romanticism. Back in Munich, when they had made their preparations for the visit, they had concentrated on this night. Little Sisi was more simply dressed, in a plain pale-pink frock, and seemed very childlike next to the handsome figure of her sister.

The Emperor did not join in the first dance—nor did the two Bavarian princesses. For the second dance, a polka, Archduchess Sophie begged Franz Joseph's aide-de-camp, Hugo von Weckbecker, to "dance with Princess Elisabeth, who heretofore had only taken lessons from the dancing master and required an experienced guide for her first debut [sic]." Weckbecker: "She presented me to the charming Princess, who was stricken with extreme embarrassment and told me shyly that she did not know whether and how she would manage without the dancing master." Weckbecker reassured the young girl, though he himself was "a little anxious, for I knew that in general—in spite of dancing masters—Bavarian princesses were not good dancers. . . . Fortunately, Princess Elisabeth was musical and therefore at least kept time well." It was with some astonishment that Weckbecker observed the young Emperor who, quite contrary to his usual habit, sat out this dance as well, instead merely watching the dancing Sisi, who "floated past, sylphlike, on my arm." After the dance, Weckbecker whispered to a friend, "I suspect I've just been dancing with our future Empress."[16]

The Emperor danced the cotillion with young Sisi and afterward presented her with his nosegay—a traditional sign that she was the chosen one. Every one of the onlookers understood—except Sisi herself. In answer to the question whether this mark of attention had not struck her as significant she said, "No, it only made me feel self-conscious."

Sophie described Sisi's appearance at length to her sister Marie.

In her beautiful hair she wore a large comb that held back her braids, she wears her hair fashionably combed away from her face. The little one's bearing is so charming, so modest, so impeccable, so graceful yes almost humble, when she dances with the Emperor. She was like a rosebud, unfolding under the rays of the sun, sitting beside the Emperor during the cotillion. She seemed to me so attractive, so childishly unpretentious and yet quite unaffected with him. It was only the crowd of people that intimidated her.

On August 18, Franz Joseph's birthday was celebrated in the bosom of the assembled family. Archduchess Sophie wrote to Marie of Saxony, "At the family dinner the Emperor was so proud that Sisi, who was allowed to sit next to him, had eaten with such a hearty appetite! In the afternoon we went on an excursion to Wolfgang. We also walked a little ways on foot. I was in my barouche with the two children and the Emperor. He must like them very much to stand it for so long in the closed barouche! Helene chattered a great deal and very amusingly, the girl has a great deal of charm for me. . . ."

After the stroll, the Emperor requested his mother to make tentative inquiries of Sisi's mother "if she would have him," but he also insisted that the two mothers were not to exert any pressure. "My situation is so difficult that, God knows, it is no pleasure to share it with me." To which Sophie replied, "But my dear child, how can you think that a woman would not be only too happy to lighten your situation with her charm and cheerfulness?"

Sophie then formally informed her sister Ludovika of Franz Joseph's intentions; Ludovika, "moved, pressed my hand, for in her great humility, she had always doubted whether the Emperor would truly consider one of her daughters." When Sisi's mother asked her if she could love the Emperor, she replied (according to Archduchess Sophie), "How could anyone not love *that* man?" Then she burst into tears and vowed that she would do everything in her power to make the Emperor happy and "to be the most loving child" to Aunt Sophie. "But," she said, "how can he possibly think of me? After all, I'm so unimportant!" And a short time later, "I love the Emperor so much! If only he were not the Emperor!" Sophie's comment: "That is what intimidates her—her future position. The Emperor was literally enraptured when I told him these moving words by his bride, since they express such deep and unassuming understanding for him."

How the talk between mother and daughter really went and whether Ludovika's and Sophie's recollections are to be believed must remain an open question. When Ludovika was later asked whether the girl's feelings had actually been considered in this decision, she always gave the same answer: "One does not send the Emperor of Austria packing."[17]

Each of the nine Bavarian sisters had at one time or another suffered from a broken heart. Each of them knew that, as an eligible princess, she was a political pawn and had no choice but to accept the man selected for her. In order not to confuse the young girls, not to plunge them into conflicts, the reading of love stories was strictly forbidden at the Bavarian court. Even the German classics were banned for the same reason.

Ludovika herself had been an outstanding beauty in her youth. Some even went so far as to claim that she had been far more beautiful than any of her daughters, including Elisabeth. She had suffered from a love affair with Prince Miguel of Braganza, later King of Portugal, whom she was not allowed to marry for political reasons. It was the family that chose the marriage with her cousin Max. He told her frankly that he did not love her and was marrying her merely because he was afraid of his forceful grandfather. He had been hopelessly in love with a nonaristocratic woman, whom he was forbidden to marry for reasons of rank.

The marriage between Max and Ludovika was unhappy from the very first day. Ludovika later told her children that she had spent her first wedding anniversary weeping from morning to night. Only gradually did she learn to tolerate her husband's restlessness and his many affairs and to remain alone with the growing brood of children. Much later, after she was widowed, she told her grandchildren that, starting with their golden wedding anniversary, Max had been good to her. Fifty bitter years had preceded that day. Elisabeth had grown up hearing her mother's complaints about the unhappy marriage, and she had often heard Ludovika's bitter statement, "When one is married, one feels so abandoned."

Archduchess Sophie was hardly more fortunate. She was forced to marry Archduke Franz Karl, "weak in body and mind," brother of the ailing Emperor Ferdinand. In Bavaria, it was said that Sophie had spent many nights in tears in despair and fear of this marriage. When her governess reported this state of affairs to Sophie's mother, she was unmoved and replied, "What do you want? The matter was decided at the Congress of Vienna!"

When Sophie saw that her fate had been irrevocably sealed, she coura-geously declared that from now on she would be happy with the Archduke. Emperor Franz told her that "given his son's condition, she would herself have to handle everything." And so she did, becoming an independent, energetic woman. She loved her good-natured husband "like a child that has to be taken care of," and she raised her four sons well. As a young woman, she enjoyed a close friendship with Napoleon's son, the Duke of Reichstadt, whom she nursed touchingly during his fatal illness. Viennese gossip turned the young man into the father of her second son, Archduke Ferdinand Max. In all probability, this gossip had no basis in fact; but it does show that the pretty Archduchess was considered quite capable of a romantic interlude.

Thus, like most princesses of their time, the mothers of the young couple had been forced to renounce love. Of course, they did their duty—even in tears. They could not help but regard the engagement in Bad Ischl as a rare instance of great good fortune: Franz Joseph loved his future bride, as was plain to see. He was young and good-looking, not feebleminded like his father and uncle. He was the Emperor of Austria. The young girl would have no difficulty adjusting to her situation, which, compared to the lots of both mothers, was enviable. No, really, "one does not send the Emperor of Austria packing."

Archduchess Sophie was still entirely caught up in eighteenth-century thinking. She had no high opinion of individualism, let alone emotion, as an element in court politics—in contrast to her daughter-in-law-to-be. On one occasion, Sophie wrote to Princess Metternich that one should not believe "that individual personalities have any significance." She had always noticed that one person was replaced by another, without making the slightest difference in the world.[18] Now, whether the future Empress was named Helene or Elisabeth made little difference, according to this view. Both came from the same family, were equal in rank, were both Catholic and Sophie's nieces—and that last was all that mattered in the end.

Ludovika communicated Sisi's acceptance to her sister Sophie in writing. On August 19, at eight o'clock in the morning, the Emperor beaming with happiness, appeared at his bride's rooms at the hotel. Ludovika wrote about the meeting to a relative: "I left him alone with Sisi, since he wanted to speak to her himself, and when he came back to my room, he looked quite pleased, quite cheerful, and she did too—as is proper for a happy bride."[19]

Ludovika's excitement was every bit as great as her gratitude to Sophie: "It is such prodigious joy, and yet such a weighty and important situation, that I am very moved in every respect. She is so young, so inexperienced, but I hope that forbearance will be shown to such extreme youth! . . . Aunt

Sophie is so very good and kind to her, and what a consolation for me to be able to hand her over to such a dear sister as a second mother."

Nevertheless, Elisabeth later always referred to this situation with great bitterness, saying, "Marriage is an absurd arrangement. One is sold as a fifteen-year-old child and makes a vow one does not understand and then regrets for thirty years or more, and which one can never undo again."[20]

In August 1853, however, those who were present looked on this imperial engagement, in Count Hübner's words, as "a simple, lovely, and noble idyll."[21]

The young couple left the hotel arm in arm to breakfast with the Archduchess and of course the rest of the family, all of whom observed the pair with interest and approval—with the exception of Archduke Karl Ludwig, who had lost the love of his youth. Franz Joseph took this occasion to introduce his adjutants to the fifteen-year-old girl, especially Karl Count Grünne, whose judgment he valued very highly, including his views in matters concerning women.

At eleven o'clock, the party repaired in a body to the parish church. The congregation watched reverently as Archduchess Sophie held back at the door, granting precedence to her young niece: Sisi was pledged to an emperor, and from this time on, she stood higher in rank than the emperor's mother. With this noble gesture, Sophie expressed her respect for the imperial hierarchy. Sisi, to be sure, hardly understood. Self-conscious and bashful, she entered the church, unpleasantly affected by the attention she aroused. Sophie: "The priest welcomed us with holy water, his eyes filled with tears! On the moment we entered the church, the national anthem was struck up." After the benediction, Emperor Franz Joseph gently took the girl by the hand, led her to the priest, and requested of him, "I beseech you, Reverend, bless us, this is my bride."

The priest's blessing was followed by the good wishes of all those present on this historic occasion.[22] Count Grünne then made a speech in honor of the young couple. Weckbecker: "The Princess was so moved and self-conscious that she was barely able to respond."[23] Everyone was in a state of high emotion. The Emperor found it difficult to take his future bride away from the hearty crowd.

Duchess Ludovika, however, was so worried about her daughter's future that even on this day she complained to Weckbecker, who was a total stranger to her, "with how much trepidation she looked on the hard task facing her daughter Elisabeth, since she was ascending the throne literally straight from the nursery. She also harbored concern because of the severe judgments of the ladies of the Viennese aristocracy." That these fears were only too justified soon became evident.

Dinner was taken in Hallstatt. Afterward, the party went for a drive. After the previous day's rain, the landscape was ravishing. Mountains and cliffs were bathed in the light of the setting sun. The lake glimmered. The Emperor took Sisi's hand and explained the sights to her. Queen Elise of Prussia was enchanted: "It's so lovely, so much young happiness in such a wonderful landscape."[24] Sophie reported to her sister Marie of Saxony in a letter how tenderly the Emperor had wrapped his betrothed in his military cloak, so fearful was he that she might catch a chill, and how he had confessed to his mother, "I can't tell you how happy I am!"

That night Bad Ischl was lit up by ten thousand candles and by lamps in the Austrian and Bavarian colors. On the Siriuskogl, multicolored lanterns sketched a classical temple in the sky, enclosing the initials *FJ* and *E* in a bridal wreath. This was the first time that young Sisi experienced the jubilation of a benevolent, loyal people gathered in the streets to welcome its future Empress.

The Emperor's happiness is clearly evident in every report on those days in Bad Ischl. Of Sisi's feelings we unfortunately know very little, except that she was very embarrassed, very quiet, and constantly in tears. Sophie commented to her sister, "You cannot imagine how charming Sisi is when she cries!" One party followed on the heels of the last. The young girl was presented with gifts from all sides. The Emperor gave her jewelry with precious gems, among them a magnificent blossoming tendril made of diamonds and emeralds, which she could braid into her hair. Sisi, who was visibly growing more elegant, stood at the center of Bad Ischl's social life. She was the cynosure of all eyes; her charm was widely praised.

The young Emperor was gentle, circumspect, and generous in the consideration he showed his childlike fiancée. To give her pleasure, he even had a swing put up in the garden of the summer estate, and the girl used it with childish glee. Since he saw how much Sisi was afraid of every new strange face, the Emperor arranged for the magnificent coach, drawn by five piebald horses, to be driven not by a coachman but by his adjutant general, Grünne.[25] He had noticed that the girl had already grown accustomed to this man, the Emperor's closest confidant, and that she was fond of him.

Grünne was forty-five years old at that time, and one of the most influential men in the monarchy, an important member of the widely deplored Kamarilla at the Viennese court. As head of the military chancellery, he was the top officer in the Austrian army after the emperor. Grünne accompanied his young master on all trips, was his closest political adviser, and had unique insight into the Emperor's private life. To this day it is asserted in Viennese society that it was Grünne who arranged romantic adventures for the young Emperor. (After all, Franz Joseph was hardly an inexperienced stripling by the time he became engaged to be married.) The fact that Sisi trusted Grünne from the first gave the Emperor much satisfaction, and he took pleasure in making his adjutant general the guardian angel of his young love during these coach rides à trois.

Three more balls were scheduled in Bad Ischl. According to Sophie's diary, Sisi continued to be bashful and tractable. When Countess Sophie Esterházy, who was soon to head the Empress's household, extended her good wishes, saying, "We are so grateful to Your Royal Highness for making the Emperor so happy," Sisi replied, "You will have to be very patient with me for a while."[26]

Unlike the prospective bride, the rest of the young people in the imperial family were in high spirits. During the cotillion they set off rockets and firecrackers; poor Ludovika, whose nerves were badly strained, fled in horror to her sister's bedroom. The Duchess had still not decided whether to be pleased at the great honor granted her daughter or distressed at the prospect of the emotional burdens in store for the fifteen-year-old girl.

Helene was another source of worry to her mother. The girl was upset and unhappy. She was already eighteen—rather old, therefore, for the preliminaries of a new match. Even Sophie's magnificent gift, a cross of diamonds and turquoise, and the assurance that Sophie continued to find her extraordinarily charming, could not console Helene. She longed to be back home in Bavaria.

So did Duchess Ludovika, who wrote about her concern to her Bavarian relatives: "Life here is extremely busy. Sisi especially is not at all accustomed to it yet, especially the late hours. I am pleasantly surprised at the way she becomes resigned to speaking to so many strangers and that, in spite of her embarrassment, she maintains such calm."[27]

The bride's father, Duke Max, was informed of the engagement by telegram, as was the King of Bavaria. As head of the Wittelsbach family, the King's official approval of the engagement of his cousin was required.

Franz Joseph's letter to Czar Nicholas is remarkable, vouchsafing as it does an intimacy and affection between the two sovereigns that goes a long way toward explaining the Czar's subsequent disappointment in Franz

Joseph's attitude during the Crimean War. "In the rapture of my joy, dear precious friend, I make haste to speak to you of my happiness. I say my happiness, because I am convinced that my bride has all the virtues and all those properties of mind and heart that will make me happy."[28]

Finally, papal dispensation for the marriage had to be applied for; the bride and groom were, after all, first cousins. No one seems to have been concerned about this circumstance. Elisabeth's parents, too, were closely related—both were members of the Wittelsbach family, and second cousins. Nor, given the state of medical knowledge at the time, did anyone realize that the children of this imperial marriage, especially the hoped-for crown prince, would one day have to bear the full burden of the Wittelsbach heritage as a result of this intermingling of family members.

The Wittelsbach line was not free of hereditary taints. There were several cases of mental illness. Duke Max's father, Duke Pius (that is, Sisi's grandfather), was feebleminded and crippled. At times he led a dissolute life, once landing in police custody after a brawl, and he ended his pitiful days as a hermit, living in total solitude.[29] (The fact that the two sons of the Bavarian King, Crown Prince Ludwig and Prince Otto, were also mentally ill was not yet known in 1853, since both were still children. Besides, the hereditary debility was attributed to the maternal line, with which the ducal line was not connected.)

On August 24, the *Wiener Zeitung* published an official statement:

> His Imperial and Royal Apostolic Highness, our most gracious Lord and Emperor, Franz Joseph I, during His Majesty's stay in Bad Ischl, offered his hand to Her Most Serene Highness, Princess Elisabeth Amalie Eugenie, Duchess of Bavaria, daughter of Their Royal Highnesses Duke Maximilian Joseph and Duchess Ludovika, née Royal Princess of Bavaria, after obtaining the approval of His Majesty, King Maximilian II of Bavaria, as well as Their Serene Highnesses the parents of the Princess-bride, and entered on an engagement. May the blessing of the Almighty rest on this event, so happy and joyful for the Imperial House and the Empire.

The report caused a sensation. For a long time, the Viennese, especially in high society, had racked their brains about who would be their empress. Many princesses had been discussed. Elisabeth of Bavaria had never figured in the speculations. Impatiently, the city waited for the first portraits of the imperial bride. During the long hours little Sisi spent sitting for painters and illustrators, the smitten groom kept her company. He sat endlessly by her side, watching her proudly.

Since Vienna knew so little about the future Empress, gossip flourished. The first thing that always happened with newcomers to the Viennese court was critical scrutiny of the Almanach de Gotha. And here the imperial bride was not proof against criticism, for her ancestral line included a Princess Arenberg (the mother of her father, Duke Max). Though the Arenbergs were a family of the high aristocracy, they were not royal— not, that is, a family fit to furnish marriage partners to the House of Habsburg. Grandmother Arenberg, in her turn, was related to all sorts of other aristocratic but not royal families: the Schwarzenbergs, the Windisch-Graetzes, the Lobkovics, Schönburgs, Neippergs, Esterházys. The future Empress, therefore, was not above aristocratic society but merely a part of it—through complex family relations with nonroyal houses. Elisabeth, then, could not meet the one essential condition to unchallenged acceptability at the Viennese court—a flawless pedigree. She would be made to feel this lack only too soon.

Her father also provided ample grounds for talk. His circus riding, his chumminess with the bourgeoisie and with peasants, his disregard for the aristocratic world, his far from refined stag parties in Possenhofen and Munich—all were subjects of gossip. It was said that Duke Max let his children run wild, that though they could ride like little circus artistes, they were barely able to put together a sensible sentence in French, let alone carry on a *conversation*. The parquet floors of the Viennese court were notoriously slippery.

It goes without saying that Duke Max's castles were also subjected to critical scrutiny. The new palace on the Ludwigstrasse, built by the popular architect Leo Klenze, was unquestionably in keeping with the Duke's position. But the summer castle of Possenhofen on Lake Starnberg was far less distinguished. It was not long before Vienna heard of the "beggars' household" that was said to be the future Empress's family background.

Even twenty years later Elisabeth's lady-in-waiting Countess Marie Festetics was still disturbed by these defamatory slanders. She liked Possenhofen: "The house is simple but well kept, clean, attractive, the cuisine is good, I found no pomp, everything is agreeably old-fashioned, but elegant and without a trace of a beggar's household, such as my counterparts of then and now made so much of."

The Countess was especially enthusiastic about the situation of the little castle on Lake Starnberg. She extolled the moonlight on the calm waters and the birdsong that woke her from sleep in the mornings: "they rejoiced as if it were spring—I rushed to the window—the view is delightful, deep, deep blue the waters—a paradise of trees, and green *all over,* and across the lake, on the other side, handsome mountains—everything loveliness and sun—the garden filled with flowers—the old house wreathed in wild vines and ivy—so poetic—so beautiful." And the lady-in-waiting, who loved her Empress, continued: "yes, her home could not be otherwise, to allow her dreaminess, her love of nature—to develop to this extent!"[30]

Dreaminess and a love of nature were qualities Elisabeth exhibited even as a child. All the romantic tales of her childhood summers in Possenhofen are true. Love of nature was one of the few shared traits that united Franz Joseph and Elisabeth.

The "divine sojourn in Ischl," to use Franz Joseph's words, lasted until August 31. The parting—which, Elisabeth noted in her diary, was "very tender"—took place in festively decorated Salzburg. To commemorate the engagement, Archduchess Sophie decided to buy the rented villa where the couple had met and to renovate and expand it into the "imperial villa," to be used for the imperial family's yearly summer vacation. The ground plan of the mansion was changed by the addition of two wings into the shape of an *E*—for Elisabeth.

Franz Joseph's happiness lasted even beyond his return "to the desk-bound paper existence here, with its cares and troubles." He even enjoyed sitting for the painter Schwager: "to the extent that I normally find it boring to be painted, I now look forward to every sitting, since I am reminded of Sisi's sittings in Ischl, and Schwager always brings me her portrait." He confessed to Archduchess Sophie that his thoughts clung "with infinite longing to the west."[31] The young Emperor's happy frame of mind also affected domestic policy: The state of siege, in effect since the Revolution of 1848, was now lifted at least in the three cities of Vienna, Graz, and Prague.

(It may appear like a sign of things to come that, shortly after Elisabeth became a part of Austria's history, the Crown of St. Stephen was recovered. In 1848 it had been buried by Kossuth. The holiest relic of the Hungarian nation was solemnly returned to Budapest—for some, an emblem of reconciliation between Austria and Hungary, though the bond could not be sealed until the Austrian emperor was crowned with this Hungarian symbol. That aim was accomplished by Elisabeth in 1867—her one political feat.)

Sisi was now subjected to an extensive course of study. It was especially necessary that she learn French and Italian as quickly as possible. All that had been neglected in her schooling and upbringing was now to be remedied in the few months that remained before the wedding. Duchess Ludovika was worried, because the lessons were not progressing very well: "Unfortunately, my children have no facility in learning foreign languages, and in social circles here, the speaking of French is noticeably decreasing."[32]

The most important subject Sisi had to study was Austrian history. Three times a week the historian Count Johann Mailáth visited her in order to read to her personally from his major work, *Geschichte des österreichischen Kaiserstaates* (History of the Austrian Empire). Mailath was a short man, very lively and amusing, approaching seventy. He lived in Munich on the income from his books, in very modest, even shabby circumstances. (Only a year later, his financial straits drove him to drown himself in Lake Starnberg.) As a historian, he was not without his critics, because his presentation of history was highly imaginative and uncritical. Among the liberal Hungarians, he was unpopular because of his extremely pro-Austrian stance.

But Sisi liked him. The history lessons tended to last into the evenings, and the circle of listeners kept growing; her sister Helene and her brother Karl Theodor ("Gackel") joined, as did some of the other tutors and Duchess Ludovika. But Mailath gave his readings only "pour les beaux yeux de Sisi."[33] Even decades later, Elisabeth still talked about this teacher. In spite of his deep loyalty to the central government in Vienna, Mailath was nevertheless a proud Hungarian who related the history of Austria to the future Empress of Austria from the Hungarian point of view. He worked to instill an understanding of Hungary's special historic privileges and explained to Sisi about the old Hungarian constitution, which Emperor Franz Joseph had abolished in 1849. He, whom the Forty-Eighters thought of as one of the Old Conservatives, even tried to make the future Empress understand the advantages of the republican form of government. At least, Elisabeth was recalling Mailath some years later, when she shocked the Viennese court with the statement, "I have been told that the most appropriate form of government is that of the republic."[34] These cozy readings in history within the bosom of the ducal family in Possenhofen established in the fifteen-year-old imperial bride the soil for her subsequent political views. It would be hard to overestimate their significance.

A correspondence set in between Vienna and Munich—concerning the bride's trousseau, which had to be assembled in practically no time at all and which kept dozens of Bavarian seamstresses, embroiderers, shoemakers, and milliners busy from morn until night. Archduchess Sophie sent written suggestions, such as the advice that Sisi take better care of her teeth. No effort was to be spared to turn the little Bavarian country girl into a suitable representative of the Habsburg state.

The young woman's fear of the Hofburg, the imperial palace in Vienna, and of her new, luxurious life grew. She became almost entirely indifferent to the many new gowns, loathed the endless fittings, was unmoved by the jewelry that arrived from Vienna. She was still a child; none of the precious gifts gave her as much pleasure as did a parrot the Emperor sent to Bavaria.

Sisi was not used to being hemmed in by a rigid program all day long. Her family, worried, observed that though the girl was flattered by her success and the excessive attention suddenly paid to her, she also grew more and more silent and melancholy. She wrote elegiac poems about her beloved Possenhofen, still mourned her old love, and was afraid of the new one.

Ludovika's fears were only too well founded—and no secret. The Belgian envoy reported to Brussels, "In order to spare her daughter the exertions arising from the festivities, the mother is said to want to postpone the wedding until June. If the ceremony were to take place at an advanced season and the major part of the nobility had already departed Vienna, it would be possible to win some dispensation from the events connected with the wedding."[35] This wish—at odds with the prevailing customs in Vienna—was not granted. After all, an emperor of Austria did not get married by excluding the public simply because the future Empress was afraid of the aristocracy.

Another topic subjected to lengthy discussion was the site of the wedding—Munich or Vienna. Ludovika: "No consideration can be given to a proxy marriage, and unfortunately, the Emperor cannot come here. To have the wedding here is, unfortunately, impossible, although it is always the most pleasant! I regret this very much, for if we accompany Sisi to Vienna, that is a great undertaking, such a great court, the large family gathering, Viennese society, the parties, etc. . . . I am not made for all that . . . I do not even want to think of it, and until now, I myself don't know what is going to happen. In general, I do not like to think about Sisi's moving away, and I would wish to postpone the moment forever."[36]

Unmindful of the Emperor's feelings of love, the political crisis to the east grew increasingly complicated. On November 1, Turkey declared war on Russia. The Balkan question became acute. The significance to Austria of this conflict was not realized in Vienna; as late as October, the Austrian army was drastically reduced because funds were no longer available. During these months, Austrian policies presented an extremely confused picture.

It would appear that the politically inexperienced but all-powerful young Emperor did not in the least comprehend the consequences of his wavering. His ministers, most especially his foreign minister, Buol, were weak; nor were they given any responsibility beyond advising, the Emperor. In any case, since opinion was divided, not only among the ministers, but also at the court, Franz Joseph vacillated helplessly; firmly convinced of his imperial sovereignty, he refused to seek guidance from experienced statesmen.

His thoughts dwelled not so much on statecraft as on his bride-to-be. His mind was focused on ever new and ever more splendid gifts; in Vienna as in Bad Ischl, he tried to speed up the building renovations—though he cautioned his mother, who was supervising the work on the villa in Bad Ischl "that the whole if possible cost no more than is proposed, since I am short of funds."[37]

Franz Joseph's frequent complaints about lack of money are astonishing, coming from the ruler of such a powerful empire. But, in fact, the imperial family in Vienna commanded relatively scarce resources. For though Emperor Ferdinand the Kindly had renounced the throne in 1848 and retired to Prague, he had held on to his fortune. The immensely rich imperial estates, which each year brought in many millions of guldens, belonged not to the ruling emperor, but to the abdicated Emperor Ferdinand. Only after Ferdinand's death in 1875 did the fortune become part of Franz Joseph's estate. From 1848 to 1875—quite a considerable length of time—the resources on which the Viennese imperial family could draw were by no means unlimited; caution had to be exercised even when it came to buying and renovating a summer residence.

Furthermore, during this time the Austrian economy slid from one financial crisis into the next, all of them caused by the extremely high cost of keeping the military during years of a state of siege. All these worries were pushed aside by the Emperor, who was head over heels in love. He wrote his mother, "I can no longer wait for the moment when I am free to travel to Possenhofen to see Sisi again, I cannot stop thinking of her."[38]

Since there was no direct rail connection between Vienna and Munich as yet, the trip was arduous. Proceeding by way of Prague, Dresden, Leipzig, and Hof to Munich, it took far longer than a day. During the engagement period, the Emperor made the journey three times.

Duchess Ludovika was concerned that the Emperor might be bored in her family circle.³⁹ But Franz Joseph had eyes only for little Sisi; in a transport of gratitude, he wrote from Munich to his mother in Vienna, "Never, my dear Mama, will I be able to thank you enough for having brought about such deep happiness for me. Every day I love Sisi more, and I am ever more convinced that no one else could suit me better than she."

Mindful of Sophie's advice, the Emperor wrote about his future bride, "Besides many more important good qualities, she is a charming horseback rider—of which, however, following your wish, I first convinced myself. As you advised me, I begged my Mama-in-law not to let Sisi ride too much; but I believe that will be hard to enforce, since Sisi is unwilling to give it up. And by the way, it has a very good effect on her; for since Ischl, she has gained quite a bit of weight and never looks ill now. Thanks to her care, too, her teeth have become quite white, so that she is truly lovely."⁴⁰

No improvement, however, was yet evident in the area of public appearances. The Emperor wrote his mother that the tumultuous reception at the Munich theater "embarrassed Sisi very much." But he reassured Archduchess Sophie by telling her that at the court ball (which he found "truly brilliant" and "very animated"), matters worked out more agreeably: "the entire diplomatic corps was introduced to poor Sisi, and she made conversation charmingly, speaking with everyone."⁴¹

Sisi's engagement had raised the standing of the ducal family. Even the King of Bavaria was proud of the fact that once again a woman of the Wittelsbachs would stand beside a Habsburg emperor. After decades of discord between the royal and the ducal lines of the Wittelsbachs, the royal house now made overt efforts to court the favor of its ducal relatives. Little Elisabeth was the center of these attentions. But she was not dazzled. On the contrary: She expressed her fear of the future more and more clearly. "If only he were a tailor," she lamented, speaking of her bridegroom to her equally fearful mother.⁴²

Sisi's attachment to Franz Joseph grew. But she did not understand his cares of state. Even when he was in Munich, a courier arrived daily from Vienna with the latest news bulletins. The Belgian envoy: "The seriousness of the situation forces the Emperor to hasten his return. . . . The political situation causes him much anxiety."⁴³ At his premature departure, Sisi wept so much that "her face was all swollen."

For Christmas, which coincided with Sisi's birthday (she turned sixteen), the Emperor brought to Munich the by now obligatory jewelry, which he had selected himself, along with a portrait of himself and a small silver breakfast service for traveling, engraved with an *E* and the imperial crown.[44] He also brought a gift from Archduchess Sophie—a wreath and, in the dead of winter, a bouquet of fresh roses, "which here, where such flowers are not to be found, will have quite an effect." The Emperor wrote his mother that he had "found [Sisi] very well and blooming. She is always equally dear and attractive, and is now also learning many new and different things."[45]

During this visit, too, the Emperor's eastern policy forced him to return home precipitately. He deeply lamented the fact "that, between love and the vexing affairs, which plague me endlessly even here, all my time is taken up."[46]

Only a few days after Franz Joseph's return, the news arrived that the French and English fleets had set sail for the Black Sea. The Viennese stock market reacted with a panic. Austria's position in this conflict was still not clear. The Emperor continued to leave his "dear precious friend," the Czar, in the dark, thus offending him most deeply.

The extent to which court society remained untouched by the complications of war is astonishing. Anyone who did not happen to be a politician or had personal interests in the Balkans continued to ignore events. The preparations for the imperial wedding claimed a large share of the public interest.

The Viennese countesses, for whom the special pleasure of Carnival lay in the fact that they could win a smart young emperor as a dancing partner, suffered a deep disappointment that winter: Franz Joseph would not dance, "which is in keeping with his chivalrous sentiments," they commented, but soon they began to complain about "Carnival, which so far is very dull. Since the Emperor will not dance, the major interest falls away. So far, there have been only three balls, of secondary brilliance. Everyone seems to be waiting for the wedding festivities." And: "The countesses sorely miss the best, most splendid dancer."[47]

There was, however, a more concrete reason than love for Franz Joseph's refusal to dance: He was suffering a recurrence of the "affliction of brain disease and half-sight that appeared as a consequence of the attempt on his life"—that is, impaired vision—which compelled him to take it easier.[48]

Early in March, the marriage contract was signed. In it, Duke Max of Bavaria promised "Her Serene Highness, his daughter," a marriage portion of 50,000 guldens, "which shall be delivered even before the wedding, in Munich, to the agent especially designated for this purpose by His Imperial Majesty, in return for the appropriate receipt." Elisabeth was also to be provided "with all requirements of jewelry, gowns, gems, gold and silver utensils, in accordance with her elevated rank." The Emperor pledged himself to supplement the marriage portion with an additional 100,000 guldens. This meant that the Empress's private capital was measurably increased. He further promised to make a gift to his bride of 12,000 ducats "after the marriage has been consummated, as a morning gift." Such a gift was a long-standing custom in the imperial family. As a grant of appanage —lasting even into a possible period of widowhood—the Empress was to receive 100,000 guldens a year, intended solely for "finery, dresses, alms, and minor expenditures." The cost of everything else—that is, "the table, linens and horses, maintenance and remuneration of servants, and all household effects"—was, of course, borne by the Emperor.[49]

This stipulated appanage was five times that of Archduchess Sophie, who received a mere 20,000 guldens a year. However, three days before the wedding, the Emperor raised his mother's yearly income to 50,000.[50] (At that time, a workman—provided he could find work at all during this period of pervasive unemployment—working twelve to fourteen hours a day, earned at most 200 to 300 guldens a year, women about half that, and children only a fraction. A lieutenant's salary was 24 guldens a month, noncommissioned soldiers earned correspondingly less.)

On his last visit to Munich, four weeks before the wedding, the Emperor brought a magnificent diamond tiara inset with large opals, and a matching choker and earrings. The set was a gift from Archduchess Sophie, who had worn the tiara at her own wedding. It was worth more than 60,000 guldens—an enormous value even for the Emperor. Still in Munich, Franz Joseph wrote to his mother in Vienna that she need have no fears, the jewelry would "certainly be very carefully kept and immediately put in safekeeping."[51] Evidently Sophie had no great faith in the orderliness of her sister's household.

Sisi's letter of thanks had an extremely awkward ring: "but be assured, my dear aunt, that I am keenly aware of your great goodness to me, and that it is comforting to me to know that always and in all situations of my life I will be allowed to entrust myself to your maternal affection."[52]

Aside from the many instances of patronizing and much tactless advice, for the present Elisabeth had little cause to complain of her mother-in-law. Sophie supervised the renovations of the imperial villa in Bad Ischl, and she showered the young girl with jewelry and precious objects of every sort. Her letters to her sister in Saxony never criticized the girl; the Archduchess praised every little thing she noticed—especially Sisi's simplicity and shyness.

Sophie spent months furnishing the young couple's apartment in the greatest good taste. These living quarters in the Hofburg consisted of an anteroom, an entrance hall, a dining room, a mirrored room, a drawing room, a dressing room, and a bedroom. If one leaves aside the magnificent furnishings and the size of the drawing room, the whole was rather more like the living quarters of the haute bourgeoisie, though without bathroom, lavatory (*chaises percées* were still in vogue in the Hofburg), and without its own kitchen. All meals were taken in the bosom of the family; it never occurred to the Archduchess that a young wife might prefer having a household of her own. Sophie personally picked out the tapestries and curtains, the rugs and furniture. She placed great importance on purchasing only domestic products, to promote local trade.

Sisi was to have only the best and most expensive. Her toiletry set, for example, was made of massive gold.[53] Sophie placed in the apartment precious objects, pictures, silver, Chinese porcelain, statues, and clocks from the various collections of the Imperial House as well as from the treasure-house and the Ambrase Collection. The inventories have been preserved,[54] even down to the Emperor's personal linens, which were ample indeed. And Sophie knew very well that the bride would not be bringing a trousseau that could match the Viennese provisions.

Sophie was not one to hide her light under a bushel. Her sisters admired the Archduchess's energy. For example, Queen Marie of Saxony wrote, "My good Sophie is . . . as always, self-denial incarnate, eager to give everything away and to do without for her future daughter-in-law, and she thinks of every little thing that might contribute to the happiness and comfort of the young couple. Recently Luise [Ludovika] also wrote to me correctly that it is unlikely that a bride was ever looked after so lovingly as is her daughter."[55]

A month before the wedding, the solemn "act of renunciation" occurred in Munich. This was Sisi's waiver of any claim to the succession in the kingdom of Bavaria. The members of the royal and ducal houses, the court dignitaries and the ministers of state, all watched the sixteen-year-old girl, who sat beside the King under a canopy on the dais of the throne room, for the first time in her life. Many eyes saw little Sisi, "having bowed to Their Majesties and Their Most Serene Highnesses her parents, move to the table where the Gospel lay, which is held out to Her Royal Highness by His Excellency the Archbishop."[56] The declaration of renunciation was read out, Sisi was put under oath. Then she signed the document. The somber ceremony was a small foretaste of the formal life awaiting her in Vienna.

The bridal trousseau, twenty-five trunks of it, arrived in Vienna well ahead of the bride. The precise inventory of everything Sisi brought to Vienna has been preserved; it shows clearly that the Emperor's bride really was not a "good match." Though the inventory lists jewelry worth at least 100,000 guldens, closer scrutiny indicates that more than 90 percent of the listed pieces had been gifts from the groom and Archduchess Sophie, presented during the engagement period.

The silver effects, at that time the pride of every bride from "a good family," were more than modest, adding up only to a value of roughly 700 guldens. That amount included every washing pitcher, every silver dish no matter how small, every coffeepot.

Indeed, it could not be considered a trousseau appropriate to her rank, as stipulated in the marriage contract. If we consider the pride even brides from the haute bourgeoisie took in spreading their dowry before inquisitive eyes during this period (Sisi's daughter-in-law, Stephanie of Belgium, would take great satisfaction in doing so in her time), we will understand the many scornful looks from the Viennese court ladies, the many disparaging comments among the wealthy Austrian aristocracy. Money and property—of course, along with an impeccable pedigree, an essential precondition for acceptance at court—played an excessively large role in Vienna.

At 50,000 guldens, Sisi's wardrobe represented a considerable asset, though even here the most valuable item, a blue velvet cloak with sable trimmings and a sable muff, was a gift from the Emperor. The future Empress owned four ballgowns (two white, one pink, and one sky blue with white roses); seventeen *Putzkleider,* "fancy gowns"—that is, formal gowns with trains (starting with the wedding dress, with its overdress of silver moiré, followed by taffeta and tulle dresses in the favored colors of white and pink, but of course also a black gown for the eventuality of court mourning); fourteen silk dresses; and nineteen summer frocks, which were, following the fashion of the day, adorned with embroidered flowers or trimmed with roses, violets, straw, and ears of wheat.

It was still the time of crinolines, and Sisi had three. The hooped skirts went with a narrow waist, which even in such a slender young woman as little Sisi had to be emphasized by tight lacing and corsets; Sisi owned four of these, along with three special ones for riding, since a lady had to allow herself to be laced even for outdoor exercise.

Along with the gowns went appropriate "fancy trimmings," such as twelve "headdresses" of feathers, rose petals, apple blossoms, lace, ribbon, and pearls, as well as floral adornments and wreaths of flowers, which the ladies carried to ornament and supplement their gowns. There were sixteen hats: white and pink feathered hats, several lace and straw hats, even a garden hat with a garland of wild flowers. That last was the hat Sisi had worn in Bad Ischl, to the Emperor's great delight.

Even the underwear is listed precisely: twelve dozen (that is, a hundred forty-four) camisoles, most of them of batiste with lace, and three dozen nightgowns. The fourteen dozen stockings were of silk, though a few were made of cotton. There were ten bed jackets of muslin and silk; twelve embroidered nightcaps; three negligee caps of embroidered muslin; twenty-four night neckerchiefs; six dozen petticoats of piqué, silk, and flannel; five dozen pantalettes; twenty-four combing coats; and three bathing shirts.

The number of shoes was considerable. Only six pairs, however, were leather ankle boots; all other shoes (a hundred thirteen pairs altogether) were of velvet, taffeta, silk, or "stuff"—hardly suitable, therefore, to be worn for any length of time. It seems that it was particularly in the area of shoes that Sisi had been inadequately provided for. Hardly had she arrived in Vienna than new shoes had to be bought—for the unusually large sum of 700 guldens. The Empress of Austria was not allowed to wear a pair of shoes for more than a day. Then the shoes were given away— a custom to which young Elisabeth could not resign herself and which she later abolished.

The final grouping in the inventory was made up of "other objects." These included two fans, two umbrellas, three large and three small parasols, three pairs of rubber galoshes. Even tortoise-shell combs, clothes brushes, hairbrushes, nailbrushes, toothbrushes, and shoehorns are enumerated, along with a box of straight pins and hairpins, ribbons, and buttons.

It is not difficult to see in this list the speed, even the excitement, with which this trousseau was assembled. Ludovika had long been preparing and planning for Helene's expected great match. Improvisation would have to do for Sisi. There was no chance of falling back on previously acquired goods, one had to concentrate on the essential—and what was essential were the "fancy gowns" for gala occasions. Everything else was incidental.

To the sixteen-year-old girl, this provisioning represented luxury such as she had never known. In view of the modest style of life to which she was accustomed, her many new gowns must have made her feel immensely rich, and she never suspected that all her new worldly goods were as nothing by Viennese standards and that only too soon she would be ridiculed for her simple wardrobe. Even the enamored Emperor had written his mother from Munich in October, "With the trousseau, it seems to me, things are not moving ahead well, and I have difficulty believing that it will be pretty."[57]

It is only too understandable that clever Ludovika, who loved her children, feared for Sisi's future. She knew her daughter and the girl's flights into inwardness, her indifference to outward appearances; and she knew the Viennese court, which cared about nothing so much as outward appearances, rank, and wealth.

On the other hand, the family trusted in Elisabeth's good star. She had been born one of fortune's darlings: at Christmas time, on a Sunday; furthermore, at her birth she already had a tooth—a "lucky tooth," as they said in Bavaria. Elisabeth:

> *Ich bin ein Sonntagskind, ein Kind der Sonne;*
> *Die goldnen Strahlen wand sie mir zum Throne,*
> *Mit ihrem Glanze flocht sie meine Krone,*
> *In ihrem Lichte ist es, dass ich wohne.*[58]

[I am Sunday's child, a child of the sun; / Her golden rays she wove into my throne, / With her glow she wove my crown, / It is in her light that I live.]

CHAPTER TWO

WEDDING IN VIENNA

The danger that Austria would be actively involved in the Crimean War was acute. The summer of 1853 had seen a bad harvest. There were famine, unemployment, poverty to an extent unimaginable today, and a lack of political freedom. The glitter of an imperial wedding would allow all this misery to be forgotten for a brief moment and could nourish hopes for more lenient rule. Many of the commemorative pamphlets contain blatant appeals to the young Empress to mediate between the people and their Emperor; one such screed, for example, referring obviously to 1848, notes, "You are elected by Heaven to crown the reconciliation between a prince and his people and to link forever the parted lovers. What man, wielding the sword of justice, cannot accomplish, woman bearing the frond of mercy will bring about." And again: "In a confused, tempestuous time, you and your house shall become the beacon that rescues the shipwrecked from perdition, the altar at which we devotedly kneel, to which we look for aid."[1] The various national groups under the Austrian crown, equally afflicted by misery and poverty, hoped for a justice-loving, benevolent empress: "We believe that you will become the mediator between him and us, that you will say what we, timid, do not dare to admit, that by your gentle hand many a matter will be steered to the good."[2]

During the past few months little Sisi had learned "many and different things": the languages of polite society, problems of protocol, a smattering of Austrian history. She had learned to dress correctly and to become a better dancer. She cleaned her teeth more carefully than before. But she had not the slightest idea of the life led by Austrians outside the court, whether or not they had work, whether or not the children in her new empire had enough to eat. She had barely heard of the impending war in the east.

By nature, Elisabeth was warmhearted and fair-minded. Like her sisters and brothers, she had been encouraged from childhood to care for the poor and afflicted. She was devoid of aristocratic pride, was familiar with the homes of the poor around Possenhofen. Most important, she was not superficial in her thinking; quite the contrary: From childhood on, she had a tendency to brood: She wasted little time on appearances, trying instead to fathom the "natural," the "truth" of things. Though as yet she thought as a child, this was a characteristic which nevertheless developed early and which she kept to the end of her life.

All these good traits, which Sisi demonstrated throughout her unbridled but loving childhood and by her sensitive temperament, were now worthless, even a drawback. To lack aristocratic pride was seen in Vienna not as an advantage but as a deficiency. So was any lack of respect for the formalities. The Viennese court, even the sovereignty of the Emperor and the high position of the imperial family, were based in large part on protocol and ceremony. Truth and authenticity were not important here. The aspects Sisi saw as pure formalities had great political significance after 1848: They raised the ruling family far above ordinary mortals, allowing it to become unapproachable, untouchable; the family was a visible expression of God's grace. From the day of the engagement, the warmhearted creature the peoples of Austria had hoped for was turned into a public figure representing the Viennese court—though, granted, the most beautiful one Austria had ever had. The seeds of all future conflicts were already sown during these months before the wedding. All had their origin in the discrepancy between a clear-thinking, sensitive woman and her exploitation as a court figure, and a court figure above.

On April 20, 1854, Duchess Elisabeth of Bavaria left her native city of Munich. The future Empress was not informed that on this very day a crucial event in the Crimean War occurred. Austria and Prussia concluded a pact to force Russia to retreat from the Danube duchies. Franz Joseph thus set his course against Russia but did not join the Western Powers, in this way antagonizing both sides. Austrian troops were deployed on the Russian border.

After a mass in the private chapel of the Duke's Munich palace, Sisi began by saying good-bye to the servants. For each one she had a little gift, to each one she gave her hand in farewell. As Empress of Austria, she would no longer be allowed such behavior. Very soon, in the rarefied air of the Viennese court, she would be allowed to "put out her hand for kissing" only to very specifically selected and privileged members of the aristocracy; she could not simply shake hands with anyone she took a liking to, as she was used to doing in Bavaria. At this parting the tears flowed freely—on both sides.

The family farewells were followed by the appearance of the ruling King of Bavaria, Max II, and his predecessor, Ludwig I (who had been forced to abdicate in 1848 as a result of the scandal involving Lola Montez), wearing the uniforms of Austrian regiments. With them were their wives and other members from the royal branch of the Wittelsbachs. A huge crowd had gathered on the Ludwigstrasse outside the Duke's palace. Touched by the thunderous shouts of joy of the Munich populace, Sisi rose to her feet in the carriage, her face bathed in tears, and waved her handkerchief.

The journey took three full days (with two overnight stops). First, the party was taken by carriage from Munich to Straubing. In Straubing, a Danube steamer lay waiting, and here the travelers experienced the first reception to include local officials, bands, girls dressed all in white, congratulations and speeches, the waving of flags, bouquets of flowers. This scene was to be repeated at every subsequent stop.

On April 21, at about two o'clock in the afternoon, the steamer docked in Passau. A triumphal arch had been erected at the Bavarian border. An imperial deputation welcomed the future Empress. Two festively decorated steamers escorted her from the border through Upper Austria. At six o'clock in the evening, the ships arrived in Linz, the first stop on Austrian soil. The governor and the mayor, the military, the guilds and the schoolchildren, the clergy and the aristocracy, a choir, all had arranged for a splendid reception. What was unexpected was that the Emperor came in person to welcome his bride. Early that morning he had taken the steamer from Vienna to Linz to surprise her—a gesture not on the program.

That evening, there was a gala performance at the Linz theater of *Die Rosen der Elisabeth* (The Roses of Elisabeth), then an illumination of the town, a torchlight parade, and choral selections. The Emperor left Linz at four thirty in the morning of April 22, ahead of his bride, to be able to welcome her once more at the official reception in Vienna.

The large side-wheeler *Franz Joseph* set sail with the wedding party from Linz at eight o'clock in the morning. It was surely the most splendid vessel ever to have plied the Danube. Its 140-horsepower engines, which had been manufactured in London, caused a sensation that was duly celebrated in the newspapers of the time. The ship's appointments were imperial: The walls of the bride's cabin were covered in crimson velvet; the deck was transformed into a living flower garden with a rose arbor, where Sisi could retire. Rose garlands were looped over the ship's sides down to the surface of the water. Blue-and-white Bavarian flags rippled next to the red-white-red of Austria and the black-and-yellow Habsburg colors. All other river traffic was prohibited on this special day.

The baroque convent of Melk, Castle Dürnstein, the towns of Stein, Krems, Tulln, and finally Kosterneuburg—an idyllic history-laden landscape—were festively decorated for the young Rose of Bavaria. Work was stopped everywhere. Schoolchildren, peasants, workmen, women lined the shores. At every landing stage, the local honoraries were assembled—the mayors, the teachers, the priests. Everywhere the imperial anthem was drowned out by gun salutes.

Each one of these tens of thousands of people who lined the banks wanted to see the bride. It was the third day of the journey. She was exhausted from all the new impressions. Nevertheless, she bravely stayed at her post, waved her lace handkerchief, smiled. She still, after all, had her mother by her side, her help and her refuge. Her brothers and sisters were also still with her, now and then joking to ease her nervousness. But Sisi was very pale, very quiet, very anxious.

Before arriving in Nussdorf near Vienna, the wedding party changed clothes. A spectacular reception was awaiting them. The empire's dignitaries, the members of the House of Habsburg-Lothringen, the aristocracy, representatives of the municipality—all stood ready under a splendid arch of triumph to receive the future Empress in a manner befitting her station. She slipped out of her traveling outfit and put on one of her "fancy gowns," a filmy pink silk dress with a full crinoline; with it she wore a white lace cape and a small white hat.

The thunder of cannons and the peal of the bells in every church of Vienna announced the arrival in Nussdorf of the Emperor's bride on April 22 around four o'clock in the afternoon. Even before the ship had properly docked, Emperor Franz Joseph bounded from the riverbank onto the boat to welcome his Sisi. In his marshal's uniform with the wide ribbon of the Bavarian Order of Hubertus, he looked extremely handsome. Tens of thousands watched as the young Emperor embraced his bride and kissed her heartily.

Never before and never again was a Habsburg bride welcomed both with such ceremony and with such heartfelt affection. During this love scene, many an observer was reminded of the good marriage, which had become proverbial in Austria, between Maria Theresia and her "Franzl." Chroniclers, at any rate, did not omit to mention that they felt "as if this time the gentle spirit of Maria Theresia floated above her illustrious grandson."[3] The joy at the sight was open and honest—delight in the bride's girlish though pale appearance.

The Viennese had had to wait long enough for a young, representative empress. The previous year, Napoleon III had married the beautiful Eugénie and turned Paris into the center of European glamour. Now, at last, Vienna would catch up with Paris—or so it was hoped. A young and beautiful empress would bring new sparkle to Vienna's social life, which had slumbered for so long, and would serve as an international attraction. In this way, Vienna might become a fashion center second only to Paris. Such an eventuality meant especially a hope for an impetus to the languishing trades and crafts in Austria and for an increase in employment.

The future Empress could not complain of a cool reception by the populace. The simple people who lined the banks of the Danube and stood along the heights of the Leopoldsberg in order to see the Duchess of Bavaria offered her their trust. The Emperor's evident fondness confirmed them in their hope for better times and a more benevolent ruler; surely now the "reactionary" influence of Archduchess Sophie would be held at bay by the young Empress and would give way to more liberal tendencies.

Archduchess Sophie, the "secret Empress," boarded the ship immediately after the Emperor. The official part of the reception began. The bride kissed the hand of her aunt and future mother-in-law. She was welcomed by the rest of the family—the Emperor's brothers, countless new aunts and uncles, cousins. Then she disembarked, leaving on the arm of her groom. Great shouts of jubilation, gun salutes, music, waving flags. A brief stop at the gold-ornamented Triumphhalle (Hall of Triumph), the interior of which was "splendidly decorated with mirrored walls, flowers, hangings, like a fairy temple." A resting place among flowers for Her Most Serene Highness, the imperial bride; platforms for the dignitaries along the sides, the delegates of foreign nations with their ladies on the right, the Viennese municipal council, the high clergy, the high nobility, the high military, the ministers, and the provincial governors to the left.

Then the coach procession from Nussdorf to Schönbrunn assembled: at its head, the Emperor with Duke Max; in the second coach, Sisi with Sophie; in the third, Ludovika with Archduke Franz Karl, the Emperor's father; immediately following, the remaining "Most Serene Highnesses, the family members." The procession drove under a number of triumphal arches through Döbling, Währing, Hernals, across the Schmelz to Mariahilferstrasse and on to Schönbrunn. Franz Joseph personally opened the carriage door and led his bride into his summer residence, the magnificent baroque castle dating from the time of Maria Theresia, with more than 1,400 rooms fitted out in the utmost splendor.

A complex ceremonial began to unfold in the Great Salon: first, Sophie introduced the archduchesses to Sisi, then the Emperor did the same for the male members of the House of Habsburg. (Sophie noted in her diary, not without pride, that besides her three younger sons and her husband, there were fifteen other archdukes.) Archduke Ferdinand Max, the Emperor's younger brother, assumed the task of acquainting the Wittelsbach and Habsburg families with each other. Then came the introduction of the high court officials. All this occupied considerable time.

With great solemnity, the Emperor next presented the wedding gifts, beginning with his gift to the bride, a diamond crown with a matching diamond waist ornament—a so-called corsage. The crown was a splendid example of the old goldsmiths' art, inset with emeralds; the modern resetting alone had cost 100,000 guldens.[4] (A few days before Sisi's arrival, it had accidentally been dropped—an occurrence seen by many as a bad omen —and repaired in a great hurry.) Another diamond tiara was sent by the former Emperor, Ferdinand, from Prague. The widow of Emperor Franz (an aunt of both bride and groom) also gave diamonds that befitted the occasion.

Sisi's two Bavarian "ladies," who were no longer required in Vienna, were given precious parting gifts. Their place was now taken by a personal household. It was headed by Countess Sophie Esterházy, née Princess Liechtenstein, a close confidante of Archduchess Sophie. At the time, she was fifty-six years old—seven years older than Sophie; a puritanical woman with punctilious respect for outward form, she was, for all practical purposes, assigned the job of governess to the young Empress. From the first moment, Sisi took an intense dislike to Countess Esterházy, who was viewed critically by other contemporaries as well; for example, the Emperor's aide-de-camp, Weckbecker, noted, "on the one hand, she treated the young Empress a little too much like a governess, while on the other, she saw her principal task as introducing the incipient sovereign to all sorts of gossip about the families of the high aristocracy, for which the Bavarian Princess naturally could summon up only slight interest."[5]

Elisabeth had more confidence in her chief steward, Prince Lobkowitz. Nor did she dislike the two young ladies-in-waiting, Countesses Paula Bellegarde and Karoline Lamberg. Sophie made it clear to Sisi from the outset that, as Empress, she would not be allowed to establish any personal ties with these young women. Sisi's "household" consisted of a secretary, a lady of the bedchamber, two lady's maids, two chambermaids, one valet de chambre, a porter, four footmen, one houseman, and a chamber woman. This staff, of course, was for the Empress's exclusive service. The Emperor had his own household, far larger and entirely separate from that of the Empress.

The chronicles report that on the very same evening, "the lovely Princess was gracious enough to show herself, in charming condescension and friendliness, to the loudly cheering populace"—she appeared on the large balcony of Schönbrunn Castle. That night, a large court banquet was held with all the splendor of the old empire.

From her arrival in the afternoon until late into the night, the sixteen-year-old, exhausted from her journey, was constantly under the eyes of complete strangers, not all of them well disposed toward her. The cordiality that had surged her way from the many who waved at her from the shore had given way here, in the circle of the court aristocracy, to a rather skeptical curiosity. After all, Sisi had not yet grown into the full beauty of her later years; she was ungainly, intimidated, not at all what the Viennese court might have imagined when they thought about a future empress. The exertions of this day of arrival, however, were only the beginning.

For the very next day, April 23, the traditional solemn entrance of the Emperor's bride into Vienna was celebrated. This entry began, not at Schönbrunn Castle, but at Maria Theresia's old town palace, the "Favorita" (the present Theresianum), which the imperial family hardly used at all otherwise. The solemn ritual of dressing for the event took hours—that, too, was something Sisi would now have to grow accustomed to. Many coaches carrying family members and the elite of the court appointees drove from Schönbrunn to the Favorita in the morning and assembled there for the solemn entrance, for which a highly complicated ceremonial was prescribed.

When, in the late afternoon, the moment had finally arrived for the bride and her mother to get into the state carriage pulled by eight Lipizzaners, Sisi was wearing another one of her fancy gowns—pink threaded through with silver, with a train, garlands of roses—the new diamond tiara in her hair. Her exhaustion was plain to see; within the glass coach, she wept ceaselessly. And instead of greeting a beaming imperial bride, the Viennese forming a cordon of honor welcomed a sobbing young girl sitting next to an equally intimidated mother of the bride.

The piebalds' manes were plaited with red and gold tassels, their heads sported tufts of white plumes, and their harness was gold-embroidered. Two footmen in full regalia, white-wigged, walked alongside each carriage door and each horse. The bride's coach was followed by the state coaches of the chief stewards, of the chamberlains and palace ladies on duty, and of the privy councillors. Each was drawn by six horses and was attended by footmen preceding and alongside the carriages.

Everything down to the last detail was arranged according to rank at court. Six "imperial and royal court trumpeters on horse," court forerunners and pages, the mounted guards, the auxiliary bodyguard "with colors and drums," grenadiers, cuirassiers, and court gillies escorted the sovereign bride, who hardly knew how to appreciate the magnificence all around her.

When the procession neared the city walls, the artillery salvos fell silent, and all the bells in the city began to peal. Every house along the route was decked out with bunting and flowers. All along the way platforms had been erected for the curious onlookers. The most striking element of the procession was the elegance of the Hungarian magnates. They wore their national costume, resplendent with gold and precious stones. Even their servants' liveries were of unparalleled elegance, as were their state carriages, pulled by six horses each. The Swiss envoy, Tschudi, wrote that "except for the Congress, such extraordinary splendor was never yet seen" in the capital of Austria.[6]

Less than five years had passed since the Revolution had raised barricades in the exact same spot where the stands for the onlookers now stood. "Freedom of the press," "constitution"—these were the demands the Emperor had not met. The revolutionaries were executed, had emigrated, were jailed, or had come to an arrangement with the absolutist government. The ominous sign "Property of the Nation" had long ago stopped hanging

from the Hofburg. Absolutism was celebrating its triumphs with an imperial wedding—and the people cheered.

Nevertheless, the Emperor had seized the occasion of the joyful event
to make some gestures of conciliation to the revolutionaries of 1848. The
Wiener Zeitung of April 23 printed an official communiqué pardoning over
two hundred "prisoners condemned to confinement as a consequence of
political crimes." The sentences of another hundred were reduced by half.
Additionally, a general amnesty was declared "for all crimes of lèse majesté
and offenses against the public order" and the "treasonable activities" of
1848 in Galicia and the uprising that broke out in Lemberg in November
1848. The state of siege was lifted in Hungary, Lombardy, and Venetia.

The Emperor's most valuable gift to his impoverished nation, however,
was the sum of 200,000 guldens, intended to "ease the existing state of
emergency" on the occasion of his wedding: 25,000 guldens for Bohemia,
particularly for the inhabitants of the Erzgebirge and the Riesengebirge
and the poor of Prague; 6,000 guldens for the Moravian factory districts
and the poor of Brno; 4,000 for the poor of Silesia; 25,000 for the poor
of Galicia. The Tyrol received 50,000 guldens for grain purchases and for
those injured by the vine disease in the southern Tyrol; Croatia, 10,000;
Dalmatia and the Coastland, 15,000 each; "my capital city, Vienna," for
the support of "the working class and the poor, who suffer most especially
from the current rise in prices," 50,000. The provinces of Hungary and
Northern Italy, where there was unrest, received nothing.

A veritable shower of medals rained on meritorious officials of the
monarchy. That all these proofs of favor were linked to the wedding and
the person of the new Empress makes the warm reception accorded the
bride even more understandable.

Whether Sisi took any notice of these gifts is highly questionable.
Sobbing, she arrived at her new home, the Hofburg in Vienna. As she
descended from the carriage, she stumbled because her tiara caught in the
doorframe. This embarrassing mishap occurred in full sight of the entire
imperial family, solemnly assembled to receive her outside the Hofburg.
Nevertheless, Archduchess Sophie found little Sisi *"ravissante"*—enchanting—as she noted in her diary. "The demeanor of the dear child was
perfect, full of a sweet and gracious dignity." In the Amalienhof apartments "the imperial and royal generals and the officers' corps, along with
the male royal household and the ladies," were waiting to pay their
respects to the illustrious ladies and gentlemen. With this, the ceremonies
of the day came to an end, and Sisi had to prepare for the climax: the

wedding on the following day, at seven o'clock in the evening, in the Augustinerkirche.

In every church of the monarchy, divine services marked the occasion of the imperial nuptials. On the morning of the great day, a solemn mass in St. Stephen's Cathedral was attended by "the elite of all stations." A collection taken up to mark the occasion of the wedding was so amply subscribed that forty couples married on the same day as the Emperor were given a wedding gift of 500 guldens each—about twice a worker's yearly income. In many cities and towns, needy children were clothed, the poor were fed, firewood and bread were distributed. The Austrian national anthem had a new second stanza added:

> *An des Kaisers Seite waltet,*
> *Ihm verwandt durch Stamm und Sinn,*
> *Reich an Reiz, der nie veraltet,*
> *Unsere holde Kaiserin.*
> *Was das Glück zuhöchst gepriesen,*
> *Ström auf sie der Himmel aus!*
> *Heil Franz Joseph, Heil Elisen,*
> *Segen Habsburgs ganzem Haus!*

[At the Emperor's side, / Linked to him by tribe and feeling, / Rich in charm that never withers, / Rules our lovely Empress. / What fortune has praised most highly, / Let Heaven shower on her! / Hail Franz Joseph, Hail Elise, / Blessings on Habsburg's entire House!]

There was a proliferation of poetic invention concerning the "angelic nature" and beauty of the new Empress. Besides thousands of festive broadsides in various languages, eighty-three commemorative pamphlets in Elisabeth's honor were published in 1854, among them sixty-one in German, eleven in Italian, two in Magyar, four in Czech, two in Polish, and one each in Serbo-Croatian, Latin, and English.[7]

They made an uncommonly handsome couple as they were joined in the Augustinerkirche, bright as day with the light of 15,000 candles and draped in red velvet. The historians vied with each other in describing the splendor that stretched as far as the eye could see: "All that the utmost in luxury, combined with the greatest of riches and truly imperial splendor, is able to offer dazzles the eye here. In particular, in regard to the jewels, one can surely say that a sea of precious stones and pearls billowed past the marveling eyes of the assembled crowd. Especially the diamonds seemed to multiply a thousandfold in the glow of the sumptuous illumination and made a magical impression by the wealth of their color."[8]

The Belgian envoy sounded rather complacent in his report to Brussels: "In a city where not long ago the revolutionary spirit wrought so much devastation, it was not an idle act to unfold the entire splendor of the monarchy."[9]

The Archbishop of Vienna, Cardinal Othmar, Ritter von Rauscher, performed the marriage ceremony with the assistance of more than seventy bishops and prelates. At the moment when the rings were exchanged, a battalion of grenadiers mounted on the roof of the church released the first salvo, which was followed by a thunder of cannons, proclaiming that the Duchess Elisabeth of Bavaria had been transformed into the Empress of Austria. The seemingly endless and flowery wedding address earned Rauscher the nickname "Cardinal Plauscher" (blabbermouth).

On the same occasion, Rauscher, a confidant of Archduchess Sophie, could not forego referring to 1848 with abhorrence: "In the first bloom of youth, he [Franz Joseph] threw himself against those demonic forces that threatened destruction to all that humanity holds sacred. Victory followed wherever he trod." From now on, he continued, the Emperor would also be the paragon of Christian family life.[10]

When the religious rites had finally been weathered, and the ceremonial procession had returned the bridal pair to the Hofburg, the machinery of court protocol was set in motion. The victorious generals of 1848 were the first to be admitted to an audience with the imperial couple: Radetzky, Windisch-Graetz, Nugent, Jelačić.

In the audience chamber, the ambassadors and envoys were waiting. Foreign Minister Buol had the great honor of introducing each one to the new Empress. After completion of this long audience, Their Majesties moved to the Hall of Mirrors. There the ladies of the diplomatic corps were waiting in full regalia to be introduced to the Empress.

"Thereupon Their Majesties with the Imperial Family and the Royal Household on Duty proceeded to the Hall of Ceremony in order to receive the congratulatory delegation." Empress and Emperor "were gracious enough to chat with those present. The chatelaine made the introductions: 'The ladies responsible for the palace and the living quarters; further, the royal and imperial first steward and the gentlemen of the royal household.' Thereupon the ladies were led up for the kiss on the hand."[11]

At the sight of so many strangers, the young Empress panicked and fled to an adjoining room, where she broke out in tears. We can easily imagine the whispering among the ladies in full regalia waiting for the bride in the audience chamber.[12] When Sisi finally joined the reception exhausted and unsteady, her face tear-stained, she provided new food for gossip. For she was too timid to make conversation with each of the ladies presented to her. According to protocol, however, no one was allowed to speak to the Empress except to reply to questions. A most awkward situation, which Countess Esterházy finally salvaged by requesting the ladies to address a few words to the Empress.

And the worst was yet to come. When Sisi caught sight of her two cousins Adelgunde and Hildegard from Bavaria among the huge crowd of strangers, she refused them the obligatory kiss on the hand, wishing to hug them instead. When the outraged expressions around her told her that once again she had committed an error, she defended herself: "But we are cousins!" Archduchess Sophie could not, of course, accept this reason for an offense against protocol; she reminded Sisi of her exalted position and insisted that the protocol—that is, the kiss on the hand of the Empress— be observed.[13]

The first causes of conflict in the imperial family could not be overlooked. The differences in the couple's lives up to that time were too great. To Franz Joseph and his mother, the rigid formality was a matter of everyday practice, even indispensable to demonstrating the power of the crown. That the young Empress would have to learn to accustom herself to the ceremonial was a matter of course. Most young girls would gladly have accepted this magnificent burden, even enjoyed it.

Elisabeth, however, had inherited the Wittelsbach family traits to an extreme degree: high intelligence coupled with an excessive sensibility and a strong desire for freedom. Until this time, she had been able to develop her natural tendencies freely and had had practically no obligations imposed on her. And with the exception of the household help, she had never actually seen anyone work. As far as her father, Max, was concerned, as a general, he was a member of the Bavarian army; but this position by no means took up much of his time or energies. He lived on a generous grant of 250,000 guldens a year, neglected his family and paternal obligations, and did only what he felt like doing. A sixteen-year-old girl from such a background could hardly be faulted for lacking a sense of duty.

Titles, honors, money—these were concepts that held no meaning for young Elisabeth. She was made entirely of feeling, and her childish imagination had none but purely sentimental expectations of her future marriage. A rude awakening in Vienna was only too inevitable.

The exertions of the wedding-day protocol ended with the illumination of the "capital and residence"—an obligatory part of all the most exalted festivities. Great crowds came from the outskirts to the inner city to witness this popular display. One chronicler reported that "the area around the gates was constantly enveloped in dense clouds of dust, caused by the movement of so many thousands." The most magnificent illuminations were in Kohlmarkt and Michaelerplatz, where the open two-horse carriage bearing the young couple appeared in the course of the evening. "It seemed that the entire street had been transformed into a ballroom."[14]

Connoisseurs of the situation at court, however, noticed that even on this wedding day not everything was as rosy as it seemed. One eyewitness, Baron Karl Kübeck, wrote in his diary on April 24, "On the podium and among the spectators, jubilation and expectant joy. Behind the scenes, increasingly somber, very somber signs."[15]

A gala banquet took place between ten and eleven o'clock at night. Only then did the public festivities end. Sophie: "Louise [Ludovika] and I led the young bride to her rooms. I left her with her mother and stayed in the small room next to the bedroom until she was in bed. Then I fetched my son and led him to his young wife, whom I saw once more, to wish her a good night. She hid her pretty face, surrounded by the masses of her beautiful hair, in her pillow, as a frightened bird hides in its nest."[16]

This *coucher,* normally attended with great ceremony, was, in court terms, decidedly familial and intimate. Other bridal couples at other European courts had to suffer a great deal more protocol in equivalent situations. King Johann of Saxony, for example, wrote about his bridal night with Sisi's Aunt Amalie: "All the married princesses and their chatelaines escorted the bride home, assisted at her toilet, and said a prayer, whereupon she was taken to her bed. Now the bride's chatelaine had the job of informing me that I could come in. Accompanied by all the married princes, I entered the bedroom and had to get into bed in the presence of all these princes, princesses, and ladies. When the families and their entourages had left, I arose again to make my actual night toilet."[17] In the case of the young Emperor and his bride, the two mothers rejected those ceremonies that were too complicated and too embarrassing. But even the little that remained was too much for the sensitive girl after such a strenuous day.

The following morning the pair did not remain alone for long. Even at breakfast they were interrupted by Archduchess Sophie, who brought along Duchess Ludovika. Sophie wrote in her diary, "We found the young couple at breakfast in the pretty writing room, my son beaming and all over the picture of sweet happiness (praise be to God!), Sisi emotional as she embraced her mother. At first we intended leaving them again, but the Emperor held us back with a touching eagerness."

Whether this last statement can be taken at face value is open to doubt. The two mothers—people commanding respect from the young, overly courteous Emperor—had interrupted the couple's first breakfast, had inquisitively scrutinized their expressions, and then suddenly and politely announced that they were leaving. What choice did the Emperor have but to request them to stay? A fairly obvious situation to anyone familiar with Viennese customs. Sophie's diary continues with the revealing sentence, "Thereafter a confidential talk between each child and its mother." This clearly means that Sophie subjected her son to a detailed inquisition even while he was still at breakfast. In the course of it she would learn that the performance of marital duties had not yet been accomplished—a fact known all over the court before the day was out. Footmen and chambermaids were reliable informants.

Even the imperial bedchamber enjoyed little privacy. Everyone knew on which night (the third) Sisi became a woman. The following morning, the young Empress was bidden to appear at a family breakfast in her mother-in-law's apartments, although in her shame and embarrassment, she was reluctant to go. According to Sophie's diary, that morning the Emperor climbed the stairs to his parents' apartments alone and "waited for his dear Sisi to arise."[18] He did not understand his young wife's wish that they remain alone rather than presenting themselves to the assembled family, who had been watching every movement of the bridal couple for days.

Much later, Elisabeth explained this embarrassing situation to her then lady-in-waiting, Countess Marie Festetics. "The Emperor was so used to obeying her that he gave in to this demand as well. But it was horrible for me. I went only for his sake."[19] In later years Elisabeth repeatedly referred to this particular morning.

During the day, it was her duty to receive deputations from Lower and Upper Austria, Styria, Carinthia, Carniola, and Bukovina, standing between her husband and her mother-in-law. Even Sophie found these audiences so tiring that she "simply couldn't" and needed fortifying in between. All meals were official events, preceded by a change of clothes.

At the audience for the Hungarian deputation, Sisi wore Hungarian national costume for the first time—a pink dress with a black velvet bodice and magnificent lace trimmings. It was, oddly enough, a gift from her mother-in-law. Archduchess Sophie, whose feelings for Hungary were anything but benevolent, admired her daughter-in-law's beauty particularly in this dress. "She and the Emperor in his hussar's uniform made such a handsome and gracious couple," she confided to her diary.

On the evening of April 27 a large court ball took place. The young wife had to withstand the inquisitive looks of the "socially acceptable" aristocracy. The news of the current status of the imperial marriage had already made the rounds. "Her Majesty," this time dressed all in white, her new diamond belt around her waist, a tiara and a wreath of white roses in her hair, sat with "His Majesty" under a canopy of red velvet and listened to "Master Strauss" letting "his tunes ring out." Both Their Majesties danced several times—not with each other, of course, but with the personages designated by protocol. Archduchess Sophie did not forget to note in her diary that the Emperor had to "prompt" his young wife in the figures of the dance.[20] Sisi's dancing skills could not yet measure up to the standards of the Viennese court. At the high point of the ball, the cotillion, Strauss's "Elisabethklänge" was heard for the first time. As tribute to the bride and groom, both the imperial anthem and the Bavarian anthem were woven into the composition.

Duchess Ludovika remained remarkably objective, unaffected by so much glitter, in her report to Bavaria. "Yesterday's court ball was very nice, enormously crowded, brilliant, but the rooms are too small for here, there was such pushing and shoving that one was almost crushed. Many beautiful women and much jewelry make all the festivities glitter." Ludovika saw very clearly that this magnificence meant only work for her daughter. "I see little of Sisi, she is much in demand, and I very much fear to embarrass the Emperor, a young married couple should be left alone."[21] But there was to be no minute of the day that the young couple was left in peace.

The Emperor, dutiful as always, was disciplined enough to see to his paperwork and give audiences in between festivities. The Austrian ambassador in Paris, Count Alexander Hübner, for example, that same day spent more than an hour with the Emperor discussing the Eastern question. He found him "physically and mentally matured" and wrote in his diary, "How cheerful, happy, and so very openly in love he looked! It was a joy to watch him. May God preserve him!"[22] Archduchess Sophie expressed quite similar sentiments in her diary. She repeatedly emphasized how much in love and how happy her Franzi was.

What the court ball was to society, the celebration in the Prater the following day was to the people. The open state carriages bearing the imperial and ducal families drove through the hurly-burly of the park, along the principal avenue, decorated with Japanese lanterns, and through the Wurstelprater to the Feuerwerksplatz, where the Circus Renz was giving a gala performance. This time the Empress's pleasure was visible to all. She enjoyed the acrobats' tricks, especially those of the horseback riders in medieval costumes, and the famous handsome horses of the Renz family. Elisabeth's love for the Circus Renz, which was kindled that night, remained with her to the end of her life.

Four days after the wedding, Elisabeth was so exhausted by all the gala activities that for her sake the Emperor canceled all the planned receptions, taking her instead to the Prater in the afternoon, driving the phaeton himself.

But Elisabeth drew the greatest comfort from her brothers and sisters, who spent a few more days in Vienna before returning to Bavaria. She especially liked being with her older sister Helene, with whom Sisi could talk freely. Ludovika wrote to Marie of Saxony, "As long as the sisters [Sisi and Helene] were together, they were inseparable, and always spoke English, but took no part in our conversations, which was not at all nice of them . . . although it got them into trouble . . . more than once."[23]

The two girls used English as something like a secret language. At the Viennese court, English was not customarily spoken. Neither the Emperor nor Archduchess Sophie knew the language. The annoyance at the sisters' mysterious conversations was therefore entirely understandable. But anyone could also see how steadfast was the love between them—even after the engagement in Bad Ischl, such an unhappy episode in Helene's life.

The festival week concluded with a municipal ball in the Winterreitschule (Winter Riding School) and the Redoutensäle (Masked-Ball Halls), which were connected specifically for this occasion by breaking through the walls. Once again Johann Strauss provided the music. Once again Sisi felt herself the target of thousands of eyes. As the new Empress, after all, she was supposed to be seen by as many people as possible as soon as possible.

Ceremonial controlled even the honeymoon, which, once the festivities were concluded, the couple spent in Laxenburg Castle outside Vienna. Since punctually every morning the Emperor drove to his desk in the Hofburg in Vienna, the young woman was left alone all day long in Laxenburg—that is, isolated within a large circle of people ready to educate and serve her. Archduchess Sophie joined her daughter-in-law every day "to keep her company."

Sisi's sisters, including Helene, returned to Bavaria. Sisi was homesick and wrote sad poems during her Laxenburg honeymoon. One she entitled "Sehnsucht" (Longing).

> Es kehrt der junge Frühling wieder
> Und schmückt den Baum mit frischem Grün
> Und lehrt den Vögeln neue Lieder
> Und macht die Blumen schöner blüh'n.
>
> Doch was ist mir die Frühlingswonne
> Hier in dem fernen, fremden Land?
> Ich sehn' mich nach der Heimat Sonne,
> Ich sehn' mich nach der Isar Strand.[24]

[Fresh spring returns / And trims the trees with new green / And teaches new songs to the birds / And makes the flowers bloom more beautifully. // But what is springtime bliss to me / Here in the faraway, strange land? / I long for the sun of home, / I long for the banks of the Isar.]

The theme that recurred from then on was that of the caged bird or the butterfly far from home, finding only unhappiness and the absence of freedom. This despairing cry for freedom is threaded through all of the young Empress's verses. Two weeks after the wedding, on May 8, 1854, she wrote:

> Oh, dass ich nie den Pfad verlassen,
> Der mich zur Freiheit hätt' geführt.
> Oh, dass ich auf der breiten Strassen
> Der Eitelkeit mich nie verirrt!
>
> Ich bin erwacht in einem Kerker,
> Und Fesseln sind an meiner Hand.
> Und meine Sehnsucht immer stärker—
> Und Freiheit! Du, mir abgewandt!
>
> Ich bin erwacht aus einem Rausche,
> Der meinen Geist gefangenhielt,
> Und fluche fruchtlos diesem Tausche,
> Bei dem ich Freiheit! Dich—verspielt.[25]

[Oh, had I but never left the path / That would have led me
to freedom. / Oh, that on the broad avenues / Of vanity I had
never strayed! // I have awakened in a dungeon, / With chains on
my hands. / And my longing ever stronger— / And freedom!
You, turned from me! // I have awakened from a rapture, /
Which held my spirit captive, / And vainly do I curse this
exchange, / In which I gambled away you—freedom!—away.]

But the young Empress shed tears, not only over her home and her
freedom, but also over her first love. That she did so even during the
honeymoon weeks with Franz Joseph indicates that there were additional
problems, about which we can only speculate.

Reluctantly and sadly, Sisi began to obey the rules of the court, even
if she never acknowledged the propriety of such rigid etiquette. Later, she
told her lady-in-waiting "how afraid she had been in the world of strangers, of exalted personages—how everything had seemed so different!—
how she missed her home and her sisters and brothers!—the whole carefree,
innocent existence of Possenhofen!—The natural, the simple was to disappear under the unnatural pressure of exaggerated etiquette—in a word—
how everything dealt only with 'seeming' and not with 'being'—and how
difficult everything had often been."[26]

In Vienna, Sisi's health became very precarious. For months she suffered
from severe coughing fits and from anxiety attacks whenever she had to
go down steep stairs.[27] It is quite probable that her constant ailments had
psychological origins.

A mere two weeks after the wedding, Sisi's longing for her sisters and
brothers was so great that she requested the Emperor almost beseechingly
to invite her favorite brother, Karl Theodor, to spend a few days in Vienna.
When the Emperor agreed, she wept for joy.

She felt trapped in a gilded cage. The jewelry, the beautiful dresses—
they were merely a burden to her. For they meant fittings, making choices,
constant dressing and changing. There were battles over little things.
Elisabeth refused to give away her shoes after wearing them once. The
chambermaids sneered: The new Empress was unfamiliar with the simplest
time-honored customs practiced at the court of Vienna. She did not like
to have the waiting women dress her. She had been raised to be independent, and she was very shy; the lady's maids were still strangers to her. On
this point, too, she was unable to get her way.

Conflicts with the secret Empress, Archduchess Sophie, usually turned,
in Sisi's opinion, on trivialities, and they hurt her all the more for being

so trivial. Thus, the young couple liked to wander alone through the halls and twisting corridors of the Hofburg to the old Burgtheater, which was part of the castle. This innocent pleasure, however, was immediately forbidden by Archduchess Sophie. For the Emperor and Empress were entitled to be escorted to the theater by carefully specified court officials.[28] Sophie was always concerned with upholding imperial dignity. The fact that in this matter the Emperor did not dare to object additionally offended the already high-strung Sisi.

Sophie was accustomed to making all the decisions in family and political matters. And she was accustomed to commanding obedience. Her husband depended on her mind. From their earliest childhood on, her four sons—Franz Joseph, Ferdinand Maximilian, Karl Ludwig, and Ludwig Viktor—acknowledged Sophie's authority as supreme and never dared to resist her. It was Sophie to whom Franz Joseph owed his position. She had persuaded her husband, the rightful heir to the throne, to renounce it. She had made her son what he was—a fully trained, dutiful, and extremely industrious young man of personal integrity, who espoused her political principles: the divine right of kings, absolute rule by the monarch, suppression of any manifestations of the popular will, rejection of parliamentarianism, close ties between church and state. Now she felt it to be her duty to turn her sixteen-year-old niece into an empress who would fulfill *her* conception in the service of the empire and the dynasty.

In later years, Elisabeth understood that Sophie was not motivated by malice, and she declared to a lady-in-waiting, "that the Archduchess surely meant so well in everything—but that the paths were arduous and the manner harsh—that the Emperor suffered from it as well and that she always wanted to control . . . and how from the first day she was an obstacle to her contentment and happiness and interfered in everything and how she made it harder for them to be—undisturbed—together!"[29]

All her life, Archduchess Sophie had longed for a position such as her sixteen-year-old niece now assumed. She could not help being offended, even outraged, at the way in which the young Empress looked on her high standing as only a burden and something that robbed her of her personal liberty. Sophie paid no attention whatever to Sisi's very obvious depressions; she did not even take them seriously. She saw only the expression, radiant with joy, of her enamored "Franzi."

Queen Marie of Saxony confirmed this attitude. "The news from Vienna sounds indescribably happy and makes me happy. . . . Both happy mothers have written me veritable *books* about it."[30] Sophie also wrote to Bavaria about "our dear young couple," who, in the "rural seclusion" of Laxenburg "spent the happiest honeymoon. The truly Christian domestic happiness of my children is a heartwarming sight."[31]

Nevertheless, there is no trace of domestic happiness in the Empress's statements made in later years. Whenever she visited Laxenburg, Sisi never forgot to refer to her sad honeymoon. For example, Marie Valerie, her younger daughter, noted in her diary, "Mama showed us the desk at which she wrote so much to Possi [Possenhofen] and cried so much, so much, because she was homesick."[32]

Similarly, Marie Festetics wrote in her diary in Laxenburg,

> Elisabeth went from room to room—said of each what it was —but without more detailed commentary, until finally she stopped in a corner room where a desk stood between windows and a desk chair before it; she stood quiet as a mouse for a long time—suddenly she said: ". . . Here I wept a lot, Marie. The mere thought of that time constricts my heart. I was here after my wedding. . . . I felt so abandoned, so lonely. Of course the Emperor could not be here during the day, early every morning he went to Vienna. At six o'clock he returned for dinner. Until then I was alone all day long and was afraid of the moment when Archduchess Sophie came. For she came every day, to spy on what I was doing at any hour. I was completely *à la merci* of this completely malicious woman. Everything I did was bad. She passed disparaging judgments on anyone I loved. She found out everything because she never stopped prying. The whole house feared her so much that everyone trembled. Of course they told her everything. The smallest thing was an affair of state."[33]

Elisabeth's complaints continued in the same vein. Surely as far as Sophie's malice went, they were exaggerated. For that the Archduchess meant well, even though she employed the wrong means, is made sufficiently clear by Sophie's diary. On the other hand, Elisabeth's stories show very obviously the paramount position Sophie occupied in the imperial family during the 1850s. Archduchess Sophie "scolded" not only the young Empress, "but also the Emperor, like schoolchildren," the astonished Countess Festetics learned from Elisabeth.

Once I requested the Emperor to take me along to Vienna. I spent the whole day there with him. For one day I did not see her . . . but no sooner had we arrived back home in the evening, than she came running over. She forbade me to do anything like that ever again. She reviled me so much because it is unseemly for an Empress to go running after her husband and to drive back and forth like a cadet. Of course, after that it was stopped.

Even here in Laxenburg, during the so-called honeymoon, the young couple was hardly ever alone for their only shared meal of the day. For example, one of the imperial aides-de-camp, Hugo von Weckbecker, had the job of sitting next to the Empress and was supposed to "endeavor to engage her in conversation, since she was still too timid and was now to be educated in the social graces."[34] Countess Esterházy, acting on Sophie's orders, also never left Sisi's side, so as to be able to correct every misstep immediately.

The Emperor and Empress took their first trip early in June, traveling to Moravia and Bohemia. It was an act of gratitude and recognition for proffered aid and loyalty. In 1848, the imperial family had fled riot-torn Vienna and gone to Olmütz in Moravia. There, an important event in Austrian history had taken place: Emperor Ferdinand's renunciation of the throne ("I was glad to do it") and the accession of Franz Joseph, eighteen years old at the time.

The privileged position of the Bohemian lands during this time can also be seen in the fact that the first new language Sisi was expected to learn was Bohemian. Archduchess Sophie once noted in her diary that Sisi could already "count in Bohemian," though later there was very little mention of Sisi's progress in the language.

Sisi had no choice but to grow used to the extensive retinue that always accompanied the imperial couple on all travels. There were aides-de-camp, military officers, household troops, clergy, the personal physician Dr. Johann Seeburger, Adjutant General Grünne. Then there was Sisi's personal entourage: chief steward and chatelaine, two ladies-in-waiting, a secretary. All these people brought along their own servants—valets, hairdressers, bathing attendants, footmen.

A rail line—the Nordbahn (Northern Railway)—had already been built along the stretch from Vienna through Brno to Prague, which was of great economic importance. The flower-bedecked locomotive Proserpina brought the imperial couple to Brno, the capital of Moravia, in a mere four hours. They were greeted with arches of triumph, girls dressed all in white, waving flags, speeches by dignitaries and the Emperor in German and in Czech, festive illumination, gala performances at the theater, a public festival in Brno's Augarten with sack races and ropedancers, a torchlight parade. A parade in Moravian costume featured a colorful float bearing a bride and groom and the entire rustic wedding party. They presented the Emperor and Empress with gifts—including a bottle of local wine, vintage 1746.

Here in Moravia, young Elisabeth made her debut in the role of sovereign. She visited orphanages, schools, and a charity hospital. Wherever she went, she made "a highly favorable impression by her gracious condescension and kindness," as the *Wiener Zeitung* reported the following day. The simple and natural manner in which the young Empress was able to speak with people from the lower classes was noticed, and it nourished the hope that some day this woman would espouse social problems.

Two days later, arrival in Prague: guard of honor made up of mine workers, the guilds, and the trades of this highly industrialized land. Franz Joseph and Elisabeth stayed in Hradčany Castle, the old seat of the kings of Bohemia; and it was here that they received the homage of the nobility, the city, the university, the army, and the regional deputations. The new Queen of Bohemia was also introduced to the "socially acceptable ladies" —those, that is, who could furnish proof of sixteen highly aristocratic ancestors and who were therefore worthy to attend court functions.

Exactly as happened in the Viennese Hofburg, in Hradčany Castle in Prague the schedule was crammed with hours of audiences and official dinners. The newspapers allow us to reconstruct the imperial couple's daily ordeal in precise detail. The Emperor permitted himself no rest, used as he was from childhood to fulfilling his duties. He expected the same readiness to meet obligations from his young wife, whose health was not the best.

So the sixteen-year-old girl received delegations and petitioners, such as the deputation from the Erzgebirge. The *Wiener Zeitung* noted with some emotion, "But when the President movingly described the poverty of the mountain people, the beautiful eyes of the lovely sovereign filled with tears, and Her Majesty was hardly able to master her inner emotion. What a deeply affecting impression this new proof of her angelic gentleness had on those present is indescribable, it was a solemn moment."[35]

The young couple laid the cornerstone for a church; opened a target shoot; and visited a home for deaf-mutes, an insane asylum, and an agricultural fair. At this last they were given a demonstration of a new baking oven (the baker made them a pretzel in the shape of the Austrian eagle) and a new centrifugal pump before they inspected the horned-cattle breeds. At the fair, it was said, "Their Very Majesties enchanted all those present by their amiability and interest."

In spite of many events featuring the populace, however, the powerful Bohemian nobility clearly set the tone of this imperial visit. In his speeches, Emperor Franz Joseph laid particular stress on the significance of the Bohemian nobility: "I am convinced that in future, too, the Bohemian nobility will remain a pillar of my throne and realm."[36] For months now the first families of Bohemia had spared no effort and no expense to arrange one of the most splendid functions in old Austria: a carrousel—a tournament on horseback executed by trained cavalrymen—featuring a gala joust in late-medieval costume. It was held in the great riding academy of the Waldstein Palace. The Bohemian nobility furnished the horsemen. The climax of the event was the reenactment of the entrance of Ferdinand III and his consort into Prague in 1637. The costumes and armor, patterned on old illustrations, had cost more than 100,000 guldens.

All her life Elisabeth had a strong dislike of the Bohemian aristocracy. Whether this feeling was connected with her first visit to Prague we do not know. But the Bohemian nobility—Schwarzenberg, Waldstein, Lobkovics, Mittrowsky, Khevenhüller, Liechtenstein, Auersperg, Kinsky, Kaunitz, Nostitz, Clam-Martinitz—set the tone at the court of Vienna as well. The contempt shown in Vienna to the little Duchess from Bavaria may well have been echoed in Prague.

As happened wherever the Emperor visited, great military parades were arranged in Prague as well, including even a field maneuver. The *Wiener Zeitung* noted, "Her Majesty the Empress also followed the imposing martial spectacle with unmistakable interest and, heedless of repeated rain showers, remained in the open carriage to the end."[37] While the Emperor reviewed the parade on horseback, Sisi was driven around in a two-horse state carriage—exactly like Archduchess Sophie, who knew very well that her Franzi loved nothing so much as these splendid military march-pasts. During her five weeks of marriage Sisi had already seen more parades and drills than in all her previous life, although her father was a general.

Prague also became the center of a visit to other family members—the abdicated Emperor Ferdinand and Empress Maria Anna, who had their summer residence at Ploschkowitz Castle near Prague. Empress Maria Anna devotedly cared for her husband, who was severely afflicted with epilepsy and feeblemindedness. Landgravine Therese Fürstenberg, a lady-in-waiting, described him as follows: "he was short, carried his large head at a slight tilt, his small eyes had an uncertain look, and his lip sagged considerably; he always nodded in a friendly and benevolent way and asked the same thing twenty times; a sad sight." To ease the boredom of his lonely days, the ex-Emperor spent hours every day playing dominoes.[38]

The family ties between the former and the ruling Emperor, who were uncle and nephew, were rather formal. Since the transfer of the throne in Olmütz, Ferdinand had retired completely from politics in order to avoid any difficulties with both the young Emperor and with the "secret Empress," Archduchess Sophie. He did not come to Vienna even for the wedding, merely sending a generous present. Emperor Ferdinand, a man of personal integrity and genuine kindliness, still had many supporters in the monarchy. His appearance in Vienna might well have given rise to demonstrations of sympathy. That the young couple's first visit abroad included the former Emperor and Empress was also an expression of gratitude on the part of the young Emperor to his predecessor.

In conclusion of the visit to Bohemia, Emperor Franz Joseph met with the kings of Prussia and Saxony in Count Thun's castle in Tetschen-Bodenbach. Both kings were related by marriage to Franz Joseph as well as to Elisabeth and had known both from childhood. The meeting of the three monarchs, however, had a political significance beyond the personal: The King of Saxony presented the young Emperor with a comprehensive memorandum concerning the Eastern crisis and warned him—unsuccessfully—to stick with his anti-Russian policy. The King of Prussia's vast retinue included Otto von Bismarck, at that time representing the Prussian assembly in the German Diet in Frankfurt.

Even after two strenuous weeks in Bohemia, the imperial couple was given no opportunity to rest. The day after their return was Corpus Christi Day, a holiday that became the occasion of political demonstrations during Franz Joseph's reign. The Emperor headed the procession, walking just behind the holy statues, to show his close ties to the Catholic Church against all the liberal and anticlerical tendencies of 1848. The army also played an important part. According to the *Wiener Zeitung,* "In all the streets through which the procession made its way, the military stood in ranks; these same also paraded massively on several squares."[39] After the procession, the troops marched past the Emperor on the Burgplatz. Sensitive liberal temperaments could only see this event jointly organized by state, church, and army as a provocation.

The young Empress showed no understanding for the imperial splendor unfolded on the occasion of a religious feast day. Her religious attitude, schooled at home, agreed with none of what she was expected to exhibit here. Though Sisi's family was Catholic, it was nevertheless very tolerant and rather liberal. The fusing of religion and politics was completely foreign to her.

"But would it not be enough if I merely appeared at the church?" she demurred. "I think that I am still too young and too inexperienced to be able to take the place of an empress in full dignity at this sort of public celebration; all the more so since I have had described to me the imposing majestic presence of the former empress [Maria Anna, the wife of Ferdinand] on such occasions. Perhaps in a few years I will be able to rise to such heights."[40]

But her objections were in vain. She was the principal attraction of the church feast—in full court regalia, her dress ending in a long train, a diamond tiara in her hair. Tens of thousands had come to Vienna from the provinces expressly for this event. Even the approach of the gala state coach, drawn by eight white horses, to St. Stephen's Cathedral was a triumphal procession. Archduchess Sophie commented on Sisi's appearance: "The Empress's bearing was delightful, devout, collected, almost humble."[41]

But Sisi's discontent grew. There was no one to whom she could have poured out her heart. According to Sophie's expressed wishes, Sisi was not allowed to confide in anyone, for to do so would have compromised her sovereign position as Empress. Emperor Franz Joseph could not see the isolation from which his wife suffered as anything out of the ordinary. Accustomed to such separateness from childhood, he accepted it as a natural side effect—even more, as the natural expression—of his exalted position, as his mother had taught him. A family member, Archduchess Marie Mainer, many years later explained to Sisi's daughter Marie Valerie that it had been Sophie's "system to isolate Papa and his brothers, to keep them far from any intimacy with the rest of the family; keeping them on an island, she thought she was providing them with greater authority over the others, preserving them from influences." Valerie's response to this communication is also recorded in her diary. "Now I see the reason why Papa stands so very alone, takes no pleasure in dealings with relatives, is therefore dependent on the advice of strangers, often unreliable men. I always thought that I should blame Mama for it."[42]

The conversation between Marie Mainer and Marie Valerie mentioned only relations with family members—that is, the "august house." The much greater difficulties of contact with people of a lower station—let alone the so-called people—require no elucidation. This absolute isolation, this elevation above the crowd, was something the young Empress could not deal with at all. She could not reconcile the discrepancies between her turbulent but loving family life in Bavaria and the exalted existence of an imperial majesty.

Her education and her personality made Sisi almost uniquely suited to the role of benevolent "mother of the people." The fact that her best traits were now being forcibly suppressed can be ascribed to the rigid system of Archduchess Sophie and her exaggerated idea of the divine right of the Habsburgs. In all likelihood, the Habsburg court of the late eighteenth century (under Maria Theresia, Joseph II, and Leopold II) would have found it much easier to accept a personality like that of young Elisabeth, since that court was considerably more "progressive"—closer to the people, and more enlightened than the court of the 1850s.

Nor would the difficulties have been so great if anyone had taken the trouble to instruct the young Empress in at least current political events, making her feel that she belonged. Enough was happening: In August, Austrian troops marched into Walachia and forced the Russians to abandon the occupied territories. From week to week, the political situation became more critical. The Empress, however, knew nothing. Her time was taken up with enduring dancing lessons, learning foreign languages, practicing conversation, and listening to her chatelaine, who, as Weckbecker noted, spent hours discussing the gossip of court society. What was evident was that the insecure and uneducated young Empress was thought to be somewhat deficient in intelligence—doing her a grave injustice.

During this early period, there was only one person who paid serious attention to Sisi: Karl Count Grünne, Franz Joseph's older friend and adjutant general, one of the most powerful and most universally hated figures of the monarchy. With Grünne, who was probably the best judge of horses of his day and also headed the imperial stables, the young Empress went riding—always a bright spot in her unhappy days at the Viennese court. It was therefore all the more painful when she had to give up the rides only a few weeks after the wedding: There were signs that she was pregnant.

Even in this psychologically taxing situation, Sisi remained alone. For hours she busied herself with the animals she had brought from Possenhofen. They alone, especially her parrots, were able to alleviate her homesickness. This pastime of the childlike Empress was another occupation of which Archduchess Sophie did not approve. She suggested to the Emperor that he take the parrots away from Sisi so that she would not "look askance" at a bird, condemning her baby to end up looking like a parrot.[43]

This and similar prohibitions voiced by her mother-in-law, which the Emperor usually followed without protest, reinforced Elisabeth's great sensibility. She began literally to talk herself into hostility to her aunt and mother-in-law; she exaggerated in the process, she felt persecuted.

The complaints of the early months of pregnancy affected the delicate sixteen-year-old to their full extent. Emperor Franz Joseph reported to his mother, "Sisi could not come, since yesterday she was quite miserable. She even had to leave church and then vomited several times, furthermore she suffered from headache and spent almost the entire day resting on her bed; only in the evening did she take tea with me on our terrace on a beautiful evening. Since Wednesday she had been feeling very well, so that I already feared our expectations would be dashed, but now I am confident again, though it pains me to see her suffer so."[44]

In Possenhofen, Ludovika was extremely worried about her daughter, but she did not dare to visit her for fear of fanning Sisi's homesickness to even greater heights. Zealously she wrote letters, and as early as the end of June, she sent "caring advice and recommendations for precautions from a mother's heart to her little daughter, who is already expecting."[45]

Not until the next summer in Bad Ischl did she see Sisi again. Earlier, she expressed her indecision in a letter to Marie of Saxony. "I have been invited by Sophie and the good Emperor. But I do not know whether it is sensible for a number of reasons, it would be difficult for me personally from a financial aspect. Whether it would be good for Sisi to be with us again so soon? . . . That is why I have not yet decided, although I often feel such great longing for her!!!"[46]

The arrival of the Bavarian relatives in Bad Ischl was not without its comic aspects. "Empress Elisabeth, Ischl. Arriving with Spatz and Gackel. Mimi"—so read the telegram from Possenhofen, with the notation of the time when the train would be arriving in Lambach, the railroad station closest to Bad Ischl. A carriage was to meet the travelers there. When Ludovika (whom Sisi always called Mimi) and her children Mathilde (nicknamed Spatz) and Karl Theodor (Gackel) and their servants detrained in Lambach, no carriage was waiting. Great consternation. After a while, a servant from the Hotel Elisabeth in Bad Ischl timidly approached the disconcerted travelers. He was carrying two cages, one in each hand, for the expected birds (*Spatz* means "sparrow," and *Gackel* means "rooster"), which had been heralded by a traveler named Mimi. The misunderstanding was soon cleared up. And Ludovika arrived at the imperial villa in Bad Ischl in a garishly lacquered carriage from the hotel, to be received with great astonishment, since no one had had any notice that she was arriving.[47]

Ludovika's self-confidence was not bolstered by these events. They only increased her fear of her energetic sister, Sophie. Ludovika, deferential and diffident, relied absolutely on her sister's judgment. When Sophie went to Dresden and the Emperor to Vienna to look after his affairs, while Ludovika remained behind in Bad Ischl with Sisi, Ludovika felt helpless: "Now I wish twice as much that Sophie were here; for she really is the life and soul of everything, and without her one does not know to whom to turn. One also sees what great love attaches the Emperor to his mother, it is a wonderful relationship."[48]

About her daughter, Ludovika wrote to Bavaria, "I found Sisi grown larger and heavier, although her condition is not very evident yet, on the whole she is well, though afflicted with a great deal of queasiness, which sometimes depresses her a little, but she never complains and tries only too hard to conceal this discomfort; but it often makes her more quiet, but the change of coloring, which cannot be concealed, most readily reveals her condition."[49]

In Bad Ischl, the young Empress had no household of her own. Even when her mother-in-law was away, Sisi was under constant observation. Franz Joseph's twelve-year-old brother, Archduke Ludwig Viktor, once wrote indignantly to Archduchess Sophie, "Dear Mama, since you went away, strange things are going on here, to Papa's [Franz Karl's] great consternation; that is, the Empress and Lenza [Joseph Legrenzi, the Emperor's chief valet de chambre] do as they like. Poor Papa complains to me every morning at breakfast . . . poor Zehkorn [court clerk in Sophie's service] runs around like crazy. . . . Countess Esterházy and Paula [Bellegarde] wring their hands."[50] This letter allows us to draw some conclusions about the attitude within the family concerning the Empress.

During her pregnancy, the sixteen-year-old grew even more depressed, especially because Sophie forced her over and over to appear in public. Later, Elisabeth was to tell Marie Festetics, "Hardly had she arrived than she dragged me out into the garden and declared that it was my duty to show off my stomach, so that the people could see that I really was pregnant. It was awful. Instead, it seemed to me a blessing to be alone and able to weep."[51]

Archduchess Sophie firmly took all the necessary preparations for the forthcoming blessed event into her own hands. She decided where the nurseries were to be installed: not near the imperial couple, but next to her own apartments, which she ordered redecorated at the same time. Thus, even months before the birth, she decided that Elisabeth was to be separated from her child. For the "baby chamber" was accessible from the imperial apartments only by way of several steep staircases and drafty corridors, and at the same time was so closely connected to Sophie's apartments that the young mother could not visit her child without Sophie's being present.

Nor did Elisabeth have a say in the selection of the "Aja." Sophie chose Baroness Karoline von Welden, the widow of the artillery commander who had distinguished himself in the suppression of the uprising in Hungary in 1848–1849. Baroness von Welden had no children of her own and no experience of child rearing. Her choice was a purely political decision and a recognition of the Baroness's late husband's merits. The principal work in the nursery was left to Leopoldine Nischer, whom Sophie prepared for her task in repeated discussions.

In all these decisions the young Empress was not only bypassed but even treated like a child. She was to do her duty: appear in public until she dropped, and have a baby as soon as possible—although she was only sixteen. That she had desires and needs, that she wanted to be acknowledged as a person in her own right, not even the enamored Emperor recognized.

The crisis in the East was still acute. Reinforcements were sent to the Russian border. The Czar of Russia turned into an enemy once and for all. Franz Joseph wrote his mother, "It is hard to have to oppose former friends, however in politics it is not possible to do otherwise, and in the East, Russia is always our natural enemy."[52]

Austria lost her old ally, Russia, without gaining new friends in the West. The country would have to pay dearly for her political isolation during the subsequent wars waged by Franz Joseph—in 1859 in the cause of Lombardy, in 1866 in the cause of Venetia and predominance in Germany, and even, finally, in 1914. The fact that this infinitely complex political situation happened to coincide with the Emperor's wedding and the early years of his marriage is surely not without its tragic aspects. The emotional and mental stress on the Emperor left him far too little time for his young wife. His constant absences allowed the differences between Sophie and Elisabeth to grow into irreconcilable antagonisms, which had their full effect on the imperial marriage.

The bankrupt state was not able to raise the monies required for mobilization. A "national loan" of 500 million guldens was floated. Proud and self-confident, Franz Joseph wrote his mother, "We will deal with the feared revolution even without Russia, and a country that in one year manages without difficulty to enlist 200,000 recruits and brings about a loan of more than 500 million guldens within its borders is not yet so very wasted by revolution."[53] Nevertheless, such good judges of the situation as Baron Kübeck deeply regretted that the Emperor and his mother held completely erroneous ideas about the methods used to extort the money from the provinces, which were causing great bitterness throughout the realm. "The Emperor seemed to me very cheerful and wholly subject to the deceptions spread around him." And: "The way every population group talks about the methods used to raise the levy seems to be unknown in these regions."[54]

In the spring of 1855, the new minister of finance, Baron Karl von Bruck, faced an unusual situation; for the upkeep of the army alone, every year 36 million guldens more were spent than the entire income raised by the state.[55]

In order to raise funds for the mobilization for the Crimean War in addition to the moneys procured by taxes, the loan, and shady bank manipulations, in 1856 Austria sold her railroads and coal mines to a French banker—a highly dubious business, since only about half the sum the railroads had cost was realized. (The sale was soon to prove calamitous, especially in the Northern Italian provinces. For in the 1859 war with France—that is, three years later—Austria could not count on the reliability of the French railroad personnel for troop transports, while Napoleon III could be all the more confident. The railroads had subsequently to be bought back by Austria at a far higher price.[56]) Rising prices and famine were rampant in all the Austrian provinces. Epidemics of cholera broke out, first among the troops concentrated in Walachia. The imperial family had no idea what was happening among the ordinary people. Archduchess Sophie was just as persuaded by the ideas of an absolute monarchy as was her son who, though he dutifully read his files, had no knowledge of human nature nor felt any need of such knowledge.

For the uninformed young Empress, the Crimean War was merely an occasion for jealousy. For the Emperor often spent hours with his mother discussing the political situation, while little Sisi felt neglected and discriminated against for being too immature. Later, Elisabeth repeatedly told her children, as if to justify herself, about these difficult early years of her marriage. Even Sisi's younger daughter, Marie Valerie, knew "about Mama's sad youth, how Grandmama Sophie stood between her and Papa, always claimed his confidence, and in a way forever made impossible their getting to know each other and an understanding between Papa and Mama."[57] But since the young woman, as all her letters as well as Sophie's diaries for the early period show, was extremely shy and lacking in self-confidence, was even submissive to her imperial consort, these differences could not be aired. Sisi suffered in silence, wept, composed melancholy verses. Franz Joseph, for his part, believed fully in "my complete domestic happiness."[58]

That the young couple were different not only by temperament and upbringing but also in their tastes became increasingly clear as the days passed. As an example we need only mention *A Midsummer Night's Dream;* this was Sisi's favorite play, and eventually she committed great sections of it to memory. Franz Joseph to Sophie: "Yesterday I went with Sisi to the *Midsummer Night's Dream* by Shakespeare in the Burgtheater. . . . It was quite boring and very stupid. Only Beckmann wearing a donkey's head was amusing."[59]

Even as a child, Sisi had read a great deal. And though she was uneducated about court conditions (at least as far as ceremonial and French conversation went), she nevertheless, unlike Franz Joseph, took a lively interest in literature and history. Writing about the early period, Weckbecker related that during one railway journey he had told the young Empress "what I knew about the history of the places, especially of Wiener Neustadt. She listened with interest, and clearly it captured her more than the gossip of Countess Esterházy."[60]

Only a few months after the resplendent wedding, the intoxication of novelty had worn off. The young Empress had to prove herself and withstand criticism, in spite of her tender years, both as "mother of the country"—although she knew next to nothing about "her" country—and most especially as first lady among the Austrian nobility. And here Elisabeth failed. The Viennese nobility sharply criticized this Empress, so clearly not "well brought up." Even family members, such as Prince Alexander of Hesse, considered Sisi beautiful but stupid. In November 1854, he wrote in his diary that, in spite of her advanced pregnancy, the Empress was very beautiful but "After her stereotypical questions, 'Have you been here long?' 'How long will you be staying in Vienna?' apparently a little *bûche,* a word the French are in the habit of using to designate people of low intelligence."[61]

There was constant talk about the Empress's lack of accomplishments: that she had not mastered protocol, that she did not dance well enough, that she dressed with insufficient elegance. Not once did her critics deal with intellectual or social skills; books and learning had no place in the world of the court. And as the American envoy John Motley wrote, the famous salon at court was in no way a criterion for intelligence. "But I think that no reasonable being ought to like a salon. There are three topics —the Opera, the Prater, the Burg Theatre; when these are exhausted, you are floored. Conversazioni where the one thing that does not exist is conversation, are not the most cheerful of institutions."[62] The American envoy failed to mention that the aristocrats' principal occupation was gossip—for everyone knew everyone else and was, for all practical purposes, related to everyone else. As a diplomat, after all, he was no more a part of the inner circle at court than was the young Empress, who, because of her station, had to remain above this family tattle, and who, by virtue of her origins and upbringing, had no points of contact with such conversations. She stood outside, and whether she wanted to or not, she had to allow herself to be criticized and measured against the norms of the Viennese court.

CHAPTER THREE

THE NEWLYWEDS

Problematic as Sisi's position at the court of Vienna and her relations with her mother-in-law, Archduchess Sophie, might have been, the relationship between the Emperor and Empress was excellent. It was impossible to ignore the fact that Franz Joseph was deeply in love. And there can be scarcely any doubt that Sisi returned her husband's feelings and was happy with him.

The couple's first child was a girl, little Sophie. We have Archduchess Sophie to thank for a detailed description of the birth; her diary records a veritable idyll.

On the morning of March 5, 1855, the Emperor woke his mother at seven o'clock because Sisi's pains had started. Taking along a piece of needlework, Sophie sat outside the imperial bedchamber and waited, "and the Emperor went back and forth between her and me," she wrote.

When, around eleven o'clock, the pains grew stronger, Sophie joined the Emperor at her daughter-in-law's bedside, observing the couple's every move.

> Sisi held my son's hand between her own two and once kissed it with a lively and respectful tenderness; this was so touching and made him weep; he kissed her ceaselessly, comforted her and lamented with her, and looked at me at every pain to see if it satisfied me. When they grew stronger each time and the birth began, I told him so, to give Sisi and my son new courage. I held the dear child's head, the chamberwoman Pilat held her knees, and the midwife held her from behind. Finally, after a few good long labor pains, the head appeared, and immediately after that, the child was born (after three o'clock) and cried like a six-week-old baby. The young mother, with an expression of such touching bliss, said to me, 'oh, now everything is all right, now I don't mind how much I suffered!' The Emperor burst into tears, he and Sisi did not stop kissing each other, and they embraced me with the liveliest tenderness. Sisi looked at the child with delight, and she and the young father were full of care for the child, a big, strong girl.

The Emperor accepted the congratulations of the family assembled in the anteroom. After the baby was washed and dressed, Sophie held it in her arms and sat next to Sisi's bed, as did the Emperor. They waited until Sisi fell asleep, around six o'clock. "Very contented and cheerful," the imperial family took tea. The Emperor joined his younger brother Max for a cigar and a chat. Services of thanksgiving were held in all the churches.

Hardly anywhere else is Sophie's paramount position in the imperial family as evident as in this special situation. The midwife followed her orders. The Emperor, unsure of himself like any young father, anxiously searched his mother's expression for indications about the progress of the birth. Elisabeth, who had just turned seventeen, was without her mother's support, wholly at her mother-in-law's mercy. Nevertheless, even during the strongest labor pains, her demeanor was one of "reverent, respectful tenderness" for Franz Joseph, as Sophie wrote.[1] It was such demeanor that Archduchess Sophie expected as a matter of course from the young Empress in every situation, even in this extraordinary one.

Sisi's later complaints that the child had been taken from her right after the birth must, however, be taken with certain reservations. At least during the first few weeks after the birth, matters cannot have been quite so bad. Three weeks after her confinement, the young Empress wrote to a relative in Bavaria, "My little one really is already very charming and gives the Emperor and me enormous joy. At first it seemed very strange to me to have a baby of my own; it is like an entirely new joy, and I have the little one with me all day long, except when she is carried for a walk, which happens often while the fine weather holds."[2]

But, of course, the young mother had to submit to her mother-in-law's regime without remonstrating—just as the Emperor was used to doing from childhood. The child was given the name Sophie, her grandmother being the godmother. Sisi was not consulted on this decision, either.

Until her death in 1857, little Sophie held a special place in her grandmother's heart. Pages of the diary are covered with the details of infant care. Everything aroused the grandmotherly pride of the Archduchess, who was normally so cool: The slightest development, every new tooth became worthy of being recorded in the Archduchess's diary. Of course, this grandmotherly ardor—her possessiveness—aggravated the problems within the imperial family. The seventeen-year-old, inexperienced Elisabeth, intimidated, gave ground; not even the birth of a child had been able to improve her standing at court.

Little more than a year later, in July 1856, Sisi gave birth to another girl. She was named Gisela—after the Bavarian wife of the first Christian King of Hungary, Stephen I. This time Duchess Ludovika was the godmother, though she was not present at the christening and was represented by Archduchess Sophie—giving rise to further gossip. We do not know the reason why, in spite of Sisi's pleas, Ludovika delayed for so long visiting her daughter and her first grandchildren in Vienna. We can only infer from some of Ludovika's other statements that she was anxious to forestall any jealousy on Sophie's part.

The disappointment at the fact that once again the hoped-for heir to the throne had not been born was great. The populace was probably most unhappy because the people had reason to expect especially generous benefactions at the birth of an heir to the throne, and during these bad times, the country was in desperate need of succor from any quarter.

This child, too, was handed over to her grandmother's supervision. Later, Elisabeth expressed deep regret that she did not have a close relationship with her elder children, and she always blamed her mother-in-law. Only with her fourth child, Marie Valerie, did she assert her maternal rights, and she confessed, "Only now do I understand what bliss a child means. Now I have finally had the courage to love the baby and keep it with me. My other children were taken away from me at once. I was permitted to see the children only when Archduchess Sophie gave permission. She was always present when I visited the children. Finally I gave up the struggle and went upstairs only rarely."[3]

No matter how insignificant Sisi's position at court was, her popularity among the populace kept growing. This popularity also had a political basis. For after the Emperor's marriage, some cautious efforts at liberalization were undertaken. The state of siege in the larger cities was gradually raised, and these proclamations always occurred on the occasion of family events, such as the Emperor's wedding and the births of his children. Political prisoners were released before they had served their full term or were granted amnesty.

The new military penal statute of January 1855—that is, only a few months after the Emperor's wedding—also brought some easing of restrictions. This law abolished among others the punishment, still practiced in Austria, of running the gauntlet. Popular belief would have it that it was the young Empress who had asked her husband to do away with this torture as a wedding present to her. The sources furnish no proofs for the theory; but it is very likely that the extremely sensitive young Empress witnessed such a punishment during one of the numerous military visits or at least heard about it.[4] And it was thoroughly in character for her to have spoken out forcefully against such cruelty. The abolition of keeping prisoners in chains was also attributed to Elisabeth's initiative. No one had any doubt that these measures could not be attributed to Archduchess Sophie's influence. For she continued to advocate extreme harshness toward the revolutionaries of 1848 and all other insurgents. Patriotic Austrians loyal to the Emperor were only too ready to believe in the benevolent influence of a new Empress who was in sympathy with the people.

Whether Elisabeth truly had such a direct influence on the Emperor we do not know. But there is no doubt that under his rapturous love and the happiness of his new marriage, the Emperor grew more gentle and yielding, and for that reason if no other, he showed himself less firmly opposed than before to liberalizations, which were overdue.

The very young Empress became something like a political hope for all those who felt uneasy under the neo-absolutist regime. The opponents of the Concordat also soon rallied around the Empress. The signing of the Concordat of 1855 constituted a high point of political Catholicism in Austria, at the same time that it was a triumph for Archduchess Sophie, who was thus able to impose her concept of a Catholic empire: The state yielded to the church the power over the regulation of marriage and over the schools. From this time on, the church had the ultimate decision, not only over the contents of the curriculum (from history to mathematics), but also over the selection of teachers. Even the drawing master and the physical-education teacher had to meet the first requirement—that of being good Catholics (which was checked out down to the taking of the sacraments). Otherwise, they would not be given posts. The Concordat was throwing down the gauntlet to all non-Catholics and Liberals, as well as to scientists, artists, and writers, whose work was severely impeded.

The opponents of the Concordat believed that they had found a sympathizer in the young Empress—whose conflicts with Archduchess Sophie could no longer be kept secret. They may have been right up to a point. Thus, a characteristic story made the rounds in 1856. The small Lutheran congregation in Attersee wished to erect a steeple on its little church, as was recently permitted, and it needed funds for the project. The pastor turned to the court, which happened to be in residence in nearby Bad Ischl, and he met with the Empress herself. Later, the liberal *Wiener Tageblatt* reported that the young Empress had begun the interview by expressing her surprise "that the Protestants are for the first time being allowed to build steeples on top of their churches. Where I come from," she said in a cordial way, "your coreligionists have enjoyed these rights, as I know, for fifty years already. My late grandfather [King Maximilian I of Bavaria] used state funds to let the Protestants build the handsome church on the Karlsplatz in Munich. The Queen of Bavaria [Marie, the wife of Maximilian II] is also a Protestant, and my grandmother on my mother's side was a Lutheran. Bavaria is an arch-Catholic nation, but the Protestants among us surely have no cause to complain about discrimination or infringements."

The Empress made a generous donation, though it was said to have "caused great surprise in clerical circles." The quarrelsome Bishop Franz Joseph Rüdiger of Linz was said to have "requested a formal clarification of whether the matter was true as reported." The newspaper of the clericals in Linz presented the "incident" from the viewpoint "as if the Empress had not been precisely informed about the actual purpose of the donation, and as if it had been presented to her that the subject was a poor congregation in general terms, but not that it was a Protestant one. The pastor, however, defended himself with a 'correction' in the official Linz newspaper."[5]

With this innocent donation for a Protestant steeple, Elisabeth became marked, whether she wanted to be or not, as an adherent of tolerance in religious questions and as opposing the Concordat. From then on, one faction placed its hopes in her, while the other—and this was the "clerical" party of her mother-in-law, Archduchess Sophie—saw her as an opponent. Sisi's relations to the court and the aristocracy were anything but improved by these hopes of the Liberals.

Sisi's behavior within the family circle also gradually changed. She was becoming ever less submissive, ever less quiet. She was more and more aware of her exalted position: She was the Empress, the first lady of the land.

This also meant that she dared to oppose her mother-in-law, who had ruled unchallenged until that time. Of course, the first bone of contention was influence in the imperial nursery. At first, Sisi received no support from the Emperor. It was not until 1856, when she was alone with her husband during a journey through Carinthia and Styria, that Sisi insisted that the children be allowed to be near her. Far from the Hofburg, far from the daily shared meals with her mother-in-law, she finally felt strong enough to free the Emperor from his excessive servility toward his adored mother and to remind him for once of his wife's needs.

An open quarrel now broke out between Sisi and Sophie over the two little girls. Sophie resisted Sisi's urgent pleas to move the nurseries. She raised a number of objections (the rooms in question did not get enough sunlight, and similar concerns). When Sisi would not give in, Archduchess Sophie threatened to move out of the Hofburg—her strongest weapon. And this time the young Empress managed to pull her husband to her side —to judge from Franz Joseph's letters, it was the first and only time that the Emperor rebuked the mother he adored.

Shortly after his return from the trip he had taken with his wife, he wrote to Sophie:

> I beg you most earnestly to judge Sisi with forbearance if perhaps she is too jealous a mother—after all, she is such a devoted wife and mother! If you would be gracious enough to think about the matter calmly, you will perhaps understand our feelings of pain at seeing our children enclosed in your apart-ments with an almost joint anteroom, while poor Sisi, who is often so heavy, must pant her way up the stairs, only rarely to find the children alone, even to find them among strangers if you were gracious enough to show off the children, which shortens especially the few moments I have to spend with the

children—aside from the fact that showing off the children, thereby making them conceited, horrifies me; wherein, by the way, I may be wrong. By the way, it never occurs to Sisi to wish to deprive you of the children, and she specifically asked me to write to you and tell you that they will always be entirely at your disposal.[6]

For the first time, Elisabeth was able to get her way. The trip was a complete success and brought the couple closer again. Both deeply enjoyed the beauty of the mountains—one of the few things Franz Joseph and Elisabeth had in common. Wherever they went, the young couple aroused admiration for the simple and natural way they appeared in the rural landscape: the Emperor in lederhosen and the traditional hat with a chamois tuft, the Empress wearing a tight-fitting loden suit and sturdy mountain-climbing boots, a loden hat on her head. There was no court ceremonial here, and even the Emperor, who was so formal and stilted in Vienna, behaved casually and showed that he had preserved a certain measure of spontaneity and joie de vivre.

The two made an excursion on foot into the mountains. Elisabeth, who was an experienced mountain climber but was still weak from her last confinement, rested at the site of today's Glocknerhaus after a three-hour hike and enjoyed the view of the peak of the Grossglockner. This place was given the name Elisabethruhe—Elisabeth's rest. Franz Joseph went on as far as the Pasterze glacier.

From that time on, shared trips provided happy occasions for Elisabeth to be alone with her husband and to strengthen her influence.

But even if Sisi had won a battle, the war with her mother-in-law, which went on for decades, consumed a great deal of energy—all the more so as the Archduchess could always count on support from the court, unlike the young Empress.

Sophie never managed to train Elisabeth according to her precepts. The long, embittered struggle, however, deprived the monarchy and the imperial family of a highly promising, talented personality by driving Elisabeth into isolation.

Countess Marie Festetics—who, granted, could judge the situation only on the basis of the Empress's stories—wrote about the Archduchess: "Her ambition always made her come between the two married people—always forcing a decision between mother and wife, and it is only by God's grace that an open break did not occur. She wanted to break the influence of the Empress over the Emperor. That was a dangerous gamble. The Emperor loves the Empress. . . . The Empress has nothing but her rights and her noblesse to aid her."[7]

The Peace of Paris, signed in the spring of 1856, ended the Crimean War and brought a radical change in the system of European nations: Russia lost her dominant position to the France of Napoleon III. The earlier close friendship between Russia and Austria had turned into enmity, to Prussia's advantage. These effects were unfortunate for Austria. But another factor, little considered until that time, made itself painfully felt: The seedbed of the Italian unification movement, Piedmont, had furnished France with 15,000 soldiers during the Crimean War and thereby won Napoleon III as protector of the Irredentist movement. The Austrian provinces of Lombardy and Venetia were more threatened than ever, as were the Central Italian states of Tuscany and Modena, which were ruled by Habsburgs and stood under Austrian military protection. The Italian unification movement saw Austrian rule in Italy as the greatest obstacle to the achievement of its goals.

Franz Joseph continued to reject any attempt to relinquish the Italian provinces through advantageous treaties or sale—though opinion was unanimous that they could not be maintained. In 1854, Ernst II of Coburg also tried to urge these ideas propounded by Napoleon III on the young Emperor, for "it was not to be expected that Italy would ever be pacified." Prince Ernst: "The Emperor seemed to become very disturbed at this report and most decisively rejected any thought of ceding Italian territories."[8] And four years later, the Swiss envoy reported to Bern "that the Emperor would sacrifice his last man and his last thaler to defend Venetia."[9] War over Italy thus became inevitable sooner or later.

For the present, the Emperor hoped that he would be able to hold on to the insurgent provinces by strong military power. To demonstrate imperial sovereignty, the Emperor and Empress traveled to Northern Italy in the winter of 1856–1857, living for four months in the old royal palaces of Milan and Venice and there displaying the full magnificence of the court and the military.

On this occasion, too, there were quarrels within the imperial family. Elisabeth was unwilling to leave her children for such a long period. Against the Archduchess's strong opposition, she succeeded to the extent that the older daughter, Sophie, who was two years old, accompanied her parents to Italy. Elisabeth justified her wish by declaring that the Northern Italian air would be good for the delicate child in the winter months. The Italian newspapers, however, conjectured that the child had been brought along primarily as a safeguard against assassination attempts.[10] Archduchess Sophie, for her part, complained of the dangers of the journey for the child; she was not entirely wrong.

The trip started by rail from Vienna to Leibach. There, the thirty-seven coaches that had been brought along were unloaded, and the journey continued by post-horse and ship.

In Italy, Sisi could not possibly stay away from politics. Until this time, during all her trips to the provinces—to Bohemia, Styria, Carinthia, and of course Salzburg, which was crisscrossed during the weeks in Bad Ischl —Sisi encountered a populace that received its imperial rulers, if not with enthusiasm, at least amiably. But now she was met by contempt, even hatred.

The Italian people, suffering under the Austrian military administration, longed for the nationalist Italy advocated by Cavour and Garibaldi. There had been attempts at putsches, executions. The taxes the once rich lands had to pay to Austria were oppressive (although by this time the military occupation of the country cost far more than could be raised by taxes— even from the onetime richest province, Lombardy). The Emperor and Empress were made to feel all these dissatisfactions. The Austrian military authorities carefully arranged the receptions. The imperial couple invariably appeared with a large military retinue, intended as a demonstration of power. But the Italians regarded these entourages as hostile provocations. The military authorities were in a state of full alert; the Emperor's and Empress's visit practically invited assassination attempts. But as always in such situations, the young Emperor showed great courage, as did the Empress. Behaving irreproachably, she overlooked acts of sabotage and hostility among the populace.

She had good reason to be afraid. In Trieste, a huge imperial crown, made of crystal, shattered on the ship. No one believed that it was an unfortunate accident; everyone believed it to be sabotage. But happy as the young Empress was to cancel official receptions in Vienna, in Northern Italy she carried out her schedule all the more rigidly, leaving her husband's side at most for purely military inspections.

In Venice, where the Emperor's ship, escorted by six powerful men-of-war, lay at anchor, the military reception was splendid, but when the imperial couple with little Sophie crossed the broad St. Mark's Place on their way to San Marco, not a single *"Evviva"* went up from the large crowd gathered there. Only the Austrian soldiers cried out "Hail" and "Hurrah." The Italians demonstrated by remaining silent. The English consul reported to London, "The only emotion shown by the people was merely curiosity to see the Empress, whose reputation of being wonderfully beautiful had, of course, arrived here as well."[11]

The majority of the Italian nobility stayed away from the imperial receptions. Those who attended in spite of the boycott were reviled in the streets. During the festivities at the Teatro Fenice, the boxes of the most eminent families remained empty. In the course of the imperial stay in Venice, however, the mood brightened, especially when the Emperor removed one of the greatest vexations to the Italian nobility by rescinding the confiscation of the property of political refugees and granting amnesty to political prisoners.

Franz Joseph did not neglect to praise the services of his young wife. From Venice he wrote to Archduchess Sophie, "The populace was very correct, without exhibiting any special enthusiasm. Since then, the mood has brightened very much for various reasons, especially the good impression made by Sisi."[12] In Vienna, the Emperor's statement that Sisi's beauty "conquered Italy better than his soldiers and cannons had been able to do" soon made the rounds.[13]

In the other cities, the receptions were no more cordial—not in Vicenza; not in Verona, where the Austrian troops were headquartered; not in Brescia; and not in Milan. In the last city, the officials even tried to pay those who lived in the country to come to the city and line up to welcome the Emperor and Empress. The nobility of Lombardy maintained its iron resolve. The imperial receptions were attended by only about a fifth of those who had been invited. At the gala performance at La Scala, servants sat in the boxes instead of their aristocratic employers—an enormous insult.

The Emperor relaxed from the strain of these constant affronts by going on long troop inspections. His interest centered, not on the treasures of Venice and Milan, but on the fortifications, arsenals, barracks, men-of-war, and battle sites. Only too frequently the young Empress, who was once again ailing, was compelled to accompany him.

Field Marshal Radetzky—who was, by then, ninety years old—could hardly be said to have firm control over the regiment in Northern Italy. Since the Emperor found him "terribly changed and reverting to childhood,"[14] Franz Joseph decided to pension him with full honors and to introduce separate military and civilian administrations in the Italian provinces. Archduke Ferdinand Max, the Emperor's younger brother, twenty-four years old, was assigned the difficult task of going to Milan as civilian governor. Franz Joseph to his mother: "Our Lord will help, and time along with Max's tact will do much."[15]

Unfortunately, since we have none of Sisi's letters from this period, we do not know whether she commented on political questions during this first visit to Italy. All we know is that her opinion on the Italian question was less optimistic than her husband's. This information comes from her brother Karl Theodor, who visited her in Venice and took back to Bavaria a very negative vision of Austria's position in these provinces.[16]

Only a few weeks after their return from Italy, the imperial couple visited another unquiet province—Hungary. Relations between Vienna and Budapest were tense. Minister of the Interior Alexander Bach conceived the ambitious plan of turning all of Austria into a unified, centrally ruled realm and to bring refractory Hungary "into line." The old Hungarian constitution had been abolished. The revolutionaries of 1848 had emigrated, their goods had been confiscated. The Viennese court, represented by Archduchess Sophie as well as by the military governor of Hungary, Archduke Albrecht, harbored extremely anti-Hungarian sentiments.

The young Empress was Hungary's hope. It was known that, influenced by Count Mailath, she cared about Hungarian history, with a special interest in the liberation movements. The political relaxations on the occasion of the imperial wedding had made a favorable impression. Elisabeth's opposition to Archduchess Sophie was sufficiently well known. The Hungarians now hoped that these circumstances could be exploited to their advantage.

The journey proceeded by ship down the Danube from Vienna by way of Pressburg to Budapest. This time, Sisi had insisted on taking both children along, again against her mother-in-law's protests. According to Franz Joseph, before the departure, little Sophie had come down with a fever and a slight case of diarrhea. The doctors had assured the parents that these symptoms were related to teething.[17]

The receptions, the military parades, the first court ball held in the castle at Budapest after many years—all these were carried out with the usual display of splendor, but they were handicapped by rather moderate enthusiasm among the Hungarians. All those who attended agreed only on the beauty of Elisabeth, not yet twenty years old. Nor was it difficult to recognize how susceptible she was to the magnates' compliments. The Hungarian nobles in their diamond-studded costumes and their extraordinarily self-confident, proud bearing were so strikingly different from the Viennese aristocracy, almost opposites, that from the first moment the young Empress developed a liking for Hungary. At the court ball, she enthusiastically watched the Hungarian dances, which she had never seen before, and then she danced a quadrille herself—first with Archduke Wilhelm and then with Count Nikolaus Esterházy, who would subsequently become her favorite companion at the hunt. The Hungarians' appreciation of the young Empress was returned. From this time on, the Hungarians ascribed any political relaxations to the Empress's favorable influence, just as they laid every harassment at Archduchess Sophie's door.

Elisabeth championed the Hungarian cause even then. It is true that during the trip, the Emperor refused to accept a petition from the nobility to reintroduce the old Hungarian constitution; but the return of prominent emigrants, such as Gyula Andrássy, who came back from Paris, was made easier, and some of the confiscated estates were released. Cautious indications of further liberalization were evident, although the Emperor persisted in his rigidly centralist policy.

Morale in Hungary improved gradually in the course of the visit. The mood brightened especially whenever the Empress appeared in public— when, for example, she attended one of the military reviews, appearing on horseback at her husband's side. Her riding skills found many admirers in Hungary. Count Franz Folliot de Crenneville, who was one of the party, however, was scandalized at having to see an empress on horseback. "This riding performance, entirely unsuitable to the dignity of an empress, made a painful impression on me," he wrote to his wife.[18]

Just when the Emperor and Empress were about to set out for the Hungarian provinces, as had been arranged, ten-month-old Gisela suddenly came down with a fever and diarrhea. The trip was postponed. When Gisela recovered, two-year-old Sophie fell ill. Her parents were very worried. Franz Joseph to his mother: "She slept only 1 1/2 hours all night, is very nervous, and keeps crying constantly, it's enough to break your heart."[19]

Dr. Seeburger, the personal physician, reassured the Emperor and Empress. Franz Joseph found the leisure to go hunting and, as he proudly wrote his mother, to shoot "72 herons and cormorants." The couple started on the trip to the interior; after five days, however, it was broken off in Debrecen because the news of little Sophie grew worse.

For eleven hours, the nineteen-year-old Empress watched in despair as her child died. "Our little one is an angel in heaven. After a long struggle, she finally passed away at nine thirty. We are devastated," the Emperor telegraphed his mother from Budapest on May 29, 1857.[20] The young couple returned to Vienna with the body of the child.

Elisabeth was inconsolable. After a suitable period, the Emperor became resigned; but Sisi withdrew from everyone, sought solitude, wept for days, even weeks, refused all nourishment, abandoned herself completely to her grief. In view of her despondency, no one dared openly to reproach her. But the relationship with her mother-in-law, whose favorite little Sophie had been, grew frosty. After all, it was the young Empress who had taken the children to Hungary against the expressed wishes, even the opposition, of the Archduchess.

In the following weeks and months, a significant change took place in Elisabeth. After this misfortune, for which she did not feel blameless, she gave up the struggle for the daughter who was left her, little Gisela. It seemed as if she were no longer willing even to acknowledge the existence of this child. She paid no attention to the little girl, abandoning the field entirely to Grandmama Sophie.

Sisi's emotional state and her weak physical constitution gave ample grounds for worry in the summer of 1857. Since neither Franz Joseph nor Sophie could think what was to be done, Duchess Ludovika was summoned to Vienna. She arrived with three of Sisi's younger sisters. Ludovika: "The company of her young, cheerful sisters seemed to do Sisi much good; since parting from us was so hard for her, she made me promise to come to Ischl if at all possible."[21]

Even six months later, Sisi had not become reconciled to her loss. The Emperor wrote his mother, "Poor Sisi is much affected by all the memories that confront her here [in Vienna] on all sides, and she cries a great deal. Yesterday Gisela, visiting with Sisi, sat in the little red armchair of our poor little one, which stands in the den, and at that, both of us cried, but Gisela, happy at this new place of honor, kept laughing so charmingly."[22]

It was just during this difficult time that Emperor Franz Joseph's younger brother, Archduke Ferdinand Max, married Charlotte (Carlotta), the daughter of the King of the Belgians. Sisi's new sister-in-law was not only beautiful and intelligent, but also enormously rich. Furthermore, she had an impeccable pedigree. Sophie and her faction now did all they could to pit the new wife of Max, who was next in line to the throne, against the Empress, who was descended from a far more humble family. In their correspondence and their talks, and in her diary, Sophie could not find enough praise for Carlotta's upbringing, her beauty, her cleverness, but most of all for the affection she showed her husband and her mother-in-law. With every word, Sisi could not help but feel scolded. "Charlotte is charming, beautiful, attractive, loving, and gentle to me. I feel as if I had always loved her. . . . I thank God with all my heart for the charming wife He has given Max and for the additional child He has given us," reads

Sophie's diary.[23] That the two sisters-in-law took a cordial dislike to each other is not very surprising. Elisabeth's position at court notably deteriorated.

In December 1857 the Empress gave signs of the new pregnancy everyone had hoped for. A letter from Ludovika to her sister Sophie gives some indication of the discord between Sophie and Elisabeth. "As far as Sisi's expectations are concerned, they have given me great reassurance, great joy," Ludovika wrote, but added, "You say that they have freed you from many a worry—were these worries related to the physical or the moral? If an improvement that satisfies you has set in, I am immensely pleased." And the very next day, Ludovika wrote to Sophie again about her "great reassurance that Sisi has now become so reasonable and conscientious about lacing and tight clothes, a matter that always worried and bothered me; I myself believe that it can have an effect on one's mood; for an uncomfortable feeling, like constant embarrassment, may truly put one out of sorts."[24]

Starvation diets and her beloved riding had to be abandoned now, to Sophie's great satisfaction. Instead, Sisi was supposed to go for long walks. Franz Joseph went with her as often as he could find the time. The harmony between the couple had not suffered even during the recent difficult months. Franz Joseph showed his love for his young wife openly.

Sophie, of course, found repeated cause to complain of the young Empress. Submissive and anxious, Ludovika wrote letters like the following: "I want to be able to hope that all situations have turned out to be more pleasant than in the previous year, that you have cause to be more satisfied, which is always so close to my heart."[25]

During these same months, Ludovika was deeply agitated about all her beautiful, difficult daughters. The oldest, Helene, cast aside at the engagement in Bad Ischl, was now twenty-two years old. Ludovika: "She would have been a good wife and mother; now she, and all of us, has given it up entirely, though she remains very cheerful."[26] Helene filled her time chiefly with painting and "also visits the poor and the sick in the villages a lot." Abruptly, a suitor for Helene's hand turned up in the person of the Hereditary Prince Maximilian of Thurn und Taxis. The King of Bavaria hesitated to give his permission for the marriage because the Thurn und Taxis family was not of equal rank. Ludovika wrote urgent letters to her daughter in Vienna. Sisi was to intervene with the Emperor on her sister's behalf, and he in turn was to be put in a good word with the King of Bavaria. No matter how diffident the Empress was in other situations—for her family she would do anything. She diligently wrote hither and yon, comforting her mother and Helene. A remnant of a guilty conscience because of Helene's failed marriage plans may also have played a part in her efforts. Finally, in 1858, the marriage occurred.

In the winter of 1857, Sisi's younger sister Marie was considered a match of great beauty. One suitor who applied for her hand was the Crown Prince of Naples—whom no one from the Bavarian family had ever met, of course. Once again, the correspondence with Vienna increased. Ludovika: Marie "thinks that you have the most detailed and reliable information about the young man, and she needs to be reassured, since she knows no one, and the thought of belonging to a man whom she does not know and who does not know her makes her so afraid. . . . That he is not pretty she already knows." This fact, which could not be denied, Sisi had found out from Habsburg relatives who had been to Southern Italy.

Ludovika also feared that the "great piety" of the suitor might "scare off" young Marie, but, she quickly added, surely to reassure Sophie about the loose ideas held in Possenhofen, that she hoped this piety would, "little by little," make Marie "herself increasingly more pious."[27]

Once again a swarm of new teachers traveled in and out of Possenhofen. Once again a country girl had to be drilled in court manners. And once again a Bavarian duchess was not very happy with all her new obligations: learning Italian, receiving ladies "to get used to talking." Since the girl was not yet "formed" (that is, had not started her menses), the doctors tried all their skills on her, treating her with leeches and hot baths.

Ludovika complained, as always bereft of any help from her Max. "The thought of the separation grows ever harder for me now, although I must wish that it will not be drawn out, for surely it is better that she comes young into this altogether different, foreign situation, she will find and adapt herself all the more readily and with less difficulty."[28]

Unfortunately, the only clues we have so far to Sisi's efforts on behalf of her sister come from the voluminous letters of Archduchess Ludovika. Sisi's own letters (and the young Empress was a most diligent correspondent when her Bavarian family was concerned) are still not accessible to historians.

On August 21, 1858, in Laxenburg, the Empress was delivered of the Crown Prince. He was named Rudolf, after the Habsburg ancestor who, in 1278, won the Austrian dominions from King Ottokar of Bohemia and invested his sons with them. As had been the case in naming Gisela, the imperial family reached far back into medieval history, thus affirming its tradition. Around this same time, Franz Joseph also had the grave of Rudolf of Habsburg in Speyer restored at his own expense. He still hoped to be able to reestablish the old tradition of Habsburg rule over all of Germany, which Emperor Franz had relinquished in 1806 with the retirement of the crown of the Holy Roman Empire. The choice of name for the Crown Prince was politically motivated.

The joy at a crown prince, hoped for such a long time, was overwhelming at court and genuine among the people, if for no other reason than because this birth was the occasion of generous donations. The Emperor gave his wife a triple strand of pearls worth 75,000 guldens. He laid the Order of the Golden Fleece in little Rudolf's cradle, and on the first day of the child's life, his father made him a colonel in the army. "I want my son, granted me by God's grace, from his entry into the world to be a member of my brave army."[29] This was not only a demonstration of the military state, which angered so many "civilians," but also a decision about the newborn Prince: Whether he liked it or not, he would have to be a soldier. The subsequent conflicts between father and son had their source in that determination.

The Emperor had warm words of thanks for the good wishes proffered by his capital and residential city. "Heaven has given me a child who will one day find a new, larger, and more elegant Vienna. However, though the city will change, the Prince will nevertheless find no change in the loyal hearts of old, and therefore he will meet with the Viennese of old, who, should it become necessary, will prove to him as well their tested willingness to make sacrifices."[30]

For the Crown Prince was born at the time Vienna was being transformed. The medieval city walls were being torn down. Their place was taken by a broad, splendid avenue that enclosed the inner city like a ring, the Ringstrasse. The constrictions of the old town, squeezed inside the walls, was intended to make way for the grandeur and spaciousness of a modern city connected to its outskirts.

That such a monument in stone to a new time and a crown prince was not, however, in itself enough was hinted by Franz Grillparzer in one of his quatrains.

> *Wiens Wälle fallen in den Sand;*
> *Wer wird in engen Mauern leben!*
> *Auch ist ja schon das ganze Land*
> *Von einer chinesischen umgeben.*[31]

[Vienna's ramparts fall to the sand; / Who would live in narrow walls! / Especially as the entire land / Is already surrounded by a Chinese one.]

Public pressure on the Emperor increased to create a modern state, and especially to grant a constitution.

The birth was a difficult one. Elisabeth recovered slowly, especially as she was not allowed to nurse the baby and therefore suffered from milk congestion and fevers. In this instance, too, no exception was made, in spite of Sisi's pleas. As previously arranged, the child was fed exclusively by the wet nurse, Marianka, an "exceedingly beautiful" (according to Sophie) peasant woman from Moravia. Sisi's convalescence took longer than normal. The fever recurred for weeks after the birth, weakening her immensely. Under these circumstances, there could be no question of the child's being in his mother's care. As she had done earlier, Grandmother Sophie once again assumed full responsibility for the nursery.

Since Sisi's health did not improve by fall and winter, Duchess Ludovika was summoned to Austria once more. She arrived with several of the Empress's younger sisters, and she also brought along the old family physician, Dr. Fischer, in whom the young Empress had more confidence than she did in Dr. Seeburger. Dr. Fischer's diagnosis is not known. Sophie's diary, too, is filled with remarks concerning Sisi's illness, but no clear-cut symptoms (except for frequent fevers, general weakness, and lack of appetite) are recorded.

The old enmity between mother-in-law and daughter-in-law was not diminished by the birth of the Crown Prince. Matters grew so grave that Sophie complained to Ludovika, who for her part lamented, "Your letter made me feel very bad in one respect, I thought it was going much better and such things as you wrote me were no longer happening. It is a real sorrow to me that it always remains the same, and the years bring no change. It is an incomprehensible way to behave, an injustice that bothers me and makes me afraid, my only grief whenever I think joyfully of this happy situation, where everything is so arranged for happiness and the grateful enjoyment of such unusual happiness."[32]

The only times Sisi's illness disappeared were when someone from the Bavarian family was with her. In January 1859, her younger sister Marie —now married by proxy to the Crown Prince of Naples—stopped off in Vienna on her way to her new home. The beauty of the seventeen-year-old bride was admired even by Archduchess Sophie. "Her beautiful eyes hold an expression of sweet melancholy which, if that is possible, makes her more beautiful still."[33]

Marie spent two weeks in Vienna, lavishly spoiled by the Empress. "Sisi writes such happy letters . . . and Marie as well, it really must be a joy to see them together," Ludovika wrote to Sophie.[34] Sisi took her younger sister to the Burgtheater, to the Prater, to the Circus Renz. The two spent many hours alone chatting. "It was almost as if fate, well aware what was in store for our poor Maria in future, wished to grant her a few day's delay," Sisi was to say later.[35]

Ludovika, to be sure, worried that this strange solitary wedding trip would delude her daughter too much about the earnestness of life. "I am only afraid that Marie is having too good a time in Vienna, and I hope she will not compare her future position with Sisi's, especially her relationship with her dear Emperor; God grant that she, too, will find marital happiness, but anyway it is not easy to withstand comparison with the Emperor. My hope lies in Marie's gentle, submissive, more kindly nature."[36]

Ludovika was still completely caught up in the old court ways of thinking. An alliance with the Neapolitan royal house meant a brilliant match for a duchess from Bavaria. Ludovika could not help knowing that the throne, supported by a harsh, even cruel, absolutist regime was threatened by revolts of every sort, though she may have been ignorant of the full extent. King Ferdinand II ("King Bomba") was adamantly set against even the slightest liberalization and insisted on the divine right of his royal position. His reasons for marrying his son to young Marie were entirely political: The marriage turned the future King of the Two Sicilies into the brother-in-law of the Emperor of Austria. Given the threats from Garibaldi's partisans to the south and the Sardinian troops to the north, support from the leading absolutist power on the Continent was politically advantageous. In these revolutionary times, the princes clustered as close together as possible.

In spite of her poor health, Elisabeth accompanied her younger sister as far as Trieste. Their older brother Duke Ludwig ("Louis") also traveled with them. With great astonishment, the three witnessed the medieval ceremonies with which the Neapolitans received their future Queen. A silk ribbon had been stretched across the center of the large hall of the Governor's Palace in Trieste to symbolize the border between Bavaria and Naples. A large table under the ribbon had two of its legs in "Bavaria" and two in "Naples." Marie was led to an armchair at the Bavarian end of the table. The two doors, decorated with coats of arms and flags, now opened to admit the two delegations with an honor guard of Neapolitan and Bavarian soldiers respectively. Across the silk ribbon the authorized representatives exchanged the documents, bowed solemnly to each other, and passed the documents on to the attendants. The Bavarian representative now spoke the parting words to Marie. All Bavarians were allowed to kiss Marie's hand once more. Then the silk ribbon was lowered, and Marie had to move to the "Neapolitan" armchair. The Neapolitan delegation was presented to her, then Marie was taken to the royal yacht, *Fulminante*. [37]

A tearful parting of the sisters followed in the ship's cabin. Now Maria Sophia, the seventeen-year-old Princess of Calabria, Crown Princess of the Two Sicilies, set sail for Bari with total strangers, people whose language she barely understood. The only living creature from her home that was by her side was her canary. What was waiting for her was an unhappy marriage, revolution, and expulsion from her kingdom.

Sisi's brother Ludwig responded to the unhappiness of his two (imperial and royal) sisters in his own way. A few months after the spectacle in Trieste, he broke out of the rigid mold of court life. Against the wishes of the King of Bavaria and the ducal family, he married his love of many years, the bourgeois actress Henriette Mendel, with whom he already had a daughter. For her sake, he even renounced his birthright of primogeniture and considerable sources of income.

By now, Sisi was rejecting the court mentality so sharply that she made a point of welcoming her brother's marriage, and she established a pointedly intimate relationship with the sister-in-law who was scorned in aristocratic circles. She maintained these loving ties to the end of her life.

Matters went far worse for her little sister Marie than Elisabeth had feared. The bridegroom was mentally and physically enfeebled, was a religious fanatic, and was impotent. Since King Ferdinand II died only a few months after Marie's arrival, the seventeen-year-old became Queen— at the side of a sickly, anxiety-ridden King, in a kingdom threatened by revolution and external enemies. Ludovika soon sent photographs "of Marie and her king. He must be horrible; . . . Marie looks so pale and haggard."[38]

All Italy was in revolt, the unification movement was unstoppable. The Kingdom of the Two Sicilies was not the only area threatened; the Habsburg principalities in Tuscany and Modena and the Austrian provinces in Northern Italy—Lombardy and Venetia—were also at risk. Backed by a secret pact with France, Piedmont fanned the political unrest with every means, to provoke Austria into military intervention.

Austrian politics fell helplessly into the trap of this maneuver. On April 23, 1859, Emperor Franz Joseph sent an ultimatum to Turin, demanding that the Sardinian "army be put on peacetime status and the partisans be dismissed." The ultimatum was rejected by Cavour and seized on as the welcome occasion for warfare with Austria. This was the first time Emperor Franz Joseph issued an ultimatum that resulted in bloody war for which the country was militarily and politically ill prepared. This demand was not unlike the later ultimatum to Serbia issued in the summer of 1914.

Austrian troops marched into Piedmont—and were seen as the aggressors by all the world. France came to the aid of the little country. Franz Joseph expressed his outrage at Napoleon III. "Once again we stand on the threshold of a time when total destruction of the existing order is hurled into the world, no longer only by sectarian groups, but now also by thrones."

Now, when war had already broken out, he tried to gain help from the German Confederation, and most especially from Prussia—"I speak as a prince in the German Confederation when I point out to you our common danger."[39]

But there could be no thought of Greater German solidarity. Prussian policies had quite other aims. A weakening of the Austrian rivals suited Berlin only too well. Austria was left without help. The situation was hopeless.

New taxes were levied to finance this war. The Swiss envoy reported to Bern, "This is a harsh blow to the populace of Vienna and the monarchy, and the rise in food costs, as well as increases in ground rents and house rents—which had already spiraled to an unprecedented height, soon exceeding conditions in Paris—are now being increased again by a considerable amount. There is no end in sight, and this will not improve the mood."[40]

"For lack of participation," for example, the Kunstverein (Art Society) had to close its exhibitions. "Like trade and business, art, too, is on the brink of ruin," one Viennese correspondent noted.[41] Further examples could be cited endlessly.

The fact that at this very time the Emperor and Empress, surrounded by all the archdukes and archduchesses, went to the horse races in the Prater and graciously allowed themselves to be cheered was not likely to improve morale. Untouched by the war in Italy, by the misery of the people, a wondrously beautiful young Empress appeared and solemnly handed out the state prizes.

The Habsburg relatives, rulers in Tuscany and Modena, and their families were forced to flee. They sought refuge in Vienna. These numerous Italian Habsburgs were now permanent guests at the family dinner table in the Hofburg. They described their experiences at great length and fanned the anger at the revolution.

The imperial family clung to its illusions for a long time and formed erroneous opinions on what was happening. As late as May, Franz Joseph prettified the situation, telling Sophie that the French had lost a thousand men to the cold and lack of food. Sophie: "poor people, and in such an unjust cause. In Germany the armies are being rallied."[42]

During these days, Archduchess Sophie sent 85,000 cigars, at a cost of 500 guldens, to the troops in Northern Italy.[43] Whether they ever reached their destination is uncertain. Supplies were so poorly controlled that the Austrian soldiers often had to go into battle on an empty stomach, while behind the scenes, profiteers helped themselves to purloined goods. In spite of great bravery among the troops ravaged by hunger and a lack of organization, the generals' incompetence lost the Battle of Magenta.

In the elegant Viennese salons, the ladies rolled bandages. Among them were the young Empress, Archduchess Sophie, and all the ladies of the court. Every day long trains brought countless numbers of the wounded and the sick from the theater of war. "They cursed and damned the generals who commanded them in Italy, and Gyulai in particular was the object of satirical poems and defilement," Prince Khevenhüller recorded in his diary.[44]

After the embarrassing and bloody defeat at Magenta, Count Franz Gyulai, the commanding general and a close friend of Grünne's, was removed from the supreme command. When the Emperor recognized Austria's hopeless situation, he traveled to Northern Italy to cheer the soldiers by his presence. He still insisted that Austria was fighting for a "just cause against infamy and treason," but increasingly he admitted to himself the seriousness of the situation. "We are faced with an enemy who is superior to us in numbers and very brave, who will employ any means, even the most evil, who is allied to the revolution and thus gains reinforcements, we are betrayed on all sides in our own country."[45]

Franz Joseph dealt with this situation entirely as a soldier whose duty it is to go to war. Nevertheless, this decision, born of military romanticism, showed that he "was wanting a deeper insight into the nature of his actual position as a ruler," his biographer Joseph Redlich noted.[46] For the departure of the absolute ruler from Vienna also meant that diplomatic negotiations, especially those with the German princes, were interrupted, thwarting any opportunity for a nonmilitary accord. Just before his departure, Franz Joseph asked the aged Prince Metternich how he was to word his will and what regency was to be provided for in case of his death.

The Emperor's parting was heartrending. The children were driven to the railroad station in a six-horse carriage to wave at their father one last time. In her diary, Leopoldine Nischer, the baby nurse, described the dense crowd gathered around the carriage. "Also a number of weeping women thronged to the window, calling, 'the poor children,' so that the little ones began to feel quite frightened."[47]

Gisela was barely three years old, the Crown Prince a mere eight months.

Elisabeth accompanied her husband as far as Mürzzuschlag; when she left, she implored his retinue, especially Count Grünne, "You will surely always remember your promise to take good care of the Emperor; that is my only comfort in this terrible time, that you will do so always and on every occasion. If I did not have this assurance, I would have to be deathly afraid." That Sisi, too, was convinced that in these difficult times, the Emperor's place was properly in Vienna rather than on the field of battle in Italy is revealed in her letter to Grünne. "But you will surely do whatever is in your power to persuade the Emperor to return quickly and remind him at every opportunity that he is so sorely needed in Vienna as well. If you knew how much I worry, you would feel very sorry for me."[48]

"The Empress's discomposure surpasses imagination," Leopoldine Nischer wrote. "Since yesterday [after her return from Mürzzuschlag], she has not stopped crying, will not eat, and always remains alone—at best, with the children." The mother's despair also affected the children. The nurse worried because "poor Gisela [is] somewhat disconcerted by the unceasing tears. Last night she sat very quietly in a corner, and her eyes were damp. When I asked her what was the matter, she said: 'Gisela has to cry too for dear Papa.' "

Like most Austrians, the nurse also had family members in the army in Italy. Her brother-in-law died several days after the Battle of Magenta, her oldest son survived the Battle of Solferino.

Sisi was in a state of hysterical despondency. Ludovika: "her letters are soaked in tears!"[49] She begged the Emperor for permission to follow him to Italy. Franz Joseph: "Unfortunately, I cannot grant your wish for the present, infinitely much as I would like to. There is no place for women in the restless life at headquarters, I cannot head my army with a bad example."[50]

He tried to calm his wife, who was ailing again. "I beg you, my angel, if you love me, do not grieve so much, take care of yourself, distract yourself as much as you can, go riding, drive with caution and care, and preserve for me your dear precious health, so that when I come back, I will find you quite well and we can be quite happy."[51]

Still in Verona, he wrote to Ludovika asking her to be so kind as to travel to Vienna, or at least to send her younger daughter, Mathilde, to cheer Sisi up.

Once again, Dr. Fischer came from Bavaria, this time at the request of a completely perplexed Sophie. Ludovika was outraged and almost apologized to her sister for her difficult daughter: "if only it were recognized that you do everything, how well disposed you are to others! God grant that things will be different again!"[52]

Once again, the Empress went on starvation diets, rode horseback for hours every day, turned inward, and fled the family teas and dinners Archduchess Sophie gave.

The number of Elisabeth's critics grew. By now, even the imperial physican, Dr. Seeburger, was among them. He "poured out his reproaches and complaints about the Empress who, according to him, did not meet her obligations either as an empress or as a woman; though she was essentially idle, her contacts with the children were very casual, and though she sorrows and weeps for the absent noble Emperor, she rides horseback for hours, to the detriment of her health; between her and Archduchess Sophy an icy abyss yawns."[53]

The governor of the castle criticized "the Empress's bearing, because she smoked as she was being driven about, so that I grew truly uneasy at having to hear such things," wrote the minister of police, Baron Johann Kempen in his diary.[54] Even Queen Victoria of England heard of the shocking fact that the young Austrian Empress—like her sister Marie of Naples—smoked. Such tittle-tattle reveals the extent of the gossip.[55]

The Emperor cautiously reminded his wife of her obligations. "I beg you, for the love you bear me, pull yourself together, show yourself in the city sometimes, visit institutions. You have no idea what a great help you can be to me in this way. It will put heart into the people in Vienna and keep up the good spirit I require so urgently. See to it through Countess Esterházy that the Ladies' Aid Society sends as much as possible, especially bandages for the many, very many wounded, perhaps also some wine."[56]

Franz Joseph's reports of military details, as well as the names of the dead and wounded, covered many pages, none of which could comfort the

Empress: "The fighting was so bitter that whole piles of the dead lay about. The many officers who lost their lives will be hard to replace."[57]

On June 18, the Emperor issued a directive to the army that caused an enormous sensation. In it, the Emperor "immediately" assumed "supreme command over my armies in the field against the enemy." He wished "to continue, at the head of my brave troops, the struggle Austria is forced to wage for her honor and rights."

The decision by the twenty-nine-year-old strategically inexperienced Emperor in this precarious situation aroused vehement criticism, which was to prove justified only too soon. For the next battle, that of Solferino, was the bloodiest, sustaining the greatest losses, of the whole unfortunate war. It sealed Austria's final defeat. The horror of the battlefield of Solferino under the burning sun was beyond all imagining. (It was here that, shaken by the helplessness of the wounded, Henri Dunant decided to found what became the Red Cross.)

The Emperor's insufficient strategic skills, combined with overly hasty decisions to retreat, were the elements most responsible for the defeat. The ugly phrase "lions led by asses" made the rounds and was applied most especially to the Emperor.[58] Since the beginning of his reign, the interest Franz Joseph had shown in the army was unsurpassed. No other department had so much money spent on it (and debts run up for it), and now all ambition was ending in a huge humiliation and a bloodbath.

Count Alexander Mensdorff-Pouilly wrote to his cousin, Prince Ernst of Coburg, "May the *souls* of the many fallen, in the form of dream figures, disturb the nocturnal rest of those who, now comfortably ensconced behind their desks, plan political washouts."[59]

The mood in Austria was so despairing that many people, aware of the poor political and military leadership and the unbearable burdens on the people, even wished for a defeat. Heinrich Laube, the director of the Burgtheater, who was born in northern Germany, recalled this time. "During all these wars—as well as later, in the year '66—I saw with astonishment and shock that the mood of the populace had no great objection to our being beaten. Yes, if we were politically in order—they say out loud—it would be a pleasure to see our troops victorious. But as it is, as it is! The year '48 was confiscated from us, and we gain concessions only when the government meets with difficulties caused by lost battles. I had only just become an Austrian, but this way of thinking was thoroughly repugnant to me."[60]

Emperor Franz Joseph was made to feel the full brunt of the consequences of the defeat. At no other time was the Emperor as unpopular with the people as during these months. The impoverished and angry populace blamed the terrible policies and poor strategy for tens of thousands of the dead, forced to give their lives for a province they considered foreign. Their rage went so far as to be expressed in public appeals for the Emperor's abdication and for transfer of the government to his younger, more liberal brother, Max. A revolutionary mood thus obtained even in Vienna!

The strict censorship imposed on the Austrian newspapers kept them from giving free rein to their disapproval. The foreign papers dealt all the more critically with the young Emperor. Friedrich Engels, for example, endowed him with such expressions as "arrogant youngster" and "pitiful weakling"; he wrote that the courageous Austrian soldiers had "been beaten, not by the French, but by the overbearing imbecility of their own emperor."[61]

It was only too easy to ascribe the catastrophe in Lombardy to the military and aristocratic Kamarilla surrounding the inexperienced but all-powerful Emperor. A system that identified to such an extent with the military as that of Emperor Franz Joseph could not survive so massive a military catastrophe without some damage. Franz Joseph, disheartened, wrote to his wife, "I have grown wiser by many experiences and have come to know how it feels to be a beaten general. The serious consequences of our misfortune will set in eventually, but I trust in God and am not aware of any blame, nor any error in judgment."[62]

Napoleon III, on the other hand, laid the principal blame for the defeat at Franz Joseph's door and admitted to Prince Ernst that he "regarded" the French victory "as the purest fluke. . . . His army had been in the poorest condition, and his generals had shown no aptitude for leading a large army; the Austrians had fought much better than the French and . . . there could be no doubt that they would have won Solferino if the Emperor had allowed the reserves to move forward. The Emperor of Austria, he said, was a man of great standing, *mais malheureusement il lui manque l'énergie de la volonté* [but unfortunately he lacked the will]."[63]

Even Duchess Ludovika criticized Franz Joseph's eagerness to prove himself as a military commander, writing to Marie of Saxony, "I really had not expected such a defeat one after another . . . and that it was the emperor himself who was leading the forces, I think, makes the event even sadder; I could not even approve his leaving Vienna during such difficult times, and now his return will be most unpleasant."[64]

Meanwhile, Sisi had organized a hospital for the wounded in Laxenburg. Franz Joseph: "Put the wounded wherever you want, in all the houses of Laxenburg. They will be very happy in your care. I cannot thank you enough."[65] After the bloody battles, 60,000 of the sick and wounded had to be seen to. All the hospitals in Austria were not enough by far.[66] Convents, churches, and castles had to take in the patients. It took months before the fate of the wounded soldiers was decided; they either died or survived as cripples or in good health. A great deal of money had been spent on outfitting the army. No provisions had been made for medical treatment of the wounded, however.

The young Empress was suddenly confronted with these problems. She began to inform herself thoroughly by reading the newspapers, and she arrived at a firm stance that opposed the military and the aristocratic, purely absolutist regime of her husband. We do not know precisely what personal influences had a part in this change and whether the Bavarian relatives were responsible during their visits to Vienna. But that increasingly the young Empress took an unequivocal stand on the side of the people and the newspapers was as obvious as was the fact that these political questions also began to enter into the struggle between mother-in-law and daughter-in-law. For though Elisabeth spared her husband direct reproaches, she ascribed all the evils to Archduchess Sophie's reactionary influence—as did the Austrian bourgeois intellectuals.

The twenty-one-year-old Empress even attempted to give the Emperor some political advice (which echoed the "voice of the people"): Why not conclude a peace as soon as possible? Franz Joseph, however, had no intention of listening to his wife's suggestions. He replied defensively, "Your political plan contains some very good ideas, but we must not give up hope that Prussia and Germany will yet come to our aid, and before that time, there can be no thought of negotiating with the enemy."[67]

It is astonishing how uninformed the Emperor was about the political plans and principles underlying Prussian policies. Even at this late date, when the war had long since been lost, he could still harbor such illusions. The Emperor had no recourse but to trust in God, "Who will surely guide everything for the best. He tests us severely, and we are surely only at the beginning of worse afflictions, but we must bear them with resignation and always do our duty in everything."[68]

Elisabeth's political suggestions met with little success. Her inquiry whether Grünne (who was hated in the army) would be dismissed was also answered in the negative by the Emperor. "No thought has ever been given to making a change for Count Grünne, and I do not consider it at all. In general, I beg you not to believe what the papers say, they write so many stupid and wrong things."[69] Instead, he urged his wife to eat more, to go horseback riding less, but most of all, to get more sleep. "I implore you, give up this life at once and sleep during the night, which nature intended for sleep and not for reading and writing. And do not ride so much and so vigorously."[70]

Nor were the two mothers, Ludovika and Sophie, delighted at the young Empress's interest in politics. Ludovika to Sophie: "I believe the presence of the child will fill many hours of the day, will calm her, will occupy her, animate her domestic senses, give a new direction to her habits and tastes. I would like to fan every little spark, nurture every good impulse."[71]

Only a few days after the Emperor had turned down Sisi's suggestion that he make peace quickly, he himself admitted the futility of the war. Nevertheless, the initiative for an armistice came, not from him, but from Napoleon III, the arch-scoundrel, as Franz Joseph called him.[72]

The Treaty of Villefranche obligated Austria to relinquish Lombardy, at one time her richest province, an Austrian possession since the Congress of Vienna. Though Venetia was to remain in Austrian hands, no one seriously believed that this last Italian possession could be held for long.

The Swiss envoy reported that in Vienna the peace

> made a horribly unfavorable impression. . . . The halo that until now has surmounted the Emperor has shattered even among the lower strata of the people. For ten years, the most tenuous efforts were made to maintain the costly military system and to bring it to the highest degree of perfection, and now they realize that millions upon millions of guldens were thrown away to maintain a toy and a weapon for ultramontanism and for the aristocracy. If the Emperor returns with the idea of maintaining the present system of government and to rule with the help of the Concordat and his military protégés, the monarchy would face a dismal future, this system is rotten through and through and cannot but break.[73]

In Hungary, a new revolution loomed on the horizon. Concerning conditions in Vienna, Dr. Seeburger felt that "the mood had never been worse than now, but Archduchess Sophie, to whom he [Seeburger] had told this, refused to believe him. In taverns and coffeehouses no one is afraid to slander the Emperor, but he is going hunting tomorrow in

Reichenau, and the Empress is going to the same place, to go horseback riding."[74]

Sophie's husband, Archduke Franz Karl, also labored under some misconceptions. He spoke "openly about the prevailing discontent, but at the same time he denied that it had any greater significance, because he was still being saluted. What flimsy reassurance!" Minister of Police Kempen remarked in his diary.[75] Assassination plots were uncovered, one even in the Hofburg itself; a footman had planned to murder the Emperor and Archduchess Sophie. Ludovika found the people's rage against the Emperor "as painful as it is outrageous . . . because it is directed specifically against the person of the Emperor, who is being unbelievably reviled; lies about him are spread that are so unutterably unfounded and unjust precisely against him of all people—Unfortunately, the rancor emanates largely from the military, which even abroad . . . expresses itself so bitterly about him." The sentence that follows this passage is typical for Franz Joseph's character; variations on it can be found in several contemporary sources, even in Archduchess Sophie's diary itself: "in all this," Franz Joseph "himself is, I would say, so innocent, for he is cheerful, actually that surprised me."[76]

Monstrous corruption in the military and financial systems came to light. Finance Minister Baron Karl von Bruck, devastated by the Emperor's lack of trust, slit his throat. Ministers and generals were dismissed; besides Foreign Minister Buol, they were Minister of the Interior Bach, Minister of Police Kempen, General Gyulai, General Hess. It was very difficult for the Emperor "to allay the enormous mania for reorganizing and casting aside," as he complained to his mother.[77]

At the center of the criticism stood the Emperor's adjutant general, his closest personal and political intimate and friend, Count Karl Grünne. He considered himself his sovereign's whipping boy and accepted the blame that was by rights the Emperor's. Even Ludovika knew: "The main hatred is directed at Grün[ne], because it is said that he deliberately kept him in ignorance of all the sad things that happened, about the terrible negligence, blunders, and fraud."[78]

Some years later, the liberal *Neues Wiener Tagblatt* wrote, "The name Grünne enjoyed an unpopularity that almost bordered on popularity." He had been, the newspaper claimed, a "nonsystematic dictator," a "head of government *extra statum*," with the "halo of a vice emperor." In the Council of Ministers, he had represented "often also the voice of the monarch."[79]

Under the pressure of popular opinion, the Emperor was forced to dismiss Grünne from his posts of adjutant general and head of the military chancellery—though he did so with great proofs of favor. Grünne did retain the office of chief equerry.

Sisi's friendship with Grünne remained unaffected by politics. After his dismissal, she wished him "especially a better happier time than the last has been. I still cannot accept that now everything is so very different from before, and especially to see a different person in your place, but my only consolation is that we have not lost you altogether, and you know how grateful I am to you for this."[80]

Emperor Franz Joseph exerted himself to the fullest to avert a curtailment of his absolute rule. Archduchess Sophie supported him. She abhorred the "popular will," considering it an offense against the imperial majesty. In her letters, she complained of treason and refused to admit any fault in the "system." She complained that "my poor son, hard pressed by the victory of injustice over justice, by treachery and disloyalty, nevertheless was unappreciated by many."[81]

A fair evaluation of the Empress's political attitude, which was soon made plain to a larger group, must take into account the fact that her liberalism, which was considered (at court) so taboo, her anticlericalism, her enthusiasm for the constitutional state came to the fore during Austria's darkest hour, politically speaking. In the most personal terms, it was the antithesis of the demands for divine right, absolutism, and aristocratic thinking espoused by Archduchess Sophie.

CHAPTER FOUR

FLIGHT

The political crisis of the winter of 1859–1860 went hand in hand with a serious private crisis in the life of the Emperor and Empress. In the political sphere, one piece of bad news followed on the last. Grünne's successor as adjutant general, Count Crenneville, complained, "terrible prospects—state bankruptcy—revolution—misfortune—war. Poor Emperor, indefatigably striving for the best."[1]

Emperor Franz Joseph had no intention of letting his young wife share in his worries. He continued to discuss politics only with his mother, never with Elisabeth, who was developing opposing opinions. Annoyed, the Empress had to accept a situation in which she was pushed aside like a child and her suggestions were not even acknowledged. The tug of war between Sophie and Sisi was fiercer than ever.

It can hardly seem surprising that the Emperor tried to keep out of the way of the endless quarreling of the two women in this already over-charged atmosphere and that he sought comfort elsewhere. Widespread rumors about Franz Joseph's affairs began to circulate for the first time in his marriage, which was almost six years old. However, this was a turn of events the Empress was not ready to confront. Lack of experience, excessive sensibility, jealousy of her mother-in-law, the most severe strain on her nerves caused by her husband's long absence—all contributed to her loss of self-control.

She began to provoke those around her. In the winter of 1859–1860—at the very time when the Austrian Empire was trapped in the greatest political calamities and the Emperor's unpopularity had reached unprece-dented heights—the young Empress, normally so reserved, became a bla-tant pleasure-seeker. She, who until then had strictly refused to develop any social activities at court outside the official functions, now, in the spring of 1860, organized no fewer than six balls in her apartments. She never invited more than twenty-five couples—all of them, of course, young people of the first rank with impeccable genealogies, as was required at court. The peculiarity of these balls, however, was that only the young couples were invited, not the mothers of the young women, as was customary. This meant that Archduchess Sophie, too, was excluded.

Landgravine Therese Fürstenberg, who did attend the balls, wrote that these "orphan balls" at the Empress's were very amusing, but nevertheless did irritate court society not a little: "at first one was startled at such an enormity [not inviting the mothers], nothing could be done against the Supreme will." Landgravine Therese wrote that at these balls, the Empress "danced with passion,"[2] a partiality never remarked in her before or after.

Furthermore, Sisi, who normally shunned all social events as best she could, also attended the large private balls. After a ball given by the Margrave Pallavicini, for example, she did not return to the Hofburg until six thirty in the morning, by which time the Emperor had already set out for the hunt, so that she no longer found him at home (as Archduchess Sophie noted in her diary). Political cares did not deter the Emperor, either, from going hunting as often as possible.

While court society showed no tolerance for Sisi's defiant behavior, it had all the more sympathy for a husband's romantic adventures. In the circles of the high nobility and the court, marriages of convenience and dynastic marriages were the rule. They were necessary to maintain an immaculate pedigree. Love affairs alongside these marriages of rank were common. The wives understood as much. Though for the most part they could not retaliate with affairs of their own (for similar open-mindedness was not granted to a woman), on the whole they accepted their husbands' affairs without complaint. For they were repaid by the high social position they occupied by virtue of their marriages, which, for all practical purposes, could never be dissolved.

But Elisabeth had not married Franz Joseph out of any social ambition. Purely emotional reasons (whether or not they can be called love in a fifteen-year-old) united her to the Emperor. Now she had to admit that the young Emperor was not adequate to her emotional demands (which surely seemed excessive to him, given his life), that he was betraying her. Franz Joseph was the only one, besides the children, who tied Elisabeth to the Viennese court. This one link in an otherwise alien and hostile world was now threatening to break.

Elisabeth had witnessed the unhappiness of her parents' marriage; Duchess Ludovika with her horde of children lived apart from her husband, Duke Max. As the whole family knew, he had affairs and a whole string of illegitimate children, whom he provided for generously. This marriage was characterized by decades of humiliation and total isolation of the wife and mother. The fear of such a lamentable fate as Duchess Ludovika's may have played a large part in Sisi's vehement reaction.

Disturbing news from Naples now aggravated the difficult situation. In May 1860, Garibaldi's troops conquered the island of Sicily, and a short time later, Naples, the capital of the Kingdom of the Two Sicilies was threatened. Cries for help from young Queen Marie reached Elisabeth. In June, her brothers Karl Theodor and Ludwig arrived in Vienna to discuss possible measures to aid the Bourbon kingdom. But no matter how much solidarity Emperor Franz Joseph felt for the royal house, related to him by marriage, and no matter how much he and Archduchess Sophie deplored the predicament in which this monarchy found itself—given Austria's own unfortunate situation, there could be no thought of military or financial aid. The young King and his Queen were abandoned to their fate. Elisabeth's worries about her beloved young sister, who had tried in vain to obtain Austrian help, not only further strained her already over-taxed nerves, but also placed an additional burden on the imperial marriage. In July 1860, the differences between the Emperor and Empress were so acute that Elisabeth left Vienna, taking little Gisela with her, and went to Possenhofen—for the first time in five years. This sudden trip was in the nature of flight. Sisi used the new railway line from Vienna to Munich (Kaiserin-Elisabeth-Westbahn) before its official opening, thus introducing no little chaos into the solemn celebrations.

Elisabeth was in no hurry whatever to return to Vienna. She passed the time primarily in horseback riding, and it was the Viennese stables she missed most. For her brother's horses no longer met her high expectations. They "are terribly overridden and out of hand," she wrote to Grünne, to whom she was openly affectionate. "I hope that you miss me a little and feel the absence of all my complaining, which you always tolerate so patiently."[3]

To avoid creating a stir, however, Sisi had to return to Vienna before Franz Joseph's birthday on August 18. The Emperor drove to Salzburg to meet his wife. Sisi asked two of her siblings to come with her—Karl Theodor and Mathilde—a sign that she needed support against the imperial family and still did not feel confident enough to be alone with Sophie and Franz Joseph.

In the meantime, the situation in Naples had worsened. Garibaldi had invaded the capital. Queen Marie and her sickly, weak husband retired to the fortress of Gaeta. In spite of great bravery on the part of the twenty-year-old Queen ("the heroine of Gaeta"), the fall of the fortress and the ultimate victory of the Italian unification movement was only a matter of time.

Austria's domestic policies ushered in hardly less radical changes than did her foreign policy. The call for a constitution could no longer be ignored. Characteristic of the mood is an anonymous letter delivered to the Emperor in August 1860.

A voice from God! To Emperor Franz Joseph. Why do you hesitate so long with the constitution. Why have you taken from your people what Emperor Ferdinand the Kindly gave it?!

Take the side of citizens and farmers, not merely of the nobility and the great. Imitate the great Emperor Josef II.

Take as a warning the unfortunate King of Naples.

If you continue to persist in absolutism, the same will happen to you.

Down with the Kamarilla.

Build your throne, not on bayonets, but on the love of the people.

In short do as the other German regents do, in unity there is strength.

Justitia regnorum fundamentum. With joined forces.

> Your devoted friend Martin vom guten Rath [Martin of the
> good advice].[4]

The Emperor remained helpless in the face of all political demands; outraged, he complained to his mother, "But such vileness on the one hand and cowardice on the other as rule the world now have surely never been seen before; one wonders sometimes whether everything that happens can really be happening."

He begged for "forgiveness for the fact that the banditry of Garibaldi, the thievery of Victor Emmanuel, the unprecedented sharp practices of the arch-villain in Paris, who surpasses even himself—the Reichsrat, now happily and truly buried beyond all expectation, the Hungarian nuisance, and the inexhaustible wants and needs of all the provinces, etc. claim me to such an extent and fill my poor head so much that I had hardly a moment for myself."[5]

The first concession to the Austrians thirsting for freedom was the October Diploma of 1860, the beginning of a constitution. Franz Joseph wrote to reassure his mother, who was worried about the fact that "popular opinion" was prevailing, "Though we will get a little parliamentarianism, all the power remains in my hands, and the overall situation will suit Austrian conditions very well."[6] But the Emperor, who had ruled absolutely, felt even this modest concession to be a personal humiliation. Sophie went so far as to regard this first loosening of absolute rule as the "ruin of the realm, which we are rapidly approaching."[7]

The family peace had now been broken for a year. No improvement was in sight—quite the contrary: Elisabeth's health, affected by nervous breakdowns and unrelieved starvation diets, became so fragile by the end of October 1860 that Dr. Josef Skoda, a lung specialist, determined that she would have to seek out a warmer climate at once; he felt her condition to be acutely life-threatening. She could no longer, he advised, endure the Viennese winter. During the preliminary consultations, the physician recommended Madeira as a suitable wintering place.

It is not clear why he chose Madeira; it may be that the Empress herself suggested this destination. A short time earlier, Archduke Max, Sisi's favorite brother-in-law, had returned from a trip to Brazil and a lengthy stay on Madeira and had told the imperial family many stories of the scenically beautiful island in the Atlantic. These recitals may well have inspired the Empress's eccentric wish. For in fact the Austrian monarchy contained enough resorts situated in mild climates (to mention only

Merano), where consumptives could go to be cured. Madeira, on the other hand, was not exactly famous as boasting a climate conducive to recovery from life-threatening pulmonary disease. It looked to all the world as if by choosing a distant destination, Elisabeth wanted to prevent frequent visits from the Emperor.

The form of disease was completely obscure—and remains so to this day. To the same degree that Elisabeth was healthy as a child, she began ailing from her wedding day on. Three pregnancies within four years had exhausted her body, especially the difficult birth of the Crown Prince in 1858. For years, she suffered from severe coughing attacks, which increased ominously in the winter of 1860 and probably led to the diagnosis of pulmonary disease. Her stubborn refusal to eat not only caused her to suffer from "greensickness"—anemia—but kept her physically exhausted. Her nerves could take no more. Repeatedly, she fell into crying jags that would not stop. To calm her strained nerves, she had acquired the habit of taking a great deal of exercise: daily rides over often considerable distances (for example, from Laxenburg to Vöslau, which the Emperor called "sheer foolishness"[8]), obstacle jumping to the point of complete exhaustion, hikes extending for hours, gymnastics.

The diagnosis of life-threatening "affected lungs" was received with much skepticism. Especially the Viennese relatives and the court society were not willing to believe that the Empress was really so very ill. Archduchess Therese, for example, wrote to her father, Archduke Albrecht, "One cannot get to the bottom of whether there is much or little wrong with her, since so many versions of Dr. Skoda's pronouncements are told."

Rumors were rife at court. For example, Therese again: "Yesterday, Aunt Marie visited the Empress; she brought along a large handkerchief, because she thought she would cry a lot; instead, the Empress was very merry, she is infinitely happy about going to Madeira. Aunt was so indignant that she gave the Empress a piece of her mind in a pretty blunt manner: 'the Emperor is still in Ischl.' "[9] What is astonishing is that it was exactly during the days when Dr. Skoda diagnosed a life-threatening illness that Franz Joseph went hunting in Bad Ischl and left his wife in Vienna. He did not return until November 7.

During this marital crisis, obvious to the inner circle at court, all sympathies were unequivocally with the Emperor. Archduchess Therese: "I feel infinitely sorry for him for having a wife who prefers to leave her husband and her children for six months instead of leading a quiet life in Vienna, as the doctors ordered." And after a meeting with the Emperor:

"it cuts me to the quick to see him so sad and weary. I hope that his children will give him much comfort and cheer this winter."[10]

Sisi successfully insisted that Countess Esterházy, her mother-in-law's confidante, stay behind in Vienna rather than coming to Madeira. Therese: "Countess Esterházy is being pushed aside strangely. Instead of her, young Mathilde Windisch-Graetz is traveling to Madeira; it is also strange of the latter to leave her little child." The behavior of the allegedly mortally ill woman was astonishing: "The Empress is fully occupied with her summer wardrobe for Madeira."[11]

Nothing can be found in Archduchess Sophie's diary concerning the nature of Sisi's illness, only regret that the Empress was abandoning her husband and children for so long. "She will be separated from her husband for five months, and from her children, on whom she has such a beneficial influence and whom she really raises so well," wrote Sophie of all people. "I was devastated at the news."[12]

Duchess Ludovika was also more inclined to be astonished at the bad news from Vienna than she was to believe in a potentially fatal illness. "Sisi's trip worries me a great deal," she wrote to Saxony, "and it was a great shock, for when she was here, one would not have foreseen such a necessity, although she always coughed a little, especially when she first arrived. . . . Sadly, she does not take enough care of herself and trusts too much in her strong constitution." Strange too is Ludovika's remark, "Since the stay in Madeira is said to be very quiet and, as she writes, very boring, I hope she will soon find opportunity to seek out some amusement."[13]

The Viennese court reacted with spiteful glee. It was noted with gratification that Archduchess Sophie and the Emperor grew closer again and that, for the time being, the Empress was not around to cause further annoyance. Archduchess Therese wrote, "Now the family dinners will always be at Aunt Sophie's. I believe that much as she minds that the Emperor is so lonely since his wife left, secretly she is hoping that he will join her more often and perhaps devote most of his evenings to her." Therese voiced the court position and her own view: "In Vienna, no one has any compassion for the Empress; I am sorry that she could not win the love of the people."[14] This statement, however, refers mainly to the aristocracy and to court circles. Among the common people, the young Empress was still popular.

The news of the Austrian Empress's serious illness created a sensation throughout the world in early November 1860. Offers of help came from the four corners of the earth. Since no suitable ship was available for the journey to Madeira, Queen Victoria of England made her private yacht available. Ludovika wrote about seeing her daughter again in Munich. "Sisi has become thinner and looks, if not ill, nevertheless not as blooming as last summer; but what is remarkable is the coughing, which has increased a great deal, so that one comes to believe that a warmer climate could not help but be beneficial to her."[15] These sentences are remarkably calm for the constantly excitable Ludovika and thus do not fit at all with the newspaper reports that mentioned the Austrian Empress's imminent demise.

It was also astonishing that Sisi, who was known to despise official calls, used the few hours of her stopover in Munich on formal family visits.

From Munich, Sisi's trip continued by way of Bamberg (where Franz Joseph took his leave of her) to Mainz. There she spent the night, and the following day she continued on to Antwerp, where she boarded the British royal yacht *Victoria and Albert*. Her servants and the luggage followed in the *Osborne*. It is remarkable that almost all the passengers (including the physicians) became seasick during heavy storms in the Bay of Biscay, while the allegedly fatally afflicted Empress was spared.

To this day, the strangest rumors are rife in Vienna concerning the Empress's illness before her flight to Madeira. Time and again one hears the version of a supposed venereal disease with which the Emperor is said to have infected his young wife. If that were true, the Empress really would have had to be very ill indeed in November 1860. But according to all the reports from her closest family members, she was hardly that.

Corti, Elisabeth's biographer, came closer to the mark when, discussing the difficulties of November 1860, he wrote, "the cover of illness will reduce all that, and she really is ill, her mental state also affects her body severely. And what would otherwise be a little anemia, an insignificant cough, under such circumstances, almost really an illness." Nevertheless, out of excessive loyalty to the Imperial House, Corti did not dare to allow himself to publish these sentences and crossed them from the manuscript, as he did the following sentences regarding Archduchess Sophie. "She, however, is fully informed and is merely outraged at Elisabeth, who is unmindful of her obligations and who, in her opinion, was only shamming illness in order to escape winter and to be able to pursue her peculiar habits without constraint."[16]

Modern medicine would speak less of a mental than of an emotional illness. The Empress's excessive drive to physical activity, her constant refusal to eat indicate (with all due reservations against such retrospective diagnoses) a neurotic anorexia nervosa, which is often coupled with (somewhat pubertal) rejection of sexuality. This theory would also explain the fact that Sisi seemed to recover at once whenever she removed herself from Vienna and her husband.

In Madeira, Sisi lived a quiet solitary life in a rented villa by the sea. Now and again, the Emperor sent a courier who was to inform himself about her condition and convey letters. The first of these couriers was Joseph Latour. He brought to Munich and Vienna details of Sisi's "quiet existence and the very calm, sensible suitable life she leads," as Ludovika wrote to Saxony. Sisi's mother, however, went on to mention the "very melancholy" letters from the young Empress, her unhappiness about "the great distance and long separation," especially from her children. "She longs enormously for home, for the emperor and the children."[17]

Madeira offered little distraction. The Empress did what she had liked doing best in Possenhofen: She spent the major part of her days with her animals. There were ponies, parrots, but most especially large dogs. Card playing was another pastime—which became a further occasion for gossip in Vienna. Archduchess Therese: "The couriers returned from Madeira cannot say enough about how boring it is there. Everything is divided according to hours, even the card games. From 8–9 Old Maid, from 9–10 Half Past Eleven [another popular card game]. No one talks, even loquacious Helene Taxis has given it up."

In Vienna, a photograph from Madeira was passed from hand to hand. Archduchess Therese: "The Empress is seated playing the mandolin, Helene Taxis crouches on the ground in front of her, holding the Doberman in her arms. Mathilde Windisch-Graetz stands with the horn in her hand; in the background stands Lily Hunyady, she looks thoughtfully at all the others. All the ladies in sailors' blouses and sailor hats."[18] Archduchess Sophie gave a detailed description of the same photograph in her diary. If we consider the difficult times the monarchy was passing through, the political problems weighing on the Emperor, we will understand the astonishment at this photograph, which Vienna felt to be an insult. The children were without their mother, the husband without his wife, the country without its Empress. And in Madeira, Elisabeth stared thoughtfully out to sea, complained about her situation, and played the mandolin and Old Maid. On the other hand, the doctors insisted that the Empress continue her stay on the island, postponing her return to May, when Vienna's climate would be milder.

Thus, Elisabeth continued to be bored, endlessly operating her *"Werkel"* —an Austrian expression for a barrel organ—playing especially arias from

La Traviata. She read a great deal and passed some of the time in Hungarian lessons, given her by one of her "honorary escorts," Count Imre Hunyady. Of course, it was not long before Hunyady, considered extremely dashing, fell in love with the young Empress and was promptly recalled to Vienna. The Austrian Empress's entourage was so vast, with everyone watching everyone else, so many petty jealousies raged within this small society on Madeira, which was completely cut off from the outside world, that not even the slightest emotion could go unrecognized.

In Vienna, Elisabeth's self-confidence was constantly undermined. She was treated as a pretty little fool and pushed aside whenever serious matters were discussed. Here on Madeira, it was not only her lungs that recovered, but more particularly her self-esteem. Here, she became aware of her beauty and her effect on practically every man. The handsome Count Hunyady's infatuation contributed to this process, as did that of the officers of a Russian warship that was berthed at Madeira. The Empress invited them to a dinner followed by a dance—a welcome distraction for the chronically bored entourage and ladies-in-waiting. A Russian admiral, who mentioned this invitation some time later, noted that each of the invited officers, old and young alike, had fallen in love with the Empress.

The longer the stay on Madeira lasted, the more Sisi seemed to forget the disagreements in Vienna and to long to be back with her children. She complained to Grünne, "That would be something for you, to live here, I don't think you could stand it for two weeks. If I'd known how it is here, I would sooner have chosen another place for such a long time, for even if the air leaves nothing to be desired, it takes more to live comfortably."

Once again, wanderlust seized her. Sisi to Grünne: "Anyway, I want always to be on the move, every ship I see sailing away fills me with the greatest desire to be on it, whether it is going to Brazil, to Africa, or to the Cape, it doesn't matter to me, only not to sit in one place for so long."

But she also confided in Count Grünne her fear of Vienna. "To confess to you quite openly, if I didn't have the children, the thought of having to resume the life I have led until now would be quite unendurable. Of A——[Archduchess Sophie] I think only with a shudder, and the distance only makes me detest her all the more."

It was Grünne who supplied her with the political news in which she was so interested. Sisi:

> I beg you, write me how matters now stand, whether it is probable that we will have a campaign, and how things look

domestically. The E.——[Franz Joseph] does not write me about these things. But does he know himself, or at least most of it? You cannot write me too much about all this, I beg you, do it with every courier, you give me so much pleasure, and I will be very grateful to you.

Sisi closed this and other letters to Grünne with the childlike, "Assurances of my sincere friendship, with which I remain always, Your most fond Elisabeth."[19]

That Sisi was totally uninterested in politics, as was claimed in Vienna, was not true. Sisi to Grünne from Funchal: "It seems that no campaign will break out so soon really. I also hoped that it would look better in Hungary, but according to what you wrote me, this does not seem to be the case. In the end, it will start there sooner than in Italy." (By which she meant the expected uprising in Venetia.)

"How strange it would seem to me to still be here at the time of a war, you can imagine. That is why I have pleaded with the Emperor to let me leave sooner, but since he assured me so firmly that there are no grounds for fear, I must believe him and try to remain calm."[20]

Sisi had mixed feelings about returning to Vienna. She wrote Grünne, "I regret missing May in Vienna, especially the races. On the other hand, it is pleasant to be in the city as little as possible and be with, or at least close to, someone who has surely made good use of my absence to control and supervise the E.[mperor] and the children. The beginning will not be sweet, and it will take me a little while to get used to taking up the domestic cross again."

But Sisi's sense of humor broke through again at once. "How much I look forward to riding with you in the Prater for the first time, please have Forester made ready, and for the second time, Gypsy Girl, whom I'm looking forward to especially because I have a hat that's just right for a black horse. I can see quite clearly how you'll laugh at me when you read this."[21]

During the months Sisi was living in Madeira, the fortress of Gaeta fell. The twenty-year-old Queen Marie of Naples and her husband fled to Rome. Elisabeth, who had no news, was deeply troubled about her young sister.

But while Sisi's worries were all for Marie, Archduchess Sophie was thinking in purely political terms. For her, the fall of the absolute monarchy of the Two Sicilies was a further step in the decline of all monarchies. "Now even our last consolation, the last luster of the monarchic prin-

ciple, has vanished!" she lamented after the fall of Gaeta in February
1861.[22]

After a six-month separation, Franz Joseph and Elisabeth met again in
Trieste in May 1861. The friendly welcome tendered by the populace was
encouraging for the future. Ludovika wrote to her sister Sophie.

> Everywhere it looks bad, but I am glad to see that the feeling
> for our dear Emperor has, after all, changed completely, since
> I love him so dearly. . . . May God grant that Sisi will give him
> a truly happy domestic life and that in his inner self he will find
> the happiness and quiet enjoyment he so richly deserves after the
> long, sad winter. May she now, as a result of the long separation,
> learn to truly value and enjoy her good fortune, may he find
> everything in her that he deserves and needs so urgently, as balm
> and boon for the painful burden of his position, for all the
> thanklessness he has been made to feel.[23]

Ludovika hoped in vain. Sisi had been in Vienna for precisely four days
when her attacks of fever and coughing took on frightening proportions
again, especially after the first salon with the high aristocracy. As before
her trip to Madeira, the Empress was again constantly in tears, again took
refuge in solitude.

Foreign Minister Count Louis Rechberg wrote about the "Emperor's
deep distress" and the "depressed mood" at the court. "Since her return,
the Empress has the deepest aversion to any kind of nourishment. She no
longer eats anything at all, and her energies are exhausted all the more as
the cough persists and severe pain robs her of the sleep that might still be
able to keep up her energies."[24]

We cannot be certain whether it was really only the raw Viennese
climate and the exertions of public appearances that were responsible for
this total collapse or whether resumption of marital relations might not
also have played a part. In any case, after the renewed outbreak of her
illness, Sisi had a reason for keeping her bedroom door locked to her
husband.

In June, Dr. Skoda diagnosed galloping consumption and, as a last hope,
ordered a stay on Corfu. Sisi had come to know the island during the
return journey from Madeira, and she deeply admired Corfu's scenic
beauty. But the island had no more of a reputation as a place conducive
to curing pulmonary diseases than had Madeira.

This time, even Ludovika believed in a serious, even fatal, illness. She was further concerned because Sisi regularly quarreled with the doctors who were treating her. Ludovika wrote to Sophie that the doctor had not told Sisi the whole truth, "or everything would be lost and Sisi would not admit him any longer, either. . . . I am devastated."[25]

The physicians' pessimistic diagnosis may or may not have been correct; whatever the case, the state of the Empress's nerves was desperate. She even believed, as Ludovika related, that she was "nothing but a burden on the Emperor and the country, never again able to be of use to the children, yes, she may even think that if she were no longer alive, the Emperor could marry again and that, as a miserable, languishing creature, she can no longer make him happy!" Ludovika to Sophie: "Surely she also wished for the separation to spare him this sad sight? . . . If you had read the letter, after her return to Vienna, the expression of happiness to be with her Emperor, her children again! At the time, it quickened my heart—now it makes it break."[26]

Weeping, Sophie embraced the two children "because they are approaching a great misfortune, the loss of their poor mother." When Sisi left Vienna, Sophie wrote in her diary, "Sad parting from our poor Sisi, perhaps for life. She wept and was extremely emotional and begged my forgiveness in case she had not been to me as she should have been. I cannot express the anguish I felt, it broke my heart." In parting from the children's nurse, Leopoldine Nischer, Sisi entrusted the children to her care with the words, "they are the only thing that is left to the Emperor!"[27]

Fanned by newspaper reports, there was great excitement among the people of Vienna. Archduchess Therese reported that the departure of the imperial couple from Laxenburg "was very moving. A huge crowd came to the railroad station. There was a profound silence, broken only by the women's sobs. As the train slowly began to move, the people felt as if a funeral procession were riding past."[28] And in truth, as early as two days after Sisi's departure, rumors ran through Vienna to the effect that the Empress had died.[29]

Franz Joseph traveled with his wife as far as Miramar near Trieste. His brother Max went to Corfu with her, along with an entourage of thirty-three. Even on the sea journey the invalid's appetite improved.

The atmosphere between the Emperor and Empress continued tense. At the end of July, Franz Joseph sent Count Grünne to Corfu, apparently with instructions to initiate a reconciliation. The attempt failed utterly. But not only that: Elisabeth's friendship with Grünne was shattered. Whether the gossip was correct that the Empress accused the Count of acting as go-between in the Emperor's love affairs is moot. The rumors can be neither disproved nor supported by the documentary sources.

Subsequently, the Empress repeatedly spoke about her quarrel with Grünne. Thus, as late as 1872, she told Marie Festetics, "The man did so many things to me that I believe even on my deathbed I won't be able to forgive him."[30]

There are some indications that Grünne unfairly implied that the young Empress had been untrue to the Emperor. But in his fatherly way, he did not reproach her on this account, instead giving her more good advice, which infuriated the Empress all the more. Later she told her lady-in-waiting Marie Festetics about Count Grünne: "With the greatest bonhomie, he said incredible things; for example, speaking as a fatherly friend: 'Your Majesty must remember one thing, you can do as you like, but you must never write so much as a word. Anything is better than the written word.'" Elisabeth's comment, ten years after the fact: "At the time, I hardly understood, but instinct told me that such advice cannot spring from a pure heart."[31]

The upsets caused by Grünne's visit aggravated Sisi's condition. She refused to eat and fell into a deep depression. "She seems to consider herself lost, incurable," Ludovika wrote to Saxony.[32]

And after Grünne left, Elisabeth wrote to her former friend and closest intimate, "although the outcome of your journey has not brought any change in the situation, either for the Emperor or for myself, it seems that you need not fear a repetition of your long travels and your stay, which offered little relaxation." It did not seem, she continued "that we will be seeing each other again soon, or ever."[33]

As always in times of crisis, Sisi longed for her mother and her brothers and sisters. Helene Taxis decided to make the journey to Corfu. Ludovika: "Helene is making a great sacrifice, which is very hard for her, but she says the Emperor has so ardently begged her, she felt indescribably sorry for him—the poor, dear Emperor; he is said to be so unhappy and sad."[34]

By this time, Helene Taxis was the mother of two little children, whom she was reluctant to leave for such a long time. Furthermore, the political situation in the Mediterranean was anything but reassuring. Corfu and its neighboring islands, members of the "Ionian Republic," were a British protectorate with a strong anti-Greek government. (Only in 1864, two years after the expulsion of the Wittelsbach King of Greece, Otto, did England cede the Ionian Islands to Greece.) There were riots, and in

September 1861, during Sisi's stay on Corfu, there was even an attempt to assassinate Queen Amalie of Greece.

Helene's reluctance to undertake the trip was understandable. But Ludovika knew how urgently Sisi needed help from Bavaria. "Helene may be the only one who can manage it [that is, to bring a favorable influence to bear]; she was always Sisi's favorite sister."[35] In fact, the news from Corfu improved after Helene's arrival. Sisi "eats a lot of meat," wrote Ludovika, "drinks a lot of beer, is invariably cheerful, coughs little, especially since the weather, as Helene finds, has turned so very hot again, and they make very beautiful outings by water and by land."[36] At first, however, Helene had been "frightened" by Sisi's "puffiness and pallor."[37]

The news of the Empress's sudden cheerfulness was an occasion for grudging comment in Vienna: "The idea that she is ill with her nerves rather than with her chest is current again."[38] In this situation, Ludovika once more felt obliged to make her excuses to Sophie. "Of course Sisi's lot is quite a painful topic for me to mention, all the more painful because she brought it on herself by so much carelessness, yes one must almost say: presumption, since she refused to listen to any of us!"[39]

Emperor Franz Joseph, kept busy by new assassination attempts and riots in Hungary, reacted with surliness to the conflicting news and complained to his mother about "the time the correspondence with Corfu consumes."[40] In October, he traveled to Corfu to see for himself how matters stood. He reported to his mother that Sisi "has grown stronger, is, it is true, still a little puffy in the face, but mostly has a good color; she coughs very little and without any chest pains, and her nerves are much calmer." Franz Joseph and Elisabeth went for walks, but primarily he toured the fortifications, barracks, and warships; wearing "civilian clothes" and attending incognito, he observed the exercises of the English troops, "which interested me very much and, because of their stiffness, also amused me."[41]

Since Sisi's longing for her children was great but she did not dare to spend the winter in Vienna, the Emperor allowed the children to be brought to Venice, so that they could spend several months with their mother. Sophie was beside herself. "One more sacrifice for our poor martyr, their excellent father!"[42]

Sophie cited every possible reason why the children must not leave Vienna for such a long period. Most particularly, she put forward the claim that the water in Venice was bad. Thereupon, Franz Joseph ordered that fresh spring water be shipped daily from Schönbrunn to Venice. Sophie did, however, get her way in that her confidante, Countess Sophie Esterházy, accompanied the children to Venice. The Countess kept the Archduchess regularly informed, not only about the children, but especially about her daughter-in-law.

Given the circumstances, it might have been predicted that renewed discord would break out. This time the conflict was between the Empress and Countess Esterházy. Elisabeth now managed to dismiss her chatelaine, who had always placed Sophie's interest before the Empress's. For eight years Elisabeth had had to endure the presence of this woman, who was charged with the task of training Sisi. Now, at last, Elisabeth carried off a victory. Not only Sophie but also Ludovika were at a fever pitch of excitement. "It is truly very regrettable that Sisi has taken this step and altogether is so uncompromising," Ludovika wrote apologetically to Sophie in Vienna, "without any consideration, without keeping in mind that it can be harmful to her and will make a very bad impression."[43]

A very bad impression was also made on the court by Sisi's insistence on installing her lady-in-waiting Paula Bellegarde, Countess Königsegg, as the new chatelaine. The Prussian ambassador reported to Berlin that "local society" was "very embarrassed" because Countess Königsegg, "according to her rank," was "not legitimately entitled to the office."[44] Unlike Countess Esterházy, née Princess of Liechtenstein, the new chatelaine did not belong to the high nobility but was merely a countess (by birth as well as marriage). As the head of the Empress's household, she took "precedence over all the ladies of the land"—that is, even over the ladies of the high nobility. This appointment was Sisi's first, still relatively cautious, provocation of the Viennese court in questions of rank.

The political mood in Venice continued to be hostile in Austria. A German diplomat reported that "since the Empress has arrived, the populace avoids St. Mark's Square."[45]

Ludovika was anxious to see for herself what was actually wrong with her daughter. In spite of severe attacks of migraine, she responded to Sisi's urgent plea by traveling to Venice with her son Karl Theodor. She found Sisi "looking better," but without any confidence in the doctors. "These are peculiarities which I fail to understand but which worry me." The old privy councillor Dr. Fischer had also come from Munich to examine the Empress. "He says that for the moment, the lung affliction has receded into the background, but there was greensickness to such a degree that it was a total anemia, owing to which, tendencies to dropsy are appearing again."[46] At times, Sisi's feet were so swollen that she could not step on them; walking required a special effort and could be accomplished only with the support of two people. (We can only conjecture that even at this time the symptoms pointed to acute edema from undernourishment.)

But the worst was her low emotional state. Ludovika: "She is infinitely kind and loving to me, but often I find her sad . . . depressed." Ludovika was "weighed down by the thought of all that the Emperor is having to do without and how dreadfully his happiness is destroyed." Sisi's fear of wasting away with dropsy over a period of years "wrings tears from her eyes," Ludovika wrote, "and countless times she asks Gackel and me whether we found her very changed, whether she looked like someone with the dropsy! Often we do not know what to say? . . . But now and then she is quite cheerful again; my ladies find her immensely charming and in the evenings usually quite lively." Ludovika did everything to brighten her daughter's spirits, "but an old person like myself is, to be sure, not quite suited to it."

The conclusion that the physicians had probably been treating her incorrectly was now voiced. "Much has been done for her health, but unfortunately never the right thing, although it has cost such enormous sacrifices. Fischer was the only one who diagnosed her correctly always— and he was opposed to the long voyages and the hot climates!"[47]

The Emperor also twice visited his wife in Venice. He used his stays, however, mainly for troop inspections and parades, occasionally taking three-year-old Rudolf along.

When she had no visitors, Sisi struggled with her major problem: boredom. Her favorite occupation during later years, hiking, was impossible because of her chronically swollen feet. She was chained, therefore, to the house most of the time; she spent the long days playing cards, reading a little, and collecting photographs.

First she procured pictures of family members, including her favorites among the servants in her parents' home and the nursemaids who looked after the children during her absences from Vienna. She extended the collection more and more, including diplomats, court officials, aristocrats, and finally her favorite actors, as well as (true daughter of Duke Max of Bavaria) jugglers and clowns. She devoted special zeal to collecting the photographs of famous beauties, asking Austrian diplomats to send her pictures of beautiful women from Paris, London, Berlin, St. Petersburg, and Constantinople.[48]

In May 1862, after a stay of almost a year in Corfu and Venice, the Empress, still gravely ill, arrived in Reichenau an der Rax and from there, on Dr. Fischer's orders, traveled on to Bad Kissingen to take the cure— without stopping in Vienna. This time the diagnosis was dropsy. Once again, the physician in charge of the case was Dr. Fischer, who had an intimate acquaintance with the Duke of Bavaria's family, along with its many eccentricities.

Sisi's condition improved quickly under Dr. Fischer's rigorous, probably also psychologically adroit treatment. As early as July, *Die Presse* reassured "the minds of those who imagined the exalted invalid to be in the final stages of pulmonary tuberculosis," though the newspaper did mention a new diagnosis, this time a "disease of the blood-forming organs (lymph nodes and spleen)."[49]

A week later, a reporter on the same paper wrote, "I saw the Empress, who a few weeks ago had almost to be carried, repeatedly promenading for hours at the Curplatz without resting, without coughing even once, although she was engaged in conversation most of the time."[50] At the festive illumination and the fireworks which Kissingen organized on the occasion of her recovery, the Empress, in good spirits, appeared on the arm of her father, Duke Max. Max, as well as Sisi's favorite brother, Karl Theodor, had taken the Kissengen cure with her. One can only speculate about the extent of her father's concern with Sisi's health.

Yet even now Sisi did not trust herself to return to Vienna. Once again she fled to Possenhofen. Among her brothers and sisters, in the familiar, noisy, bohemian atmosphere of the manor, she summoned up her strength before the unavoidable return to the Viennese court and married life.

The court ladies who traveled with her outdid each other in relating horror stories about the "beggars' household" and loose practices of Elisabeth's parents' home. To them, Possenhofen was a place "that has caused us many a vexation." The pedigrees of the Bavarian court ladies, they pointed out, were far from impeccable. Therese Fürstenberg, one of Archduchess Sophie's ladies-in-waiting, for example, wrote to Austria, "My colleagues, five in number, with one exception owe their existence to cooks, tradesmen's daughters, and the like; they are pretty good souls on the whole, but a few nevertheless reveal their maternal heritage." The noise, she reported, was earsplitting, the table manners were impossible; "and the Duchess [that is, Elisabeth's mother], who lives for her dogs, always has some on her lap next to her or under her arm and cracks fleas on the dinner plates! But the plates are replaced at once!"[51]

Greater contrasts than those between Vienna and Possenhofen can hardly be imagined. The same lady-in-waiting described imperial family life in Vienna. "You have no idea, by the way, how boring and uncomfortable such an exalted family circle is, and yet one is inclined to believe that being among themselves would do them good; but there they sit, according to rank and speak according to rank or rather do not speak; bore each other and are glad when the family party is over. Really, it often makes you sorry to see what a sad life they lead and how they have no idea how to make it more pleasant for themselves; each one lives in isolation, alone, cultivates his boredom or pursues his 'private pleasures.' "[52]

That a young woman such as Elisabeth would try to escape this monotonous life, preferring the Possenhofen idyll, was met with a total lack of understanding at the Viennese court. After all, Elisabeth was an empress-queen, for whom such supersensitivity was not fitting.

In Possenhofen she met her "Italian" sisters, ex-Queen Marie of Naples and Countess Mathilde Trani ("Spatz"). They too had fled to "Possi," leaving their husbands behind in Rome.

That there were difficulties in Marie's marriage all the family knew. Queen Marie of Saxony, for example, wrote that the King of Naples was "very undeveloped when it comes to marital love, with all the affection and admiration he expresses to others about Marie, he is nevertheless said never to have let her near his heart, though, as she used to say, she made every effort." She hinted that the young husband suffered from phimosis (tightness or constriction of the orifice of the prepuce), making intercourse impossible.[53]

Mathilde's husband (a younger brother of the ex-King of Naples), on the other hand, was very merry and not inclined to take his marriage vows very seriously. Ludovika on her two daughters, Marie and Mathilde: "I would have wished them husbands who had more character and knew how to give them guidance, of which both are still in great need; but good as the two brothers are, they are no support to their wives."[54]

In Rome, the two sisters were constantly together, and they shared secrets. With Mathilde's help, ex-Queen Marie began a love affair with a Belgian count, an officer in the Papal Guard. Mathilde was said to console herself with a Spanish grandee. After a few happy months, retribution set in: Marie became pregnant. In dire straits, she fled to Possenhofen under the pretext of illness. Dr. Fischer took her under his wing. Poor Ludovika was in a flurry of excitement. Duke Max, however, kept his composure: "Well, all right, such things happen," he said. "What's the point of cackling?"[55]

In the midst of this situation and adding to it, Sisi came to Possenhofen. What the three sisters talked about during these weeks, in what ways they influenced each other, we do not know. Whatever the case, it is certain that their relationships had changed. Now it was the oldest, Elisabeth, at twenty-four, who was instructed by both her younger sisters. Sisi could not keep pace with Marie's and Mathilde's adventures. But with horror she also became aware of Marie's poor emotional state and her utter unhappiness following the separation from the man she loved.

Marie's regrettable frame of mind (the true cause of which no one except the closest family members knew) was described at length in the newspapers. She was observed in the pilgrimage church of Altötting, spending hours in silent prayers. It was told that, in Sisi's presence, she had said, "Oh, if only a bullet had struck me at Gaeta!"[56]

During their conversations, the sisters forgot the world around them. Sisi's ladies-in-waiting, even her new chatelaine, Countess Königsegg, were deeply offended at being so constantly ignored—"because Her Majesty grows more and more estranged from her Austrian surroundings," as Crenneville wrote in his diary.[57]

Though ex-Queen Marie had sent her Neapolitan retinue back to Naples, Elisabeth had brought a considerable body of servants to Possenhofen: hairdressers, footmen, and lesser servants, for whom there was no room in the small castle. The nearby inns had their hands full taking care of the Austrian overflow.

The unrest in his house, combined with the unremitting secret-mongering and whispering of his three older daughters, as well as the complaints of his wife, finally became too much for the hotheaded Duke Max. One of the rages for which he was famous in the family broke out; it ended with the three married daughters having to leave Possenhofen. Queen Marie of Saxony reported that her brother-in-law "suddenly was of the opinion that his daughters were a burden in his house: that is why the reunion of the children in Possi, which was such a consolation to my poor Louise (that quietly suffering bearer of her cross!) came to a quick end."[58]

In November 1862, in the Convent of St. Ursula in Augsburg, Marie gave birth in total secrecy, but she had to give the child, a girl, to its biological father. Her secret remained safe. Five months later, Marie returned to her husband in Rome. After the ex-King underwent an operation, and after Marie confessed, the marriage turned out to be fairly harmonious after all.

Duke Max's putting his foot down made it impossible for Elisabeth to remain in Possenhofen any longer. She had to return to her husband. But there were further difficulties. The Emperor and his mother were spending the summer in Bad Ischl; but Sisi refused adamantly to go anywhere near her mother-in-law. The imperial adjutant general, Count Crenneville, moaned in his diary, "Oh, women, women!!!! with or without a crown, dressed in silk or percale, have caprices and few are exempt."[59]

A few days before the Emperor's birthday on August 18, 1862, the Empress returned to Vienna on very short notice. Franz Joseph wrote his mother in Bad Ischl "how happy I am to have Sisi with me again and thus finally, after doing without for so long, to possess an 'at home.' The reception by the populace of Vienna was truly very warm and agreeable. It has been a long time since there have been such good spirits here."[60]

Even on this happy occasion, however, the newspapers did not muffle their demands to the Imperial House. "The land is glad of the recovery of its Princess," wrote the *Morgen-Post,* for example, "may the Princess also soon find cause to be pleased in the same measure at the full recovery of the country from all the wounds with which it is still afflicted, from all the evils from which it still suffers. May she live happily by the side of her imperial consort among a happy people!"[61]

The imperial couple was minutely observed. During the past two years, there had been so much gossip about Elisabeth that her every gesture was grounds for discussion. One lady-in-waiting wrote, "*His* expression as he lifted her out of the carriage I will never forget. I find her blooming but not natural looking, her expression forced and nervous *au possible,* her color so high that I find her heated, hectic, and not quite swollen anymore but very fat and changed in the face."[62]

In a letter to her father, Archduchess Therese described how Sisi received her relatives in Schönbrunn. "She was friendly but nevertheless stiff; during the trip the poor thing vomited 4 times and with it a severe migraine. She told Aunt Elisabeth that her eyes were so swollen, that she cried so terribly when she had to leave her dear Possi; she arose at 4 in the morning to walk around the garden before her departure." Therese also mentioned that one of the houses festively decorated to welcome the Empress sported the ambiguous banner, "Good, strong constitution, long life!"[63]

The fact that Sisi arrived in Vienna, not alone, but accompanied by her brothers, was also an occasion for biting comments. "The fact that Prince Karl Theodor came along is proof of how much she dreads being alone with *him* and with us." Every glance and every gesture made by the Empress and the Emperor were observed. "At least in front of us, she is very friendly with him, talkative and natural, *alla camera* there may be many differences of opinion, that becomes apparent sometimes."[64]

It was by no means true that after Sisi's return, the imperial family lived together in cozy domesticity. The children were on vacation in Reichenau; Emperor Franz Joseph had no intention of giving up the hunts, which often took him away for several days; Sisi traveled back and forth between Vienna, Reichenau, and Passau, where she met her mother and her sisters. Archduchess Sophie continued to stay in Bad Ischl, and Emperor Franz Joseph visited her there for more than two weeks, while Sisi stayed behind in Vienna and her sister Helene came to visit once more. The ladies-in-waiting were pleased whenever Helene was with the Empress: "She always has a calming effect, is herself so reasonable and decent and tells her the truth."[65]

During the nearly two years of separation from her husband and the society of the Viennese court, the Empress had changed. She had become very self-confident and brisk and had learned to assert her interests vigorously. The Emperor, living in constant fear that at the first sign of discord she might run off again and do further damage to the prestige of the August House, treated her circumspectly, showing infinite patience.

He was considerate of Sisi's sensibilities, personally protesting the constant surveillance by omnipresent police agents. He wrote firmly to his adjutant general

> I beg you to put a stop to the uniformed and supposedly secret surveillance system that surrounds us and that once again flourishes quite extraordinarily. When we go walking in the gardens, we are followed and watched at every step; when the Empress goes into her little garden or goes horseback riding, literally a regiment of guards hides behind the trees, and even when we take a pleasure drive, we find the same familiar faces wherever we end up, so that I have now invented the subterfuge of calling out a false destination to the coachman as we set off, in order to mislead the staff adjutant, and not until we have left the castle grounds do I advise the coachman where he is to go. Really, it's enough to make one laugh.
>
> Aside from the impression that must of necessity be made on the public by these measures, which betray fear and are carried out very crudely and conspicuously—living like prisoners, being constantly watched and spied upon is not to be endured. FJ[66]

Hardly had the Empress regained her health than all hopes turned on a further offspring in the imperial family. Though a crown prince was assured, the Emperor wanted a second son to secure the succession. In this situation, Sisi found support and help in her old family physician, Privy

RIGHT: Bust of Elisabeth as a twelve-year-old girl. BELOW LEFT: Archduke Max, Elisabeth's father. BELOW RIGHT: Archduchess Ludovika, Elisabeth's mother

1

2

3

4

ABOVE: Ludovika with her children Helene,
Ludwig and the newborn Elisabeth. BELOW:
Archduke Max riding in his private circus

The bridal couple

Franz Joseph showing Vienna to his bride

LEFT: Empress Sophie, mother of the Kaiser.
BELOW: Count Gyula Andrássy

8

9

The Imperial Family in 1856. From the left: Sophie with
Gisela, Franz Carl, Sisi, Franz Joseph with Sophie

11

By 1860, after six years of marriage, Elisabeth was both unwell and deeply unhappy, as this sequence of photographs by Angerer of Vienna makes clear.

12

13

14

After a long separation, Elisabeth saw her two children
Gisela and Rudolf again in Venice. Next to Sisi is
Rudolf's governess Karoline von Welden.

Two of the trio of famous Winterhalter portraits of the Empress, 1864. The third appears on the jacket.

16

17

18

ABOVE: Elisabeth's youngest child, Marie Valerie,
with the Empress's favorite niece, Baroness Marie
Wallersee, the future Countess Larisch. RIGHT:
Crown Prince Rudolf in the 1870s

19

20

Princesses Gisela and Marie Valerie in 1885

21

2

In the mid 1860s, at the height of her beauty, Sisi enjoyed being photographed—but not with her children or her husband. She would pose alone, or with her dogs.

23

2

One of the very rare photographs of Sisi smiling (Photograph by Albert of Munich)

25

27

26

Franz Joseph and Sisi as King and Queen of Hungary, with Gisela and Rudolf in Hungarian costume. In the background, Gödöllö Castle near Budapest, a gift from the people of Hungary.

Although there is no evidence that Sisi ever permitted herself to be photographed with her husband, she did pose with her beloved brother Duke Karl Theodor.

28

Sisi as Queen of Hungary

Councillor Dr. Fischer. He firmly declared that for the present, there could be no thought of "new expectations"; he advised that "repeated use of Kissingen" (with one stay at the spa a year, this meant a delay of several years at least) had to precede any such plans.[67]

In the meantime, Sisi returned to hiking and horseback riding. One of the ladies-in-waiting commented, "If one lacks inner peace altogether, one thinks that keeping on the move will make life easier, and she is by now only too used to this."[68]

Elisabeth fled into solitude. The ladies-in-waiting made fun of her "eternal promenades in the evenings alone in the little garden." As often as she could, she refused all company, getting her way, for example, in "being allowed to go alone through the gallery into the Oratorium," which was contrary to court protocol.[69] For an empress had to be an empress at all times, with appropriate entourage; she could not scurry alone through the long corridors of the Hofburg like a shy doe, as Sisi liked to do.

Nevertheless, she took part in the most important functions. She appeared at the court ball and at the Corpus Christi procession—and promptly became the center of a crowd.

The guests of the imperial family who met the young Empress during this time on public occasions were uniformly cool in their judgments. Typical is a letter from the Prussian Crown Princess Victoria, to her mother, Queen Victoria. Though she praised Sisi's beauty and amiability, she did not hold back her criticism.

> Very shy and timid, she speaks little. It is really difficult to keep a conversation going, for she seems to know very little and to have only minimal interests. The Empress neither sings nor draws or plays the piano and hardly ever speaks about her children. . . . The Emperor seems smitten with her, but I do not have the impression that she is with him. He seems most insignificant, very unassuming and simple, and he looks—as one would not believe from his paintings and photographs—old and wrinkled, while his reddish moustache and his sidewhiskers are very unbecoming to him. Franz Joseph is very little—or rather, not at all—talkative, all in all extremely "insignificant."[70]

In the fall of 1863, the "Mexican affair" was settled. Archduke Max agreed to assume the crown of Mexico, moved by his ambitious wife, Carlotta, his dissatisfaction with Austria, and his increasingly deteriorating relationship with his brother the Emperor. Archduchess Sophie—like the young Empress, who had always felt close to Max—was outraged at his willingness to undertake the adventure. Neither woman had any faith that it would turn out well. Even in the court party, hardly anyone took a rosy view of the plan, though some might have hoped that Max, who caused considerable discomfort by his liberal stance, might never return to Austria.

In his castle of Miramar near Trieste, Maximilian steeped himself in his fantasy of Mexico. Elisabeth called this residence "Max's most beautiful poem, which shows so clearly what a poetic soul his was, filled with a dream of beauty, though unfortunately also with a longing for power and fame, for everywhere were affixed insignia and allegories of the new position, intended to tell of a powerful empire the Habsburg scion founded across the seas."[71]

In April 1864, the new Emperor of Mexico and his wife set out for an uncertain, eventually tragic, future. Sophie's diary noted with gratitude that Sisi was showing deep compassion for her, the deeply stricken mother. Sophie had long ago abandoned her preference for Carlotta. By this time, she shared Elisabeth's dislike of the ambitious wife of the once so merry Max. Sophie suspected that the parting was a final one, and she wrote as much in her diary. The last dinner with Max seemed to her like a "last meal (before execution)."[72]

In February 1864, Sisi had another opportunity to demonstrate her Samaritan services. At the Nordbahnhof, the wounded from the war in Schleswig-Holstein arrived. Austria was fighting on the side of Prussia against little Denmark. Franz Joseph to Sophie: "The alliance with Prussia is the only correct policy, but they make it hard with their lack of principle and their boorish recklessness."[73] Few in Vienna understood that Schleswig-Holstein was merely another milestone in Bismarck's road to a war between Prussia and Austria.

During the Prussian-Austrian negotiations in Vienna, the Empress once again showed only too openly how much she hated public appearances. At one of the official dinners, which Bismarck attended, she even left the room on the pretext of being indisposed. The fact that she did not participate in the subsequent receptions and dinners fueled the gossip. Crenneville: "Everyone believes that she is expecting, others say she has stomach cramps because she takes cold baths after meals and laces herself too tightly, I do not know what is true in all this and only feel sorry for my good master."[74] Once again, Dr. Fischer was summoned from Munich. But Sisi's illness can hardly have been serious, for Dr. Fischer used his stay in Vienna primarily to shoot stags in the Prater, with the Emperor's permission.

Only many years later did the Empress indicate the true cause of her supposed indisposition: She was annoyed at Bismarck. In 1893, she told Konstantin Christomanos, her Greek reader, "It seems to me that Bismarck was also a follower of Schopenhauer; he could not stand women, with the possible exception of his own wife. Mainly, I believe, he despises queens. When I saw him for the first time, he was exceptionally stiff. What he really wanted was to say: The ladies may keep to their rooms."[75]

The Empress's few official appearances in public aroused enormous notice and steeped the function in question in great solemnity—the inauguration, for example, of the Ringstrasse on May 1, 1865. Seven years had passed since demolition was begun. For seven years, the "capitol and residence" had been one large building site. The old ramparts were torn down and the broad avenue took their place. The munificent new boulevard gave to Vienna an entirely new feeling of spaciousness, breadth, a link with the modern world.

For the reception of the imperial couple, a fairground with tents, platforms, flags, and flowers had been set up outside the Burgtor. The coach carrying the Emperor and Empress drove across Burgring, Schottenring, and Quai and over the Ferdinandsbrücke into the Prater. Hundreds of flower-trimmed coaches followed in a long procession past hundreds of thousands of enthusiastic spectators, who were eager especially to catch a glimpse of the young Empress.

We have no indications that Elisabeth took an interest of any kind in the restructuring of the city of Vienna. The construction of the Ringstrasse brought work and (meager) earnings to many of those who had been unemployed; but it was, of course, entirely a concern of the highest society. The demolition of the old city walls and ramparts did create a great deal of space for new housing. But except for public buildings, only splendid mansions for the richest families were put up. The notorious Viennese housing shortage was not relieved—on the contrary: The slums connected to the old ramparts (which, though they placed the poor in indescribable living conditions, nevertheless put a roof over their heads) were torn down and not replaced. The housing shortage was further aggravated by the influx of many thousands of workers employed in the construction of the Ringstrasse.

In all probability, the Empress was not well informed about social conditions in the capitol and residence (not to mention the provincial cities and the countryside). She was isolated within the court. Her freedom of movement was so restricted by protocol that it would have required great effort to stand outside so as to form a true picture. But after a few failed attempts during the early years of her marriage, Elisabeth became incapable of such efforts. Her energy flagged in proportion as she began to enjoy and exploit the advantages of her position.

The two children, Gisela and Rudolf, had now outgrown the nursery. While Gisela had a robust constitution and was of average abilities, the Crown Prince became a remarkable figure at an early age. He proved to be unusually intelligent and intellectually precocious. Even as a five-year-old, he could make himself understood, as Archduchess Sophie proudly noted, in four languages: German, Hungarian, Czech, and French. The little boy had a lively imagination and an exuberant temperament, but he also had a delicate constitution and was frequently ill. He was delicate and extremely thin, as well as anxious and in great need of love.

Franz Joseph had wished for a bold, physically strong son, who would grow into a good soldier. Little Rudolf absolutely did not fulfill these hopes. His intellectual precocity was a cause for worry rather than joy for his august father.

On the Crown Prince's sixth birthday, the two children, who had grown extremely close, were separated. Following the Habsburg custom, Rudolf was given his own all-male household, with a tutor who also undertook the Prince's military training. The separation from the nursemaid and the shared "Aja," Baroness von Welden, and particularly the separation of the two children from each other were occasions for heart-rending scenes.

Rudolf had quite obviously inherited his mother's sensibility. Since living under the strict, even sadistic control of his new tutor, Count Leopold Gondrecourt, he was almost a permanent invalid, suffering from fevers, angina, stomach colds, and similar ailments. Gondrecourt had strict orders from the Emperor to "work extremely hard" with the delicate, overly sensitive boy to make a good soldier out of him: "His Imperial Highness is physically and mentally more advanced than other children of his age, but rather vivacious and nervously irritable, therefore his intellectual development must be sensibly subdued, so that that of the body can keep pace."[76]

Gondrecourt carried out the Emperor's instructions in his own way: He drilled the anxious, sickly child to the point of exhaustion with military exercises and rigorous physical and psychological "toughening."

At this time (1864), the Empress did not yet have enough influence over her husband to be able to prevent this sort of upbringing. Later, she repeatedly complained about the children "who were no longer allowed to be with me—about whose education I was not allowed to have a say —until, with their [that is, the Crown Prince's household] rough handling and Count Gondrecourt's educational methods, they almost turned him into an idiot;—to try to turn a child of 6 into a hero through hydropathic treatments and fear is madness."[77]

The martyrdom of the little Crown Prince was nothing extraordinary for the time; rather, it was part of the normal training of a cadet. The only thing that made it worse for Rudolf was that in his case this military toughening started at an unusually early age and that—at the express wish of the Emperor—it was carried out with unusual rigor.

Archduchess Sophie's diary gives indications that, after a year of military education, little Rudolf was high-strung and ill, and that the worst—his dying—was feared. But the Archduchess saw no connection with Gondrecourt's methods, as Elisabeth did; like the Emperor, Sophie placed all the blame on Rudolf's "delicate constitution." The idea was that this constitution would be strengthened by further, always harsher toughening, ever more cruel drills.

The little Crown Prince was much too timid, much too afraid of his father to complain of the cruelties he experienced daily. Finally, one of Gondrecourt's subordinates, Joseph Latour, began to take an interest in the unhappy child and went to the Empress with his reservations. He, too, did not dare to speak to the Emperor on the matter, for everyone knew that Gondrecourt was only carrying out the Emperor's orders. At court, it was even said that Rudolf's old "Aja," Baroness von Welden, had gone on her knees to the Emperor and begged for more lenient treatment of the child. To no avail.

In this situation, when nothing less than her child's life was at stake, Elisabeth took action. Later she related, "when I learned the reason for his illness, I had to find a remedy; gathered up all my courage when I saw that it was impossible to prevail against this protégé of my mother-in-law, and told everything to the Emperor, who could not decide to take a position against his mother's will—I reached for the utmost and said that I could no longer stand by—something would have to happen! either Gondrecourt goes, or I go."

This statement is confirmed by a highly significant document, which has been preserved and which casts a revealing light on the Emperor's family life during this period. Elisabeth handed the Emperor the following ultimatum in writing.

I wish to have reserved to me absolute authority in all matters concerning the children, the choice of the people around them, the place of their residence, the complete supervision of their education, in a word, everything is to be left entirely to me to decide, until the moment of their majority. I further wish that, whatever concerns my personal affairs, such as, among others, the choice of the people around me, the place of my residence, all arrangements in the house etc. be reserved to me alone to decide. Elisabeth. Ischl, 27 August 1865.[78]

We must see this document as in the nature of Elisabeth's declaration of independence. It had taken eleven years for her to find the strength to stand her ground rather than, as before, taking flight into illness or trips abroad. Now she became vigorous—and prevailed.

Why at this particular time Elisabeth was in such a position of power may be clarified by a remark in Sophie's diary. In a confidential conversation, Sophie reported, she told her "Franzi" that she wished him a second son; but by expressing this wish she also wanted to draw him out about how matters really stood in his married life. And the Emperor responded amiably. Sophie: "And one word . . . gave me, praised be God for it a thousand times, almost the assurance that finally Sisi had united herself with him anew."[79]

Five years had passed since Sisi's flight to Madeira, years filled with cares, illness, refusals, quarrels. Now at last, a move toward a proper relationship seemed at hand—and it was at this very time that Elisabeth threatened to go away if Rudolf's military upbringing was continued.

The exceedingly sharp tone of her ultimatum reveals the new method the Empress used to deal with her husband. As recently as two years earlier, she had pined away, had sobbed and wept. Now she made demands—and he, who had earlier treated her like a child, now obeyed, at least in most instances. Archduchess Sophie also retreated more and more, since she could no longer be sure of her son, and she wept on the shoulders of relatives.

Now, when her beauty was at its height, Elisabeth had become the stronger one. She could put pressure on her husband—with refusal or with the threat of leaving Vienna again. She did not know the meaning of preserving the reputation of the dynasty or the state—which she represented as well. She saw her problems in purely personal terms, though at the same time she knew the extent to which Franz Joseph was aware of and fulfilled his obligations to the state and the dynasty. She knew very well that he would have to give in to her demands when the reputation of the August House was at stake. It was the sheerest blackmail, and Franz Joseph capitulated, because he loved his ever more beautiful and more mature wife—in spite of everything.

The court officials, especially the ladies-in-waiting who had some insight into the couple's domestic life, had much material for gossip. They bemoaned the Emperor's weakness when confronted by his wife. However, Franz Joseph exhibited the same weakness in other instances. Countess Marie Festetics was "often astonished that the Emperor gave in to some urgent strong wish on the part of someone or other among his entourage, although the form in which the wish had been expressed seemed to him indecorous." The Empress herself explained to the Countess the reason for this behavior. "The Emperor was well brought up and in his youth had a loving entourage. If someone submits a request in a respectful manner and he cannot grant it, he will know how to say no in his gracious way. But if someone approaches him roughly and demandingly, he is so surprised by this unusual manner that he lets himself be intimidated, as it were, and agrees."[80]

Now Elisabeth exploited this weakness of the Emperor without scruple. To the extent that her demands related to Rudolf's upbringing, they had a beneficial effect. To begin with, Elisabeth saw to it that the Crown Prince was given a thorough medical examination by the new imperial physician, Dr. Hermann Widerhofer. She next decided on the new tutor: Colonel Latour, who had been such an effective supplicant in the cause of little Rudolf and who had, as the future was to show, genuinely taken the boy to his heart. Under his new tutor, Rudolf flourished, regaining his health rapidly. Emotional disturbances, especially nocturnal anxiety attacks, however, stayed with him for years, indeed for the rest of his life.

Elisabeth had full confidence in Latour. She had known him for a long time; he had been among the courtiers on Madeira. Elisabeth knew that, compared to the rest of the court, he held extremely liberal views. For this reason, he was mistrusted, even hated, at court and was forced to guard against massive intrigues. He was not, after all, an aristocrat like Gondrecourt, and he was a newcomer to the military field as well. He was interested, not in drill, but in education, even for soldiers. Rudolf's military drill was reduced to the most basic exercises and to riding and shooting. Intellectual training was given precedence over the physical— exactly the reverse of what the Emperor had ordered a year earlier.

Now the Empress was the only one who determined the guidelines of the new education. It was to be "liberal," as the new teachers were expressly told.

Elisabeth also left to Latour the choice of teachers. The only criteria for selection were the educational and scholarly qualifications of the applicants. Thus, Rudolf's teachers did not have to be military men, members of the clergy, or aristocrats, as had been the custom in court educations. When it came to competence pure and simple (a revolutionary demand), the bourgeois teachers and scholars had an advantage.

This revolution actually did take place. Aside from the religion tutor, Rudolf's teachers were all bourgeois intellectuals. Since, like the majority of this class, their politics were unequivocally in the liberal camp, they were also pronouncedly antiaristocratic and anticlerical.

These teachers formed a foreign body at the Viennese court and were disliked accordingly. Gondrecourt intrigued behind the scenes against his successor, for example with Adjutant General Crenneville. He accused Latour of being capable only of "nursemaiding" his pupil but not of educating him. Furthermore, in Gondrecourt's opinion, Latour had "neither the desired sense of chivalry nor the uprightness and necessary distinguished deportment . . . to exert a beneficial influence on the mind and character of the Crown Prince in daily intercourse."[81] He requested Crenneville to intervene with the Emperor.

Time and again, Gondrecourt stressed the (indisputable) fact that his educational methods had been nothing but an expression of the Emperor's wishes. "I have the reassuring belief at all times of having done only what His Majesty ordered me to do and do not know how to reproach myself with anything in regard to my system with the Crown Prince. Furthermore, I was happy to see His Majesty approve my views on the education of the Crown Prince at any time."[82]

But the years of intrigues against Latour were without success. Elisabeth was steadfast in her protection of the pronouncedly anticourt upbringing of her son. With these teachers, Rudolf—according to the Empress's expressed will—became a first-rate and well-rounded, cultured young man, who not only understood, but also approved the democratic ideals of 1848. It was not long before he saw the "basis of the modern state," not in the aristocracy, but in the middle class. Through his bourgeois teachers, whom he admired and loved, Rudolf became an ardent liberal—and only too soon found himself in a bitter conflict with the court system over which his father presided. All the Empress's enemies, however (and by now she had a considerable number), unable to prevail against Elisabeth, now agitated against Rudolf, her son who was so like her but much weaker.

The power struggle over the Crown Prince's education did not run its course without serious discord. Once again the Empress left the Hofburg in Vienna, this time a scant two weeks before Christmas. Once again an illness was used as a pretext for the public: She was suffering from swollen glands; she was cutting a wisdom tooth. Sisi's precipitate departure to Munich (officially, to be treated by Dr. Fischer) did not make a good impression in Vienna.

Archduchess Sophie learned of her daughter-in-law's departure only through a note that arrived when Elisabeth was already on the train. The hotel reservation in Munich was also not placed until after the trip had been begun. Clearly, Sisi did not trust herself simply to stay at her father's Munich palace—mindful of the disagreements during her last visit in Bavaria.

Once again husband and children were forced to spend Christmas without the Empress; she did not return to Vienna until December 30. The Prussian envoy reported somewhat maliciously to Berlin, "In these sudden travel plans during the current time of year, we might search for some caprice in the exalted beautiful lady, which is nothing unusual in the princesses from the ducal Bavarian line (Queen of Naples, Countess Trani)."[83]

With all the understanding for the difficult situation at court, many nevertheless now doubted Elisabeth's good will. Even Sisi's favorite daughter, Marie Valerie, would later reproach her mother cautiously but firmly on this score. "How often I ask myself whether the relationship between my parents might not, after all, have turned out differently if in her youth Mama had had a serious, courageous will for it.—I mean, a woman can accomplish anything.—And yet she may be right that, given the circumstances, it was impossible to become more intimately one."[84]

Crown Prince Rudolf, however, was grateful to his mother all his life for the fact that, in this situation, so crucial to his life, she had so rigorously and successfully taken his part.

CHAPTER FIVE

THE CULT OF BEAUTY

E lisabeth derived her growing self-confidence from the circumstance of her increasingly more striking and more unusual beauty. It turned her into a worldwide celebrity in the 1860s. The legendary beauty of Empress Elisabeth grew very slowly. She had been a sturdy, boyish little girl with a round peasant face. At that time, her sister Helene was considered the great beauty in the family.

When little Sisi reached marriageable age—somewhere between fourteen and fifteen—she caused her mother great worry. In Bad Ischl, when the young Emperor asked for her hand rather than for Helene's, no one was more surprised than Sisi herself and her Bavarian family. She was pleasant, lively, and limber, but still barely matured and a little melancholy. It may have been this last—such a contrast to the merry Viennese countesses to whose company the young Emperor was accustomed—that gave her a unique charm.

Comments on the young Empress's beauty from the early years of the marriage are still rather reserved. We should not forget that Sisi was, after all, ailing (whatever the disease may have been) from the moment she came to Vienna. She went on starvation diets, she was often exhausted, severely anemic, and extremely unsure of herself in the court surroundings. All these circumstances would not enhance her appearance.

Thus, her increasing charms went unrecognized for a long time. Her figure became more rounded, especially as a result of three children born in the first four years of marriage. A great deal of physical activity and constant diets, however, kept her extremely slender and graceful. During this time, she also grew taller, until, at the considerable height of 172 centimeters (5 feet, 7.5 inches), she topped her husband by several centimeters. (Portraits of the couple do not show this difference, for painters always made adjustments rendering the Emperor taller than his wife.) All her life, Elisabeth's weight remained fairly constant at roughly 50 kilos (110 pounds)—she was thus considerably underweight. Even her waist measurement changed hardly at all in her lifetime; it was an astonishing and almost incredible 50 centimeters (19.5 inches). Elisabeth emphasized her famous tiny waist by lacing so tightly that she frequently suffered from shortness of breath, as her mother-in-law complained repeatedly. The reported hip measurement, however (62 to 65 centimeters; 24 to 25 inches) is open to doubt.[1] Apparently at the time the measurement was taken higher up on the body.

It was the common people who first recognized the young Empress's beauty. When she went riding in the Prater, crowds gathered to see her. Archduchess Sophie's diary noted with some astonishment after one such turbulent visit to the Prater, "It is the Empress who attracts them all. For she is their joy, their idol."[2] As soon as Sisi showed herself in the city, crowds gathered. Curious onlookers blocked the streets before her carriage. On one occasion, when she wanted to walk to St. Stephen's Cathedral, so many people thronged around her that she became afraid and could think of no other way out than to flee, weeping, into the vestry. Sophie: "It was almost a scandal."[3]

Foreign diplomats were also quick to remark on the Empress's extraordinary looks. As early as two years after the wedding, for example, Minister of Police Kempen confided to his diary "that the beauty of Empress Elisabeth draws many people to the court who would otherwise stay away."[4]

Sisi had a more difficult time with court society. The many elegant countesses were hardly prepared to accept the former Bavarian country girl as a beauty; the aristocratic ladies continued to find fault with this or that detail of Sisi's outward appearance. With a positively insulting eagerness, in 1857, they elected Archduke Max's bride, Carlotta, as the "beauty" of the court—putting the final touch on the already strained relationship between the sisters-in-law. To assert herself in this group of people who bore her no good will was extremely difficult for the young Empress.

The crisis in her marriage and her flights from Vienna to Madeira and Corfu marked a turning point. In her solitude far from the Viennese court, Sisi's self-confidence began to blossom. Here the shy, insecure girl from Bavaria turned into a mature young woman exceedingly conscious of her beauty. This new self-assurance intensified with time into a sense of being one of the elect, based on the recognition of her extraordinary physical looks.

In Madeira, Sisi also had an ardent admirer in Count Hunyady, whom she could use to test the power of her radiance and whom she treated as she did all his successors. She was the unapproachable, cold beauty who allowed herself to be worshiped to the point of the man's surrender, but who never permitted even the smallest liberty. With all the loveliness of her appearance, she became increasingly and emphatically dignified, even majestic—to men.

To women, on the other hand, Sisi could be very cordial, affectionate, even sisterly. But here, too, she applied one overriding criterion: She liked only beautiful women. In the early 1860s (again, beginning with her stay on Madeira) she had an intimate friendship with her lady-in-waiting who was of the same age, the beautiful Countess Lily Hunyady, Imre's sister. She made no secret of this attachment, in that she preferred Lily's company to any other, neglecting the other ladies (which gave rise to endless petty jealousies in the small royal household cut off from the rest of the world). When he visited on Corfu, Adjutant General Count Crenneville even noticed a "magnetic rapport" between the Empress and Lily Hunyady, but immediately added that this tie, "cleverly employed, could be useful"[5]— which presumably meant that he believed the Empress could be influenced through her lady-in-waiting. Unfortunately, there are not enough sources to allow us to do justice to this intimate friendship, which lasted for years.

During this time, Sisi repeatedly showed her attachments to beautiful young women, including complete strangers she happened to meet. In 1867, for example, she wrote to her son, then nine years old, from Switzerland, "We have made the acquaintance of a twelve-year-old very pretty Belgian girl, who has splendid long hair. We talk with her often, and once I even kissed her! So you can imagine how sweet she must be."[6]

The Empress took special pleasure in appearing at the side of another, hardly less beautiful woman—Lily Hunyady as well as her younger sister, ex-Queen Marie of Naples. These relationships involved a deep attachment, demonstrated publicly; thus, in 1868 in Budapest, the two beautiful sisters, Elisabeth and Marie, appeared side by side dressed exactly alike— dark silk dresses, plaid "bedouins" (a coatlike wrap, extremely fashionable at the time), and small pearl-gray silk hats—and reveled in their obvious success.[7]

Ex-Queen Marie of Naples was also the star in the album of beauties Sisi compiled for herself in Venice in 1862. Of the more than one hundred photographed beauties in the album, there were more portraits of the "heroine of Gaeta," as she was known all over the world, than of anyone else. Without a trace of envy, Elisabeth was the foremost admirer of the delicate, still very melancholy beauty of her younger sister.

At the time, there were several famous galleries of beauties, although all the others were made up of paintings. The best-known collection was the gallery of beauties that Sisi's uncle King Ludwig I of Bavaria assembled in Nymphenburg. The chief attraction of this gallery is (to this day) the portrait of the royal mistress Lola Montez, for whose sake Ludwig I abdicated in 1848. Besides Lola, however, several other favorite beauties of the art-connoisseur King are represented—primarily from the middle classes. Ludwig included only a few of the Wittelsbach family—of the nine sisters, however, none other than Sisi's mother-in-law, Archduchess Sophie, who had been a beautiful woman in her youth, and one of the most implacable opponents of Lola Montez. The notorious Montez also found a place in Sisi's photo collection—to be sure, heavily aged—and thus established a direct link to the Nymphenburg collection.

Like her Uncle Ludwig, Sisi had no high opinion of impeccable aristocratic pedigrees when it came to beauty. Like Ludwig, she accepted women of all classes into her album, even total strangers. For example, she sent a request to her brother-in-law, Archduke Ludwig Viktor, "I happen to be assembling an album of beauties and am now collecting photographs for it, only of women. Please send me whatever pretty faces you run across at Angerer's and other photographers."[8]

Austrian diplomats were also instructed to send to the foreign minister photographs of beautiful women for the Empress. This request aroused immediate skepticism and astonishment; no one was ready to believe that it really was the Empress who wanted the pictures. And many a respectable ministry official came under suspicion of wanting them for himself.

From London, Berlin, and St. Petersburg, the ambassadors sent portraits of beautiful women from the very best society: photographs taken in the foremost studios, artfully arranged, with mirrors, draperies, or scenery framing a lady, dressed in the latest fashion and striking a pose.

The task set the envoy in Constantinople was much harder to fulfill than that of his colleagues. His instructions from Vienna read, "H. M. the Empress desires to receive for her private collection photographic portraits of beautiful women from the preeminent capitals of Europe. Her Supreme Majesty would place special value on possessing, along with such portraits of Oriental beauties, photographs of beautiful women from the world of the Turkish harems. I shall not fail to inform you of this her desire, insofar as local conditions allow, to fulfill it by prompt posting of such portraits executed in the usual form of calling cards."[9]

The ambassador's reply to the foreign minister expressed considerable perplexity concerning the desired ladies of the harem. "The matter is more difficult than it may seem, namely in regard to Turkish women, who, with very few exceptions, do not allow themselves to be photographed and can least be persuaded to do so by their husbands."[10] But finally several likenesses traveled from Constantinoppe to Vienna, of exceedingly strange ladies of questionable beauty (by Viennese standards), whose antecedents (whether from the harem or not) were simply left open.

The pictures that arrived from Paris were quite unexpectedly ordinary. They did not depict ladies from the circles of the famously beautiful Empress Eugénie, nor did they show off the latest Parisian fashions. Instead, many dozens of wallet-sized photographs arrived displaying the likenesses of acrobats, actresses, dancers, circus equestriennes in extremely scanty clothes and remarkably unrestrained, even scandalous poses. The Empress's instructions had not been entirely clear, and the definition of *beauty* was flexible. One can hardly accuse this Parisian consignment of malicious intentions—although a certain mockery could not be ignored by initiates: Still another way had been found to allude to Sisi's inadequately noble origins and the circus predilections of her Bavarian family.

Quite independent of the fashion of the season, the legend of Empress Elisabeth's extraordinary beauty grew. It originated among the public, the observers outside the court, the foreign diplomats. Each of Sisi's rare public appearances during the 1860s turned into a sensation, cause for endless talk. No matter how much the Viennese aristocracy objected that Sisi's dresses were not always at the zenith of whatever the fashion trend was, it became impossible to deny or dispute her unusual beauty. By the mid-1860s, there was not a single lady in Viennese society who could consider herself a match for Elisabeth.

Sisi's success was overwhelming. In 1864, for example, she went to Dresden for her brother Karl Theodor's wedding. After the court ball, Archduke Ludwig Viktor reported to Vienna that Sisi was "stunningly beautiful, also the people here acted insane. I have never seen anyone having such an effect before." Sisi wore a white dress embroidered with stars, her famous large diamond stars in her hair, on her breast a corsage of camellias. Her sister "Helene, a very pale copy of the Empress, in a star dress also," wrote Ludwig Viktor. At the wedding, the main attraction was not the bride, but Elisabeth. This time she appeared in a lilac dress embroidered with silver clover leaves, with a cape of silver lace, a diamond tiara on her intricately dressed hair. Ludwig Viktor: "the people here are so flabbergasted at our lady sovereign!!! they're right."[11]

Queen Marie of Saxony wrote to a friend, "You can have no idea of the enthusiasm aroused here by the Empress's beauty and graciousness; never before have I seen my Saxons *so* excited! They thought, spoke, heard only her praises."[12]

During this time, Franz Winterhalter painted the three famous portraits of the Empress. Countless reproductions, especially of the painting depicting her in a ballgown, with the diamond stars in her hair, spread the news of Sisi's beauty throughout the world. Many, many letters by visitors to Vienna mention Sisi. Hardly any other tale from Vienna was as interesting as learning from an eyewitness whether the Empress was truly as beautiful as it was said.

In 1864, for example, the American envoy to Vienna wrote to his mother at home, "The Empress, as I have often told you before, is a wonder of beauty—tall, beautifully formed, with a profusion of bright brown hair, a low Greek forehead, gentle eyes, very red lips, a sweet smile, a low musical voice, and a manner partly timid, partly gracious."[13]

And a year later, having sat next to Sisi at table during a court dinner, he wrote:

> Well, she was perfectly charming: She is in great beauty this year—more radiant, lambent, exquisite than ever. In the midst of the dinner, while she was prattling away very amiably, she suddenly said, "I am so clumsy," and began to blush in the most adorable manner, like a school-girl. She had upset a glass of

Roman punch on the tablecloth; and the Emperor coming to the rescue, very heroically upset another, so that there was a great mess. Napkins were brought, damages repaired, but the mantling colour on her cheek was certainly not less natural than the spontaneous, half-confused laughter with which she greeted the little incident, amid the solemn hush of all the rest. How I do wish that I was a "sentimental sort of fellow." What pretty and poetic things I would say. How many sonnets I would have composed to those majestic eyebrows.[14]

The reputation of her extraordinary looks became more burdensome the more it grew. For, as many eyewitnesses reveal, Sisi had to stand her ground against the curious and critical glances of the people at every public appearance, not unlike an actress, to whom she was frequently compared. Her clothing, her jewelry, her hair: Everything furnished endless matter for discussion. Every flaw, even the slightest, in her looks or her dress was noted and commented on. Every second, Elisabeth had to live up to her reputation as the greatest beauty of the monarchy. But there is not the least indication that she enjoyed the splash she made, as others in her situation would have done. Quite the contrary: Her innate timidity and unsociability were not relieved by these public appearances; instead, they were reinforced to such a degree that she developed a virtual terror of strangers.

Anxious and tense, she made efforts to conceal such flaws in her beauty as her bad teeth. Archduchess Sophie had noted and criticized this defect even before the engagement in Bad Ischl. Nor could it be corrected by the most expensive dentists throughout her life. Elisabeth's self-consciousness because of this blemish was so great that, from her first day in Vienna, she parted her lips as little as possible whenever she spoke. Her enunciation was therefore extremely indistinct, almost unintelligible, and she spoke so softly that, as many contemporaries complained, she was given more to whispering than to speaking. This habit made conversation in the salon extremely difficult; for hardly anyone could understand the Empress's words.

Her lack of gregariousness at public functions was cause for many a piece of gossip in society. The Prussian Crown Princess Victoria, for example, in 1863 wrote her mother, Queen Victoria, "The Empress of Austria speaks very softly, since she is quite shy. Recently she said to a gentleman who was very hard of hearing: 'Are you married?' The gentleman answered: 'Sometimes.' The Empress said: 'Do you have any children?' and the unfortunate man bellowed: 'From time to time.' "[15]

Finally, Sisi abandoned her pitiful attempts at conversation and contented herself with appearing with her lips resolutely closed. Her silence was judged to express lack of intelligence, bolstering her reputation of being "beautiful but dumb." Sisi, for her part, in her extreme sensibility, felt this criticism acutely and turned even more from the real or imagined hostility of her surroundings into her self-chosen isolation. Even ten years after the fact, the wife of the Belgian envoy wrote about the time she had been presented to the Empress. "She is extremely pretty: wonderful figure and hair which, they say, reaches to her heels. Her conversation is not as brilliant as her shape."[16]

The people believed that they had a right to stare in wonder at this marvel. The awareness of owning, as it were, a "fairy Empress" famous the world over swelled feelings of nationalist pride. The excessively shy Elisabeth withdrew from this possessive thinking. She cultivated her beauty exclusively for herself, to keep up her self-assurance. She was not vain in the sense that she needed, let alone enjoyed, the admiration of the masses. She viewed her body as a work of art too precious to be exhibited to all the world, all the curious lookers and gapers.

Her beauty gave her a sense of being one of the elect, of being different. Her aestheticism, directed at her physical appearance, made her the foremost admirer of her own beauty. Her narcissism was as evident as her shyness. She flatly refused to be "merely a spectacle for the Viennese theater audiences," as Marie Festetics wrote. When the Countess assured the Empress "how happy the people are when they see Your Majesty," Elisabeth, unmoved, replied, "Oh, yes, they're curious—whenever there's something to see, they come running, for the monkey dancing at the hurdy-gurdy just as much as for me. That is their love!"[17]

Sisi was obsessed with her hair, which over the years changed color from dark blond to chestnut brown and grew down to her heels. To manage this mass, to keep it healthy and to arrange it in artful styles, required immense skill on the part of the hairdresser. Sisi's complicated crown of hair, with long braids twisted on top of her head, was repeatedly—and almost always vainly—imitated. Hardly any other woman had such healthy, strong hair, so much time and patience to care for it, and such an artist for a hairdresser as did Elisabeth. The expense was huge. Washing it every three weeks (with always newer precious essences, until eventually cognac and egg became the preferred mixture) took up a whole day, leaving the Empress unavailable for any other concerns. The daily regimen of hair care could not be accomplished in much less than three hours.

The hairdresser became an important person at court; Elisabeth's mood depended in large part on her skills. For nothing could put the Empress out of sorts more easily than strands of hair falling out, having it poorly styled, or dealing with a hairdresser she did not like.

She found her favorite hairdresser, Fanny Angerer, at the Burgtheater. During a comedy she noticed the unusually handsome coiffure of the leading actress, Helene Gabillon. She asked for the name of the artist. It was the very young Fanny, "a girl of striking appearance" and "lively wit." She was the daughter of a hairdresser recently employed at the Hofburgtheater.[18] There were long discussions pro and con concerning her appointment at court. These disputes reached the outside world. Finally, in April 1863, in the "News of the Day" column, the *Morgen-Post* carried the following item.

> The question, pending for a long time, whether a man or a woman hairdresser would assume service with Her Majesty the Empress has finally been settled. Fräulein Angerer relinquishes the Order of Coiffeurs to Court Actresses and the honorarium assigned to it and receives instead a compensation of 2,000 fl. a year to devote herself to the most exalted service as imperial hairdresser, whereby, time permitting, other artistic earnings are not excluded.[19]

The yearly salary of 2,000 guldens was very high, corresponding roughly to that of a university professor. The highest salary paid at the imperial theater to such stars as Joseph Lewinsky and Charlotte Wolter was an annual 3,000 guldens. Archduchess Sophie was incensed at the smug tone of the newspaper item and in her diary grumbled about "impertinent court news."[20]

Henceforth, Fanny Angerer was the most famous hairdresser of the monarchy; her part in Sisi's beauty was not to be underestimated. The ladies of high society virtually sued for Fanny's favor, so that they, too, might, on special occasions, obtain her services. (These engagements brought Fanny the "other artistic earnings" the *Morgen-Post* had mockingly mentioned.)

But Fanny Angerer knew not only how to concoct the most tasteful and artfully braided hairstyles in Vienna, but also how to treat the notoriously difficult Empress with the utmost tact. She also employed tricks; for example, she cunningly secreted the combed-out hairs under her apron on a piece of adhesive tape—and could therefore often show the Empress a clean comb at the end of the day's work. Soon Sisi let no one but Fanny Angerer touch her hair; she even refused to appear at an official function if Fanny was ill and unavailable.

Fanny kept the Empress in a kind of thrall. If she was annoyed for any reason, she pleaded illness and sent a different hairdresser to the Empress, or a chambermaid took over the task. Whenever this happened, the Empress was devastated. Elisabeth to Christomanos: "After several such days of hairdressing, I am quite worn down. She knows that and waits for a capitulation. I am a slave to my hair."[21]

Elisabeth also took a strong personal interest in young Fanny, and when it came to her marriage, Elisabeth took a very active role. The hairdresser fell in love with a middle-class bank official but could not marry him because to do so would have gone against court rules. She would therefore have had to leave, something Sisi wanted to prevent at any cost. Only Elisabeth's personal intervention with her husband the Emperor managed to get the exception granted; Fanny was allowed to marry and still retain her position. Her groom was also given employment at court.

This move made Hugo Feifalik's fortune. He advanced to be the Empress's private secretary and then to the position of her Reisemarschall—travel supervisor, as it were—and of course Fanny was taken along on all of Elisabeth's many trips. Next he served as Regierungsrat—something like a senior executive officer—then he became treasurer of the Sternkreuzorden (Order of the Star Cross) and court councillor. Finally, he had a knighthood conferred on him. The Feifaliks had a strong though subtle influence on the Empress for thirty years. It can be recognized mainly in the jealousy Feifalik aroused among the ladies of the court, especially Countess Festetics.

As the decades passed, the Empress's "supreme" trust made Frau Feifalik not only conceited and arrogant, as Marie Festetics repeatedly complained, but also enormously genteel and stately—in any case, far more stately than the Empress herself. More than once, Elisabeth took advantage of Feifalik's faultless bearing to use her as a double. In this way, she could disappear, unrecognized, among the crowd, while Fanny Feifalik officially accepted the jubilation; of course, this ruse could be practiced only abroad, where Elisabeth was not so easily recognized. Thus, in 1885, Elisabeth had her hairdresser ride around the harbor of Smyrna in the boat of honor, accepting the homage of the worthies of the city, while she herself went ashore by barge and took a sight-seeing tour of the town.[22] As late as 1894, there was another such deception, at the Marseilles railroad station. Many people crowded the platform to watch the departure of the Empress of Austria. Countess Irma Sztaray, a lady-in-waiting, reported

> Under normal circumstances, Her Majesty felt extremely ill at ease, but this time she was entirely delighted, because the people's curiosity was fully satisfied—before she ever appeared. . . . Frau F., the Empress's hairdresser, walked up and down the platform with a most stately bearing, thus playing the Empress to the best of her ability. . . . Her Majesty found this interlude very amusing. "Let's not interrupt my good F.," she said, and quickly and unnoticed, boarded the train.[23]

Elisabeth considered her hair her crowning glory. She was proud of nothing so much as the cascade that enveloped her like a cloak when it was loosened. To the end of her life, Elisabeth made the daily hairdressing a "sacred ritual," as Christomanos floridly put it. (During the 1890s it was his job to engage the Empress in Greek conversation and translation practice during the hours her hair was being dressed.) Christomanos:

> Behind the Empress's armchair stood the hairdresser [Fanny Feifalik] in a black dress with a long train, a white apron of spider webs tied in front; though a servant herself, of an imposing appearance, with traces of faded beauty on her face, and eyes filled with sinister intrigues. . . . With her white hands she burrowed in the waves of hair, raised them and ran her fingertips over them as she might over velvet and silk, twisted them around her arms like rivers she wanted to capture because they did not want to run but to fly.

There follows a long-winded description of the actual hairdressing.

> Then in a silver bowl she brought her mistress's dead hair for inspection, and the looks of the mistress and her servant crossed for a second—containing a slight reproach in that of the mistress, guilt and remorse speaking in that of the servant. Then the white lace robe was lifted from the falling shoulders, and the black Empress, like the statue of a goddess, rose from the sheltering garment. Then the mistress lowered her head—the

servant sank into the ground, softly whispering: "I lay myself at Your Majesty's feet," and so the sacred ritual was completed.

"I am aware of my hair," Elisabeth told Christomanos. "It is like a foreign body on my head."

Christomanos: "Your Majesty wears her hair like a crown instead of the crown."

To which Elisabeth replied, "Except that any other crown is more easily laid aside."[24]

The weight of these masses was so great that sometimes it caused Elisabeth to have a headache. On such mornings, she remained in her apartments for hours, her hair held up high with ribbons. This method decreased the weight on her head, and allowed air to circulate.

The older Elisabeth grew, the more strenuous became her struggle to hold on to her looks. The methods and the time spent on care became ever more lavish. By constant diets, Elisabeth managed to remain willowy and slender; hours of daily exercise kept her supple and graceful. Her skin care was a highly complicated process. Since there was no cosmetic industry such as exists today, the ladies who took pride in their appearance had to depend on beauty products they mixed themselves according to more or less secret recipes. All this required enormous expenditures of time and money.

The constant occupation with these "outward appearances," so essential to Elisabeth's sense of self, degenerated into a virtual obsession with beauty. In later years, Elisabeth's niece Marie Larisch characterized this maliciously as "an all-consuming passionate love": "She worshiped her beauty like a heathen his idols and was on her knees to it. The sight of the perfection of her body gave her aesthetic pleasure; everything that marred this beauty was displeasing and repulsive to her. . . . She saw it as her life's work to remain young, and all her thoughts turned on the best method for preserving her beauty."[25]

Marie Larisch recorded the means with which the Empress attempted to keep up her beauty: nightly face masks with raw veal, during strawberry season a strawberry mask, warm olive-oil baths to maintain the smoothness of her skin. "But once the oil was almost boiling, and she barely escaped the dreadful death of many a Christian martyr. Often she slept with damp cloths over her hips to maintain her slenderness, and for the same reason, she drank a dreadful mixture of five or six egg whites with salt."[26]

Sisi needed as much as three hours a day for dressing (occasionally several times in one day). The famous lacing alone frequently took an hour, until the desired wasp waist was slight enough. To do justice to her reputation of a proverbially narrow waist, Sisi made use of unusual methods, shocking for her time; beginning in the 1870s, for example, she gave up petticoats, wearing only thin "pantalettes" made of the finest doeskin. She had herself sewn into her dresses—each time she changed clothes.

The fact that these outrageously time-consuming preparations for public appearances became increasingly burdensome and arduous for her may explain in no small part why more and more she avoided being "harnessed" to function as the premier showpiece of the empire. Other empresses before her had not been under an obligation to uphold a reputation of fabulous looks. They could afford to appear in public simply attired, or with hair less carefully dressed without incurring criticism. Such behavior became all the more impossible for Elisabeth the more brightly shone her reputation for beauty.

The course of Sisi's day during the 1870s and 1880s was unusual for an empress. In summer, she rose around five, in winter, around six o'clock, and she began her day with a cold bath and massage. This was followed by gymnastics and exercise and a meager breakfast, sometimes taken with her younger daughter, Valerie. Then, while her hair was being dressed, she used the time for reading and for writing letters and for studying Hungarian. Then came dressing (either in her fencing costume, if she intended to fence, or her riding habit, if she was going to the riding school to practice). All these activities amply filled the morning. At dinner, however, the Empress made up for lost time; her meal, often consisting of no more than a thin gravy, was consumed in a few minutes. After the meal, she went for a walk lasting several hours—more accurately, a forced march at great speed over huge distances—on which she was accompanied by a lady-in-waiting. Around five in the afternoon, after another change of clothing and hair combing, Marie Valerie came to play. Then, if there was no way to avoid it, Elisabeth appeared at the family dinner table around seven o'clock—and there, usually for the only time during the day, she saw her husband. But this meeting did not last long; for Elisabeth retired at the earliest opportunity, to indulge in her daily chat with her friend Ida Ferenczy, who also prepared the Empress for bed and loosened her hair.

Every official obligation, no matter how insignificant, was considered a disruption of the schedule. The Empress lived entirely for her beauty and health. There was no room in her day for court and family duties (except for concern with Valerie).

When the first signs of aging appeared—wrinkles and weather-beaten skin caused by her diets and the time spent out of doors, and aching joints —Sisi was determined to hold on to her widely praised beauty by force. She tortured her slight body with hours of physical exercise—at the barre, at the rings, with dumbbells and weights of every description.

Wherever she lived, Elisabeth installed exercise rooms, which she used daily for long periods at a time. The first news of this innovation, in the 1860s, caused a sensation—and incredible astonishment. No one could readily conjure up an image of an empress of Austria as she lived and breathed, in an exercise outfit at the parallel bars or the barre. And so the newspapers printed grotesquely false reports, such as the following: "It must surely be of great interest to learn that the Great Hall in the Hofburg has been turned into an exercise ground. Every form of gymnastic equipment can be found in it: swings, parallel bars, barres, monkey bars, etc. Almost daily for 2 hours, His Majesty the Emperor and the exalted archdukes, along with gentlemen from the royal court including even the aged Baron Hess, all of them in gymnastic costume, disport themselves. . . . "[27] The fact that it was not the male members of the August House, but the Empress who spent several hours a day exercising seemed unthinkable even to the journalists of 1864.

Franz Joseph's rage at such articles is completely understandable—quite aside from the fact that the site where the exercises were said to take place was one of the most impressive rooms in the Hofburg, the very one where, for a time, Emperor Franz Joseph delivered his official addresses. "Whether the matter is not too silly to be retracted as a lie, I leave to you to decide," the Emperor wrote to Crenneville. In any case, one must "find some method to make the editors of the *Fremdenblatt* feel the impropriety of their actions through selective harassment."[28]

Elisabeth rose above the gossip and held rigorously to her daily hours of exercising. For a woman of her day, this was really scandalous behavior. At times, she took pleasure in shocking unsuspecting people with her gymnastic exercises; on New Year's Day of 1892 (when Elisabeth was fifty-four years old), for example, Christomanos wrote in his diary, "This morning before her drive she had me called back to the salon. At the open door between the salon and her boudoir, ropes, bars, and rings were installed. When I saw her, she was just raising herself on the handrings. She wore a black silk dress with a long train, hemmed with magnificent black ostrich feathers. I had never before seen her so imposing. Hanging on the ropes, she made a fantastic impression, like a creature somewhere between snake and bird." In order to let herself back down, she had to jump over a rope stretched above the ground. " 'This rope,' she said, 'is there to make sure that I don't forget how to leap. My father was a mighty hunter before the Lord, and he wanted us to learn to leap like the mountain goats.' " Then she begged the astonished student to continue his reading of the *Odyssey* and explained to him that she was so formally dressed because she was about to receive some archduchesses. "If the archduchesses knew that I did my exercises in this dress, they would turn to stone."

Proudly, Elisabeth always spoke of her father's teachings (though she did not get along at all well with the man himself). He had taught his daughters the right way to walk, she told Christomanos. "We were to keep only one model in mind: the butterflies. My sisters Alençon and the Queen of Naples are famous in Paris for the way they walk. But we do not walk as queens are supposed to walk. The Bourbons, who hardly ever went out on foot, acquired an odd way of walking—like proud geese. They walk like true kings."[29] Here, as in all things, naturalness was Elisabeth's ideal. And she used even this occasion to polemicize against the unnaturalness of the "true kings."

The success both of rigorous dieting and of exercising could not, however, be ignored. To the nineteenth century, which stamped even thirty-year-old women as matrons, especially when they had borne several children, Empress Elisabeth was an extraordinary phenomenon. For roughly thirty years—an unheard-of length of time—the reputation of her beauty persisted.

Even the appearances of the forty-year-old Empress at the major balls were of almost fabulous splendor: Diamond stars in her hair, her tall, slender figure clothed in the most splendid gowns that European dressmakers could contrive, she stood at the center of the court bustle and brilliance, "not as if she were in a ballroom among all the people, but as if she were standing alone on a rock at the ocean, so lost is her glance into the distance" —so unapproachable and so unreal. To the admiring remark of her niece Marie Larisch that she was like Titania, Queen of the Fairies, Elisabeth, however, replied with her usual irony, "Not Titania but a seagull that has been caught and cowers in its cage."[30]

Wherever Elisabeth appeared, she stole the show from the other women. When the Italian King and Queen visited Vienna in 1881, Alexander Hübner, writing about the meeting of the two queens, noted, "poor Queen Margherita seemed a soubrette next to a demigoddess."[31]

And Elisabeth's youngest daughter, Marie Valerie, often could hardly contain her pride in her beautiful mother; for example, in 1882, she wrote in her diary, "Dinner. Mama black pearl bodice, black feather in her hair and a gold chain around her throat. Oh! she was so beautiful. Nor did Mama look much older than me."[32] (This last was surely an exaggeration —since at the time Elisabeth was not quite forty-five years old, while Valerie was fourteen.)

That always and everywhere Sisi's beauty expressed sovereignty was mentioned by many contemporaries, including the German Emperor Wilhelm II: "she did not sit down, she lowered her body; she did not stand up, she rose. . . . "[33]

Sisi's confidante, Marie Festetics, was another admirer.

> One never grows tired when one goes out with her. At her side it is delightful, and so it is behind her. Looking alone is enough. She is the embodiment of the idea of loveliness. At one time I will think that she is like a lily, then again like a swan, then I see a fairy—oh, no, a sprite—and finally—no! an empress! From the top of her head to the soles of her feet a royal woman!! In everything excellent and noble. And then I remember all the gossip, and I think there may be much envy in it. She is so enchantingly beautiful and charming.

But Festetics noticed something else about the Empress, who was only thirty-four at the time. "What I miss in her is joy in life. A serenity overlies her that is quite striking in a young person!"[34]

Sisi's esoteric, overly sensitive nature was coupled with a considerable arrogance. She showed this aspect of her personality in a hurtful way whenever and wherever it suited her, especially to her critics at court.

In the course of time, her ill humor increasingly turned into contempt for any public appearances. During the 1880s, Sisi spoke with her close friend and fellow poet Queen Elisabeth of Romania (Carmen Sylva) about the value of her position. She described it as exceedingly low; she held appearing in public to be no more than playacting. Queen Elisabeth remarked, astonished, "Your great beauty does not help you and does not relieve you of any of your shyness!"

To which Sisi replied, "I am not shy, it merely bores me! So they hang beautiful clothes on me and much jewelry, and then I step outside and say a few words to the people, and then I rush to my room, tear it all off, and write."[35]

The clever Countess Festetics, who knew and loved her Empress more than most, wrote in her diary in the late 1860s that Elisabeth had all the virtues but that a wicked fairy had transformed each one into its opposite:

"Beauty!—Loveliness!—Grace!—Elegance!—Simplicity!—Goodness!
—Magnanimity!—Spirit!—Wit!—Humor!—Astuteness!—Cleverness!" And now the curse: "for everything turns against you—even your
beauty will bring you nothing but sorrow, and your high spirit will
penetrate so deep—so deep that it will lead you astray."[36]

But this is to anticipate subsequent events. In the mid-1860s, Elisabeth
was a beauty in her late twenties. She enjoyed the awareness of her power,
triumphed over her Viennese adversaries, and took it as a natural tribute
that her husband was her foremost and most ardent admirer. The relationship between the couple had changed since the years of flight; Elisabeth
was now the stronger and could influence the Emperor with feminine
wiles. The Viennese court observed this turn of events with deep concern.
Archduchess Sophie still stood to one side. Her influence on the Emperor
was barely noticeable.

Sisi had brought about these changes, not by achievement, courtesy, or
intelligence, but solely by her beauty. The excessive significance she ascribed to her outward appearance is therefore understandable. In the mid-
1860s—at the height of her perfection—she knew very clearly: This beauty
was her power and could be employed as a tool for the fulfillment of her
wishes. That she knew how to employ this tool successfully was to be
demonstrated before long not only within the family circle, but also in
Austrian politics.

CHAPTER SIX

HUNGARY

E lisabeth's sympathies for Hungary must have had their roots in her opposition to the Viennese court. The Viennese aristocracy —those people, that is, in whom the Empress saw her principal enemies (probably correctly)—consisted to a large extent of Bohemian families. These families set the tone in Vienna, furnished the high dignitaries and functionaries at the court, controlled social life, and had a powerful champion and friend in Archduchess Sophie. The Emperor's mother continued to express her gratitude for the loyalty of the Bohemian lands during the Revolution of 1848. She insisted that the young Empress also behave gratefully toward the Bohemians—especially by learning to speak Bohemian. But precisely because this request came from the Archduchess, Sisi did not get far in the language. She could barely recite the numbers, much less manage to hold short memorized speeches in Czech.

The more Sisi's relations with court society and her mother-in-law worsened, and the more critical she felt about their neo-absolutism, the greater became her interest in the Hungarians. During the 1850s it was they who persisted in strict opposition to the Viennese court—even including the Hungarian nobility. A relatively large section of the Hungarian aristocracy (in contrast to the Bohemian aristocracy) had taken part in the Revolution. Their estates were confiscated, and many were still living in exile. It was not until the late 1850s that the former revolutionaries returned to Budapest—after the Emperor had restored their property and remitted their prison sentences, even (as in the case of Gyula Andrássy) rescinded the death sentences. For the Viennese court, they were and remained revolutionaries. Archduchess Sophie in particular never concealed the fact that she considered the Magyars as a whole, and especially the Magyar aristocrats, a rebellious people because they expressed a self-confidence and pride that an absolute ruler by divine right, such as Archduchess Sophie imagined him, could hardly tolerate in his subjects.

After the Revolution had been quelled, Hungary was "forcibly brought into line." The country's ancient special rights and her old constitution were "forfeited." She was administered and centrally ruled from Vienna, which proved a constant irritant. From 1848 to 1867—almost twenty years —Hungary was an insurgent, unquiet province. Though she was kept in line with strong military force, she nevertheless successfully refused such duties as paying taxes to Vienna. During these years, there were even wide-ranging agreements with foreign powers (including and especially with Prussia) to support Hungary in her resistance to the government in Vienna. Streams of money flowed into the land along subterranean routes to fan the insurrection. Every trip he took to Hungary was dangerous to the young Emperor.

That the Hungarians of all social classes and parties were undeterred in their demand that Franz Joseph be crowned King of Hungary made them especially unpopular in Vienna. A precondition to coronation was the guarantee of the old Hungarian constitution—and nothing was as suspect after the suppression of the 1848 Revolution as the demand for a constitution, which signified a qualification of the absolute powers of the ruler and concession to the detested popular will (or, in the case of the old Hungarian constitution, to the feudal power of the estates).

When, however, Austria lost Lombardy in 1859 (here, too, the aristocrats were the insurgents who turned the tide) and was unable to hold Venetia, Hungary moved closer to center stage. It became clear that in a potential confrontation between Austria and Prussia on the German question, Hungary could become extremely dangerous. Therefore cautious discussions were begun in Vienna concerning the possibility of making some concessions without losing face.

At first Elisabeth knew very few Hungarians; besides her teacher in Bavaria, the historian Count Mailath, there were the magnates who had officially greeted her on the occasion of her 1857 trip to Hungary and who had cheered her (perhaps more as a beautiful woman than as the Empress of Austria) at that time. Rudolf had had a Hungarian wet nurse, to whom Sisi could barely make herself understood. Then, on Madeira, there was the romantic interlude with Imre Hunyady, who taught the Empress her first words of Hungarian. Finally, years of friendship linked her to Imre's sister Lily. It is certain that this favorite lady-in-waiting talked to the Empress about her homeland during the many lonely hours on Madeira and Corfu.

After her return from Corfu—in February 1863, to be precise—Sisi insisted on having regular Hungarian lessons. In Possenhofen it was said that Archduchess Sophie, even Emperor Franz Joseph, did not want to allow it, claiming that Hungarian was too difficult, Sisi would never be able to learn it (since she had already had such great trouble with Czech). This interdiction only made her more determined.[1] She would show her critics.

Until that time, the court had found fault with Elisabeth's insufficient knowledge of languages. The Viennese aristocracy was especially amused by her rote phrases of French and Italian, which she trotted out at the court salons. Archduchess Ludovika, too, believed her daughter to have no talent for languages. The astonishment at Sisi's rapid progress was therefore great. "Sisi is making unbelievable progress in Hungarian," the Emperor wrote his mother only a few months later.[2]

This progress was by no means attributable only to her teacher of Hungarian, Professor Homoky, a clergyman. Rather, the prime cause was a delicate Hungarian country girl whom the Empress took into her most immediate circle in 1864: Ida Ferenczy. It is almost impossible to overestimate the importance of this woman in Sisi's life. For thirty-four years—until Elisabeth's death—Ida (who was four years younger than the Empress) remained Sisi's closest confidante. Ida knew all her secrets, was the go-between for her most private correspondence, was altogether indispensable—not only as a servant, but also as a close friend.

It remains a mystery to this day how this twenty-three-year-old daughter of the landed gentry arrived at the Viennese court in the first place. Max Falk, a Hungarian journalist, related in his memoirs that the Viennese court had compiled a list of six young Hungarian noblewomen considered suitable for the position of companion to the Empress. The list resulted from several tests of strength among the various factions. When the final list—calligraphed—was presented to the Empress, a seventh name, entered in another hand, had allegedly been added. This was the name of Ida Ferenczy—a name, therefore, in no way chosen by the court.[3]

This story of a mysterious stranger who placed the name of a simple country girl on a list of the high aristocracy seems exceedingly dramatic, but it serves to show the significance the Hungarians later attributed to Ida. A plainer version implies that Countess Almassy, who compiled the list, remembered the Ferenczy family from Kecskemét, and because they were friends of hers, she placed the name of one of the family's five daughters on the list.[4] This, in turn, can have happened only behind the court's back, since Ida did not fulfill one of the principal qualifications for the position —membership in the higher nobility.

Because of her lowly origins, Ida could not become a lady-in-waiting. Someone thought up the subterfuge of first naming Ida to be a canoness, which entitled her at least to the title of *Frau*, and then to appoint her officially "reader to Her Majesty," beginning with a monthly salary of 150 guldens in addition to board and lodging. Of course, Ida never read to the Empress.

Sisi's letters to Ida, filled with tenderness, are usually headed by the address (in Hungarian), "My sweet Ida!" The letters are exceedingly long (to her husband, for example, Sisi wrote much shorter and usually more sober notes) and contain such remarkable sentences as "I think of you so much, during the long hairdressing, during my walks, and a thousand times a day."[5] (Only fragments of Elisabeth's letters to Ida Ferenczy survive. Ida burned most of them, presumably the most significant ones; the few that were preserved were destroyed during the Second World War except for a few scraps.)

One thing is certain: Little Ida was an intimate of the Hungarian liberals who were working for a "compromise." Chief among these were Gyula Andrássy and Ferencz Deák. And Ida's entry into the Viennese Hofburg was the beginning of Sisi's enthusiasm for what the Hungarians called *conciliation*—reestablishment of the old Hungarian special privileges, and Franz Joseph's coronation as King of Hungary. Conversely, Ida Ferenczy kept the Hungarians minutely informed concerning the relative strengths within the imperial family.

This relationship between the Empress of Austria and Ida Ferenczy, so crucial in political terms, was certainly carefully cultivated on the part of Hungary (that is, especially by Andrássy and Deák). They were very clever at exploiting for their own purposes the young Empress's isolation at the Viennese court and her differences with the anti-Hungarian Archduchess Sophie. In the conflict between the Empress and the court, Ida was the first person who from the outset unequivocally sided with Sisi. She made no attempts at mediation, as Count Grünne had done in his time. She had no family ties to the high nobility, as did the ladies-in-waiting who, until this time, had constituted the Empress's entire world. (Even Sisi's friend Lily Hunyady, by now married to Count Walterskirchen, belonged to a faction of the Viennese aristocracy in spite of her Hungarian origins.) Ida stayed far away from all gossip, remained aloof from everyone at court, even distant, was devoted with her whole heart and soul to her mistress and friend (and remained so even after Elisabeth's death). No wonder that Ida Ferenczy soon became one of the most bitterly hated people in the Hofburg. Given Sisi's unshakable affection, however, the dislike did not particularly trouble Ida.

The twenty-seven-year-old Empress spent many hours a day with her new "reader." Ida had to be present especially during the hairdressing and hair washing—and to use the time for Hungarian conversation, which the chambermaids and hairdressers in the room did not understand. Hungarian became something like a secret code between the two women. After only a few weeks, Countess Almassy wrote to Hungary, "Ida is delighted with the Empress's good pronunciation, she is also said to speak Hungarian quite fluently—in a word, they are both pleased with each other."[6]

As the first step toward a reconciliation between the King and Hungary, the politicians proposed a visit by Franz Joseph to Budapest. Ida had spent only a few weeks with the Empress when she persuaded her mistress of the necessity of such a visit.

In June 1865, Franz Joseph, after months of urging on the part of the Hungarians (and of his wife), actually did go to Budapest and started to make concessions. He began by abolishing military jurisdiction, which still governed Hungary instead of civil law; then he proclaimed an amnesty for offenses against the laws governing the press.

These small steps, however, were not enough to satisfy the Hungarians. They did not drop their demand for reestablishment of the Hungarian constitution and for the coronation. On this point, all the Hungarian parties were agreed. They closed ranks behind Deák—as did the Hungarians who lived in Vienna, and each in his way worked for conciliation.

Ida Ferenczy was not only an enthusiastic partisan of Deák; she also knew him through her family. Ida's admiration for the "sage" was passed on to the Empress. In June 1866, Ida sent to Hungary for a portrait of Deák with his signature in his own hand. "I will say in confidence that Her Majesty wishes to have it, but it must not become known, so that the newspapers will not write about it, which is not permitted," she noted in her request.[7] Deák's picture hung over Elisabeth's bed in the Hofburg until her death.

In the mid-1860s, for reasons of age, Deák passed on his most important political offices to Count Gyula Andrássy. Andrássy, too, kept up a regular correspondence with Ida Ferenczy, assuming the role of fatherly friend. Elisabeth knew Gyula Andrássy quite well from Ida's stories long before meeting him. She was informed not only about his political ideas, but also about his adventurous private life, which frequently merged with his political activities. Andrássy did not return to Hungary from exile until 1858—after the amnesty of his death sentence.

In 1849, at Schwechat, Andrássy fought with Kossuth against the imperial troops. In the 1860s, his followers tended to minimize this part of his past as a "youthful prank," but understandably, it kept the mistrust of him alive at the Viennese court. Also in 1849, wearing the uniform of a colonel in the Honved (the Hungarian national army, which fought against the imperial troops), he had gone to Constantinople on instructions from the revolutionary government in order to prevent the handing over of the Hungarian emigrants to Austria (a mission he executed successfully). When the Austrian and Russian troops were victorious against the Honved, Andrássy was condemned to death for high treason. His name was nailed to the gallows by the executioner—a further romantic detail to delight the ladies of the Parisian salons, who fluttered around the "handsome hanged man" *(le beau pendu)* in his exile.

In exile, first in London, then in Paris, Andrássy flourished. Unlike so many of his compatriots, he had no need to earn a living by odd jobs. His mother sent ample funds from Hungary, and the fact that he was not only an aristocrat but also a most witty companion, with splendid good looks and perfect fluency in Hungarian, German, French, and English opened the doors to all the distinguished homes.

In England he could immediately afford to acquire saddle horses and to play "with delightful elegance the homeless person" on Derby Day, as his adversaries mocked.[8] There is no need to mention that always and everywhere he exploited the quick effect of his charm to extract political information.

The court of Napoleon III knew Andrássy as few others did. It was also in Paris that he met his wife. Of course, she was an aristocrat, a Hungarian, and the most celebrated beauty after Empress Eugénie: Countess Katinka Kendeffy. With her, Andrássy returned to Budapest as the adored Martyr of the Revolution—and immediately won a place for himself politically, without having to work for it. Offices and honors were virtually heaped on him.

The years as an émigré had put him in touch with the powerful men in Europe. He was skilled in making his way in Western European diplomatic circles. The liberal Hungarian party—which was deeply rooted among the simple people, thanks to Deák—needed a man like Andrássy, who had ties to both the aristocracy and ruling circles abroad. Further, Andrássy was a man with the very best connections to the press (after all, he had written for years for the newspaper *Pesti Naplo*) and renowned as a witty speaker. His political adages became widely quoted, such as his pronouncement on the neo-absolutism of the young Emperor Franz Joseph, "The new Austria resembled a pyramid that had been stood on its head; can it come as a surprise, then, that it cannot stand straight?" As early as 1861, when Austria was still vigorously defending her positions in Italy and Germany, Andrássy coined the remark, which would become famous, that "the double-headed eagle will not flutter over Rome, Tuscany, Hessia, and Holstein, where the imperial government sent it, perhaps for the glory of the army, but not in the interest of the people's welfare." The "defensive position of Austria was a European interest"—this was a renunciation of the Italian and German policies, espousing instead concentration on the lands of the Danube monarchy.[9]

Andrássy was a man of large ideas and concepts, no friend of painstaking detail. But he defended his ideas with confidence and spirit. Few men in public life deserve the epithet of "political sensualist" as much as Andrássy. He was as vain as a prima donna and assiduously cultivated the image of being irresistible—irresistible to his compatriots, who admired him; irresistible especially to women, who chased after him.

A great many contradictory statements apply to Andrássy's personality. The Hungarians turned him into a national hero, non-Hungarians often saw him as a villain. Count Hübner, for example, who knew him in Paris, wrote in his diary, "Personally he is not unlikable, he has a touch of the bohemian and the gentleman, of the sportsman and gambler. He looks like a conspirator, and yet, at the same moment, like a man who says everything that is going through his mind. He is the boldest liar of his day and at the same time the most indiscreet of braggarts."[10]

Andrássy's and Elisabeth's paths first crossed in January 1866. She was twenty-eight years old, Andrássy was forty-two.

Hungarian matters were in a state of flux. After the Emperor had made concessions during his visit to Hungary, a delegation of the Hungarian parliament, headed by the Prince Primate, traveled from Vienna to officially invite the Empress for a visit and to bring belated good wishes on her birthday (which she had, once again, spent in Munich). Andrássy was a member of this delegation, being at that time vice president of the Hungarian Chamber of Deputies. The deputation, preceded by imperial and royal court and chamber heralds, strode ceremoniously through the anterooms, and the ranks of Imperial and Royal Household Guards, to reach the apartments of Her Majesty. In the last anteroom, they were greeted by the Empress's chamberlain, who led them into the audience chamber. The encounter was marked by theatrical effects. Andrássy, wearing the gold-embroidered ceremonial dress of the Magyar aristocracy (the so-called Attila), his coat embroidered with precious gems, spurs on his boots, a tiger skin over his shoulders, was flanked by the Prince Primate, the Greek-Orthodox bishop, and other deputies. Even in this normally ornate setting, he stood out by virtue of his casual, man-of-the-world appearance, his somewhat gypsylike wild aura.

Sisi presented herself as a fairy-tale princess. Her Hungarian national costume was given a romantic interpretation: The white silk dress and black bodice were trimmed with rich lacings of diamonds and pearls. Over it she wore a white lace apron, and on her head a Hungarian bonnet. A diamond crown adorned her forehead. She stood under the canopy, surrounded by her chatelaine and eight specially selected attendant ladies, most of them Hungarian. She was every inch the Queen of Hungary.

To everyone's astonishment, the improvised speech in which she expressed her gratitude for Hungary's good wishes was in faultless Hungarian. Enthusiastic shouts of *"Elje!"* followed her address.

That evening, the Hungarian deputation was invited to dine at court. For this occasion, Sisi made her appearance in a white dress with a train, pearls braided into her long hair. At the after-dinner reception, both Franz Joseph and Elisabeth "were gracious enough to converse with each member of the deputation individually at some length," as the newspapers reported. It was the first conversation between the Empress and Gyula Andrássy—

in Hungarian, of course. Later, Andrássy made public the details of his conversation with the Empress, including Elisabeth's widely quoted statement, "You see, when the Emperor's affairs in Italy go badly, it pains me; but when the same thing happens with Hungary, that is death to me."[11]

Ida Ferenczy had done her job well. Andrássy knew that in Elisabeth he had found an advocate of the Hungarians' special demands. These were anything but modest, taking the rights of the non-Hungarian peoples of the monarchy not at all into consideration. Emperor Ferdinand, Franz Joseph's predecessor, had himself crowned twice: as King of Bohemia in Prague and as King of Hungary in Pressburg. Now, however, the matter was restricted to coronation as King of Hungary and to Hungary's demands (from the Bohemian point of view, quite outrageous) for parity with everything that was non-Hungarian (that is, a significantly larger as well as economically much more important region).

To the displeasure of the Viennese Court Party, in late January 1866, the Emperor and Empress undertook a visit to Hungary that was to last several weeks. It was Sisi's first sight of Budapest since 1857—that is, in nine years. The times had changed, the climate between Vienna and Budapest had not improved. A solution to the years-long conflict was to be hoped for in the near future.

The program for the Hungarian visit was a strenuous one for the visitors from Vienna. While Elisabeth groaned about every official reception in Vienna, feeling it to be a burden and a limitation of her personal freedom, she disciplined herself here in Hungary, submitting to her role as queen. Admittedly, Gyula Andrássy was always near her. And wicked tongues sent word from Budapest to Vienna on how well the two conversed with each other during the receptions and salons—speaking in Hungarian, of course, so that Sisi's ladies-in-waiting understood none of it. Adjutant General Crenneville, who was along on the trip, wrote angrily to his wife in Vienna that during the court ball, in the royal castle of Budapest, the Empress had spoken for a quarter of an hour in Hungarian with Andrássy, and he stressed this piece of news by following it with three exclamation points.[12]

With displeasure and malicious glee, the Viennese court officials took note of the underside of the glittering facade of Hungary. Crenneville, for example, found fault with the magnates' "soiled costumes, some highly ridiculous Attilas," and continued with a long tirade about the "shameless" czardas danced at the court ball—"but as an *épouseur,* I would never marry a girl who dances like this, and I would leave my wife if she forgot herself in public with a strange man, as is done during the so-called decent czardas of yesterday's court ball." Crenneville also criticized "the elegant but half-naked get-up of the ladies."[13]

This liberality, this lack of reticence and the openly flaunted temperament of the Hungarian aristocracy, however, was precisely what attracted and clearly excited the young Empress after the strict life at the Viennese court. Sisi bloomed under the huzzahs of the common people of Hungary and the admiring glances of the Hungarian nobility. All the liberality, all the elegance, all the charm of Hungary, however, crystallized for her in Gyula Andrássy.

She was an overt, overwhelming success. Even Franz Joseph wrote appreciatively to his mother in Vienna, "Sisi is of great help to me with her courtesy, her exquisite tact, and her good Hungarian, in which the people are less reluctant to hear some rebuke from lovely lips."[14]

The undisputed high point of the visit was Elisabeth's address to the Hungarian national diet in faultless Hungarian. At the words, "May the Almighty attend your activities with His richest blessing," she folded her hands. Her eyes filled with tears of emotion. One of the magnates described the moment "as so moving that the deputies could not utter the *Elje,* and tears streamed down the cheeks of the old and young." The malicious commentary of the imperial head of Cabinet, Baron Adolf von Braun, on the same moment: "One cannot deny that the Hungarians have heart—if only it would last."[15]

But even here in Budapest, Sisi fell ill again. The symptoms were the same familiar ones: paroxysms of weeping, coughing, debility. She was forced to keep to her rooms for a week—to the disappointment of the many who had come to the capital for the sole purpose of seeing the "Queen." Franz Joseph to Archduchess Sophie: "Our ball was once again very brilliant and crowded, but actually a disappointment, since many people came from every corner of the country only to see Sisi and be presented to her, and they found me alone."[16]

The longer the imperial visit to Budapest lasted, the more ill-humored the commentaries in Vienna grew. Archduke Albrecht, head of the conservative Court Party, wrote in outrage to Count Crenneville, "If only there were a way to prevent the overly long stay of the supreme imperial couple, which is sure to be damaging! Whatever could possibly have been achieved by it was achieved in the first 8 to 10 days, and now the repetition is injurious as well to the first good impression, as imperial dignity and renown are being totally destroyed thereby." The blame for the Emperor's behavior, too partial to Hungary, was assigned to none other than the Empress: "By now the mood here [that is, in Vienna] grows so bitter against both Their Majesties personally and especially against Her Majesty when the public . . . reads detailed accounts about devotions and courtesies that were never granted to the local nobility and the Viennese, much less other provinces!"[17]

Franz Joseph saw to it that the answer sent to his great-uncle expressed considerable irritation: "The stay here in no way threatens the monarch's personal renown, since the Emperor knows perfectly well what he wants and what he will never grant—being, as he is, not the Emperor of Vienna but considering himself at home in each of his kingdoms and lands equally."[18]

The political concessions to Hungary produced anything but agreement from the Viennese court. In his letters to Vienna, Crenneville gave free rein to his vexation, and he did not suppress his contemptuous expressions about "the gallows expressions of Deák and company."[19]

After a stay of five weeks, the Emperor and Empress returned to Vienna early in March.

The news that the beautiful Empress—inspired by Ida's enthusiasm—had cast an eye on Gyula Andrássy spread through Hungary like wildfire. Such gossip surely contributed to solidifying Andrássy's position in domestic affairs. Elisabeth was a woman in her late twenties, in full flower. She had given birth to three children but was dissatisfied, unfulfilled, and thirsting for freedom. There were problems in her marriage. In Vienna, she certainly did not feel at ease. A man such as Gyula Andrássy—in everything the opposite of her husband—could become dangerous to her. Ida's passion for Andrássy confirmed Sisi in her very obvious infatuation. And all these feelings, erupting so unexpectedly, she now put at the service of Hungary's cause—for an adventure in the ordinary sense was out of the question for a woman in her position.

Andrássy continued to be charged with the negotiations for conciliation and traveled back and forth between Budapest and Vienna. An intense political correspondence between Andrássy and the Empress began. Of course, they did not write to each other directly; Ida Ferenczy was the intermediary. These letters were worded in guarded and convoluted terms. The Empress was rarely mentioned by name; usually she was called "your sister"; Andrássy appeared as "the friend." Thus, even if one of the letters were intercepted, it would be impossible to decode its message. For the same reason, today's historian finds it difficult to extract useful facts from the few letters that have survived.

Andrássy was under constant observation, especially during his visits to Vienna. That it was not possible for him to call on the Empress privately goes without saying; but that he was also reluctant to visit Ida Ferenczy's apartments shows the degree of secrecy. Andrássy to Ida: "I wanted to come up to you, but since I assume that all my steps are being followed, I did not unnecessarily want to show the paths along which Providence is now doing its work."[20]

The political situation, especially relations with Prussia, worsened rapidly during these weeks. There were long conferences about possible preparations for war. Ludwig von Benedek was named commander in chief of the troops in Bohemia, while Archduke Albrecht was assigned to head the armies in Northern Italy.

Franz Joseph and Elisabeth did not agree on the person in Berlin responsible for the anti-Austrian sentiments. Elisabeth wrote to her mother, very childishly, "It really would be a mercy if the King of Prussia were to die suddenly, it would prevent a great deal of misfortune."[21] Franz Joseph knew better who was fanning the flames in Berlin: "As long as Bismarck remains, there will be no real peace."[22] As early as April 1866, Prussia concluded a secret treaty against Austria with the new Kingdom of Italy. Bismarck now fomented the conflict over Schleswig-Holstein so cleverly that war became inevitable. Supremacy in Germany was at stake.

For fear that France would also involve herself in the war and strengthen the Italian position, Austria concluded a secret treaty with Napoleon III on June 12. In return for assurance of French neutrality, Austria ceded the province of Venetia to France. France intended to pass the province on to Italy. The peculiar situation, then, was that the Austrian troops in Italy paid a high price in blood fighting for a province that the Emperor had already given away (though the generals were unaware of the true state of affairs).

A declaration of war followed on June 15, 1866. In the northern sector, Prussia fought against Austria, Saxony, Bavaria, Württemberg, Baden, Hanover, and Hesse-Kassel—for all practical purposes, that is, against the rest of Germany. Hardly anyone in Europe gave the Prussian armies a chance against such numerical superiority. But the immense military strength of Austria existed only on paper. The German allies did not amount to much; only Saxony entered the war at full strength; all the other German states had problems, especially Bavaria. At the height of the crisis, young King Ludwig II, disgusted by the political dealings, retired to his Rose Island in Lake Starnberg. For days, the ministers were unable to have an audience with their King. Instead, Ludwig used the time to set off a splendid fireworks display on the lake. The Austrian envoy reported to Vienna, "One begins to think that the King is demented."[23]

Even Elisabeth, who was always ready to defend her Bavarian family, did not conceal her disapproval. She wrote to her mother in Possenhofen, "I hear the King has gone away again. If only he would pay a little more attention to the government, now that times are so bad!"[24]

During these worrisome days, the Empress was in Vienna, by her husband's side. Now at last she forgot her troubles, her "caprices" and minor ailments. She was informed about political and military events and daily wrote long letters to her son in Bad Ischl in order to keep the eight-year-old up to date on events—including even such horror stories as one occurrence after the victory at Custozza at the end of June 1866. "The Piedmontese behave quite inhumanly to the prisoners, they kill the wounded, enlisted men as well as officers, yes they even hanged a few riflemen, two could still be saved, but one went mad. Uncle Albrecht threatened them with retaliation."[25] But Venetia could not be regained.

From the northern sector—Bohemia—one piece of bad news followed on the last. Once again the generals failed. Once again the equipment and provisions turned out to be inadequate.

Emperor Franz Joseph preserved a remarkable calm. Elisabeth to Rudolf: "In spite of the sad times and the many cares of state, dear Papa looks well, thank God, has an admirable calm and confidence in the future, although the Prussian needle guns are enormously successful. . . . This afternoon Papa had detailed news of the most recent battles, and they are better than he thought they would be, only the losses are terrible, since the troops are too brave and too fiery, so that an order was issued for them to wait with their bayonet attacks until the artillery has done its work."[26]

On July 1, the Empress wrote with great caution to her son's tutor, Colonel Latour ("Tell Rudolf as much as you consider advisable"): "Unfortunately, the situation is such that I can no longer send you news by telegraph, but to keep my promise, I want to let you know by letter how matters stand with us now. The northern army suffered terribly from the most recent battles, with a loss of 20,000 men, almost all staff and higher officers have been shot out of their regiments. The Saxons, too, are badly beaten."[27] Elisabeth: "The Emperor is admirable, always uniformly calm and collected. . . . The news I send you is bad, but one must not lose courage."

The day after the decisive Battle of Königgrätz (July 3), Elisabeth wrote to Latour, "Last night we received the news that dashed our last hopes . . . the losses are said to be terrible." There followed details of wounded relatives and friends: "Archduke Wilhelm suffered a head wound; Count Festetics's foot was shot away, it has already been amputated; then Colonel

Müller was hit, Count Grünne [the son of Karl Grünne] is also said to be gravely wounded. . . . No one yet knows, I think, what will happen next, God grant only that no peace is concluded, we have nothing more to lose, so it is better to perish with honor." Then Elisabeth expressed compassion for "the poor child," Rudolf, "whose future is such a sad one."[28]

The horrifying details from Königgrätz surpassed all imagination. Landgravine Fürstenberg: "It is the bloodiest war known to history." The Austrians "were doused with bullets so hard that they fell by the company, it was as if sand were being thrown in their faces; it must have been a horrible bloodbath. Let God put an end to it, no matter how and through whom."[29]

The battle was the biggest military encounter of modern history to date. Around 450,000 men were in the field—more than took part in the "Battle of the Nations" against Napoleon at Leipzig. This one battle and this one day turned Prussia into a European Great Power.[30]

Daily, trains filled with the wounded arrived at the Nordbahnhof. The Empress was busy from morning to night giving comfort. Both her mother-in-law and the public appreciated Elisabeth's activities. Landgravine Therese Fürstenberg: "The Empress edifies and astonishes all the world by the truly maternal manner in which she devotes herself to the care of the wounded and the hospitals; it was time for her to win back the hearts of the public; she is doing a good job."[31]

Daily the Prussian troops moved closer to Vienna. Whoever could afford to do so, fled the city, taking valuables to safety. The court was packing as well. Starting on July 10, the most important files of the Foreign Ministry and the Cabinet Chancellery, and the most valuable manuscripts in the Court Library were shipped to Budapest. The most valuable paintings were removed from the walls. The furs of the imperial family and, of course, the crown insignia were also sent to Hungary.

The Swiss envoy informed Bern that the Emperor would personally assume the command in any impending battle outside the gates of Vienna. The crisis in Austria was so acute, he wrote, that there was already talk in Vienna of a regency by the Empress.[32]

Elisabeth, too, left Vienna on July 9 (that is, a mere six days after Königgrätz) and traveled to Budapest. Three days later, she returned to Vienna briefly to get the children, who had been brought to the capital from Bad Ischl.

Archduchess Sophie was outraged at this decision. In her considered opinion, the children were much safer in Bad Ischl, besides being able to enjoy the salubrious mountain air. She feared that "the humid air and the bad water of Budapest" could harm the Crown Prince's health. The fact that Hungary had been picked for the imperial family's sanctuary was more than an annoyance to Sophie.[33] In any case, she refused to join them and remained in Bad Ischl, moving all her valuables there.

Sisi's choice of Hungary as a haven from this precarious, even desperate situation was a political decision of the greatest import. After all, it was just at this time that Bismarck, sparing no expense, essayed his support of the Klapka Legion, which aimed at separating Hungary from Austria and exploiting Austria's desolate situation for a nationalist uprising. According to prevailing opinion, revolution in Hungary would signal the end of the Austrian monarchy.

Sisi's journey to Hungary was carefully calculated: Of all the members of the imperial family, she maintained the best relations with Hungary. And these relations were now sorely needed. It is not known who was behind the plan. Considering the furious opposition of Archduchess Sophie, it is even likely that the whole action—a deeply political maneuver —can be ascribed to none other than the usually so apolitical Empress herself, and that this time she was able to get her way. It was also an essential part of the calculation that she took the children with her. The parallels to Maria Theresia's cry for help to the Hungarians in Pressburg in 1741 (holding the little successor to the throne in her arms) was pointed out soon enough in the Hungarian newspapers—and its significance should not be underestimated.

A further gesture that attracted a great deal of attention on the part of the Empress occurred during her farewells at the Vienna railroad station: she publicly kissed the hand of her husband, who had been humiliated on every side. Franz Joseph's popularity had fallen to an all-time low during these sad weeks. The populace, harried by war and misery, accused him of placing the interests of the dynasty before those of the state. The rumor was making the rounds that Emperor Maximilian was returning from Mexico to assume the regency in Austria. Shouts were heard, directed at the Emperor, "*Viva* Maximilian!"—that is, a demand for abdication. The phrase, "Let the Prussians come, we'll build golden bridges for them" was even heard.[34] In this situation, the Empress, usually so critical, stood by her husband.

In Hungary, Elisabeth and the children were received enthusiastically. Deák, Andrássy, and other leading political figures came to greet them at the railway station. Deák referred to the glittering reception accorded the Emperor and Empress during their most recent visit to Hungary when he said, "I would consider it cowardice to turn our backs on the Empress in her misfortune after we came forward to meet her when the affairs of the dynasty were still favorable."[35]

In Budapest, Elisabeth was entirely under Hungarian influence. Her daily, increasingly firm letters put pressure on her husband, supported the Hungarian demands, and urged Franz Joseph to make haste. Her first objective was to arrange a personal meeting between the Emperor and Deák.

Sisi was a willing, almost fanatical tool of Andrássy and his policies. He was extremely clever at making her feel that she was the savior of Austria (and Hungary). On July 15, she wrote the Emperor that she had just come from a meeting with Andrássy

> alone, of course. He expressed his views clearly and precisely. I understood them and gained the conviction that, if you trust him, but *entirely,* we, and not Hungary alone, but the monarchy, can still be saved. But you must *at least* speak with him yourself, and I mean at once, for each day can shape events in such a way that in the end he would no longer assume it; at such a moment it really does require a very large sacrifice to do it. So speak with him at once. You can do so frankly, for I can give you this assurance, you are not dealing with a man who wants to play a part at any price, who strives for a position, quite the contrary, he is jeopardizing his present position, which is a handsome one. But like any man of honor, he is also prepared, at the moment when the state is facing ruin, to contribute all in his power to salvage it; whatever he has, his reason, his influence in the country, he will place at your feet. For the last time, I beg you in the name of Rudolf, do not let the last opportunity slip by.

The letter continued in the same tone. At no other time in her life did Elisabeth write such long letters to her husband as she did now, when it was a matter of Hungary (and Andrássy's will). For the sake of Hungary (and Andrássy), she worded her political preferences so sharply as to approximate blackmail:

> I beg you, send me a telegram the minute you receive my letter whether Andrássy should take the evening train to Vienna. I am asking him to come again tomorrow to Paula [Königsegg, her

chatelaine], where I will give him an answer. If you say "No,"
if you are unwilling at the final hour even to listen to disinterested advice any longer, then you are in fact acting un . . . ly
to us all. In that case, you will be forever spared my further p
. . . and ms. [pleas and molestations], and I have nothing to fall
back on but to reassure myself with the knowledge that, whatever happens, I will one day be able honestly to tell Rudolf, "I
did all in my power. Your misfortune does not weigh on my
conscience."[36]

Franz Joseph capitulated. Against his better judgment and the advice of
his mother and his ministers in Vienna, he acceded to his wife's rigorous
demands.

Gyula Andrássy called on the Emperor on July 17, bringing with him
a long letter from Sisi to her husband. The interview lasted an hour and
a half. According to Franz Joseph, Andrássy spoke "very frankly and
cleverly, developed all his views, and begged me most of all to speak with
the old man"—that is, with Fèrencz Deák.

Franz Joseph's suspicion of Andrássy, however, was deep-seated: "For
the rest, I found him, as always, too imprecise in his views and without
the necessary consideration of the other parts of the monarchy. He covets
a great deal and offers too little at the present crucial moment." On the
other hand, the Emperor praised Andrássy's "great frankness and level-
headedness": "but I fear that he has neither the strength nor can find the
means in his country to carry out his present intentions."[37]

Andrássy's pronounced liberal policies ran completely counter to the
principles of the Viennese court as well as those of the Emperor. It was
obvious that adopting any such new policy for Hungary would also affect
the other parts of the monarchy. For this reason, the Hungarian demands
were supported by constitutionalists and liberals in the other parts of the
monarchy.

On July 19, "the old man," Ferencz Deák, also arrived at the Hofburg.
The Emperor found him "Much clearer than A[ndrássy] and taking the
rest of the monarchy much more into account. But I gained the same
impression from him as I did from A. They covet everything in the widest
sense and offer no guarantees of success, only hopes and probabilities, and
they do not promise to hold out should they be unable to carry through
their intentions in the country and are outflanked by the left." Franz Joseph
had "great respect for his honesty, frankness, and dynastic loyalty . . .

however, courage, decisiveness, and endurance in misfortune is not granted this man."[38]

The Emperor felt hard-pressed on all sides. At court, anti-Hungarian sentiment was strong; but his wife regularly sent impassioned letters pleading the Hungarian cause. The Prussians were at the gates of Pressburg. A scalding heat lay over Vienna. Trains full of the wounded arrived daily.

Many exiled kings and princes from Italy and Germany had taken refuge at the Viennese court. There was much political discussion and much argument. Aggression filled the air. But the Emperor "intends to hold out to the last," wrote Archduke Ludwig Viktor to his mother, Archduchess Sophie.[39] In these days, Franz Joseph's letters to his wife ended in a signature different from his usual closing. Instead of the standard wording, "Your ever-loving Franz," the letters now read piteously, "Your devoted little man," "Your manikin," or "Your little one who loves you so much" —formulations the Emperor kept up for the rest of her life.

Hope for help from France was equally vain. Napoleon III had been given an enormous present—Venetia—and he had received it even before the war and without having to promise help in return. It never crossed Napoleon's mind now to come to Austria's aid. After all, he had never obligated himself to do so. Archduke Ludwig Viktor heaped reproaches on King Johann of Saxony on this score: "Uncle Johann, to whom today . . . I spoke my mind about Venetia, now deeply regrets having given this advice, since Napoleon does absolutely nothing for us and since now it is all over unless we get an armistice."[40] Finally, through French intermediaries, a cease-fire—for five days, to begin with—was arranged.

The southern army continued to fight in Northern Italy. On July 21, the news of the brilliant Austrian naval victory at Lissa, under Admiral Wilhelm von Tegetthoff, arrived. This victory gave particular satisfaction to Archduchess Sophie, since it was her son Max who, as commander in chief of the navy, had insisted on instituting important reforms before leaving Austria.

The newspapers made a great fuss over the victory and tried to elevate the dark mood that prevailed in Austria. The public was still unaware that Venetia was lost and that the victory was just as pointless as that of Custozza. But the mood in Vienna continued to be tense.

The decimated and exhausted troops of the northern army longed for peace every bit as much as the severely distressed populace. Of course, no one in Vienna knew that the Prussians, too, had exhausted their strength because cholera had broken out; this circumstance could not, therefore, be used in Vienna's favor during the negotiations.

Franz Joseph was already making his personal plans for the armistice. When he wrote to his wife, he expressed great longing for her and begged her to go to Bad Ischl with the children, "for your presence in Hungary would no longer be necessary, since thereafter, the political question there must be attacked, and the country will calm down." In Bad Ischl, he added, he would be able "perhaps sometimes to visit" his family, "for I, too, could profit from a day or so of rest."[41]

But Elisabeth remained in Budapest and continued to write her urgent letters. Franz Joseph's patience began to show signs of exhaustion.

The peace negotiations dragged on. Everyone realized that Austria's position of supremacy in Germany had come to an end. Franz Joseph to his wife: "In any case, we will withdraw from Germany entirely, whether it is demanded or not, and after what we have learned through bitter experience about our dear German allies, I consider this a fortunate turn of events for Austria."[42]

On July 29, Archduke Ludwig Viktor wrote to his mother:

> Peace would seem to be just about assured. At first, this gave me no joy. But then I read several letters from military men who were always very much in favor of the war and yet think now that we cannot carry on any longer, since the troops are too worn out and too discouraged by their lack of needle guns. Furthermore, it is said to be very necessary to make peace because of Hungary, since that country is not at all what it should be. . . . Bismarck, since he is clever and the King is trapped in his stupid arrogance, is now said to be much more malleable than the latter. For the time being, however, they are in Nikolsburg with poor Alinchen and are said to be ravaging the place.[43]

Of course, Archduke Ludwig Viktor failed to mention that it was not only Countess Alinchen Mensdorff who was suffering because the King of Prussia was quartered on her estate, but that whole provinces groaned under the yoke of Prussian occupation. Franz Joseph to Elisabeth: "The Prussians wreak havoc in the provinces they have occupied, so that a famine is imminent therefore and constant cries for help from there are heard here. It is heartrending."[44]

The Emperor himself then informed his wife about the principal provisions of the Truce of Nikolsburg. It allowed "the integrity of Austria and Saxony [to be] preserved, we leave Germany entirely and pay 20 million thalers. What the Prussians do in the rest of Germany and what they will steal, I do not know, nor does it concern us further."[45]

In this situation, too, Franz Joseph begged his wife to visit him in Vienna. "Now I have a pretty request. If you could visit me! It would make me infinitely happy."[46]

Elisabeth actually did go to Vienna for a few days. But her visit was not an unmixed pleasure to the Emperor. The Hungarian affairs completely occupied her mind. Once again she used the opportunity to put political pressure on her husband. Franz Joseph continued reluctant to give in to the Hungarians' demands, plagued as he was by scruples concerning the Bohemians. He stalled Andrássy, who was in Vienna for an audience, with the words, "I will study the matter thoroughly and think it over."[47]

The following day, Empress Elisabeth invited Andrássy to an interview at Schönbrunn. Andrássy did not know whether she was speaking on the Emperor's instructions or on her own initiative (the latter is more probable). On July 30, 1866, he entered the following sentence in his diary: "What is certain is that if the matter is successful, Hungary will be more beholden to the Beautiful Providence [a phrase by which he always meant the Empress] that watches over her than she suspects."[48]

In the interview, Elisabeth showed herself more pessimistic, going so far as to state that she harbored no hope of seeing her efforts crowned by success. Thus she made it very clear to Andrássy that she did not approve of the Emperor's position. Nevertheless, Andrássy was given one more long audience with the Emperor; he was also allowed to submit a memorandum concerning the reorganization of the monarchy in the spirit of dualism (rather than feudalism).

Sisi's harsh demands on behalf of Hungary embittered the Emperor during these few shared days and cast a dark cloud over their relationship at the time. Franz Joseph to his wife after her renewed departure for Budapest: "Even though you were quite angry and importunate, I still love you so infinitely much that I cannot live without you."[49] And two days later, a little irritable: "I am very happy that you are now resting well and sleeping late, though I do not believe that your stay here and my company have tired you so much."[50] The tensions escalated into a serious quarrel when Sisi adamantly continued to refuse to leave Budapest with the children. Instead, she suggested that the Emperor visit her in Budapest.

It is necessary to imagine Austria's military and political situation and the countless cares weighing the Emperor down. No peace had yet been made with Italy; in fact, a resumption of the fighting had to be expected. Negotiations with Prussia were still up in the air. The Hungarian Legion fanned the flames of unrest in Hungary. The Bohemian lands needed immediate aid with food. Cholera and typhoid fever ravaged the downcast Austrian soldiers. In this desperate situation, the Empress of Austria not only refused to be with her husband; she even reproached him for not returning her visit. Elisabeth completely ignored her obligation as mother of the country and indulged herself in the role of neglected, sulking wife. Under the spell of the Hungarians, she worked with unparalleled fanaticism and energy toward one goal and one goal only: conciliation of the sort envisioned by Deák and Andrássy.

The Emperor, on the other hand, in spite of the Hungarian demands, was forced to consider the needs of the other provinces as well; in the current situation, these actually had a much greater claim to consideration than Hungary. For the Bohemian villages and countryside were devastated by battles, sickness, hunger, and misery, while Hungary was practically untouched by the war. Franz Joseph appealed in vain to Sisi's understanding "that it would go counter to my duty for me to adopt your exclusively Hungarian point of view and to discriminate against those lands which, in unswerving loyalty, have endured unspeakable suffering and which now more than ever require special consideration and care."

But Elisabeth gave no sign whatever of affection for her "lonely manikin" in Vienna. With the transparent excuse that the Viennese air was unhealthy, she continued to stay in Budapest. Franz Joseph, resigned: "so I simply have to console myself and once again bear my soul in patience and continue alone, as I have become used to being. In this respect, I have already learned to put up with a great deal, and finally one gets used to it. I shall not waste another word on this point, otherwise our correspondence will become too tedious, as you quite rightly note, and I shall calmly await your decision."[51]

Sisi's selfishness did not stop there. In a time of extreme need and the most exigent thrift, she conceived the intense desire to buy a castle in Hungary. By the terms of the Truce of Nikolsburg, Austria had obligated herself to pay 20 million thalers as the precondition for withdrawal of the Prussian troops. For the Emperor, the most urgent matter was "to pay them, so as to get them out of the country they are ruining."[52] In every area, the small as well as the large, there would have to be economies in order to raise the huge sum. The spending reductions went hand in hand with discharges. The populace, already decimated and famished by war, now also had to struggle against massive unemployment.

Instead of concerning herself with these hardships, the Empress saw nothing but her own comfort and her own need to establish herself more solidly in her beloved Hungary. The villa she rented at present was too small for longer stays in the country, the Budapest castle was too hot in summer; she wanted a castle in the countryside, and she knew exactly which one: Gödöllö.

In the midst of armistice negotiations with Italy, Franz Joseph wrote his wife:

> If you like, you can go to Gödöllö to visit the wounded. But do not look at it as if we wanted to buy it, for I have no money now, and in these hard times, we must economize rigorously. Even the family holdings have been terribly devastated by the Prussians, and it will take years before they recover. I have reduced the court budget for next year to 5 million, so that we have to economize by 2 million. Almost half the stables have to be sold, and we have to live in very reduced circumstances."[53]

During these various excitements, the news suddenly arrived that Empress Carlotta of Mexico had descended on Paris in order to ask Napoleon III for help for her hard-pressed empire. Franz Joseph's first reaction: "I only hope that she does not come here, for at the present moment, she is all we need."[54] Serious worry about Maximilian did not seem called for. In his regular letters to Archduchess Sophie, he always pictured his situation in optimistic terms. The fact that in the meantime the insurgent natives had put the Emperor—who, though well-meaning, was a stranger to the country—on the defensive was not known in Vienna. All the problems in far-off Mexico had been pushed into the background by the unfortunate events in Austria. Furthermore, it took six to eight weeks for mail from Mexico to reach Vienna. No one could know precisely what was really happening, and it was therefore reassuring to believe that matters could not be so very bad.

When the Emperor's birthday on August 18 approached, Sisi had no choice but to go to Vienna, a trip that occasioned Franz Joseph's almost abject gratitude. "I thank you with all my heart for being so good and paying me another visit. . . . Be good to me when you get here, for I am so sad and lonely and in great need of some cheering up."[55] The children, however, remained in Budapest. Landgravine Fürstenberg, at that time still lady-in-waiting to Archduchess Sophie: "They did not even bring the children to see him for the day from Pest! That does hurt 'my lady' [Archduchess Sophie]."[56]

Elisabeth actually spent only one day in Vienna. August 19 was St. Stephen's Day, the festival of Hungary's patron saint, and on that day she was back in Hungary. Franz Joseph after her departure: "Oh! If only I could be united soon with my family and experience somewhat better times. I am very melancholy, and my courage ebbs ever more the closer we come to peace and I can see more clearly the internal difficulties that will have to be overcome. My sense of duty alone keeps me going, as well as the gentle hope that perhaps, after all, one day better times will emerge from the European entanglements that are now beginning."[57]

In the meantime, cholera had begun to spread to Hungary. The epidemic had already claimed some deaths. Nevertheless, Sisi, usually so concerned with her health, remained in Budapest with her children. Franz Joseph wrote her: "I miss you terribly, for with you I can still talk, and then you cheer me up sometimes, though at the moment I find that you are a little troubling."[58]

Finally, in late August, the Peace of Prague was concluded with Prussia. It was not until October, however, that the peace with Italy came about. In spite of Austrian victories, Venetia was lost. First ceded to France, the province, in a plebiscite, joined Italy. Prussia annexed Hanover, the Electorate of Hesse, Schleswig-Holstein, Nassau, and Frankfurt am Main; it established the North German Confederation (which also included Saxony, the former Austrian ally), and concluded an alliance with the South German states. After a thousand years of shared history, Austria left Germany.

Not until the beginning of September—that is, after a stay of almost two months—did Elisabeth and her children leave Budapest for Vienna.

During all these crucial months, Ida Ferenczy did not leave the Empress's side. In the autumn of 1866, another Hungarian was added to Elisabeth's intimate circle; this was Max Falk, a journalist then living in Vienna. Employed by a savings bank, he also wrote articles for the Budapest newspaper *Pesti Naplo;* he was a close friend of Andrássy—and known to the police. In 1860, the Vienna constabulary had instigated a house search, confiscated his entire correspondence, and carried it off in two flour sacks.[59] Falk had spent some time in a Viennese prison for offenses against the press laws and had written widely read articles on the experience.

The astonishment of Countess Königsegg can be imagined when the

Empress ordered her to ask Max Falk of all people to give her Hungarian lessons. The Countess was anti-Hungarian in any case, and Falk was Jewish to boot. He, too, was taken aback at the request. "I replied that, thank God, I was long since past the time when I was forced to 'give lessons.' But Her Majesty's wish, I added, was not only my command, but also a high honor."

The daily meetings were no more than a pretext or a profitable side effect. The issue at hand was the matter of Hungary—in Andrássy's sense. Obviously Max Falk would not teach Elisabeth, whose Hungarian was excellent, grammar. He suggested that he would recite the history of Hungary to her, "the more remote periods as briefly as possible, the more recent ones in greater detail"; furthermore, he would make her more familiar with Hungarian literature, and for "homework" he assigned translations into Hungarian.

Subsequently, Falk wrote that "the lessons in the narrower sense of the word receded further and further into the background. . . . We began occasionally to discuss current events, then very gradually moved on to politics, and with a few cautious forward steps, we arrived at Hungarian affairs."

Falk established a connection with another liberal politician and writer, Josef Eötvös. In this matter, too, he proceeded with extreme caution, first reading the Empress some of Eötvös's poems, then arousing the Empress's curiosity about a banned poem. The Empress to Falk: "What do you mean, banned? So even an Eötvös is already banned? But do tell me what the poem says." Falk: "I had been ready for this moment for a long time, and the manuscript of 'Zaszlotarto' [The Standard-Bearer] had been in my pocket for several days. I read the poem to Her Majesty, who liked it extraordinarily; she took the manuscript from me and kept it." The poem dealt with the symbolism of the Hungarian flag as the sign of national freedom and independence.

Sisi also expressed a wish for the banned pamphlet by the Hungarian national hero Stefan Széchenyi, *A Look at the Anonymous Backward Look*, published in London in the late 1850s; the printed sheets had been smuggled into Hungary one by one. When Falk was reluctant to bring the pamphlet to the Hofburg, the Empress took from a drawer still another banned brochure, which had appeared in 1867 and caused a secret scandal, *The Collapse of Austria*. The anonymous author, the son of an imperial official (as Elisabeth knew), addressed hate-filled tirades, bolstered with the most accurate facts about Austrian policies of recent years, blaming especially the Kamarilla around Count Grünne, as well as the young Emperor. He concluded with the sentence, "The collapse of Austria is a European necessity!" The significance of these daily conversations with Falk can hardly be overestimated. There are clear parallels to the subsequent meetings of young Crown Prince Rudolf with the journalist Moritz Szeps during the 1880s. Both—Elisabeth as well as Rudolf—were interested in politics but uninformed. The information that was officially kept from them they managed to obtain by private means. In both cases, the political informants—Falk and Szeps—seized the opportunity for massive political indoctrination.

Elisabeth asked Falk for Eötvös's letters, and Falk informed Eötvös to that effect. Eötvös, in turn, began to write accordingly, "and so, in the form of letters directed to me, so many things were expressed to Her Majesty she would hardly have learned about in any other way," Falk reported.

During the coronation year, Max Falk returned to Hungary. He became editor in chief of the German-language liberal daily *Pester Lloyd,* where he supported the policies of his friend Andrássy. Before long, he was a leading member of the Hungarian diet and became one of the most powerful men in Hungary.

Unexpectedly, disturbing news arrived early in October. Empress Carlotta of Mexico had gone to Rome to ask the Pope to aid the Catholic Mexican empire, having been refused by Napoleon III. But the Pope saw no way of helping, and he treated Carlotta with great coolness. She had a mental collapse and fell prey to delusions. An alienist and two attendants took her to Castle Miramar outside Trieste, where she remained in excellent physical health and lived to 1927—without ever seeing her Max again or learning of his tragic end. She no longer had any links with the court in Vienna.

After some hesitation, Max decided to remain in Mexico, in spite of the difficulties of his situation. Archduchess Sophie approved of his choice, though she worried about him, her favorite son:

> Fortunately he is making the sacrifice for his country of remaining there, which at the moment is an urgent necessity. For were Max to leave, the country could immediately become the prey of party anarchy. Recently he wrote to me that the interest and the devotion shown him are deeply affecting. By staying, he acts honorably, in contrast to the bad behavior of Louis Napoleon [Napoleon III]. And if one day he is forced to yield to the

machinations of the United States and leave his post, he will do that with honor, too.[60]

The idea that a member of the House of Habsburg could be put to death was unthinkable to Archduchess Sophie, even in Mexico, a land that seemed so foreign, so eerily strange.

The ladies-in-waiting critically and compassionately observed the many misfortunes that befell the imperial family: "how these poor things here, of whom one is a quasi member, are afflicted by blow after blow and pressed by sorrow after sorrow! and how they *cannot* have true joy because they are unfamiliar with any sort of family life and only their innate elasticity helps them through it, one feels terribly sorry for them! ... These are the important figures of our world who, seen close up, are no more than the most piteous unfortunates."[61]

At this time, however, cares closer to home were still most pressing. In late October, Emperor Franz Joseph visited Bohemia, which had been heavily devastated by the war. Elisabeth did not go with him. She, who had done so much for Hungary in this year, acknowledged no obligation to prove herself, during these unhappy times, a good Queen of Bohemia as well.

The visit to the Bohemian battlefields depressed the Emperor deeply. The villages were destroyed, hundreds of thousands of people were homeless. The broad fields around Königgrätz, Trautenau, and Chlum were trampled hard by the combatants—not so much as a blade of grass would grow on them, so that famine was inevitable. On the battlefield itself, no fewer than 23,000 soldiers and 4,000 horses were interred; because of the heat and the danger of epidemic, no proper burial had been possible. Finally, after four months, thorough disinfecting of the entire area removed the stench of corpses.[62]

How desolate, as well as politically volatile, the mood in Bohemia was became clear through an assassination attempt on the Emperor in the Czech theater in Prague. Franz Joseph's position was no longer undisputed. Evil was brewing. Czech nationalism grew in proportion to the preference shown the Magyars. The Empress, too, realized—although not until much later—the significance of the Bohemian anger. "I do not hold it against the Czechs one bit if they revolt against Austrian rule; Slavs belong with Slavs! One day, probably only after many decades, Bohemia will manage to assert her will. But even now, we are sitting on a powderkeg."[63] That Bohemia, until now relatively peaceful, was turning into a powderkeg was not the least of Elisabeth's work.

The negotiations with Hungary continued. Gyula Andrássy continued to travel back and forth between Vienna and Budapest, negotiating here and there, in constant communication with the Empress through Ida Ferenczy. Elisabeth's daily sessions with Max Falk also continued, as did Eötvöss frequent letters to Falk, which Sisi continued to peruse.

Discussions at court about the Hungarians' demands and their method of winning them through the Empress were heated and angry. The Bohemians felt relegated to the background, although Archduchess Sophie espoused their cause. But Sophie's influence had waned considerably in recent times, while Sisi's star had risen in the political as well as the private arena.

The concept of dualism—a large realm with two equally powerful political centers, Budapest and Vienna—was predicated on the elimination of the Slavs. Dualism assigned the political power of the state to two factions: the Hungarians, who were free to dominate all other nationalities in their section of the country (Transleithania); and the Germans, who would hold the same power over the proportionately much larger Slavic population in Cisleithania (the river Leitha being seen as the boundary). This division of power inflicted a great wrong on the Austrian Slavs. The objections of the uniformly pro-Bohemian Viennese Court Party to the Hungarian claims to power were more than justified.

Once again, Archduke Albrecht became the spokesman for the Court Party. He was one of the most important and most influential—and one of the most intelligent—Habsburgs of the nineteenth century. He was older by thirteen years than his great-nephew Franz Joseph, and his huge fortune dwarfed that of the Emperor. Now, after his 1866 victory at Custozza, which was widely and enthusiastically hailed, he possessed quite enough authority to make his voice heard in Austrian politics.

Since his term as military governor of Hungary, the field marshal was one of the most cordially hated men in Hungary. In these critical months, open opposition to the Empress came not from the Emperor or any of the ministers, but from Archduke Albrecht alone. Extremely violent confrontations ensued. Rumors were rife in public about vehement scenes between the two. No fewer than six reports on this conflict alone came to the information bureau.[64] (No details about the matter are known, however; all the documents dealing with this fundamental political quarrel concerning the future of the Danube monarchy were subsequently removed from the bureau and are still missing.)

The discussions at court turned on the assessments of the Revolution of 1848. At the time, the imperial family had fled from Vienna to Olmütz and there had found loyalty and devotion, while the Hungarians, with their army of rebels (which included young Andrássy) marched on Vienna and the Emperor.

Now, suddenly, in the context of the Hungarians' demands and constant political negotiations, 1848 was presented in quite a different light: Now the Hungarians spoke only of the wrong the Emperor had done to them at the time. The former revolutionaries—such as Andrássy—were celebrated as martyrs and heroes of the nation, while the Emperor who had pronounced his death sentence was depicted as the villain.

In this situation, too, the Empress, was partisan. Not only in the family circle, but also in conversations with such Hungarians as Bishop Mihály Horváth, she left no doubt whatever in her criticism of Franz Joseph, but at the same time she tried cleverly to bridge the old chasms: "Believe me, if it were in our power, my husband and I would be the first to bring Ludwig Battyany and the blood witnesses of Arad back to life."[65]

Archduchess Sophie and Archduke Albrecht took up their old positions: They had no compassion for those who were hanged in 1849. As far as these Habsburgs were concerned, the dead were all of them merely rebels against the rightful rule of the Emperor.

Even the little Crown Prince was drawn into the dispute. Sophie had to tell him about 1848; "he always wanted to hear all the details," she wrote in her diary.[66] The Crown Prince also had a fondness for the romantic stories his adored mother told him about the heroes of the Hungarian revolution. The long stay in Hungary deeply influenced the eight-year-old's intellectual and emotional development. He had an opportunity to witness the enthusiasm of the populace for his beautiful and politically active mother, and he, too, fell under Gyula Andrássy's spell. Andrássy became his mentor, his political idol—and remained so to the end of Rudolf's life.

Once again, the Emperor found himself trapped between Sophie and Elisabeth. And this time what was at stake was not family affairs but politics of the highest magnitude. It was a matter of nothing less than the question of Austria's future—whether Germans and Hungarians alone should really share the power and thus disadvantage all other nationalities, or whether other solutions, which would include Bohemia, would have to be found.

In Vienna, the Empress employed her usual methods: She had toothaches or headaches whenever an official reception was in the offing. She did not appear at the solemn Easter vigil. She did not conceal her utter contempt for Vienna; but whenever a Hungarian came to the court, she sparkled in her full beauty, in matchless charm.

She kept her distance from her husband. Franz Joseph, for his part, was so much in love with his wife that he felt compelled to show his infinite, even abject gratitude for the slightest favor. And Elisabeth missed no trick to impose her will on the Emperor.

In February 1867, Prime Minister Richard Belcredi handed in his resignation (which was accepted). He did not mince words to explain his decision in a letter to the Emperor: "A constitutionalism that is based from the outset on the rule of only the Germans and Hungarians—definitely a minority—will never lead more than a fictive life in Austria." He reminded the Emperor of his promise "that *before* a definite decision is taken concerning the question of conciliation, the countervailing opinions of the other kingdoms and provinces would be solicited. I consider it a point of honor to remain true to this promise and would have to see a great political error in the nonfulfillment of same."[67]

As a former governor of Bohemia, Count Belcredi was not free to take any other attitude. His notes accuse the Empress of using the Emperor's frame of mind during these months of misfortune "to support with renewed vigor the specific and selfish Hungarian endeavors, which she has patronized for a long time but hitherto without success." Belcredi (and he was only one of many) charged the Empress with having abandoned her husband and pressuring him during the unfortunate months after König-grätz. "To be separated from his family at such moments of heavy testing is to live in torment for anyone, but especially for a monarch, for whom intimate relations with others are made so much more difficult. Whenever I went to see him and found him totally isolated in the vast chambers of the castle, this always made the most painful impression on me."[68]

Belcredi was followed as prime minister by Foreign Minister Ferdinand Beust, who thus exercised vast authority. Andrássy's hopes of at least taking over the Foreign Ministry from Beust came to naught. Self-confident as he was, he told the Empress during one of their many political conversations that she should not interpret it as lack of modesty on his part if he harbored the conviction that at this particular moment, he was the only man who could be useful. Elisabeth barely let him finish: "How often I have told the Emperor as much!"[69]

Having had no luck with the Foreign Ministry, Andrássy now urged Elisabeth to advocate the prompt naming of a Hungarian ministry with extensive responsibility—under his, Andrássy's, leadership, of course.

Archduchess Sophie resigned herself; early in February, her diary records, "It seems that an arrangement is being made with Hungary and concessions will be granted!"[70]

In mid-February 1867, the Hungarians pushed through the "conciliation." The old Hungarian constitution was reestablished. The empire of Austria became the Dual Monarchy of Austria-Hungary, with two capitals (Vienna and Budapest), two parliaments, two cabinets. Only the minister of war, the foreign minister, and the minister of finance served both sectors (though the last of these acted in the dual capacity only for financial affairs that applied to the total empire). According to the highly complex governmental structure, the Hungarians—who, in contrast to the peoples of the western half of the monarchy, represented a comparatively self-contained national bloc—were given excessive power, out of all proportion to their number in the total population. The costs were split in a ratio of 70 percent for Cisleithania and 30 percent for Hungary. This distribution formula, however, was to be renegotiated every ten years (a provision that eventually proved a major handicap). Now nothing stood in the way of Franz Joseph's coronation as King of Hungary.

On February 17, 1867, Gyula Andrássy was named the first constitutional prime minister of Hungary. On that day, Ferencz Deák enunciated his memorable expression of thanks to "my friend Andrássy, the man of providence truly bestowed upon us by God's grace." In this context, it is important to remember that at this time the Empress was frequently apostrophized as "the Beautiful Providence granted to the Hungarian fatherland." In Hungary, this and other analogies underlined the belief that two people above all others were responsible for the reorganization of the monarchy: Andrássy and Elisabeth. Conciliation was their joint achievement.

The Bohemia and Moravian diets, on the other hand, had to be shut down in March "because of the advancing concessions to Hungary!!" as Sophie angrily noted.[71] The marshal of Bohemia, Count Hugo Salm, and Prince Edmund Schwarzenberg came to dinner with Archduchess Sophie and gave vent to their powerless resentments. Equally powerless in the face of the decision taken by the Emperor and his prime minister, Beust, were the political figures in Vienna.

Elisabeth's Hungarian friends in Vienna, especially Ida Ferenczy and Max Falk, complained of the court's spiteful acts, expressed primarily in pettinesses. For example, the court carriage, which came every day during the spring to take Max Falk from the offices of the First Austrian Savings

Bank to Schönbrunn, began to arrive late on most days. During spells of warm weather, a closed carriage, upholstered in velvet, was sent; and when the spring rains poured down, an open carriage stood waiting outside the bank. Falk observed court protocol by wearing top hat and tails, with a starched shirt, whenever he called on the Empress; now he was forced to give his lessons sopping wet one day, bathed in perspiration on another. The Empress repaid him with cordiality and friendship, and with her allegiance to the Hungarian cause.[72]

Elisabeth's first visit to Hungary after conciliation was truly a triumphal procession. Josef Eötvös, now minister of culture in Andrássy's government, wrote Max Falk from Budapest, "Your high-born pupil was received among us with flowers. Day by day the enthusiasm grows. Firmly as I believe that never before has a country had a queen more deserving of it, I also know that there has never before been one so beloved. . . . I was always convinced that when a crown breaks, as the Hungarian crown broke in 1848, it can only be welded together again by the flames of feeling aroused in the hearts of the people." For centuries, he went on, Hungarians had hoped "that the nation would love a member of the dynasty truly, with all its heart; and now that we have achieved as much, I have no further misgivings about the future."[73]

Elisabeth paid homage to the compromise by displaying marital affection. Her letters to Franz Joseph from this period are full of tenderness; one from Budapest, for example, reads, "My beloved Emperor! Today I am also very sad, without you it is infinitely empty here. Every minute I think you will walk through the door or I will hurry to you. But I firmly hope that you will return soon, if only the coronation would take place on the 5th."[74] At this time, Sisi was composing all her letters to her husband and her children in Hungarian.

In May 1867, the Emperor, in a throne address, retroactively requested the Imperial Council to grant approval of the conciliation with Hungary, at the same time promising the western half of the empire—the kingdoms and provinces represented in the Imperial Council, as it was to be awkwardly phrased from then on—a further development of the constitution beyond the provisions of the October Diploma of 1860 and the February Patent of 1861, for the new order must, "as its essential consequence, provide the same security for the remaining kingdoms and provinces." He promised the non-Hungarian provinces "every extension of autonomy that corresponds to their wishes and without endangering the total monarchy that can be granted." Franz Joseph characterized the reorganization as "a work of peace and harmony" and begged that "a veil of forgetfulness" be spread "over the recent past, which left deep wounds in the empire."[75]

Weeks before the coronation, the preparations began. Day after day, the Viennese could watch as great quantities of boxes and chests, rugs, even carefully wrapped state coaches, were loaded onto Danube steamers and sent from Vienna to Budapest. From china through flatware to table linens and furniture, everything necessary to housekeeping at the imperial court had to be sent to the castle in Budapest. At the very least, during the celebrations, more than a thousand people had to be provided with meals. The carriage and horses for the equipages were shipped by the same route.

In Budapest, there were different problems. In no time at all (and at horrendous prices, as the diplomats groaned), lodgings had to be found and made ready for the many visitors. The police were kept fully occupied with clearing Budapest of suspicious characters and followers of Kossuth during the festivities. (From his exile, Kossuth had let it be known in no uncertain terms that he would continue to advocate Hungarian independence and that he rejected both the compromise and Franz Joseph's coronation.)

The coronation (June 8, 1867) began at four o'clock in the morning with a twenty-one-gun salute from the Citadel of St. Gerhardsberg (Saint Gerhard's Mountain). At that early hour, people were already streaming from the countryside to the city, to line the streets. The ladies of the magnates kept their dressmakers and hairdressers working through the night to make certain to be ready promptly at six o'clock, when they began to wait in long lines of carriages to drive to the Church of St. Matthew in Budapest.

At seven o'clock, the coronation procession set out from the castle. Eleven standard-bearers, chosen from among the high nobility, preceded Gyula Andrássy, wearing on his chest the large cross of the Order of St. Stephen and carrying the holy crown of Hungary. He was followed by gonfaloniers bearing the state insignia resting on red velvet pillows. Then came Franz Joseph.

The undisputed highlight of the procession was the Queen. All the Hungarian newspapers described her appearance in detail; *Pester Lloyd,* for example, reported, "On her head the diamond crown, the glittering symbol of sovereignty, but the expression of humility in her bowed bearing and traces of the deepest emotion on her noble features—thus she walked—or rather floated—along, as if one of the paintings that adorn the sacred chambers had stepped out of its frame and come to life. The appearance of the Queen here at the holy site produced a deep and lasting impression."[76]

At the solemn cathedral services, Franz Joseph was anointed King by the Primate of Hungary, but it was Andrássy—representing the palatine—who placed the crown on Franz Joseph's head. Elisabeth, too, was anointed, but the crown, following an old custom, was held over her right shoulder —by Andrássy.

The ceremonies were accompanied by the singing of traditional psalms and one modern composition; years earlier, in anticipation of a royal coronation and at the request of the Prince Primate of Hungary, Franz Liszt had composed a coronation mass bursting with nationalist fire. Liszt traveled from Rome to Budapest specifically for the performance, but, as *Pester Lloyd* objected, he was not allowed to conduct his own work because of the "strict ceremonial." The fact that a non-Hungarian conductor and the Imperial Court Choir from Vienna performed this nationalist Hungarian work aroused considerable anger.[77]

A further highlight of the endless festivities was the ceremonial procession at the conclusion of the coronation across the suspension bridge from Buda to Pest. (At the time, the two cities were still separate; they were not combined into Budapest until 1873—five years later.) On this occasion, the ladies were spectators. All the participants in the procession were on horseback. The King rode his coronation white steed. Ludwig von Przibram, an eyewitness, reported:

> What was offered here in the way of splendor of national costumes, in opulence of harnesses and saddles, in value of the gems in clasps, sword belts and pins, in antique weapons, swords studded with turquoise, rubies, and pearls, and so forth, corresponded more to the image of an Oriental display of magnificence than to the descriptions of the impoverishment and exhaustion of the country. The overall impression, however, was nevertheless that of a feudal-aristocratic military review. One truly believed oneself transported to the Middle Ages at the sight of these national barons and gonfaloniers, laden with splendor, followed in silent submission by the beweaponed vassals and men in their service. Most particularly the several mountain tribes, variously clad in hauberks and bearskins, their most striking adornment being animal heads or buffalo horns, recalling the time when Christian Europe was forced to defend itself against incursions from the pagan East. No trace of the bourgeois elements, of guilds, trades.[78]

The luxuriousness formed a harsh contrast to the extremely bad times. Thus, one Hungarian banker, for example, bought a set of antique buttons to go with a splendid Attila for his son, who was riding in the procession; the buttons alone cost 40,000 guldens. Count Edmund Batthyány had Karl Telepy, a painter, reconstruct his costume from medieval drawings. Under it, he wore a silver coat of mail made up of 18,000 links assembled painstakingly by hand. Count Edmund Zichy wore his famous emerald jewelry, valued far above 100,000 guldens, with some stones the size of hen's eggs. Count Lajos Batthyány had a massive silver harness made; the horse blanket alone weighed twenty-four pounds.[79] All this at a time when the Hungarian peasants lived in the most dire poverty.

Foreign observers found many an occasion for criticism behind all the pageantry; thus the Swiss envoy wrote, "The entire procession, in spite of its splendor and genuine grandeur, nevertheless affected the detached observer somewhat like a carnival prank, to which impression the archbishops on horseback contributed most especially. This piece of the Middle Ages simply does not suit our times, neither our level of evolution nor current political events."[80]

What was peculiar about the mounted bishops was described by Przibram: Some of them had been strapped to their horses so that they would not fall off. "Now, if, to top it all off, a horse became excited by the noise and the shots, or if a loose girth slipped, more than one of these riders anxiously threw his arms around his mount's neck, causing the towering headdress that was preventively tied under his chin to dangle from his nape, which contributed not a little to the amusement of the public lining the route."[81]

Countess de Jonghe, the wife of the Belgian envoy, also described the splendor of the festivities. "The Hungarian costumes transform Vulcan into Adonis"; but she also saw the reverse side: "When I saw the handsome gentlemen in their everyday dress: boots, a sort of buttoned-up frock coat, an ugly little neckerchief, rarely a shirt, they seemed to me to present quite a soiled appearance. . . . In all that, there remained a remnant of barbarism."[82]

The solemn procession finally halted before the platform for taking the oath. Here Franz Joseph, garbed in the nearly thousand-year-old cloak and wearing the crown, spoke the formal words: "We shall uphold intact the rights, the constitution, the lawful independence and territorial integrity of Hungary and her attendant lands."

The King's traditional horseback ride to Coronation Hill was followed by a lavish banquet, at which the guests helped themselves generously but Their Majesties took nothing but a little wine. As with all the ceremonies of that day, here, too, Andrássy remained close by the King and Queen. At this banquet, for example, it was his assigned function before and after the meal to pour water into a bowl held by pages, while the Prince Primate handed Their Majesties a towel to dry their hands.

The part played by the people in the ceremonies was mainly that of spectators. Only one event, the Night Festival, held on the common meadow, was open to everyone. Ludwig von Przibram: "Oxen and muttons were roasted on the spit or on veritable funeral pyres; the wine flowed from butts, goulash simmered in giant vats; a mixture of fish, bacon, and paprika was ladled from pots the size of wagon wheels; and all these pleasures were offered free." At the center of all the hubbub, "the figure of the monarch, surrounded by a crowd of men and women, most of them in peasant dress, some of them on their knees, others with their arms raised high, shouting '*Elje!*' and throughout, the twittering fiddles of a gypsy band playing wildly, the whole thing illuminated by the firelight of one of the open pyres—truly a romantic sight."[83]

Two acts of mercy issued after the coronation transported "all Hungary into an almost frenetic enthusiasm," as the Swiss envoy wrote. The first was a general amnesty for all political crimes since 1848 as well as reversion of all confiscated estates. "The amnesty is one of the most unconditional ever issued in the empire, for not a single convict or conspirator was excluded. Even Kossuth and Klapka, if only they swear loyalty to the crowned king and obedience to the laws of the land, can return quite freely to their fatherland."[84] (A short time later, the Emperor issued a corresponding amnesty for the western half of the empire.)

The second great act of mercy was a provocation to all non–Hungarians and to those who had been loyal partisans of the imperial cause in 1848–1849. The traditional coronation gift—a sum of 100,000 guldens—was, at Andrássy's request, passed on to the widows, orphans, and disabled veterans of the Honved—the same nationalist Hungarian army that had fought the imperial forces in 1848–1849. This gift was to be a sign of the Emperor's reconciliation with the nationalist ideas of 1848. The bitter commentary of Crenneville (and many other Austrians): "It is a base act. I would rather be dead than live to see such dishonor! Where is this leading us? To follow the suggestions of such a scoundrel is not governing. Andrássy deserves the gallows even more than he did in 1849."[85] At Andrássy's instigation (he himself had been a Honved officer), the Honved was revived as the Royal

Hungarian Militia, though with the provision that in case of war, it would be subordinate to the common imperial and royal forces. It was never suggested that a similar concession be made to any other nationalist group. A major part in these imperial mercies was ascribed, surely not incorrectly, to Elisabeth's efforts. The Swiss envoy noted that Elisabeth was "currently the most popular figure in all of Hungary."[86]

As a coronation gift, the Hungarian nation presented the Emperor and Empress with Gödöllö Castle to use as their private residence. About an hour's drive from Budapest, the eighteenth-century structure held about a hundred rooms. It was surrounded by a forest of roughly 10,000 hectares, eminently suitable for hunting.

The gift represented a triumph for Elisabeth. After all, Emperor Franz Joseph had turned down her fervent request for this very same castle because he was short of funds. Now Andrássy of all people—in the name of the Hungarian nation—was fulfilling her dream. She showed her gratitude by spending many, many months of each year not in Vienna, but in Gödöllö or Budapest.

Elisabeth's greatest gift to Hungary and to her husband, now the crowned King of Hungary and constitutional monarch, was her readiness to abandon her stubborn refusal to have another child. All the same, the fact that she offered this great sacrifice exclusively for the Hungarian nation was left in no doubt, to understandable anger in Cisleithania. Nor did she conceal the fact that she was determined to see this child treated differently from her older children, who were raised by Archduchess Sophie.

About three months before the expected birth, Elisabeth left Vienna and settled in Budapest, where everything had been made ready for the confinement. The two older children—Gisela and Rudolf—remained in Vienna. Emperor Franz Joseph shuttled back and forth between Vienna and Budapest, to spend time alternately with his children and his wife.

This most private decision to have another child grew out of the most political of motives, and it had political consequences, since it increased the contrast between Transleithania and Cisleithania. The Swiss envoy reported to Bern, "The more, however, the Empress tried to win the Hungarians' sympathies, the more she lost those of the population of the Austrian lands, and the wish was universally voiced that the child she was expecting might be a girl, for there was no denying that, in spite of the Pragmatic Sanction and all the subsequently concluded pacts, a boy born to the Queen of Hungary in the castle in Budapest would become the future King of Hungary, and thus, in time, a separation of the Hungarian crown lands from Austria would be effected."[87]

Ten months after the coronation, in April 1868, Sisi's last child, Marie Valerie, was born in Budapest. In Vienna, there was great relief.

Viennese gossip dealt at great length with this "only" child, determined to recognize none other than Gyula Andrássy as the father. When these tales reached the Empress's ears, they only increased her hatred of the Viennese court.[88] Franz Joseph's paternity cannot be in doubt; it is proven by several intimate letters from the Empress to her husband; and then there is the indisputable fact that Marie Valerie, even more than the other children, resembled the Emperor. In spite of the immense curiosity and almost criminal inquisitiveness of a great many court appointees in an effort to establish an "indiscretion" on the part of the Empress with Andrássy, such attempts have never succeeded. Both the Empress and Andrássy were under constant sharp surveillance by innumerable court members. There can be no doubt that the two loved each other; but that their feelings led even once to a definite "lapse" is, according to the sources, quite unthinkable—quite aside from the fact that Elisabeth was not a woman who found anything in physical love that seemed worth the effort, and that in any and every situation, Andrássy never stopped being the carefully calculating politician.

The christening in the Budapest castle was a large Hungarian celebration, beginning with the arrival of the state coaches of the aristocracy, everything in full ceremonial ritual. Andrássy, as Hungarian prime minister, accompanied by Chancellor Beust, was the only one who drove his carriage directly into the courtyard; during the drive, he was hailed enthusiastically, as always happened wherever he went in Hungary.

The godparents were two of Elisabeth's sisters, ex-Queen Marie of Naples (who proudly wore the Gaeta Medal and who, to everyone's surprise, answered the Prince Primate in Hungarian—using phrases Elisabeth had earlier laboriously taught her to memorize) and Countess Mathilde Trani.

To conclude the festivities, there was a target shoot by the Budapest marksmen, in which the King and Andrássy also participated. Franz Joseph's best shot was a modest "two," and here, too, he was outdone by Andrássy, who, with a "four," brought off the best score of the afternoon.[89]

Not surprisingly, in Vienna, these new Hungarian celebrations aroused unfavorable comments. Archduchess Therese, for example, wrote her father, Archduke Albrecht, "This Hungarian christening truly outrages me, but most of all because the Emperor was so coolly received at the theater. That act shows what an ungrateful nation this is!"[90]

Little Valerie—who was soon known in Vienna only as "the only child"

—was not very warmly welcomed in Cisleithania. Crenneville maliciously wrote about "the Hungarian child. She looks like any other baby, she did not cry, which does not prove Hungarian nationality."[91]

Elisabeth devoted herself to her youngest child with an excessive, exclusive love. A few years later, she told her lady-in-waiting, Countess Festetics, "Now I know what happiness a child brings—now that I have finally had the courage to love her and keep her with me."[92]

Sisi's love of her youngest child seemed so out of all proportion even to Countess Festetics (who was exceedingly well disposed toward the Empress) that she worried: "There is no moderation in her, and she suffers from this ecstasy rather than gaining happiness from it—a trembling fear for her [Valerie's] health, then again the feeling that attempts were being made to turn the little girl against her."[93] Little Valerie's precarious health during the next few years kept everyone around Elisabeth breathless, for the mother reacted with unbounded anxiety to every toothache, every slight cough.

The Empress also demonstrated her preference for Hungary in the next few years to such an extent that it was close to a provocation. Thus, she ordered that a mass be said on the name day of St. Stephen, the patron saint of the Magyars, in, of all places, the parish church of Bad Ischl. Landgravine Fürstenberg: "this little demonstration was attended by *no one* else in the family, *elle seule et ses fidèles*" [only she and her trusty cohorts]. According to the Landgravine, the occasion provided the people of Bad Ischl "with the greatest amusement, especially because there is no Sunday or holiday that she attends the parish church."[94]

For the rest of her life, the Empress kept up her relations with the great men of Hungary—Deák, Andrássy, Falk, Eötvös. Nor did she leave any doubt that she recognized their greatness: "Today Deák comes to dinner, a great honor for me," she wrote the Emperor in 1869.[95] Needless to say, none of the great men of Austria—in politics, the arts, or the sciences— was ever invited to dinner by the Empress, much less having her consider such a visit an honor. The scene of the Queen weeping at the bier of the dead Deák in 1876 became one of Hungary's patriotic icons.

The correspondence between Elisabeth and Andrássy (now as before by way of Ida Ferenczy) was kept up until Andrássy's death in 1890. Andrássy's adoration of the Empress was never in question and can be read in every line of his letters. "You know," he once wrote to Ida, "that I have very many masters—the King, the Lower House, the Upper House, etc. —but only one mistress, and precisely because I know only one woman who can command me, I obey with great pleasure."[96]

Elisabeth's frequent and lengthy stays in Hungary led to constant jealousies in Austria. Another bitter complaint was addressed to the Emperor's loss of authority. The same circles that at one time not only accepted but also approved Archduchess Sophie's influence now criticized Franz Joseph's obvious weakness in the face of his equally energetic wife. Elisabeth had gone too far; she had too clearly demonstrated her power over her imperial spouse.

For her part, the Empress, vulnerable to all criticism, made the disgruntlement of the Viennese court her excuse for withdrawing even more and working herself up into hatred of Vienna. Her private letters are full of derogatory remarks about Vienna and Austria. In 1869, for example, she wrote to Ida Ferenczy that her sister Mathilde was just as unable "to stand whatever is Austrian as can another"—by which she meant herself.[97]

Her Hungarian followers, such as Countess Festetics, for their part now accused the court of having "driven" the Empress "into solitude": "And all because of the unfortunate Compromise with Hungary? It has happened —yes! it was her work—but is it such a great crime to give back to the Emperor a country, one half the monarchy? Is it so delightful to govern with powder and gunshot and with the gallows? Can it be worthy of a noble man to forbid speech to a land that has been promised a constitution?"[98] Here Marie Festetics expressed what could be heard from most Hungarians in endlessly new formulations. No matter how much the Viennese might object, the Hungarians, from the lowliest to the magnates, would not hear a word against their Queen.

Independent of all nationalist jealousies and independent of the person of the Empress, the establishment of the new Dual Monarchy of Austria-Hungary in the Compromise of 1867 met with objections from many "Old Austrians." In 1876, for example, Baron Prokesch-Osten, an Orientalist, wrote to Alexander von Warsberg, a respected writer; the head of the Imperial Cabinet Chancellery, Baron von Braun, considered this letter of such importance that he copied it in his own hand. "For individuals as for nations and states, there is a calamity they bring on themselves. Partition has dealt Austria the death blow. Everything that happens now is its inevitable consequence, and it is immaterial whether she hurries to her future with clear-sighted or blinded eyes—it can only be one and the same."[99]

Opinions of whether the Compromise with Hungary was to be seen as a positive or negative event from the Austrian point of view are divided to this day, more than a hundred years later. True, the alternative in all probability would have been the secession of Hungary from Austria, with events paralleling those in Italy. Discussions of the Compromise therefore inevitably focus on whether Hungary's remaining with Austria was positive or negative. By now, the arguments pro and con have assumed sizable proportions.[100] From the Bohemian view (as well as the south Slavonic, Polish, Slovakian, and so on), however, the Compromise with Hungary could be regarded only as an unfavorable development.

On the other hand, the catastrophe of Königgrätz and the Compromise with liberally governed Hungary resulted in a weakening of imperial power. Emperor Franz Joseph was demoted to the rank of a constitutional monarch. The new constitution and the liberties he granted in 1867 both in Austria and in Hungary were the precondition for the flowering experienced in the economy and the sciences during the subsequent liberal era. The Austrian Empire, governed according to the strict principles of divine right, was transformed into the modern Dual Monarchy of Austria-Hungary, provided with generous liberal laws, headed by Emperor Franz Joseph as a faithful constitutional ruler.

CHAPTER SEVEN

THE BURDENS OF
PUBLIC APPEARANCE

Elisabeth's triumphs in the mid-1860s—Rudolf's liberal upbringing and the Compromise with Hungary—angered court society in Vienna to such a degree that the gulf became unbridgeable. Sisi, for her part, more than ever avoided the Viennese "prison fortress" because she was made to feel the general dislike only too clearly.

Not even the new misfortune in the Habsburg family, the death of Emperor Maximilian of Mexico, was able to melt the icy fronts. At the beginning of July 1867, the news arrived that Max had been shot to death in Querétaro. Archduchess Sophie, aged sixty-two, was unable to surmount this reverse of fortunes. Max had been her favorite son. Her only consolation was "that she had always advised him against, had never for a moment approved" his going to Mexico.[1] She knew that in the final hours of his life, he had behaved with dignity, devoutness, and heroism. "But the memory of the torments he had to undergo, of his friendlessness far from us goes with me through my life and is an indescribable pain."[2] Sophie's spirit was broken. She lived on for another five years—years filled with grieving for her Max. She grew even more pious, giving up all fights, even against her daughter-in-law Elisabeth.

Franz Joseph's mourning for his younger brother was kept within limits. Especially while he was the successor to the throne, Max had been a thoroughly troublesome and dangerous rival. He had everything Franz Joseph lacked—imagination, charm, an interest in science and the arts, liberal tendencies even in politics. Among the common people, Max had always been the favorite brother. It was he in whom the opponents of absolutism set their hopes—as the Emperor knew only too well. Franz Joseph was probably not the right person to console his deeply stricken mother.

In this situation, the expectations placed on the Empress were all the greater. At one time, Max had been her favorite in-law—that is, until his marriage to the beautiful Carlotta. Elisabeth had had no more understanding for the Mexican adventure than Sophie. The misfortune in Mexico might have brought about an understanding between the two women. But these hopes, too, were dashed. Finally, it was Duchess Ludovika who took Sophie in for several weeks in Possenhofen in order to comfort her.

Sophie vehemently refused to meet the "murderer of her son," Napoleon III, who traveled to Salzburg in August 1867 to express his condolences. Sophie could not forgive the French ruler and his wife for having lured Max into the Mexican adventure and then, when he was in difficulties, failing to come to his aid.

Elisabeth had different reasons for wanting to stay far away from this meeting, with its enormous potential for sensationalism. Once again, she claimed ill health, but she was already considering the possibility that she was pregnant (it was a month after the Hungarian coronation) and wrote her husband, "Perhaps I am expecting. During this uncertainty, the Salzburg visit is very depressing. I could weep all day long, that is how infinitely sad I am. My dear soul, comfort me, I need it very much. I have lost all interest, I do not want to go riding or walking, all, all is vanity."[3]

This time, her complaints accomplished nothing. The meeting in Salzburg took place. But the political results of it were meager indeed. The Franco-Austrian alliance against Prussia (which Bismarck feared) did not come about. In the circle around Archduchess Sophie, even the ladies-in-waiting mocked the "parvenu" Napoleon and the very inferior Eugénie, born a mere countess. Therese Fürstenberg: "And all this time they sit cozily together in Salzburg, the representatives of strict legitimacy and the representatives of exactly the opposite, our modest imperial couple, who go to sleep at nine o'clock, and the French, accustomed to splendor and festivities."[4]

It was true: The French far outdid the Austrians when it came to social pastimes. Count Hans Wilczek, who was present at this conference, reported, for example, that during a luncheon at Hellbrunn, the Empress Elisabeth's flatware suddenly disappeared: "The astonishment was great, it could only be a conjuring trick, but which one of us was clever enough to carry it out?" Then Emperor Napoleon, smiling, admitted, "In my lifetime I have acquired various talents, and I make use of them to amuse my friends when cheerfulness begins to flag."[5] As so often at the Viennese court, this time the conversation at table around Franz Joseph and Elisabeth had come to a halt, and Napoleon III had very cleverly dispelled the awkwardness with his sleight of hand.

The meeting at Salzburg turned out to be unproductive; but the two empresses attracted universal attention. They were said to be the two most beautiful women of their day; everyone felt qualified to judge which of the two was more outstanding.

Elisabeth and Eugénie (bowing to the political circumstances) gave no signs of friendship, let alone intimacy, in public. Nevertheless, they understood each other far better than gossip of their alleged rivalry would have it. Count Wilczek reported that one afternoon in Salzburg, Elisabeth paid a call, inconspicuously and entirely privately, on Empress Eugénie, and he, Wilczek, had been made to stand guard outside the door to keep away all other visitors. When Napoleon III himself asked for admittance, the Count's story continued, he became uncertain and went to ask Eugénie whether her strict orders to admit no one really applied to her imperial consort as well. Wilczek: "I opened the door very quietly and had to go through two empty rooms of the apartment, even through the bedroom to the dressing room, where the door was ajar. Across from it there was a large mirror, and with their backs turned to the door behind which I stood, the two empresses were busy with two tape measures, measuring surely the most handsome calves to be found in all of Europe at the time. The sight was indescribable, and I shall not forget it as long as I live."[6]

Empress Eugénie's feet were the talk of Europe. For she wore such short skirts (Austrian observers considered them *demi-monde*) that her ankles were visible. Sisi, on the other hand, appeared in rather old-fashioned, floor-length gowns and preserved the dignity of an imperial majesty.

The opinion prevailed that though Eugénie, who was the older by thirteen years, had more regular features, Elisabeth was by far the more lovely. Other observers, however, discovered qualities in Eugénie other than beauty. "But what conferred to a particular charm on her features," wrote Prince Hohenlohe-Ingelfingen, "was an expression of spirit and assuredness which one misses in her always shy neighbor."[7]

Elisabeth did not accept Napoleon III's return invitation to Paris for the World's Exhibition; by this time she was unquestionably pregnant and had an excuse for letting her husband go alone. In this way, she also avoided a meeting with Pauline Metternich, who, as the wife of the Austrian ambassador in Paris, brilliantly organized the imperial visit and chalked up a triumphant success.

Elisabeth's self-confidence was also evidenced by the fact that, as if it were the most natural thing in the world, she regularly went for fairly long stays in Bavaria. She appeared more and more infrequently in the imperial summer resort of Bad Ischl. She showed openly that in Bavaria she felt better than in Austria and that she enjoyed the turbulent family life around Duchess Ludovika more than the cold and boring life of Vienna.

Cheerfully Elisabeth assured her son Rudolf, six years old at the time, that she went "daily with Grandmama to the house chapel, where a Franciscan reads the mass much more quickly than our Sunday mass,"[8] a remark not calculated to give great pleasure to Archduchess Sophie, who always read these letters. Sisi described her life among her brothers and sisters, who gathered every evening. The next to arrive was "Uncle Mapperl [Max Emanuel of Bavaria] with a pile of books, if it lasts a long time, everyone falls asleep, we spray Sophie with water, to make her very angry, and that is the only entertainment." She often sat up late into the night with her youngest sister, Sophie, she reported, when all the others were already asleep, "and talked ourselves dry, which we could not do all day long."[9] The ladies-in-waiting kept noting the Empress's "infatuation" with Possenhofen.[10]

It was particularly during the 1860s and 1870s that Elisabeth's relationship to her sisters was extremely close. She helped wherever she could, traveled to Zurich for Mathilde's confinement in 1867 and to Rome in 1870 for Marie's; she paid much more attention to her sisters than to her children Gisela and Rudolf. The entourage that accompanied her to Bavaria found the Empress in the family circle "so nice to her sisters and brothers that it is a joy to see her so."[11]

It was true that her son and her older daughter interested Sisi less than ever. The children's first visit to the theater, even Gisela's first-communion celebration, the many significant events in the life of these healthy and well-brought-up children, all took place under the eyes of their father, their grandmother, their tutors and ladies-in-waiting, but not their mother. Therese Fürstenberg found the two children "adorable": They are very good, darling creatures, such nice, friendly children, as if they belonged entirely to the father!"[12] It was their father who, in spite of his many obligations, took the time to go for walks with the children, to take Rudolf along when he went hunting and to go with him to the swimming school or the Circus Renz. Therese Fürstenberg: "The Emperor, barely arrived, yesterday took his children to Renz; that would not have happened if the dragon's lair had not been empty."[13] This was intended to mean that not only did Elisabeth not look after her children, but that she also monopolized her husband to such an extent that there was no time to do things together with the children when she was in Vienna. Therese Fürstenberg mentioned "circumstances which one would rather not bring to light and which are aggravated to the point of being incredible by the stays in Bavaria and the massive intercourse with her sisters."

On another occasion she wrote "that one does not know whether one is dealing with malice, buffoonery, or foolishness, so that one would like to hide so as not to be a witness to it; and one cannot admire enough the inexhaustible forbearance and goodness of 'my lady' [Archduchess Sophie]."[14] Even Valerie's English governess, in whom Elisabeth believed to have a loyal supporter, remarked disdainfully, "The princesses of Possenhofen are all like the women of the demimonde."[15]

The sisters emphasized their resemblance to Elisabeth. Marie Festetics: "Figure—veil—hairstyle—clothes—habits—one never knows 'which is which'!" Even Marie "speaks softly. I almost could not help smiling, she is so eager to resemble the Empress." Mathilde and Sophie were hardly inferior to the two beautiful older sisters. Only Helene was an exception. Marie Festetics found her too severe, "and she looks as if she were a caricature . . . of one of the sisters."[16] If only because of this underlined resemblance, every appearance of the five in Vienna was like a demonstration of their mutual understanding. Sisi's conflicts seemed almost to proliferate, for none of them managed to bridge the gap with Viennese society.

Sisi and her younger daughter spent the greater part of the year in Hungary or in Bavaria, leaving the Emperor alone in Vienna to fulfill all the duties of public appearances. This way of life gave rise to endless criticism, such as Crenneville's diary note for Maundy Thursday, 1869:

"Church service and washing of feet. H. M. [His Majesty] alone, since the Queen!! is in residence in Budapest."[17]

Over and over the Empress disappointed the Viennese by refusing to attend major events. In May 1869, for example, the new opera house, one of the handsomest and most costly buildings in the new Ringstrasse, was opened. With great devotion, the architects had built a special salon for the Empress and furnished it. It was in Renaissance style, with violet silk covering the walls and rich gold ornaments. Everything was arranged to Sisi's taste. Along the walls hung huge paintings of Possenhofen and Lake Starnberg. The imposing table was engraved with Elisabeth's monogram. The ceiling was ornamented with three paintings on themes from Weber's *Oberon*. The center painting depicted Oberon and Titania as rulers of the fairy kingdom, riding in a shell drawn by swans[18]—a very sensitive reference to Elisabeth's favorite play, *A Midsummer Night's Dream* and its world of fairies, which Weber's opera also presented. And since Elisabeth showed no particular interest in music (with the exception of Hungarian gypsy tunes), this roundabout route by way of literature was necessary—even as it shows clearly to what great length the artists went to fitting out the salon of the Empress.

The opening date of the new Vienna Opera was postponed to accommodate Elisabeth, who was, once again, staying in Budapest longer than expected. As if there had not been enough scandal associated with the new building (public criticism of the new opera had cost both architects their lives: A year before the opening, Eduard van der Nüll committed suicide, and August Siccard von Siccardsburg died of grief a few months later), the Empress caused further outrage on the day of the opening. Although she had accepted the invitation and was back in Vienna in good time, she sent her regrets on the shortest of notice, just before the beginning of *Don Giovanni,* the inaugural production—giving as her reason the very threadbare excuse of a sudden "indisposition."

After this resounding failure, Elisabeth made amends by appearing at the Corpus Christi procession for the first time in seven years. Countess de Jonghe wrote to Brussels, "One was furious; if she had not participated this morning, a revolution would surely have broken out." At seven o'clock in the morning, Elisabeth had to stand ready at St. Stephen's Cathedral in full regalia—mauve-colored dress with train, embroidered in silver and studded with diamonds, and her hair in a complicated arrangement. Since the time it took to drive from Schönbrunn into the city has to be added to the three hours of dressing and hair combing, the Empress must have risen at three o'clock—the middle of the night—to march (though, of course, expressing piety and humility in her bearing) at the heart of the procession, the cynosure of all eyes in the midst of her equally sumptuously attired entourage. Countess de Jonghe: "The poor woman's dress was low-cut, and a gentle but quite chilly breeze was blowing. Twelve princesses followed, all with long trains and low necklines. If they are not all ill by tonight, they are very lucky." All the spectators were agreed on Elisabeth's beauty. Countess de Jonghe: "The Empress's walk resembled the glide of a beautiful swan on the water. To the last moment, one was sure she would not appear, for this beauty loves neither the sun nor being in public."[19]

Not only the spectators, but also the participants in these court spectacles expressed annoyance at Elisabeth's frequent regretful refusals. For when the Empress declined to appear, the ladies-in-waiting, for example, were also deprived of an opportunity to parade publicly in her entourage—in splendidly embroidered capes over gala gowns, adorned with the best pieces from the family jewels.

At the Maundy Thursday ceremonies, still others were disadvantaged. It was the Emperor's custom to perform the washing of the feet of twelve old men from the poorhouse, who were then treated to a lavish meal and given equally lavish presents. The Empress performed the same duty on twelve poor old women. But since the Emperor was generally the only one to perform this act of public humility, every year twelve poor old women were deprived of the enjoyment of charitable gifts and the events of this great celebration. Counting at least forty Maundy Thursdays without the Empress, the total amounts to a considerable number of neglected people.

The Empress had her own methods for visits to orphanages, hospitals, and poorhouses. Here, too, she set no great store by representing the court at ceremonial receptions addressed by the directors of the institutions, nor did she care for adulatory newspapers reports of imperial visits to the poor and the infirm. She always arrived unannounced, accompanied only by a lady-in-waiting. What was important to her was the business at hand: to make her own way to the inmates, to observe whether they were being adequately treated and cared for. For example, she always asked for samples from the institutional kitchens, tasted the morsels, praised and criticized. She spoke at length with the patients, inquired about their families, and helped out with money and encouragement wherever she could.

The Empress's approach angered both the institution supervisors and the court organization (which she simply bypassed), but she was an enormous success with the patients themselves. She was seen as a good fairy, especially because of her very plain and humane way of dealing with simple people. Her every word was eagerly received and retold in the families for generations."[20]

Nurturing the poor and infirm was a tradition in the Bavarian ducal family. It differed from the social appearances of the Austrian imperial family particularly in being personal and not limited to institutions. This was the tradition Elisabeth tried to carry on.

But increasingly, she linked these visits to her fascination with aberrations of every kind. Even as a young woman, visiting Verona, she sought out the Negro Education Institute, a missionary school in which black slaves whose freedom had been bought were trained and then sent back to Africa with Christian missions. Her visit to a cholera hospital in Munich in 1874 was not the fulfillment of a charitable duty but was occasioned by pure curiosity. This visit was also utterly thoughtless, because of the risk of contagion; it took place without the Emperor's knowledge. Accompanied by the loyal Countess Festetics, Elisabeth walked along the rows of beds of the dying. She held the hand of one young man who died only hours later; she remarked to Countess Festetics, "He is dying, and one day he will happily welcome me there."[21] This was the same Elisabeth who, in Vienna, exhibited unparalleled fastidiousness by fleeing at the mere threat of cholera.

More and more clearly, she gave preference to insane asylums— even abroad, where there was no question of representing the crown; her visits were purely private. She inquired at length about the histories of the patients. At that time, treatment of the insane was still in its infancy. It was considered sufficient in most cases to keep the patients locked up, to feed them and care for them. Elisabeth had a burning interest in new therapeutic experiments; she was, for example, present on one occasion when a patient was hypnotized—at the time, a new and sensational procedure.

This striking interest in mental illness and its treatment might have indicated the beginning of a commitment. But Elisabeth never took the step leading to active support of new therapies, though in 1871 she proposed a singular name-day wish to the Emperor: "Since you have asked me what would give me pleasure, I beg you for either a young Bengal tiger (Zoological Garden in Berlin, 3 cubs) or a locket. What I would like best of all is a fully equipped insane asylum. Now you have enough choices." And four days later: "My thanks in advance for the locket. . . . Unfortunately, you appear not to have given the other two things a moment's consideration."[22] Elisabeth's interest in insane asylums was seen as another of her many bizarre ways, frequently ridiculed and disparaged as completely unsuitable to an empress.

Elisabeth exhibited equally unsuitable behavior at the few visits she paid to artists, such as the most sought-after painter of Vienna at the time, Hans Makart, who had just garnered a great deal of attention with his monumental canvas, *Caterina Cornaro* (today in the Hermes Villa in the Tiergarten in Lainz). One day, unannounced, the Empress arrived at Makart's studio. William Unger, a student of Makart's who happened to be present, described the scene.

> For a long time, she stood silently, as she had come, almost motionless, before the painting of *Caterina Cornaro*. I am certain that I observed that it made an impression on the Empress, but she found not a word to say to Makart, and it was also not in his nature to . . . break the silence by a casual remark. Finally, the Empress turned to him with the question, "As I hear, you have a brace of Scottish greyhounds, may I see them?" Makart had the dogs brought in. The Empress, who herself owned a brace of magnificent examples of this breed, . . . looked at the animals for a time, expressed her thanks, and then took her leave; she lost not a word on the picture.[23]

Elisabeth's excessive shyness could appear insulting at such times.

Especially when dealing with the nobility, she made absolutely no effort, provoking quite unnecessary animosities. Scornfully, she commented on the mindless "chatter" of the ladies of the court—those worthy of being admitted to her private rooms among them—and the court dignitaries. Her silences during the salons were an increasingly clear expression of contempt, though not of her lack of competence. Her behavior was interpreted as eccentricity. She did not adapt to the order of the court, allowing herself an occasional ironic joke, at times, when the correct stiffness of the person she was speaking to annoyed her enough, even annoying him with a mocking smile.

Beginning in 1867, Sisi stayed away from politics—whether or not by her own choice cannot be gathered from the sources. Even in the critical summer of 1870, after the outbreak of the Franco-Prussian War, she showed little interest in the extremely tense situation and the heated discussions in Vienna. Some saw in this war a chance for Austria to make good the setback of 1866 and to fight against Prussia on the side of France. Bavaria (committed by treaties concluded in 1866) stood on the side of

Prussia, as did the other South German lands which, four years earlier, had been allied with Austria against Prussia. Intervention on the part of Austria on the side of France would therefore have taken her into the war against her former German allies, not against Prussia alone. The situation was extremely difficult, nor was Austria's military situation propitious. The quick successes of the Prussian army soon demolished any hope of wrestling Prussia to the ground. Austria-Hungary remained neutral.

Even in this tense situation, family relations in the imperial household improved hardly at all. Quite the contrary: Elisabeth, refusing to spend the summer in Bad Ischl with her mother-in-law, took the children to Neuberg on the Mürz. Elisabeth to Franz Joseph: "to spend the entire summer with your Mama—you will understand that I would prefer to avoid it."[24]

Elisabeth worried especially about her three brothers, who were at the front—on the Prussian side against France. As far as Austria's future was concerned, in any case, she was most pessimistic. In August 1870, she wrote to her husband, "But perhaps we will vegetate for a couple of years more before our turn comes. What do you think?"[25]

In September 1870, the Republic was proclaimed in Paris. Napoleon III's empire was toppled. The troops of the new Italy marched into Rome and put an end to what was left of the Papal States. Sisi's sister, the ex-Queen of Naples, fled from Rome to Bavaria. In none of these events, not even the proclamation of Wilhelm I as Emperor of Germany in Versailles, did Elisabeth take much of an interest. The people in her entourage, already in a state of deep excitement, felt further irritated in the fall of 1870 when, once again (this time with her two daughters, Gisela and Valerie), she left Vienna and went to Merano for the winter.

This time, Archduchess Sophie, usually very reticent in this regard, confided to her diary her distress about her daughter-in-law and complained of the "news that Sisi wants to spend the winter far from Vienna again and take her two daughters along to Merano to spend the winter. My poor son. And Rudolf complains at having to be separated from his sisters for such a long time."[26] Crown Prince Rudolf, by now twelve years old, for the first time expressed opposition to his mother. He wrote to his grandmother Sophie, of all people, "so poor Papa must be separated in this difficult time from dear Mama. I assume with joy the handsome office of being dear Papa's sole support!" Sophie incorporated these sentiments in her diary.[27]

The Crown Prince's disappointment is surely understandable. Elisabeth's stay in Merano lasted from October 17, 1870, to June 5, 1871 (with one short interruption in March 1871, when she went to Vienna because of the death of her sister-in-law Marie Annunziata). The Emperor was compelled to travel to Merano if he wanted to see his wife and daughters. The following summer—1871—Elisabeth spent largely in Bavaria and Bad Ischl. As early as October 1871, she went to Merano again, and there she remained (with one short intermission in Budapest because of Gisela's engagement) until May 15, 1872. The Bavarian sisters took turns staying with her.

The recently engaged lady-in-waiting, Countess Marie Festetics, went along to Merano. She had hesitated for a long time before accepting the post—though it was surely a great honor to be offered it. The Empress's charm was captivating, she reflected, "but if one 10th of what Bellegarde [Crenneville's successor as the imperial adjutant general] says is true—I have a most uneasy feeling." It took Gyula Andrássy to dispel the stern Countess's reservations and assure her that it was her duty to make the sacrifice for her fatherland (that is, Hungary) by agreeing to become a lady-in-waiting: "You can accomplish much good—and the Queen is in need of loyalty."[28] If it required so much encouragement to a Hungarian woman to place herself near the Empress, one can easily picture the reservations of the Austrian, and most especially the Bohemian aristocracy.

Countess Festetics had heard so many negative things that now she noted with astonishment and sheer surprise that, though Elisabeth was determined to get away from Vienna, on her travels she lived very quietly and that there was no sign of any sort of adventure. Festetics wrote in her diary, "until now I see only that the Empress goes walking a great deal with her large dog . . . that she wears a thick blue veil—that if she takes anyone along, it is Ferenczy and she avoids people—all that is highly regrettable —but really nothing bad."[29]

One of the few entertainments was characteristic of Elisabeth. The Empress sent a carriage for the 400-pound giantess Eugénie, who was exhibited in a stall in Merano, to have her brought to her residence, Castle Trattmansdorff, so she could view her.[30]

On one of their walks, Elisabeth asked the Countess (of course, speaking in Hungarian), "Aren't you surprised that I live like a hermit?" And she went on to explain

> I have no alternative but to choose this life. In the great world,
> I have been so persecuted, so many evil things have been said
> about me, I have been so maligned, been so deeply offended and
> hurt—and God sees my soul, sees that I have never done any-
> thing evil. So I thought I would find a society that does not

disturb my peace and offers me pleasure. The forest does not
hurt me. . . . Nature is much more rewarding than humanity.[31]

After one of her conversations with the Empress, Marie Festetics's diary
notes, "She is not at all banal, and one can sense her contemplative life in
everything she says! How sad that she fritters away all her time with
brooding and has no need to do anything. She has a talent for intellectual
activity and altogether a thirst for freedom which finds any limitation
terrible."[32] Over and over, the lady-in-waiting praised Elisabeth's human
warmth and her outstanding intellectual abilities, which revealed themselves in an often sarcastic but always apt wit. But Marie Festetics also saw
the negative traits: "In 'Her' there is everything, but as in a disordered
museum—pure treasures, which go unused. Nor does she know what to
do with them."[33]

On the other hand, the Countess had complete understanding for the
Empress's rejection of the court. As long as Marie Festetics was in Vienna,
she criticized the emptiness, formality, mendacity of life at court: "a life
that destroys the spirit." She regretted that "the futility—the decay of life
values is felt nowhere so strongly as at a court, once one accustoms oneself
to the outward brilliance and becomes so well aware of how it merely lends
glitter to the rot, like the golden tinsel on the Christmas nuts and apples;
—how well I understand the Empress's frustration."[34]

But complaints of this sort were hardly sufficient reason for the Empress
to leave Vienna for such long periods. There must have been other, more
compelling grounds, which we can only guess at. It was precisely during
this time of Elisabeth's absence that Vienna underwent a total reversal in
foreign policy. Beust, the former chancellor and foreign minister, was
dismissed. His successor was none other than Gyula Andrássy, who had
been aspiring of this office (with Elisabeth's forceful support) since 1867.
No documents from this period exist to prove any influencing control on
Elisabeth's part in Andrássy's favor. Other factors were in play as well,
especially Beust's rather belligerent attitude during the Franco-Prussian
War, while Andrássy favored a neutral position for Austria-Hungary—
and made his view prevail.

In any case, Andrássy saw himself as the savior of the monarchy. Very
similarly, Elisabeth later stated in a poem that in 1871, Andrássy had
"pulled the carriage out of the mud."[35] He formulated an entirely new
policy. While Beust had been Bismarck's great antagonist, Andrássy now
sought to find an understanding with the German Empire, thus complying
with Bismarck's intentions. Both—Bismarck as well as Andrássy—worked

toward the great goal of reconciling the enemies of Königgrätz and to conclude a German-Austrian alliance. This objective was realized in the Dual Alliance of 1879.

Precisely what happened to cause the dismissal of Count Beust and the appointment of Andrássy is not clear to this day, in spite of extensive research.[36] The principal open question concerns the role played by Elisabeth in the appointment. That she kept her distance entirely is hard to believe. For even in later years, she made her aversion to Beust and her agreement with Andrássy's policy only too clear. But her political interference had made bad blood as early as 1867, especially as it concerned Andrássy personally. Now, when this statesman was responsible not only for Hungarian affairs, but also for the foreign policy of the entire empire, the fear in Vienna was great that the liberal Andrássy might—as he had so masterfully done in 1860—use Elisabeth again for his political ends and thus grasp greater authority than any other foreign minister before or after him. This concern was understandable. It is therefore quite possible (but simply not provable, because no correspondence between the Emperor and Empress from this critical period is preserved) that, with her long absences from Vienna precisely during the critical period of Andrássy's nomination, Elisabeth was intent on foiling all discussions about her political influence. As things were, she strengthened Andrássy's position. The conservative Court Party (the one that was called the Kamarilla by the Liberals) around Archduke Albrecht and Archduchess Sophie complained about the new political course of events. Even Andrássy was unable to make any changes in Sophie's hatred of Prussia. And the logically liberal course of domestic policy—which would soon succeed in rescinding the Concordat—brought additional sad hours to the ailing old woman. On New Year's Eve of 1871, after Andrássy had become foreign minister, Sophie recorded her great bitterness in her diary: "liberalism with all its experts, all its impossibilities. May God have mercy on us!"[37]

The relationship between Elisabeth and Andrássy continued, even if nothing more about it was heard in public. The correspondence went on by way of three Hungarian intermediaries within Elisabeth's closest circle: Ida Ferenczy; the new lady-in-waiting, Countess Festetics; and the new chief chamberlain, Baron Nopcsa, who was a friend of Andrássy's. The largest and most important part of this correspondence was destroyed— probably for good reason—by Ida Ferenczy. The few letters that survive include, along with unimportant suggestions, Andrássy's request that the Empress improve relations with the German Empire to the best of her ability, especially through court visits. And in spite of all her reservations about the "Prussians," Elisabeth really did make active efforts. She maintained good, even cordial, relations with the German Crown Prince and his wife, especially with Crown Princess Victoria, who was about the same age and very prominent in politics. Elisabeth cultivated these contacts because Andrássy considered them important and appropriate, but also because the German Crown Princess, a champion of liberalism, was politically entirely on her (and Andrássy's) side. Elisabeth also continued to pass on Andrássy's wishes to her husband—when, for example, it became time to appoint a new Hungarian prime minister. "If only you could win over Tisza, he would surely be best of all. Yesterday Andrássy was still with me," she wrote in 1874.[38]

When, at the end of April 1872, displeasure at the Empress's overly long absence from Vienna grew louder, it was Andrássy who wrote to Ida Ferenczy in Merano, "I should like to ask you to bring your influence to bear on Her Majesty so that she will not remain away from the capital for long."[39] And in fact, about two weeks after receipt of the letter, Elisabeth returned to Vienna.

Though the Empress had paid little enough attention to either of her two older children, when the time came to find a suitable candidate to marry fifteen-year-old Gisela, she sprang into action. Elisabeth always bemoaned her own fate, having been married so young, and yet she gave her daughter no chance to take time with her marriage, let alone to go her own way. (It was not until she came to her youngest, Marie Valerie, that Elisabeth was generous, declaring that Valerie would be allowed to marry even a chimney sweep if she really had her heart set on it.) As Duchess Ludovika had done at one time, now Elisabeth also brought family relations into play.

Gisela was not very pretty. The royal Catholic houses of Europe, moreover, had no suitable princes to offer during the 1870s. Once more, therefore, Bavaria was considered, the candidate being Prince Leopold, the second son of Prince Luitpold. He was ten years older than Gisela.

Leopold was not free. Negotiations concerning a marriage with Princess Amalie of Coburg had been going on for a long time. This same Amalie of Coburg was adored by Sisi's youngest brother, Max Emanuel ("Mapperl"); but probably no one at the Viennese court except the Empress was aware of this. Now there was great astonishment at Elisabeth's unusual action; she invited the quasi-groom of Princess Amalie to Budapest and Gödöllö in the spring of 1872. The official occasion was a snipe hunt.

Elisabeth to Leopold: "In this way, it will, it is to be hoped, raise no questions."[40]

Leopold dragged out the negotiations with the House of Coburg because, as he said, they were unable to agree on a dowry (a matter of 50,000 guldens was at stake). Princess Amalie suspected nothing. Furthermore, as luck would have it, she happened to be in Budapest at the same time as Leopold, giving rise to many awkward situations.

Leopold's engagement to Gisela was settled after only a few days. Countess Festetics about the bride: "She is happy, as a child will be—a beautiful couple they are not."[41] The Emperor wrote to his mother, "The whole thing was simple, cordial, patriarchal, although Sisi and I simply are not patriarchs yet."[42] Sophie's comment: "The domestic happiness of the little one and the good Leopold seems assured to me, but the marriage cannot count as a great match."[43]

In spite of everything, the groom had a bad conscience; writing from Hungary, he expressed his concern to one of his aunts. "If only it does not harm A[malie]. Actually I am very concerned. . . . When I left, I met A on the stairs; she looked very cheerful. The poor thing. . . ." Leopold, however, quickly found comfort. "Fate determined it that way, and it could not be otherwise. Gisela is so nice, has her father's kind eyes."[44] For Leopold, the connection with the daughter of the Emperor of Austria was worth all the trouble. From her grandfather Archduke Franz Karl and her grandmother Sophie alone Gisela received 500,000 guldens on the occasion of her marriage.[45]

With the utmost cleverness, Elisabeth allowed a considerable length of time to pass, so that the scorned Princess Amalie might recover from her shock. Then—in May 1875—she personally, with the help of Countess Marie Festetics, negotiated the marriage of her brother to Amalie of Coburg.[46] Even on this occasion, however, Elisabeth did not suppress her poor opinion of marriage, declaring it a "strange fancy, when one is so young to give up one's freedom. But one never knows the value of what one has until one has lost it."[47] The marriage arranged by Elisabeth was a very happy one.

Whether Elisabeth made any efforts to prepare her daughter for marriage is not known. That she did not deal with such prosaic matters as the trousseau, leaving its acquisition entirely to her staff, was a matter of course. Remembering the devotion and personal commitment with which at one time Duchess Ludovika looked after young Elisabeth, how even mother-in-law Sophie spent months preparing everything for the new

Empress with the greatest care—from bed linens through the knickknacks to the rugs—one can understand why the entourage railed "at the heartlessness of the Empress," as Festetics's diary records.[48]

It was true that Gisela was colorless in every respect and not a daughter one could easily show off. She had nothing of her mother's and brother's flights of fancy. In her modesty she resembled her father, and modest as she was, she did not rebel against her mother. In the end, she became a good, calm, somewhat plump wife and mother of four. Not a single word of Elisabeth's is preserved that might indicate a loving affection for her older daughter.

Shortly after Gisela's engagement, the substitute mother of the two older children, Archduchess Sophie, who had been ill for some time, died. Thus the only person who might have paid attention to the bride, not yet sixteen years old, was removed. Sophie's death was a difficult one and took a long time. Her will to live had been broken by the death of her second son, Max. Bravely she had endured, fulfilling her duties to her husband, her children and grandchildren, and the Habsburg family. But during the last few years, she had neither taken part in political affairs, the direction of which she found deeply distasteful, nor dared to advise Elisabeth.

Sophie's ties to the Emperor continued deep and close. Everyone at the court could witness the Emperor's grief at his mother's decline. Unflaggingly solicitous, he watched at her bedside for many hours. He had straw strewn along the Burgplatz to lessen the rumble of the heavy carriages. At this time, Elisabeth was in Merano, but she interrupted her cure at the news of Sophie's imminent death and returned to Vienna.

For ten days and nights the imperial family was at Sophie's deathbed. She experienced several cerebral hemorrhages and from time to time lost the power of speech.

Countess Festetics described Sophie's hour of death. "The entire court was assembled, ministers of the imp. house, royal court. no! It was horrible." When noon passed, a certain restlessness made itself felt among the waiting group, "it increased with each minute—waiting is disconcerting! Then everyone grew hungry, death would not cross the threshold. No! I shall never forget it; at court everything is different from the way it is with other people, I know that, but death is not a ceremony—death no court appointment." Around seven o'clock in the evening the "redeeming word was spoken. Unheralded by the arrival of death, one voice said rather loudly: 'Their Supreme Majesties will proceed to dinner.' It sounded almost silly—and then all the others were excused and ran away."

But Elisabeth remained. Like the others, she had not eaten in ten hours. She stayed at the bedside until Sophie died the following morning. Marie Festetics expressed her praise: "She has brought her heart along from her forests—that is why no one understands her here, where the germ cell of all feeling must smother in the customary formality."[49]

On the morning of May 27, 1872, Archduchess Sophie—"this spiritually powerful woman," as Crenneville wrote—died. The Emperor's heavy grief was visible to all. The Swiss envoy reported to Bern, "For the Emperor, the loss of his mother is a heavy blow, since she alone still provided him with the amenities of family life, which he must lack in his immediate circle." All commentators were agreed on Sophie's political influence, especially in the important years from 1848 to 1859. Even the Swiss envoy, who had several objections to Sophie's political line, stressed as much in his report. "Without doubt, Archduchess Sophie was the most significant political figure of all the women of the imperial house after Maria Theresia."[50] All these commentaries implicitly criticized Elisabeth's inactivity as the negative contrast to Sophie's fulfillment of her duties.

Count Hübner, clearly alluding to Elisabeth, remarked in his diary that Sophie's death was "a great loss to the imperial family, to those who care about court tradition and understand its significance."[51] And after the interment, Elisabeth's devoted lady-in-waiting, Marie Festetics, overheard the cruel words, "We have buried our Empress"[52]—an unmistakable indication that in almost twenty years, Elisabeth had not managed to be accepted.

Sophie left a letter of farewell (written in 1862) in which she summarized her principles one last time, stressing the paramount position of the Emperor even within the family: "Dear children, remain, all of you, united in unalterable love and loyalty and reverence of the younger for their Emperor and lord." Nor did this document leave any doubt of her aversion to liberalism, appealing to her son: "my valued Franzi, since you are charged with a heavy responsibility for your Catholic empire, which you must *most of all* keep Catholic, though at the same time you will bestow paternal care on the several millions of different faiths." She exhorted to strength and adherence to the old principles: "Only weakness, giving up on the part of the well-intentioned, . . . encourages the pioneers of the revolution."[53]

These were the precepts of old, of the time of the divine right of kings and the time of the Concordat. In the meantime, events had passed beyond these principles. Since 1867, Austria-Hungary had a liberal constitution. The Concordat was abolished. There had been liberal school reform. Franz

Joseph was no longer an autocratic Emperor but a constitutional monarch who heeded the constitution's commands. Sophie's old enemies, the Constitution Party, the Liberals, were in power both in Austria and in Hungary. The one-time revolutionary and émigré Gyula Andrássy was the imperial and royal foreign minister. With the death of Archduchess Sophie, the era of the Catholic-conservative Habsburg state, which some mourned and others despised, had clearly come to an end. In Sophie, a symbol of the old days died.

The discord between Sophie and Elisabeth was public knowledge all over the monarchy. The extent to which these originally personal quarrels had affected politics was equally common knowledge. The death of the old Archduchess therefore meant a change in the political climate. Now, especially in Hungary, some were waiting for Elisabeth to seize her chance and become politically active. Her liberal ideas were known. Her intelligence could be relied on, as she had proven more than once, most overtly in 1867.

On the day after Sophie's funeral, Countess Festetics wrote in her diary, "without a doubt, a serious break in time! The firm bond between 'today' and the past is dissolved! Will the Empress want what she is capable of? Will she show herself now, or has she given up in the eternal struggle? —Has she become too listless, or has she lost all pleasure in the work?"[54]

The hopes (and the corresponding fears of the Court Party) were not fulfilled. Elisabeth continued to flee the court. Even Countess Festetics, who was always ready to excuse the Empress, noted with concern how much Elisabeth retired into "physical and spiritual isolation." She wrote, "All this is also nourishment to her bent to idleness. What is painful today will be comfortable in a while, and she will do less and less and people will go into battle more and more and she?—she will grow poorer and poorer for all her riches, and no one will remember that she was driven into isolation."[55]

Furthermore, Elisabeth's shyness was already—in the early 1870s— taking on grave proportions, making political as well as social activities more and more unlikely. By now Elisabeth was afraid, not only of large crowds—curious onlookers as well as hangers-on—but also of court officials. Marie Festetics: "What astonishes me every time is the fear of meeting people from the court—an aide-de-camp (let alone an adjutant general) in view is enough to unsheathe all her weapons; out come the blue veil, the large parasol, the fan, and the next path that turns off the road is taken." Before such an imminent meeting with a courtier, Elisabeth, obviously frightened, said, "My God! Let us run, I can almost hear them addressing us"—or: "Oh, dear! Bellegarde! He hates me so much that I break out in perspiration when he looks at me!" and similar remarks.[56]

The more Elisabeth fell to brooding and philosophizing, the less occupied and the more bored she grew, the more the chasm between her and the tirelessly active, dutiful Emperor widened. Marie Festetics: "He offends her . . . in spite of his adoration, and he calls whatever is enthusiasm in her, eccentricity [literally: sky-scraping]."[57]

There are dozens of witnesses to the absolutely desolate boredom of dinner with the supreme family. It truly was not easy: No one was allowed to address the Emperor, to ask him a question or simply to tell him something. But he himself maintained an icy silence, since he was not in any way a gifted conversationalist. At table, he did only what he was there to do: He ate, and as quickly and sparingly as possible. When he finished, the meal was over. No attention was paid to whether the other diners had reached even the main course or not. (The Hôtel Sacher, it was known, experienced an enormous increase in business because the archdukes, starved after a family dinner, would rush there so as finally to get some food in their stomachs.) Nor was it any better when the Empress was at table. For she ate even less than the Emperor and finished even sooner.

Elisabeth had long since given up any attempts to keep conversation going at meals. The fact is that when she had tried, she had picked the wrong subjects, attempting to engage the Emperor in talk of Schopenhauer's philosophy and Heine's poetry. She seldom took part in shared meals (since she was constantly dieting) and so escaped being with her husband—and the attendants. By now, the couple rarely met except on special occasions, such as birthday celebrations and religious holidays, when they were surrounded by ladies-in-waiting and adjutants, in an atmosphere even little Valerie complained of—as when the imperial family gathered, once a year, under the Christmas tree and felt so embarrassed and knew each other so little that they were unable to manage any conversation.

The Emperor's youngest daughter did not get to know what genuine family life was like until she herself was married and living far away from her imperial parents. Only then did Valerie realize how joyless her years at the Viennese court had been. Her diary records her enthusiasm about her first Christmas after her marriage: "The happy togetherness with the household staff made Christmas Eve such a happy occasion as I had never yet known. What a contrast with the Christmas trees in the castle, where everything was so stiff and awkward."[58]

Criticism of Viennese court life was voiced particularly by the Hungarians, who had always been suspicious of Vienna. Thus, Marie Festetics recorded, "the 10th is the court ball. What a lot of trivial matters of great importance there are—what silly little things are talked about, what striving is endemic to human nature, and how pitifully 'appearances' wreak their mischief and what value is placed in 'pinchbeck'?? one can see most hatefully at court."[59] And on another occasion, "All around, almost everyone is an egotist. Every archduke is an enclosed little court of his own with his aspirations and his little world! All of them feel the great imperial court to be something to which they, too, must bow, so it is like a pressure, and because of 'convention,' a meeting of minds, and I mean an intimate one, is out of the question, and so the good traits of each are of use to no one or to only a very few."[60]

The strict etiquette of the court can certainly be cited as a reason for this coldness and emptiness. But the same etiquette prevailed in other times as well. And other empresses—even the much busier Maria Theresia—thoroughly understood how to safeguard an area of freedom for themselves and their families. (One need think only of Queen Victoria's family life!) And this traditional task of the female members of the House of Habsburg, to cultivate an almost bourgeois family circle in the midst of court protocol, was one Elisabeth did not fulfill—in contrast to her mother-in-law. For Archduchess Sophie had managed to create some kind of family life even under these extremely unfavorable circumstances; she had done it by shared breakfasts and suppers in the more intimate circle, by long talks with the children, children-in-law, and grandchildren, by showing concern for their sorrows, by praise and criticism. Her death in 1872 therefore created a perceptible void; it is fair to say that, for all practical purposes, her passing put an end to family life in the imperial household.

Nor was it as if the Empress had rejected every form of etiquette. When it came to her own person, she was fully insistent that the rules governing behavior to an imperial majesty be observed. Countess Festetics realized as much when she wrote in her diary, "It cannot be denied that protocol is a very clever invention. Without it, Olympus would have toppled long ago. As soon as the gods show human frailties, they stop standing on their altars, and people stop bending their knees to them. The same is true for the world. But it does not have a happy effect on the images of the deities, and once idolatry no longer serves them, everything goes awry. For they will want to have both."[61]

The wedding of the Emperor's older daughter, Gisela, in April 1873 meant little more to Elisabeth than a dreaded public appearance. The bride was sixteen, the mother of the bride thirty-five years old. As usual, little notice was taken of the daughter. Elisabeth's appearance outshone the festivities. Marie Festetics: "how beautiful she was in her silver-embroidered dress; her cascading, truly shimmering hair with the glittering tiara is beyond words. But the most beautiful is not her physical being—no it is what floats above it—It is something like an atmosphere—a breath of loveliness—nobility—grace—girlishness—modesty and yet again a grandeur over 'Her' that is deeply touching."[62]

At the railroad station, there followed a great family scene to speed the newlyweds on their way. *Neues Wiener Tagblatt:* "the most touching sight was offered by Crown Prince Rudolf; he wept unceasingly and was unable either to stem the flow of tears or to suppress his sobs, even though he visibly struggled to control himself." The two older children had grown up in such isolation from the rest of the family that they had become unusually close. The separation was extremely hard on both—sixteen-year-old Gisela as well as fourteen-year-old Rudolf. Gisela, too, sobbed as she said her good-byes. The Emperor had tears in his eyes. "Nevertheless, the Princess, accompanied by her mother, walked with firm steps, greeting the deeply bowing spectators in a friendly way, toward the train compartment, which she entered."[63] By far the most composed was the mother of the bride. Her only show of emotion, while all the others sobbed and wept, was to press "her handkerchief to her tear-filled eyes."

The Empress exhibited a similar composure when, nine months later, she became a grandmother for the first time. She wrote to Ida Ferenczy about the christening of little Elisabeth (later, Countess Seefried), "Thank God, another day is past. It is bitter for me to remain here, quite alone, and unable to speak with anyone. I miss you unspeakably. Today was the christening, mother and child are so healthy that they will live to be 100. This to reassure you that the state of their health will not keep me here."[64]

Elisabeth also remained remarkably cool when Gisela gave birth to a second daughter. She wrote to her son (in Hungarian), "Gisela's child is of a rare ugliness, but very lively, it looks exactly like Gisela."[65]

The Emperor turned his first grandchild's birth into an occasion to compliment his beautiful wife. Proudly he wrote to his son-in-law, Prince Leopold, "When I look at your mother-in-law, when I think of our fox hunts, it seems very strange to me to think that she can be a grandmother already."[66]

A few weeks after Gisela's wedding, the Imperial House was faced with a task of the first order requiring public appearances: the Vienna World

Exhibition. The preparations had taken years. The rotunda, built in the Prater, as the center of the exhibition, was to be an emblem of modern Vienna. (Countess Festetics: "A monstrously large building, man only an atom before it!")

In view of the expected huge profits, speculation on the Vienna stock exchange took on hitherto unknown proportions. Even people in modest circumstances gambled their scraped-together savings. The rich (up to Archduke Ludwig Viktor, the Emperor's brother) invested millions in the hope of multiplying them many times over. For a while, their hopes were fulfilled—in pure paper profits, as it turned out soon after the opening of the exhibition. Thousands of people lost their wealth in the notorious crash of 1873. A wave of suicides among the formerly wealthy and now dirt poor accompanied the pomp of the exhibition, which failed to meet the high expectations placed in it.

But Vienna went on celebrating. Marie Festetics was outraged by the "frightening extravagance": "Almost no one appears in the same dress twice. I thought that it must be terribly rich people who were filling the boxes, foyers, and salons. One is literally blinded, so many diamonds—pearls—lace are put on show. And now gradually they are saying that with few exceptions, all of it is stock-exchange wealth, does not permanently belong to anyone—perhaps today, tomorrow no longer. Shame on the times. One grows fat on the losses of the other . . . lives on the profit that have turned the other into a beggar."[67]

Visitors were expected from every corner of the globe. Everyone, even the Emperor, was extremely nervous. For it was very difficult to lodge the many high-ranking visitors (at the expense of the Imperial House) in a manner suited to their rank and to prevent quarrels about precedence.

One of the first arrivals was Crown Prince Friedrich Wilhelm of Prussia —the same man who had been a leading general fighting the Austrians at Königgrätz. All the old feelings of hate for the enemy of 1866 had to be suppressed. The German Crown Prince and his Princess were to be received with special cordiality and with demonstrative brotherly love—along the lines of Andrássy's new policies.

And even on the opening day of the exhibition, when the tension was at its height, everything went wrong in connection with the German Crown Prince and Princess. The carriages left the visitors' quarters, the little castle of Hetzendorf, for the rotunda too soon, while the Emperor was still waiting with his entourage at the Hofburg. This meant that the Crown Prince and Princess could not, as was proper, be received at the Prater by the Emperor, their official host. Marie Festetics:

The emperor flushed deep red with anger and shouted in a passion: "but it is incredible that something of this sort should happen . . . what a mess, for him to arrive and for me not to be there. Who ordered the carriages so early, against my orders?" Count Grünne was pale to his lips but said quietly, "I did, Your Majesty." The Emperor rushed at Grünne: "I will hold you responsible for . . ." When suddenly the Empress was standing next to him. She had entered unnoticed while all of us were following the embarrassing scene in rapt silence. She had placed her hand on his arm. As if she had touched him with a magic wand, the word died on his lips, and she looked at him with such a charmingly pleading glance that the threatening frown disappeared, and pulling him away, she said, "Please let us not waste any more time, let us go."—So soft, so calm was this voice. He followed willingly.[68]

The Crown Prince's party was delayed for a while, and everything ran its planned course after all. Once again, the court had received proof of the great influence the Empress had on Franz Joseph's mood, had seen him yield as soon as she took a stand. No matter how given to outbursts of temper the Emperor might be—his wife succeeded in calming him down at her first attempt.

There were the inaugural speeches, the imperial anthem, a walk lasting for hours through the exhibition, with its many pavilions from every nation under the sun—all this in oppressive heat, with bad air and hordes of curious onlookers. Dinners, soirees, and large balls alternated with each other. Invitations and counterinvitations, courtesy calls had to be endured. After only a few days, Marie Festetics, concerned, wrote in her diary, "if the Empress will be able to endure it?—it is too much, it goes on too long. They expect too much of her."[69]

Hardly had the German Crown Prince and Princess departed than King Leopold of the Belgians arrived. Marie Festetics: "very engaging, not likable and I believe very *médisant* [a great scandalmonger]." "With so many people around, one has hardly enough strength to reflect on everything," she complained and had no chance to mention all the "lesser" royal personages: "it would be fair to say that all Germany has already been here."

The Prince and Princess of Montenegro also came: "he is a handsome robber chief, she the Princess from Trieste. . . . Everything is simply wild," the exhausted lady-in-waiting's diary notes tersely.[70]

Then Czar Alexander II arrived—with the successor to his throne and his wife, and with Grand Duke Vladimir, "seventy items of entourage," as Marie Festetics wrote, and Foreign Minister Count Gorchakov. This visit had to be organized with "extreme police protection, to which we are not accustomed."[71]

Elisabeth—along with the Emperor and the archdukes—had to be at the railway station to receive the Czar's family. She appeared in a purple silk dress, a white embroidered jacket bordered in Siberian silver fox, and a white hat, as all the Viennese newspapers reported the following day. She held punctiliously to protocol: a slight bow to the Czar, followed by a kiss on the hand of the Czarina; then an embrace and kiss for the Grand Duchess, a bow to the Grand Duke and acceptance of a kiss on her hand, then merely a "slight nod to the ladies of the entourage." She had no need to concern herself with the rest of the Russians.

Stern Count Crenneville, of all people, was chosen to look after the Russians. He complained, "What an effort it is to remember the names and faces of all the Muscovites at all the presentations."[72] Elisabeth's efforts were extremely moderate. After a dinner with the Russian visitors, Crenneville noted, "Sisi made bored faces and is stiff." Once, when she was supposed to drive to a parade with the Russian Grand Duchess, Elisabeth kept the visitor waiting in vain. "To the general regret," according to Crenneville, the Grand Duchess had to drive alone because Sisi "has to get her sleep." The Emperor came in for praise once again: "The poor master is untiringly kind, may it bear fruit vis-à-vis the false Muscovites."[73]

Then came the English successor to the throne, Edward, Prince of Wales, a favorite of the Viennese ladies but a scourge of protocol because he was never on time for any function. Nor did he otherwise submit to any constraints; Crenneville: "At the ball, it is said . . . because it was too warm, he broke a window with a chair."[74]

The German Empress Augusta also arrived. Crenneville: "Ridiculous, florid, garrulous dolled-up creature, with the voice of a corpse."[75] As hostess, it fell to Elisabeth to make special efforts for the German Empress. Crenneville: "At her side, Sisi makes the impression of a bored deaf-mute, the Emperor on the other hand dutifully amiable and touchingly attentive."[76]

Another visitor, Queen Isabella of Spain, was, according to Crenneville, "very decked out and yet ugly, taciturn. Prince of Asturia her son a bright little fellow."[77] The King and Queen of Württemberg also left an impression. "He is most insignificant," wrote Marie Festetics. "She makes a most imposing appearance . . . the only one who is a queen except for the Empress!"[78]

Marie Festetics: "This is not life, but a fantasy!!! The World Exhibition is like a purgatory that devours everything. All other interests seem to have disappeared, and the craze for making merry as wildly as possible prevails over everything else, as if in truth all seriousness had disappeared. It is almost frightening."[79]

In late July, Elisabeth retired to Payerbach near Reichenau, to the good mountain air far from the Viennese hubbub. She was criticized by the court officials, who saw how untiringly the Emperor and even the Crown Prince, not yet quite fifteen years old, fulfilled their public functions. This time, Elisabeth claimed that she was "unwell." The dates of her monthly "indisposition" were widely known at court and did, of course, have to be taken into consideration when it came to social events. Elisabeth always made a considerable fuss about this debility, and in her letters (for example, to Ida Ferenczy, but also when she wrote to the Emperor) would discuss its course in detail. Without a moment's hesitation, she would decline to participate in official events (for which special preparations had been made just with her in mind) because of her menstruation—and very openly and publicly. The ladies-in-waiting made fun of the Empress, for they were unused to such habits from the former Empress Maria Anna and from Archduchess Sophie. They saw the emphasis on Sisi's "indisposition" for what it was—another pretext for escaping from the Hofburg for a few days.

Once in Payerbach, Elisabeth decided not to return to Vienna but to go on to Bad Ischl. She had had enough of foreign princes, of soirees and balls and fireworks. She wanted her peace and quiet, wanted to take her solitary walks and horseback rides.

She proposed that her husband take a long holiday as well, and she reproached him when he would not comply. "You already spoil all the people so much that you no longer even receive thanks for your exaggerated courtesy, on the contrary. Actually you agree with me, but you won't admit it. It is always that way when you have been stupid. . . . "[80]

Elisabeth's absence caused great confusion in Vienna. After all, she was one of the main attractions of the Vienna World Exhibition. Every royal personage who visited the city naturally wished to see, not only the always diligent Emperor, but also the world-renowned Empress. With great regret, they were forced to accept the fact that Elisabeth was "unwell" and in need of pure air far from Vienna.

Only one sovereign could not be moved to accept these reasons: Nasr-ed-Din, the Shah of Persia. In late July, he arrived in Vienna with a most colorful entourage, a multitude of court dignitaries and relatives, as well as two "ladies of pleasure," as Crenneville wrote (using the phrase in English), forty wethers (gelded rams), many horses, five dogs, and four gazelles (intended as a gift to the Empress, who was known to love animals). Once again, it fell to Crenneville to look after the visitors. He referred to the Persians only as "the horde" and "the riffraff": "One can have no idea what a crew this is, by comparison, the Turks are gentlemen."[81]

The Shah was quartered in Laxenburg, where once the Emperor and Sisi had spent their honeymoon and where Crown Prince Rudolf had been born. For weeks, the place had undergone renovations, all according to specifications supplied by the "Center of the Universe." In the middle of the imperial apartments, a kitchen with an open hearth was installed, where the consecrated wethers, reserved for the Shah, could be roasted on the spit. An adjoining chamber served as a slaughtering block, where daily the butcher killed a lamb in the Shah's presence. On the parquetry floors, hearths were installed for the narghiles (long water pipes that required smoldering coals). At the last minute, a chicken coop was built because the Shah was in the habit of personally slaughtering three fat hens each morning at sunrise.

The Shah hardly ever kept to his schedule, arriving late everywhere (generally by hours, while the Emperor and his entourage stood waiting). He would give as his reason that his astrologer had told him that the stars were not auspicious for the appointment and that it was better to wait for an hour or more.

The Shah was particularly zealous and crude in his flirtations with women, and the newspapers devoted endless columns to his choice of the moment. Thus, even at the first official tour through the exhibition, with the Emperor himself acting as guide, the Shah seized the opportunity when a rather dubious young woman, out of curiosity, pushed her way close to him. *Neues Wiener Tagblatt:* "He remained standing before the charmingly smiling Dulcinea, looked her over attentively through his eyeglasses . . . pinched her arm with an amused laugh, passed his fingers over her bosom, and then nodded while dampening his lips with his tongue, as always when something pleased him." Immediately, the young woman was deferentially absorbed into the Persian entourage. Franz Joseph discreetly stared off in a different direction. Finally, *Neues Wiener Tagblatt* advised "certain good mothers" "to spare themselves the sending of letters and photographs of their daughters to the Shah's supreme master of ceremonies," for the "Center of the Universe" could not "bestow his favors on all the penniless daughters of negligent parents."[82]

The patience of the Shah's imperial host was tested to the fullest. Crenneville was at the end of his tether. The newspapers began to voice some critical remarks. In *Neues Wiener Tagblatt,* Moritz Szeps calculated the value of the Shah's diamonds, not forgetting to mention that under the "glorious rule" of the Shah, "a flat four million have died of starvation." He called the Shah a "despot steeped in blood" and spoke of "delusions of grandeur": "It strikes us as anything but chivalric for a prince to slaughter wethers with his own hands, soiling with blood the splendid chambers hallowed by history. The ritual mysteries of the Shah and his court are so unclean, so repulsive, that it is not inappropriate to give voice to feelings of pure outrage."[83]

With her departure for Payerbach, obviously the Empress had removed herself from all these strains. Since she intended to leave Payerbach not for Vienna, but for Bad Ischl, the Shah had no opportunity to meet her. He was determined, however, to see the Empress in Vienna, and he was insistent. The court feared that he would "stay himself into" a meeting with Elisabeth—that is, simply remain in Laxenburg until he could set eyes on her. The confusion was enormous; the Shah simply could not be persuaded to leave. The liberal newspapers defended Elisabeth and objected to the Emperor's excessive politeness toward such a shameless guest. "We can understand that the Austrian court observes international custom and grants the Shah the honors due a high sovereign," the cautious article read. "But the refusal of being received by the Empress might serve the Shah as an indication that offenses against manners and decency do not go unpunished." And, "But if one were to ask why Europe showed the Shah, at heart a powerless tyrant, so many marks of respect, no sensible answer would be forthcoming."[84]

The pressure—and the fear that the Shah might stay in Vienna even longer—finally became so great that Elisabeth made up her mind to appear at the Shah's farewell soiree in Schönbrunn. All day, there had been great confusion. For the Shah had let it be known that he was ill and therefore could not come to Schönbrunn. It was said "that this indisposition was seen as the first step in the threatened 'staying himself into' an audience with the Empress." Elisabeth's concession really did come at the very last moment: "Only when the hour that had been set for the party to begin had passed was it possible to send word to Laxenburg that the Shah would be allowed to present himself to the Empress. His indisposition was relieved, and the Shah went to the feast, which, as a result of this incident, began after a delay of an hour and a half."[85]

Marie Festetics: "It was very amusing when he caught sight of her the first time. Bang, he stopped short right in front of her, took out his golden eyeglasses, and calmly looked her over from the topmost curl to the tips of her toes—'ah qu'elle est belle' escaped him."[86]

Neues Wiener Tagblatt: "When Nasr-ed-Din stood before the Empress, it is said, he showed a bashfulness and self-consciousness never observed in him before, and during the hour the monarch granted him to remain at her side, he was allegedly of an almost boyish timidity in every gesture and every word."[87]

The presence of the beautiful Empress and the fireworks at the Gloriette of Schönbrunn cheered the Shah to such an extent that he declared this evening to be the highlight of his entire European trip and actually decided to return to Persia the following morning. Three days later, the Empress left as well, to go to Bad Ischl. The Emperor continued to receive the visitors to the exhibition, assisted by the Crown Prince.

In the midst of the festivities, disturbing news intruded of an outbreak of cholera. As early as July 2, Crenneville wrote to his wife, "In Schönbrunn (ne le racontez pas) a silver cleaner . . . died of cholera yesterday, they are trying to hush it up, it is said not to be an epidemic." The cases of illness increased. In spite of the secrecy, strangers became reluctant to come to the exhibition. The crowd at the rotunda in the Prater was far smaller than expected. More and more clearly, a huge financial loss loomed.

Total hysteria broke out at the Viennese court as well. At the slightest stomachache, everyone imagined himself seriously ill. Nor was the Empress, concerned with her health and highly susceptible, an exception. Whether or not it was a pretext, after returning from Bad Ischl when King Victor Emmanuel of Italy was to be feted in Vienna, she took to her bed complaining of a stomach ailment, naturally fearful of cholera. Crenneville to his wife: "Victor Emmanuel was unable to make Sisi's acquaintnace, it is a genuine stomach cold from which she suffers."[88]

According to Marie Festetics, the King of Italy was "desperate at not seeing her. Andrássy also. It gives rise to talk and articles that might better have been avoided, now that a reconciliation is being arranged."[89]

The story had made the rounds that the Empress was refusing to receive Victor Emmanuel because in 1860, he had driven her sister Marie from Naples. Foreign Minister Andrássy had no use for resentments of this sort in 1873, when he was resolutely aiming at an alliance between Austria and her former antagonist. Sisi's stomach upset lasted so long that she was also unable to lend her presence to the visit of the German Emperor Wilhelm I in October. This time she remained in Gödöllö. Since late July, Emperor Franz Joseph had single-handedly dispatched all the social duties attendant on the World Exhibition—with the exception of the farewell for the Shah.

After the Vienna World Exhibition closed, December 1873 brought still further festive events, this time in celebration of the twenty-five-year jubilee of Franz Joseph's reign. Once again there were fireworks and illuminations, solemn church services, ceremonial speeches, and an amnesty for all those in prison for lèse majesté. In Trieste and Prague, there were "a few fanatical or childish demonstrations" against the Imperial House, as the Swiss envoy reported. His overall impression of the mood in the monarchy, however, was favorable: The jubilee had "given conclusive evidence that the peoples of Austria harbor strong and warm sympathies for their monarch, who, though unfortunate in most of his wars, nevertheless in times of calm and peace is always zealous and upright in his concern for the welfare of his lands."[90]

The newspapers listed the achievements of Franz Joseph's reign—that is, since 1848. Especially the capital, Vienna, had changed during this period, and to an extent surpassing all previous centuries. The number of inhabitants had grown from 500,000 (including the suburbs, 600,000) to over a million. The expansion of the city—the demolition of the old city walls and the creation of the Ringstrasse—had brought about a modern Vienna. The regulation of the Danube was about to be completed, the time of the frequent floods was over. The *Fremdenblatt:* "In the near future, the proud merchant vessels of every nation will sail in on the broad surface of the Danube."[91] The formerly poor hygienic conditions in Vienna had been abruptly improved by the construction of the new aqueduct bringing in spring water. A great many schools, churches, and hospitals had been opened. The new university at the Schottentor was being built; the Künstlerhaus, the Musikvereingebäude, the new opera house, the Stadttheater (municipal theater), and the Volksoper had already been completed. Since 1848, Vienna had been given eleven new bridges alone.

There are no indications that the Empress took an interest in this progress within the empire, that she felt any pride. She made herself unpleasantly conspicuous by interrupting her stay in Hungary for a mere two days for the jubilee. But even during these two days, she was as inaccessible as she could manage. For her arrival at the Vienna railroad station, she wore a hat "with an impenetrable silver-gray gauze veil," the newspapers noted. At the solemn drive through Vienna of Their Majesties during the nightly "illumination," the Emperor and the Crown Prince rode in an open carriage, the Empress followed in a closed coach so that she could not be recognized.

Elisabeth's demeanor during a walk along the Ringstrasse created a great stir. Marie Festetics, who was among her companions, recalled:

> She was recognized, cheered, and surrounded. At first all went well; she smiled, thanked everyone. But people kept streaming toward her from all sides!—There was no going forward, no going back; the space around us grew narrower and narrower —the circle grew smaller and smaller, we were in mortal danger;—I begged, entreated, she and I could not breathe. Beads of perspiration born of fear stood on our foreheads. My voice could not be heard at all, and I literally shouted: "You are crushing the Empress—for God's sake, Help!—Help!—Air— air." . . . After an hour or more, we managed to make our way to the carriage—Quickly she was inside, and finally we drew a deep breath, but she was utterly exhausted and quite ill![92]

Of course, these people were friendly and not in the least malicious. Countess Festetics's terror was surely hysterical. But during the entire occurrence, Elisabeth uttered not a word, was totally passive, helpless, intimidated. There was no possibility here of an understanding between the Empress and the people. The daily papers painted a picture of the scene that differed sharply from Marie Festetics's account. No mention of the fact that the ovation had taken on a threatening dimension: "The noble lady was recognized by the public and greeted with the most enthusiastic cheers. Her Majesty was visibly touched and very gladdened by this ovation."[93]

Elisabeth's behavior on the occasion of the jubilee was strongly criticized. There was even a critical newspaper article ("The Strange Woman") that mentioned her infrequent presence in the capital. The Emperor made this article the occasion to rebuke sharply the delegation of Concordia, a journalists' association, which came to deliver its congratulations. He had, he said, "agreed to the removal of the regulations that placed barriers in the way of the free expression of opinion." But he hoped that now the press "would discuss the national situation with reasonable objectivity and in the patriotic spirit, far from intrusions in the sphere of private and family life."[94]

The louder the criticism grew, the stronger was Elisabeth's anger at Vienna and the more she talked herself into a literal persecution mania, finally seeing nothing but enemies on all sides. Marie Festetics listed these antagonists as follows:

There is the Bohemian Party, which thinks it is her fault that the Emperor will not be crowned, for she hates Bohemia because she loves Hungary!

There are the Ultramontanes, who say she is not pious enough. She holds the Emperor back, they claim, otherwise he would long ago have subordinated the state to the Church.

There are the Centralists, they say, in turn, that she is against absolutism. If her influence could be broken, it would be easy to return to the old form of government!

Dualism is said to be her work! That is the only thing in which she has a hand. I will admit that. But it was surely not to Austria's disadvantage; once everything begins to totter—He will remain King of Hungary!"[95]

Most of this is probably true. But the Empress did make enemies. She justified her stand by ascribing mistakes to others—her mother-in-law; her first chatelaine, Countess Esterházy; the Viennese court altogether. Marie Festetics (and in reading her statements, we must always bear in mind that she was an ardent admirer of Elisabeth) wrote about this quality, which intensified in subsequent years: "Even if she is wrong, she finds something to serve as a reason not to do this or that."[96] Elisabeth refused to fulfill the traditional duties, both of a wife and mother and of an empress, but lacked anything more meaningful to fill her time. Countess Festetics was worried for good reason. "She is an enthusiast, and her principal occupation is brooding. How dangerous that is. She wants to get to the bottom of everything and searches around too much, it seems to me that the healthiest mind would have to suffer from this kind of life. She needs an occupation, a position, and since the only one Sisi could have is one that is repugnant to her nature, everything in her lies fallow." The lady-in-waiting saw that Elisabeth "never [did] anything by halves": "how, with what energy, she learned Hungarian—it was a mortification. Now Archduchess Valerie fills her soul completely. But for a being with her endowments, the relationship with her child does not furnish enough intellectual nourishment, and she has little other occupation. It is clear to see how unfulfilled she is."[97]

CHAPTER EIGHT

THE QUEEN RIDES TO HOUNDS

In 1873, the year of the World Exhibition, Elisabeth met more social obligations than in any year before or after—though more under duress than of her own free will, and with many of her familiar caprices. Now she was in need of rest—far from Vienna, of course. Elisabeth wrote to her mother from Gödöllö, "here one lives so quietly without relatives and vexations, and there [in Vienna] the whole imperial family! Here, too, I am at ease as in the country, can walk alone, go for drives alone"—but especially go horseback riding.[1]

The Puszta sands seemed made for the hours of daily rides. There were still wild horses in the region. The landscape was romantic and rugged, just what Elisabeth loved. She also took part in the most difficult hunts. The wife of the Belgian envoy, Countess de Jonghe, wrote, "It is supposedly wonderful to see her at the head of all the riders and always in the most dangerous spots. The enthusiasm of the Magyars knows no bounds, they break their necks to follow more closely. Young Elemer Batthyány almost lost his life, fortunately only his horse died. Near their beautiful queen, the Hungarians become royalist to a degree that, it is said, if these hunts had begun before the elections, the government could have incurred great savings."[2]

Gödöllö was Elisabeth's empire. Here her laws prevailed, and they had little to do with questions of rank and protocol. Visitors were selected, not according to their standing among the nobility, but by their riding skills. Elisabeth collected around herself the elite of the Austro-Hungarian horsemen—young, rich aristocrats who spent their lives almost exclusively at race courses and on hunting and had no obligations or work of any kind.

For years, her favorite was Count Nikolaus Esterházy, the famous "Sports Niki." His huge estate adjoined Gödöllö. He was famous for the thoroughbreds he raised, and he supplied Elisabeth's stables with horses. During the 1860s and 1870s, Niki Esterházy was the ranking horseman of Austria-Hungary, for many years the undisputed master of the hunt, one of the founders of the Jockey Club in Vienna—besides being a dashing, good-looking bachelor and social lion, two years younger than the Empress.

"The handsome prince" Rudolf Liechtenstein, could also be found at Elisabeth's side. He was (and remained all his life) a bachelor, a little younger than the Empress, a well-known horseman and ladies' man. During the 1870s, he also distinguished himself as a composer of art songs. He was devoted to the Empress in perpetual adoration.

Count Elemer Batthyány's frequent presence at Gödöllö caused a particular sensation. For he was a son of the Hungarian prime minister whom the young Emperor Franz Joseph had executed in 1849 under humiliating circumstances. Batthyány's widow as well as Elemer refused to meet the Emperor; they went so far as to snub him openly by refusing to greet him when they met by accident.

Elisabeth never left the slightest doubt that she condemned most harshly the methods of Austrian policy and justice during the Revolution of 1848. She brought considerable understanding to young Batthyány's intransigent stance and obliged him in any way she could.

Of course, she invited Elemer to Gödöllö even when the Emperor was in residence—and, of course, Batthyány turned away whenever Franz Joseph came near him. And no matter how rigidly Franz Joseph insisted on court etiquette—here in his wife's company, he allowed Batthyány to snub him without protesting; he made desperate efforts to ignore awkward situations, and in this way he, too, showed some understanding.

Of course, Gyula Andrássy was also a frequent visitor at Gödöllö. He was still an outstanding horseman. But he could not easily keep up with the competition offered by Esterházy, Liechtenstein, and Batthyány; after all, he was the imperial and royal foreign minister, had his hands full with work, and could not spend his days on fancy riding tricks. Furthermore, by now he was past fifty. His interest in racing had waned.

Sisi also invited her niece Baroness Marie Wallersee to Gödöllö. The daughter of her brother Ludwig and the actress Henriette Mendel of Munich, Marie was not only a strikingly pretty girl (a fact which, as was well known, Sisi valued highly), but also an outstanding horsewoman. Elisabeth enjoyed provoking the nobility with the girl's presence. For in spite of her close kinship with the Empress, "little Wallersee" was not socially acceptable, because her mother was a bourgeoise and she was a "bastard." Elisabeth turned Marie into her creature, fitting her out in the latest fashions, teaching her the necessary social polish and the required haughtiness toward men. She clearly relished the sensation the beautiful young woman at her side created. Marie: "Three times a week there was a hunt. Oh, it was marvelous! On horseback, Elisabeth looked enchanting. Her hair lay in heavy braids around her head, over it she wore a top hat. Her dress fitted like a glove; she wore high laced boots with tiny spurs and she pulled three pairs of gloves over each other; the unavoidable fan was always stuck in the saddle." (The Empress used the fan swiftly whenever curious onlookers appeared, to hide her face.)

Elisabeth also made the young girl the confidante of her secrets. Marie Wallersee: "I thoroughly enjoyed the long rides with the Empress, who occasionally found pleasure in disguising herself as a boy. Of course, I had to follow her example; but I still recall the shame that tortured me when I saw myself for the first time in trousers. Elisabeth imagined that this crazy whim was not generally known in Gödöllö; in reality, everyone was talking about it. Only Franz Joseph, I believe, had no idea of what was everyone's secret."

Other habits Elisabeth cultivated in Gödöllö also soon became matters of general knowledge, at least at the Viennese court. For example, the Empress had an arena built like the one her father had had in Munich at one time. There she put her mounts through their paces and worked with circus horses. Marie: "It was a charming sight when Aunt in her black velvet riding costume led her small Arab horse around the ring in dancing step. True, for an empress, it was a somewhat uncommon occupation."[3]

Even the Bavarian family, inured to odd behavior by Max, was not a little astonished when Valerie proudly told Prince Regent Luitpold, "Uncle Luitpold, Mama on her horse can already jump through two hoops."[4]

Her instructors in these circus tricks were the most famous equestriennes from the Circus Renz, Emilie Loiset and Elise Petzold. Elise especially was a frequent guest at Gödöllö and was considered a personal confidante of the Empress. Elisabeth showed her affection for Elise (who was also known as Elise Renz in court circles) by making a gift to her of one of her favorite horses, Lord Byron, and inviting the circus equestrienne along at the most elegant hunts. When twenty-five-year-old Emilie Loiset had a fatal accident in the ring, few newspapers omitted mentioning that she had been close to the Empress of Austria.

The head of the Circus Renz, Ernst Renz, occasionally advised Elisabeth when she was buying a horse. He, too, became a celebrity in the more exalted circles because of the Empress's favors.

At Gödöllö, a former circus director named Gustav Hüttemann gave the Empress lessons in dressage. Emperor Franz Joseph put up with all these activities resignedly, even preserving his sense of humor, telling Herr Hüttemann, "Well, the roles are reversed. Tonight, the Empress takes the stage as the equestrienne. You put the horse through its paces. And I function as your equerry."

Besides the circus riders, Elisabeth also invited gypsies. Because she loved gypsy music, she ignored all the unpleasantness these visits brought with them, glossing it over generously with laughter. The men servants, including the Emperor's personal valet, were outraged: "In Gödöllö, all sorts of shady folk roamed about—filthy men, women, and children muffled in rags. Often the Empress brought a whole community to the castle, had them entertained and lavishly provided with food."[5]

All curiosities and abnormalities attracted Elisabeth's interest. Once she ordered the latest circus attraction to be sent from Budapest to Gödöllö —two black girls joined together. "But the mere thought horrified the Emperor so much that he absolutely refused to look at them," the Empress wrote to Duchess Ludovika, who was, after all, used to such things on a large scale from her Max.[6]

The more intensively and exclusively Elisabeth occupied herself with horseback riding, the more time she spent in the company of horsemen, the more dissatisfied she became with Gödöllö: The hunting season was too short, since it did not begin until after the harvest (in early September) and traditionally ended on November 3, St. Hubert's Day. The dense forests were an obstacle to the hunt. Most of all, there were too few fences and too few chances to jump; the countryside offered merely small open ditches instead of the high fences typical of the English hunts. And riding to hounds on the English model was the ne plus ultra even for Austrian gentleman riders. Whoever could not boast of successes or at least participation in English hunts—as Niki Esterházy, for example, could—was not taken seriously among the horseback elite.

Ex-Queen Marie of Naples, Sisi's beautiful sister, had already followed the fashion and (with the help of the House of Rothschild) had bought a hunting lodge in England. Now she gushed to Elisabeth about the English hunts and invited her sister to England in 1874. The official reason for this, the Empress's first trip to England, was that little Marie Valerie absolutely required ocean bathing, for which the Isle of Wight was eminently suited.

In order to forestall any political complications, Elisabeth traveled under the alias of Countess von Hohenembs. Nevertheless, she could not avoid paying a courtesy call on Queen Victoria, who was spending the summer at Osborne, also on the Isle of Wight. Elisabeth's surprise visit, on very short notice, was not convenient for the Queen. Somewhat annoyed, Victoria wrote to her daughter, "The Empress insisted on seeing me today. All of us are disappointed. I cannot call her a great beauty. She has beautiful skin, a magnificent figure, and pretty little eyes and a not very pretty nose. I must say that she looks much better in *grande tenue* [dressed in state], when she can be seen with her beautiful hair, which is to her advantage. I think Alix [the Princess of Wales] much prettier than the Empress."

The Prussian Crown Princess Victoria, the British Queen's oldest daughter, was also on the Isle of Wight, at Sandown. She, too, was disappointed by Elisabeth's visit and wrote to her mother, "The Empress of Austria also came here yesterday—she would not accept any of the refreshments she was offered. But afterwards we heard that she had gone to the hotel in Sandown and dined there, which we did find fairly strange. She did not look her best, and I believe her beauty has faded a great deal since last year, though she is still pretty! Nor was she dressed very becomingly." Victoria agreed with her mother that the English Princess Alix was prettier; "but the Empress is more striking than any lady I have ever seen. The beautiful Empress is a very strange person, as far as her daily schedule is concerned. The greatest part of the morning she spends sleeping on the sofa. She dines around 4 and rides all evening quite alone and never less than three hours and gets furious when anything else is planned. She wants to see no one or be seen anywhere."[7]

Sisi, for her part, wrote to her husband about her (only) official visiting day on Wight—"the most fatiguing day of the whole trip," she noted. "The Queen was very friendly, said nothing unpleasant, but I do not care for her. . . . I was altogether very polite, and everyone seemed astonished. But now I have done everything. Everyone understands completely that I want quiet, and they do not want to embarrass me."[8] To Duchess Ludovika she wrote that "such things bore" her. Sisi's letters in general often mentioned boredom. It was probably also the reason for her dream of faraway places. "What I would most like to do is go to America for a little while, the ocean draws me so much whenever I look at it. Valerie would like to go along, too, for she found the sea voyage charming. All the others with few exceptions were sick."[9]

Instead of paying another call on the Queen, Elisabeth sought out celebrated stud farms to look at English hunting horses, but she made no purchases. Elisabeth to her husband: "I also saw some very beautiful horses, but all of them very expensive. The one I would most have liked to have cost 25,000 fl. so naturally unaffordable."[10]

A bare two weeks later, however, she had what she wanted. A rich English lady absolutely insisted (as Sisi wrote the Emperor) on making her a present of a large English hunter. Though she had assured Lady Dudley "that it was not customary for me to accept gifts,"[11] she finally did accept. To the Emperor of Austria, this incident was an embarrassment; for Sisi it was a triumph: As had happened in 1867, when Gödöllö Castle was at stake, she was given by strangers what Franz Joseph refused her.

During her stay in London, Elisabeth went riding in Hyde Park, causing quite a stir. She visited the Wax Museum and an insane asylum. She also paid a call on another member of the British Royal Family, the Duke of Teck, but made fun of the Duchess: "She is enormously fat, I've never seen anything like it. All the time I wondered what she looked like in bed."

She went swimming in the ocean but wrote to Vienna reassuringly, "While I bathe, Marie Festetics and one of the women are always in the water, so that the onlookers at the shore and on the heights do not know which one I am. And here, too, I bathe, contrary to my custom, in a light flannel." Furthermore, she tried to persuade her very busy husband to visit her. "How unfortunate that you cannot come. After the many maneuvers, I have gratefully received the list, you could really come for two weeks, visit London, skip up to Scotland, visit the Queen, and do a little hunting near London. We have horses and everything here, so it would be a pity not to use them. Think about it for a few days before immediately saying *no* with your usual obstinacy."

Franz Joseph could not work a trip to England into his program. As usual, he relaxed by hunting, for which Elisabeth had full understanding: "I beg you, don't let anyone interfere with your plans," she wrote from England before her departure. "The hunts are such an essential recreation for you that I would be desolate if my return were to deprive you of one. I know that you love me, even without any demonstrations, and the reason we are happy together is that we never make things awkward for one another."[12]

These letters make hardly any mention of politics. On one occasion, Sisi wrote to the Emperor that she had allowed Prince Edward, the British heir, to explain the Spanish question to her. Bloody battles between Republicans and Carlists had followed the abdication of Amadeo I in 1873, and they were ended only by Alfonso XII's accession. Elisabeth found the British successor's discourse practical, "for I have not looked at a newspaper, but neither has the Crown Princess [Alexandra], which reassured me."[13]

Ex-Queen Marie of Naples introduced her older sister to members of the international hunting and racing set. At this time, the group included the Baltazzi brothers from Vienna. Because of their very real triumphs on the English racecourses, they were accepted by the highest-ranking English society, a feat they had not managed in Vienna. "One must be very careful," Marie Festetics's diary noted. "The brothers live entirely for the sport, they ride marvelously, make their way everywhere, are dangerous for us because they are entirely English and because of the horses."[14]

The lady-in-waiting knew precisely how much bad blood any accord between the Empress and such social climbers would cause. But after all, the Baltazzis—along with their equally ambitious sister, Helene Vetsera— had infiltrated the society around ex-Queen Marie of Naples. Half a step more would take them to the Empress.

The Habsburg and Baltazzi Vetsera families met for the first time in England, at the most famous racecourses of the day. Elisabeth presented a cup to Hector Baltazzi, the winner of a race on the Isle of Wight. Champagne flowed like water. It was a lively company of rich, idle, elegant people basking in the presence of a beautiful ex-queen and a still more beautiful empress. The influence of Marie of Naples on Elisabeth was especially strong during this period. Marie Festetics ascribed it to "the whole England agitation."[15]

Marie, whose only legitimate child had died soon after its birth in 1870 and who continued to feel unhappy in her marriage, had no duties of any kind. A beautiful queen in exile, financed by the House of Rothschild, she lived cheerfully for her horses and aristocratic society. Her husband was deeply devoted to his beautiful and highly intelligent wife. Marie Festetics: "Her king is for her what the baggage porter at the railroad station is for me!"[16]

According to Marie Festetics, Elisabeth was "easily influenced if it coincided with a certain convenience." Her sister Marie merely fanned her discontent. "For she finds her existence, compared with that of the Empress, so enviable—for she was so free—could do as she pleased," Countess Festetics observed, who thought no good would come of this influence. She described the beautiful ex-Queen "as a disturbing element," even as "a little evil demon,"[17] and tried to appeal to Elisabeth's sense of duty. But the lady-in-waiting failed.

This first trip to England roused Elisabeth's ambition. She became determined to shine at the great hunts like her sister. From this time on, she spent many hours a day, even in Vienna and at Gödöllö, practicing her riding and jumping.

She trained on her tall English hunter, using English hurdles, which were higher than was common on the Continent. Her equerry Allen—who was, of course, English—worked with her.

In Vienna, only the racecourse in the Freudenau was suitable to this activity. The Viennese were determined not to miss such a spectacle, and they streamed there in great crowds to watch their Empress jump hurdles. Elisabeth's popularity was not exactly enhanced by these frequent semipublic appearances. Soon she longed for a more discreet practice arena. Her stays at Gödöllö grew longer than ever—and her popularity in Vienna lower.

Then, in the summer of 1875, an event occurred that had a crucial effect on the rest of Elisabeth's life: ex-Emperor Ferdinand died without issue in Prague and named his nephew and successor, Franz Joseph, as his sole heir.

The Emperor, "totally naively," to his adjutant general, Crenneville: "All of a sudden I am a rich man!"[18] The estates in Ferdinand's holdings brought in over a million guldens a year. The cash fortune amounted to several times that.

The first outlay Franz Joseph made from his new wealth was a generous raise in Elisabeth's yearly grant and widow's pension, from 100,000 to 300,000 guldens. He made an additional gift to his wife of 2 million guldens outright.

This sum represented the beginning of the Empress's considerable personal fortune. Until that time, she had had to live on her allowance and had required her husband's consent for any additional expenses. And during the past twenty years, Emperor Franz Joseph had always had a compelling reason for thrift: wars, the reparations to be paid to Prussia after 1866, finally the crash of 1873, among others. Time and again, he had begged his wife to spend less.

These times were now over. With the income from Emperor Ferdinand's legacy, the imperial family could finally draw on unlimited resources. Franz Joseph never again refused anything his wife wanted if it could be bought. For her part, she was clever at wheedling money out of him on all conceivable occasions. From 1875 on, she increased her private fortune steadily (in spite of huge expenditures), held stocks and bonds in the state railways and the Danube Shipping Company, and acquired a number of savings accounts under aliases; one, in the First Austrian Savings Bank, for example, was held in the name of Hermengilde Haraszti.[19]

Finally, she invested some of her money with the House of Rothschild in Switzerland, thus providing for possible emergencies (such as emigration). There are no indications that the Emperor knew about these transactions.

The immediate consequence of the inheritance was that Elisabeth no longer held her desires in check. She wished to go to England for fox hunting, this time not as a spectator but as a participant. The adventure required new horses, the best to be found in Austria-Hungary.

But she still did not feel proficient enough to cut a brilliant figure on the English jumping courses—and here, too, she wanted to be the best, the most handsome, the most daring. In 1875, therefore, almost as a compromise, she added to her schedule a stay of several weeks for riding and bathing in Normandy. She stayed at the old castle of Sassetôt, the grounds of which had room for many English-style hurdles.

The official reason given by the Viennese court for this additional stay abroad was, once again, that little Marie Valerie needed ocean air to build up her strength. The Empress, it was announced, would be going with her. The fact that the entourage of sixty included the English equerry and numerous stablehands no longer aroused much surprise. Many horses were also taken along on little Valerie's vacation.

The mornings in Sassetôt were reserved for swimming. Sisi to Franz Joseph: "One bathes together with all the other bathers, men and women, however each is preoccupied with himself and it is less embarrassing. . . . Only on the first day everyone watched from the shore, that was very unpleasant."[20] In the afternoons, the Empress went riding and followed the pleasure ride with steeplechase practice.

Excursions into the surrounding countryside were only rarely undertaken. "Now, in spite of the Republic, the people here are as pushy and inquisitive as in no other country, so that it is very awkward for me wherever I go."[21] And on another occasion: "Also, while riding, I have had frequent difficulties, on the roads and in the villages, children and coachmen are all eager to frighten the horses, if one rides in the fields, of course where no damage can be done, the peasants are terribly rude." These unpleasantnesses almost turned into an affair of state. In any case, the Austrian embassy in Paris had to disclaim that the Empress of Austria had been insulted by French farmers.[22]

Countess Festetics, who was in attendance on the trip to France, was outraged to see the English riding master, Allen, encourage the Empress to ever more reckless tricks. He himself showed off by riding his horse into the high, foaming breakers—almost drowning in the process.[23]

Here in Sassetôt, the Empress had a serious riding accident, with intermittent loss of consciousness and a concussion. The Emperor, extremely worried, wanted to visit his ailing wife. But France was a republic, the political relations between the two different governments were rather cool and stiff. An imperial trip through Europe to the northern edge of France, no matter how privately conducted, would have caused unpleasantness. So Franz Joseph waited; and after a few days, the accident proved not to be life-threatening. Elisabeth to her husband from Sassetôt: "I am so sorry to have frightened you. But surely both of us are always prepared for such accidents. . . . I am already looking forward to having more horses again. Here I have too few for the work. . . . I am taking pride in showing that I have not lost heart merely because of a spill."[24] That is, Elisabeth had no intention of curbing her passion for riding—quite the reverse.

Little Marie Valerie, however, had to promise her mother that she would never get on a horse. And the Hungarian bishop Hyazinth Rónay, Valerie's tutor, copied out on a piece of tissue-thin paper the words to the Latin ninetieth psalm; from then on, the Empress always carried this paper with her in a blessed medallion. It read, "He that dwelleth in the secret place of the most High shall abide under the shadow of the Almighty. I will say of the Lord, He is my refuge and my fortress: my God; in him will I trust. . . . There shall no evil befall thee, neither shall any plague come nigh thy dwelling. For he shall give his angels charge over thee, to keep thee in all thy ways."[25]

Reactions after Elisabeth's return were uniformly negative. Gisela met her mother when she passed through Munich, "stiff, cold, formal," as Marie Festetics wrote disapprovingly. Vienna, too, was only a way station. The very next day Elisabeth went on to Gödöllö. The Emperor traveled there to see his wife again after all the excitement. He made no reproaches, wore no disapproving expression. Marie Festetics: "He is so happy that the Empress is back again, and whole, that he does not know what to do for happiness!!"[26]

Whatever Elisabeth did, Franz Joseph's affection remained unchanged. Marie Festetics: "She knows how to keep him interested in a thousand ways. And her peculiarity, her singularity may not always be easy for him to bear. But *surely* she has never bored him. *Elle sait se faire désirer,* but without pretenses. It is her way, and he is under her spell like a lover, and happy when he can touch her lightly to remind her of something!"[27]

By now, Elisabeth had prepared herself as best she could for the English hunt. She felt secure enough to keep up with the best of them. Her sister Marie was given the task of scouring the Midlands for suitable accommodations for Elisabeth and her considerable retinue. In Towcester, she found a country seat, Easton Neston, and settled on the neighboring estate herself. This time, Elisabeth brought along her riding friends: the counts Hans and Heinrich Larisch, Prince Rudolf Liechtenstein, Tassilo Festetics, Ferdinand Kinsky, and other Austrian aristocrats, all of whom, of course, brought their own horses. Such an elaborate undertaking could no longer be disguised as a necessary ocean cure for little Valerie. This second trip to England, in 1876, indisputably for the sole purpose of pleasure and sport, caused headlines all over the world—and disapproving comments in Vienna. Emperor Franz Joseph could demonstrate his personal frugality with an altogether bourgeois life-style as much as he would—with her expensive extravagances, Elisabeth completely canceled out that impression.

Early in March 1876, she arrived in England, this time feeling an urge to call on the Queen—and received a rebuff. "If I were so rude!" she huffed indignantly in a letter to Franz Joseph. "But everyone on whom I have paid calls in the evenings has been ashamed, because I was gracious, have already been everywhere."[28]

Everything had been prepared to such an extent that from the first day, Elisabeth could enjoy hunting. One of the best horsemen in England, Bay Middleton, had been engaged to pilot her. Middleton, exactly thirty years old at the time, a dashing sportsman well known for his unpolished manners, was anything but eager to take on this mission to shepherd a monarch from the Continent. Standoffish and arrogant, he showed no ambition whatever to assume this "boring position," as he called it. Finally, after much coaxing, he accepted "just this once."[29]

Elisabeth came to hear of these utterances, which were far from cordial. But no matter how sensitive she might be at other times, now she showed no anger. She was eager to show him that she really did understand something about horses and that she could ride with the best of them even though she was an empress. His self-confident, rude manner had already earned Elisabeth's respect before she met him. This sturdy, red-haired young Scotsman, who was hard of hearing and nine years her junior, was one of the few people from whom Elisabeth was willing to take orders.

The hunts were exhausting. The large, strong horses were ridden at great speeds across the high wooden fences that enclosed the fields. Ladies found it especially hard going, since they were handicapped by their long skirts and the cumbersome sidesaddles. There were only a few women in Europe who could keep up with the English hunts. Elisabeth was determined to be best, and she achieved her ambition, becoming extolled as the "Queen Riding to Hounds." Only half a dozen, perhaps, of over a hundred riders who set out would last the course. More and more frequently, the Austrian Empress, led by the sure horseman's instincts of Bay Middleton, was one of them.

Countess Festetics, however, never stopped worrying. "I tremble all day long and I grow calm only in the evening, when I know that H. M. is getting ready for bed. Touch wood, she is well, in very good humor she amuses the entire company."[30] Considering the fanaticism with which Elisabeth concentrated on the sport that captured all her energies for almost a decade, it becomes easy to understand her close personal ties to the man who was at her side in the hours of her most glittering triumphs—and to whom she owed many of them. Bay Middleton was a man who elicited Elisabeth's respect—and that meant a great deal to her.

The chief chamberlain and the ladies-in-waiting spent the weeks in England without seeing much of their Empress. Bay was always at her side. He helped her into the saddle. He pulled her out of the ditch when she tumbled. He spurred her on, and, unlike all the others, he did not try to restrain her temperament during the hunt. He was allowed to praise her, and he was allowed to criticize her—she accepted everything willingly, like a child. He also chose horses for her to buy, the most expensive ones in all of England. She had money enough, after all. Elisabeth to her husband, who was heartsick in Vienna, worrying about his wife: "Your horses are none of them worth anything, slow and dull; here quite different material is needed."[31]

Not content with causing gossip about the inseparability of Empress and guide; not content with incurring enormous expenses for horses and all that was connected with them—Elisabeth once again became responsible for diplomatic complications. Since she was unwilling to give up even one day of hunting, she announced that she would call on the Queen at Windsor on Sunday—the one day of the week when the British Royal Family made it a rule never to receive visitors. Furthermore, she did not keep to the appointed time but arrived too early—during religious services. Queen Victoria left the church in order to receive Elisabeth, "very chic, in black, with furs," and was told that Elisabeth had changed her mind and would not, as had been arranged, stay for luncheon.[32] The extremely disconcerting and discourteous visit lasted exactly three-quarters of an hour and was hardly suited to improve relations between the two ruling houses.

Worse was to come. The train that took Elisabeth and her entourage from Windsor back to London became stuck in the snow. The Empress and her people were confined to the carriage "almost four hours, in deathly fear of some later train," as Countess Festetics wrote.[33] No one had had anything to eat since early morning. Finally, the station master provided them with the bare essentials—meager enough for thirteen people. The English newspapers dealt at length with this event, criticizing Queen Victoria severely for failing to at least invite the Empress of Austria to stay to lunch. Explanations and counterexplanations followed, with much irritation on all sides.

Elisabeth aggravated the awkward situation by visiting Baron Ferdinand Rothschild the following day. She looked over his celebrated stud farm and spent more than a day in his company.

Among her horsey friends, Elisabeth was more cheerful than she could ever be in Vienna. On the last day of her stay, she gave a large party for everyone who had been helpful to her in England. Once again, she invited not only aristocrats, but everyone, from the chief chamberlain to the stableboy. This gesture won her many hearts in England—and forfeited further sympathies in Vienna. The highlight of the party, and its conclusion, was a race for the Hohenembs Cup donated by the Empress (and named for one of Elisabeth's aliases). Bay Middleton himself won the race and the cup.

At her return, the Viennese did not receive their Empress with any great affection. Everyone was now criticizing her, even the common people, who were disturbed at the stories of the great sums she spent abroad. The diplomats also joined in the general chorus of outrage. Countess de Jonghe, for example, wrote, "This woman is truly insane. If she does not turn Austria into a republic, its citizens must still be very good people. She lives exclusively for her horses. It would be good fortune if she broke her arm in such a way that it would never mend."[34]

Elisabeth spent the time between her return and her next trip to England in further riding exercises and in hunting at Göding, Pardubitz, and Gödöllö. In the summer of 1876, Bay Middleton came to Gödöllö as the Empress's guest. The Emperor was also of the party, but he did not know how to deal with Middleton—quite aside from the fact that Franz Joseph did not speak English and Middleton did not speak German or Hungarian. Elisabeth's Hungarian horsey friends were more jealous than the Emperor. Middleton soon found himself in a fairly aggressive rivalry particularly with Sisi's former favorite (or whatever the correct word is for the delicate position of principal admirer), Count Niki Esterházy. For here in Hungary, Esterházy was the first and foremost huntsman. He pointed out to Middleton the position due him by virtue of his rank, and he jealously watched that Middleton did not lay claim to too much of the Empress's time.

Everywhere in England and Ireland, Bay Middleton was the local hero, and he did not feel at ease in Gödöllö, in spite of Elisabeth's favors. Surrounded by suspicious, even hostile faces, he felt abandoned. There was also his frustration in the presence of a beautiful woman who remained unattainable and yet, at times, flirted outrageously and, just as she did in other situations, took pleasure in his helplessness.

Finally, Bay broke loose. He traveled to Budapest, shook off his companion—and disappeared. Great agitation at the castle, extreme worry on the part of the Empress, until a telegram arrived from the Budapest police commissioner with the news that one Bay Middleton, without means, was being held at the police station. He had gone to a brothel and there— ignorant of the place and the language as he was—had promptly been robbed. He returned to Gödöllö a poor repentant sinner. His rivals had triumphed. The Empress was furious, feeling personally insulted. But Bay reacted cleverly: He made a joke of the whole story, laughed at himself with the others, allowed his country charm to do its work—and Elisabeth forgave him.[35]

Niki Esterházy had celebrated too soon. For the rest of his stay, the Scotsman rode out at the Empress's side as if nothing at all had happened.

At the end of January 1878, Elisabeth went to England again—this time to Cottesbrook in Northamptonshire. Again Bay Middleton was her guide. Elisabeth to Franz Joseph: "If only you were here, I say it at every hunt, and how popular you would be thanks to your good horsemanship and your knowledge of hunting. But it would be dangerous, for you would not let Captain Middleton manage you and would leap over everything that is still being checked to see whether it is not too deep or too wide."[36]

Crown Prince Rudolf, nineteen years old at that time, did not, however, believe that riding to hounds could contribute to the popularity of the imperial family. At least, before starting out on a grand tour in England, he assured everyone that he had no intention of imitating his mother. "Truly, in England I shall avoid participating in riding to hounds, our people do not consider it a very heroic deed to break one's neck at it, and I care too much for my popularity to forfeit it for such matters."[37] It was a fact that Rudolf's horsemanship was not equal to his mother's.

Although, in the winter of 1878, mother and son were in England at the same time, they went their separate ways, as always. Elisabeth hunted in the Midlands, Rudolf underwent an exhausting schedule, inspecting and learning, in the company of his adored teacher, Professor Karl Menger, the economist. In England, he composed an anonymous pamphlet against the Austrian nobility in which he criticized the idle life of many aristocrats. It also alluded to the sport of riding and the exaggerated claims made for it. "In the late autumn, many gentlemen, as well as some ladies, travel to the hunts in Pardubitz, the principal center of the sport. The persecution of animals that takes place there in good weather is understood by a section of the nobility to be the more earnest part of life."[38]

Rudolf's few visits with his mother in England led to serious arguments concerning Bay Middleton. It was, surprisingly, ex-Queen Marie of Naples who passed on to the unsuspecting Crown Prince the gossip about a supposed affair between his mother and Middleton. She further aggravated the discord between mother and son by repeating to the Empress critical remarks the young Crown Prince had made. These, in turn, deeply hurt Elisabeth.

In her diary, Countess Festetics gave free rein to her anger at the Empress's Bavarian family. The Empress was "always the victim of her brothers and sisters," she wrote, and, "Her Majesty seems to me like Cinderella and her three wicked sisters. They are all full of envy! When they need something, they importune her. Curse and defame everything that her position gives her—but want to exploit all the advantages of her position for themselves." The sisters used Elisabeth as a "plaything, and all unpleasantness—Everything that makes her heart heavy comes from them."[39]

The Countess accused Marie of being jealous of her more beautiful, more athletic sister and wanting Bay (presumably both as trainer and as admirer) for herself. "Our sister [as Marie was known in court jargon] flirts seriously with Bay and has invited him to her house," Marie Festetics wrote to Ida Ferenczy, who had been left behind in Hungary.[40]

The Crown Prince was so outraged at what he heard that he grew abusive to Middleton—whereupon the latter was mortally offended. Finally, Countess Festetics, whom Rudolf had always liked very much, intervened and persuaded him to have a confidential talk with her. She told him, "I do not recognize your Imperial Highness at all—the English air does not become your Imperial Majesty." He laughed, "and then, like a child, he poured out his heart, half-angry, half-sad, with tears in his eyes he said that he regretted having come to England—he had lost his most beautiful illusions and felt mortally hurt and unhappy." To the lady-in-waiting's dismayed question, Rudolf replied gruffly, "and you can ask me —you of all people—"

Marie Festetics: "There was no more, for I looked at him in such astonishment that it brought him to his senses. And then he continued more calmly and told me—the most infamous thing I have ever heard. I was speechless. But my astonishment and indignation at such lies must have been so evident that, before I could even open my mouth, he, as if to apologize, blurted out, 'Aunt Marie told me.'" Marie Festetics: "All the more vile, I said icily, although inside I was boiling." Rudolf: "Yes, but why did she tell me if it is not true—and she was so nice—so good and really likes me . . . is all of it only a lie?"

The lady-in-waiting was so discreet that she did not confide the contents of the gossip to her diary: "I will not touch the matter itself—I would never forgive myself if I rescued such a story from oblivion. If the Empress knew *that!* terrible!"[41]

A vehement quarrel between the sisters ensued. They were never reconciled.

In this society of idle, mutually jealous people, for all practical purposes cut off from the rest of the world, the atmosphere grew so feverish that the Empress lost all interest in hunting and in horses for several days— and that was saying a great deal. In her outrage and anger at the proliferating quarrel, she refused to take part in several hunts and—as she did so frequently in difficult situations—took to her bed under the pretext of illness. She even found her decision quite appropriate: "Since I am not hunting for several days, people will say it is because of the Pope. This works out very well," she wrote to her husband in Vienna at a time when Pope Pius IX had just died.[42]

From then on, whenever Rudolf came to visit, Middleton was not invited, to avoid any further explosions. As soon as Rudolf left his mother's hunting lodge, matters went back to their accustomed ways. For the second time, Middleton won the cup donated and tendered by Elisabeth.

In all his letters to the Emperor, Rudolf gave no indication of any of these events. Quite the contrary: He sent his father reassurances, writing that Elisabeth "this year is riding so much more carefully and that Captain Middleton is leading more calmly." On the other hand, he did not conceal his fear, "since I have seen the English fences and have heard so much talk of accidents."[43]

These quarrels made Elisabeth lose her enthusiasm for hunting in England. From then on, she would be intent on avoiding her sister, who had a hunting lodge in Althorp as well and took part in all the large English hunts. She was determined in future to hunt in Ireland, with Bay Middleton but without the ex-Queen of Naples, in a region where it was unlikely that any member of the Imperial House would stop by on his travels.

Even aside from her excessive ambitions for her horsemanship, in the 1870s, Sisi managed to enrich Viennese court life with sensational behavior bordering on the bizarre. She had always liked surrounding herself with animals—with parrots and most especially with huge wolfhounds and greyhounds which, in spite of imperial protests, made their way into the innermost apartments of the Hofburg and never left Elisabeth's side. True, she had never acquired the Bengal tiger and its cubs from the Berlin zoo that she wanted (see page 190), any more than, a few years earlier, she had been given the dancing bear she asked for ("it costs 700 guldens").[44] Instead, as if to protest the fact that her wishes had not been met, she bought a macaque. The monkey, like her pet dogs, frightened the ladies-in-waiting and the chambermaids, but it became little Valerie's playmate, as the Empress wanted.

But soon difficulties arose. Crown Prince Rudolf wrote to his older friend, the zoologist Alfred Brehm, "Unfortunately this remarkably tame and very entertaining animal is quite sickly. Furthermore, it behaves so indecorously that it has become quite impossible to keep it in the room in the presence of ladies." The monkey was "cashiered," as Rudolf mockingly wrote, and taken to the zoo in Schönbrunn.

Next, Elisabeth asked her son to find her a new monkey, after first asking Brehm "which species of monkey was toughest as regards health and besides combines total good nature with decent behavior, and also does not make itself quite unbearable through bothersome screaming. She [the

Empress] further wished to know whether a female would be easier to keep indoors than a male." It was not, however, entirely easy for the Crown Prince to burden the respected scholar with such wishes. "Please forgive my bothering you with this matter, but you are doing a great favor to one of the most diligent readers of your book."[45] When, after a time, the Empress finally gave up her "monkey passion," as Marie Festetics wrote, not a few people at court were greatly relieved.

But soon a new interest emerged. The latest fad was Rustimo, a black-amoor the Shah of Persia (according to one of various versions) had sent as a gift. Sisi's father, Duke Max of Bavaria, had amused himself by surrounding himself with four Negro boys to frighten the Munich burghers. He went so far as to have the four pagans solemnly christened in the Frauenkirche. Whether this deed had been done from a Christian missionary spirit or in a spirit of pure mischief remains open to question.

In this area, too, Elisabeth followed in her father's footsteps. She turned the crippled Rustimo into Valerie's playmate. She even had the two photographed together, so that no one at court would remain unaware of their shared games.

On Elisabeth's express orders, Rustimo accompanied little Valerie on walks and drives; the ladies-in-waiting and the girl's tutors could not get over their outrage at this whim. Landgravine Therese Fürstenberg, for example, wrote to her sister, "The Archduchess [Valerie] recently took the blackamoor along on the promenade, he was put in the carriage with the French teacher, who sat next to the heathen feeling shamed and sad; the Archduchess always gives candy to children along the road. But now none of them dared to come near her when they saw the black boy and tried in every way to avoid the monster and his bared teeth, so as to get to the candies; all this seemed a great joke to the little girl."[46]

Even Marie Festetics found poor Rustimo "a horror . . . too big for a monkey, too little for a human being."[47] Elisabeth, however, was amused by the prompt effect of her provocation. Finally, the Empress had Rustimo christened, to invalidate all objections to the un-Christian association of her daughter with a heathen. Sisi to her mother: "Today was Rustimo's christening in Valerie's salon . . . Rudolf was godfather. It was solemn and ludicrous, there were tears and laughter. He himself was very moved and wept."[48] At Marie Wallersee's wedding to Count Georg Larisch in Gödöllö, Archduchess Valerie appeared in the church next to Rustimo—truly a successfully perpetrated outrage.

For many years, Rustimo remained part of the imperial family's inner circle. According to the ladies-in-waiting's accusations, he grew conceited and impertinent, spoiled by the beautiful Empress's extravagant favors. In 1884, he was made "announcer to the bedchamber" but fell into disfavor only a year later. In 1890, he was pensioned, and in 1891, he was sent to the charity institution in Ybbs, where he died the very next year. Little is known about Rustimo; but that his life in Vienna was a tragic one is certain even without further facts. He was an attraction, a joke, a means for Elisabeth to pique those around her. When he no longer behaved as she wanted him to, she dropped him and sent him away—like the monkey whose manners were not up to scratch.

While the Empress spent her time feuding with relatives, practicing her riding, nurturing her beauty, and complaining of boredom, Austrian soldiers were fighting partisans in Bosnia. At the Congress of Berlin, with Bismarck's support, Andrássy had won the right to occupy Bosnia and Herzegovina (which were under Turkish rule). This maneuver, piled on the serious differences created during the Crimean War, seriously angered czarist Russia. Under Andrássy's influence, Elisabeth, too, harbored no friendly feelings for the Russians. After the occupation, she wrote to her husband, "Just do not send too many Russophiles to Bosnia, such as Croatians, Bohemians, etc."[49] These words reflect her deep repugnance to all Slavs, and once again especially the Czechs.

The Austrian troops were received not as rescuing angels and saviors from the Turkish yoke, but as enemies. The number of dead and wounded rose from day to day. Once again emergency hospitals were set up, including one at Schönbrunn.

Elisabeth visited the wounded warriors. "Truly like an angel of mercy she went from bed to bed," Marie Festetics wrote. "I saw the tears trickling down the faces of the men;—no complaints crossed their lips! no word of discouragement! yes, they said—that they were *not* suffering! . . . and with glowing eyes they followed her movements and blessed her and thanked her and asked for *nothing!*"

Marie Festetics believed herself to be in agreement with the Empress when she wrote the following skeptical sentences in her diary. "I bow to this humanity that risks its life for a concept—to be beaten or shot into a cripple. . . . And almost ashamed, I ask myself—and we? what sacrifices do we bring? With our abundance, we graciously approach the beds of these half-dead men and ask whether the wounds hurt? and hand them a cigar or a friendly word to lessen the pain?—no! reflection is required here and the question who 'the great one' is?" The loyal lady-in-waiting concluded these considerations with an appreciation of the Empress: "but the Empress—she understands."[50]

But these moments of understanding did not last long. A mere two days later, Marie Festetics noted with resignation, "Life goes on! Hunting, riding academy—a great gathering there—dinners—teas. During all this, many an anxious worry, and always my mind turns to the wounded while I am playing the piano at the riding academy as everyone frolics in pleasure and merriment. . . . The Empress is charming in her efforts to entertain her guests!"[51]

Elisabeth's personality was so persuasive that she transformed even her most severe critics into admirers when she appeared officially as the Empress—as she did at the court ball of 1879. At the time, the Emperor was forty-eight years old and, according to Hübner, looked "tired and noticeably aged. 'I am growing old,' he said with a melancholy note, 'my memory is going.' " By contrast, the Empress, forty-one years old, was, again according to Hübner, "very beautiful, especially seen at a distance very poetical with her magnificent hair, which fell below her shoulders down to her waist. An empress to her fingertips."[52] But the hours Elisabeth spent "in harness," in the diamond-embroidered state gown, a tiara on her artfully dressed hair, grew more and more infrequent.

In the meantime, preparations for the trip to Ireland claimed most of Sisi's time. Nine of her horses, especially the expensive English ones Middleton had bought for her, were in England, where they were being exercised. But not even these horses were suitable for Irish conditions. On that island, jumps were taken primarily over earth embankments rather than over the high English fences. The horses had therefore to be retrained, and for this purpose they were shipped to a stable in Ireland. The reschooling of the high-bred horses, used to the Empress's slight weight, by Irish horsemen was so difficult that three of the sinfully expensive hunters perished. Middleton, who managed Elisabeth's stables in England and Ireland, provided replacements. The expenditure could hardly remain a secret, coming as it did at the time of the occupation struggles in Bosnia.

Most of the time, the Emperor was alone in Vienna. He rose at four in the morning and took all his meals alone, often quite informally while working at his desk. Consternation at the Emperor's loneliness was universal, as was condemnation of the Empress. Count Hübner's diary discusses Franz Joseph's meager distractions. "Frequently, he utilizes the last hours of the day to drive to Laxenburg. He goes there all alone, and alone he goes walking in the park. One sees this Prince, made for family life, reduced to solitude by the absence of the Empress, whom he still loves passionately."[53]

Count Crenneville and his friends also joined the universal lamentations about the Empress. "I like neither the external nor the internal, and certainly not the innermost affairs. Poor Austria, poor Emperor! He really deserves a better fate, for no one can dispute many of his outstanding traits. His greatest misfortune occurred in 1854. Without this, perhaps many things would have been avoided."[54] The mention of 1854 referred, of course, to the Emperor's marriage to Elisabeth. And on another occasion: "The papers already carry the news that the Empress is traveling to Ireland. For the Emperor's birthday, she came to Schönbrunn for not quite twenty-four hours; for the feast of Corpus Christi, she can find neither time nor inclination to make the Viennese happy by her presence!"

And:

> I do not understand how, at this time of general hardship, it is possible to think of a trip to Ireland, and how she can be allowed to do it. What an effect would it have made if the expenses of the trip (perhaps 1/2 million) had been distributed to the monarchy's aid organizations, how much hunger would have been assuaged, how many blessings would heaven have sent the benefactress? Has the master renounced all influence, all power to express a veto in his position? . . . But what is the use of complaining; I feel like shedding bitter tears over it.[55]

Once again, the loyal lady-in-waiting Marie Festetics did everything in her power to defend her mistress. "She needs absolute freedom, the quiet that comes with independence—a release from everything of this world that causes her worry and responsibility—that delivers her from the small duties, which she lacks the self-command to fulfill, and the omission of which in turn causes her to have scruples."[56] Nevertheless, Sisi's letters make no mention of scruples. Only once is there a brief hint that Elisabeth's passion for riding might be rooted in defiance of the Emperor who, after 1867, made her stay away from politics. In any case, her reproaches express great annoyance: "I no longer interfere in politics, but in these matters [having to do with horses], I do insist on having a voice."[57]

It was surely no accident that Elisabeth's single-minded preoccupation with hunting and riding coincided with the period when Andrássy, as imperial and royal foreign minister, was watched at every step—especially in the fear that, as had happened in 1866–1867, Andrássy would again engage the Empress for his purposes. Apparently at the Emperor's wish, Elisabeth avoided even the appearance of political activity—and in her way continued to be outrageous by occupying herself entirely and exclusively with horses.

Where politics was concerned, she was not in the least deferential. Her visits to Ireland were an open challenge to Queen Victoria. The incognito of a Countess von Hohenembs was of little use here. Precisely during these years, there was acute danger of Irish risings against England; the social tensions, the hatred of the poor Catholic Irish for the rich Anglican English landlords threatened to erupt into violence. The visit of a Catholic empress in this field of tension added more fuel to the fire. But Elisabeth barely acknowledged this situation, and in her letters to Vienna, she underplayed the problems. "Around here, nothing is felt of the unrests. In the western part of the island, where the harvest was bad, there is more dissatisfaction and a sort of terrorism. The landlords do not pay and maintain solidarity."[58]

She wanted to ride—everything else bored her. She committed one blunder after another. She canceled her scheduled visit to the Queen on her way through England by letter ("saw myself, under the pressure of time, compelled in great haste to make for my destination"[59]). Finally, she bestowed her presence repeatedly on Maynooth Seminary, whose priests were suspect as anti-English agitators. Of course, her visits to the seminary were a matter of good manners, and she came to apologize because during a stag hunt she and her horse had jumped the monastery wall (in the process, narrowly missing the head of the seminary's supervisor); but the repeated calls created an impression that had a poor political effect.

The nationalist Irish newspapers fully exploited Elisabeth's visit for their own purposes—to attack the British Royal House, whose members avoided setting foot in Ireland. Quite clearly, both the Empress and the people around her were almost entirely uninformed about Ireland's special position in politics and religion. The devout attitude of the Catholic Irish toward the Catholic Empress surprised even Countess Festetics, whose diary records an encounter between Elisabeth and an Irish peer.

> The Empress held out her hand, he dropped to one knee and, in evident emotion and deep respect, he kissed it. The lord was Catholic, and he welcomed her, not only as an empress, but as a Catholic leader. . . .
> In general, this stands out *very* much here. The most miserable

little village dresses up in all its finery, decorated with love, and sets up little triumphal arches. The people kneel in the streets and kiss the ground wherever she goes. It is so bad that we have to be very careful, and she *very* carefully avoids all ovations.[60]

To this day, legends abound in Ireland concerning the beautiful Empress of Austria, such as one about a mysterious fairy on horseback. And to this day, a number of Irish families cherish one of Sisi's lace handkerchiefs, which she dropped in great quantities in gratitude for small favors performed.

In March 1879, Hungary experienced a catastrophic flood, which claimed many lives. Under these circumstances, the Empress's pleasure trip could no longer be justified. "That is why I think it best to leave now," Elisabeth wrote to Franz Joseph, "and you will prefer it as well. It is the greatest sacrifice I can bring, but in this case it is necessary."[61]

Elisabeth's Irish stables, however, were maintained, and Elisabeth left her bed in Ireland, indicating her plan to return. Countess Festetics would not let even this occasion pass without fulsome praise for the Empress and accusations of the Austrian press: "if Archduchess Sophie offered the cobbler's boy a crust of bread out of her abundance, all the newspapers were full of it—if the young Empress sacrifices 14 days of her vacation (out of a mere 6 weeks) because a misfortune has struck a city—that is natural."[62]

During the return journey, the usual disaster with Queen Victoria loomed. This time, Elisabeth circumvented it with uncharacteristic reference to thrift. She wrote the Emperor, "And do you want me to spend some time in London? I would have liked to avoid it, to save the cost of the hotel stay. In this way, I would have made the whole trip both ways without having a hotel."[63] The costs of the trip amounted to 158,337 guldens and 48 kreuzers. The few guldens for the hotel bill in London, therefore, were hardly significant. But Elisabeth was inventive when it came to circumventing an official occasion such as a call on Buckingham Palace.

In April 1879, the Emperor and Empress celebrated their silver wedding anniversary—"a true family celebration of all the peoples of my empire," according to Franz Joseph. He requested that "all costly pageantry" be omitted, gifts to the poor taking its place.

But one exception was made: The city of Vienna gave its Emperor and Empress a parade, planned and organized by Hans Makart, the uncrowned king of the arts in Vienna. The procession was not a homage rendered by the nobility, like the chivalric joust in Budapest, but a demonstration of all citizens. Ten thousand people in medieval costumes, on splendid floats, paraded before the festival tent in the new Ringstrasse, preceded by an outrider representing Vienna and trumpeters on white horses. Along with the old trades of bakers, millers, butchers, cartwrights, potters, and others, the new industries were also represented. The climax of the procession was the float of the railroad men—surprising in a procession dressed in medieval costumes. Makart solved the problem by representing the railroad as a winged carriage "in which water and fire, combined, grow to that power which drives the wheel with winged speed."[64]

The comments in Vienna were by no means friendly, especially as concerned the noble lady celebrant. Elsewhere, it was said, twenty-five years of housekeeping (*ménage*) were cause for celebration, while in Vienna the festivities honored twenty-five years of stallkeeping (*manège*). The play on words became a familiar quotation during these days, repeated over and over—though only in private, of course.

At the center of the festive turbulence, Elisabeth remained unmoved. According to statements made by her niece, Marie Larisch, "most of the time [she made] a face like an Indian widow who is about to be burned; and when I told her this at a moment when we could not be overheard, she laughed, it is true, but thought that it was quite enough to have been married for twenty-five years, but that it was hardly necessary to celebrate the event."[65] The Empress walked out on the great soiree held on the eve of the anniversary after a mere quarter of an hour, leaving her husband alone to make the requisite honors.

To the Empress, this family celebration was nothing but a great bother and burden. Nor is there the least indication that she took pleasure in the Austro-Hungarian achievements of the past quarter-century. There was greater freedom. A constitution and a parliament were in force. The position of the Emperor was almost uncontested, and by now, any comparison with the other European dynasties was favorable to the House of Habsburg—as had by no means been the case during the 1850s and 1860s. A confidential letter from Bismarck to Wilhelm I of that year even put it appreciatively: "As for social conditions, Austria may have the healthiest internal conditions of all the great powers, and the rule of the Imperial House is firmly established with each and every nationality."[66]

In the midst of the patriotic joy around her, Elisabeth reacted once again as a purely private person. She bemoaned her age, her insipid marriage. She felt the disapproval of the court and complained of it.

Countess Festetics saw this attitude with increasing sorrow. "She does

not value enough the fact that she is the Empress! She has not com-
prehended the beautiful, uplifting aspect of it, for no one showed it to her;
she feels only its cool shadow side, she does not see the light, and so her
inner feelings are not in tune with external circumstances, and no calm,
no peace, no harmony can therefore enter."[67] The trusty lady-in-waiting
was still trying to make excuses for the Empress, by now over forty years
old, by citing early bad experiences—a charitable effort other eyewitnesses
were not prepared to undertake.

If Elisabeth acknowledged the criticism at all, it was only with scorn.
Early in 1880, she traveled to Ireland for a second time. By now she was
forty-two years old and a multiple grandmother, but hardened by exercise
and resilient. Since the horses were already in Ireland anyway, Elisabeth
could travel light; the freight train that followed her special train with the
saloon-dining car transported a mere forty tons of baggage.

Once again, the worried Emperor, preoccupied by a governmental
crisis, could hardly take comfort from the news of his wife, who proudly
wrote, "Rudi Liechtenstein also fell without hurting himself, and Lord
Langford, our landlord, who fell on his face, has had difficulty swallowing
ever since." And, "Middleton took a spill and so did I . . . but the ground
was very soft. Many others are said to have fallen as well . . . but since
of course I rode on, I did not see it. I saw Lord Langford standing in
another ditch fishing for his horse."[68]

Reports from Prince Liechtenstein and Countess Festetics to the Emperor also make much mention of spills, broken jaws and shins, and
daredevil leaps over moats and walls. During a particularly hazardous hunt,
Elisabeth even rode without gloves, so as to be able to control the reins
more subtly. She, who was so fastidious in Gödöllö that she wore three
pairs of gloves on top of each other, here in Ireland, at Middleton's side,
accepted hands that were roughened and bloody. That she would triumph
over all the other horsewomen and be admired accordingly was, by now,
taken for granted.

Triumphing at the hunts brought Elisabeth both an increase in self-
confidence—since she shone not as an empress, but as a horsewoman and
a beauty—and the freedom from court obligations that she sought. But
such days on horseback generally ended in despair and bitter complaints
about her life. "Why must I return to my cage? Why could I not have
broken all my bones, so as to put an end to it—to everything!"

Such outbursts, bordering on hysteria, always frightened the people
around her. In such cases, what helped was to remind Elisabeth of her

favorite daughter, Marie Valerie. Elisabeth to Marie Larisch: "I would be blaspheming if I wished to abandon her. My *kedvesem* [Hungarian: "darling"] is all I still have in the world. The only thing that has not been taken from me."[69]

In this time of unbridled thirst for life, surrounded by sporting friends, Elisabeth's cynicism deepened. Except for Middleton, there was no one around her who would have dared to speak openly. Some flattered her, manipulated her. Marie Festetics worried but was powerless: "If one's world teaches one to think small, how can one respect others without placing oneself higher? And the worst is—not to despise them as puppets. . . . With her, that is a great danger, for—anyone she does not respect is someone for whom she need have no consideration, and that is convenient!!?"[70]

Soon differences of opinion arose even between the Empress and Marie Festetics. The Countess could not warm up to Elisabeth's new friends, and she always cautiously reminded her mistress of some obligation—usually in vain.

Before her departure from Ireland, Elisabeth ordered an additional four horses to be brought from Austria, so that they could be broken in for the next season. As a matter of course, she kept her Irish stables going.

On the return trip, she made concessions to the wishes of the Viennese court. She broke the journey in London and met with Prime Minister Benjamin Disraeli and the Austrian ambassador. She was courteous and friendly. And as always when she made the effort, she immediately won all hearts. Finally, she also paid a call on the Prince of Wales and even on Queen Victoria. Nevertheless, she wrote her mother, "Unfortunately, I am supposed to visit the Queen in Windsor on my way back, the idea bores me terribly. One of the many advantages of Ireland is that there is no royalty there."[71]

In London, a telegram reached Elisabeth announcing that Crown Prince Rudolf had become engaged to the sixteen-year-old daughter of the King of the Belgians, Princess Stephanie; the engagement took place in Brussels. "Thank God that it is not a disaster," was Marie Festetics's comment on receipt of the telegram. To which Elisabeth replied, "Pray God that it is not."[72]

The news forced Elisabeth to interrupt her journey home in Brussels to tender the young couple her felicitations. She had never met young Stephanie; but she had an intense antipathy to the Belgian Royal House because it was the family of Carlotta, the former Empress of Mexico.

The short visit of congratulations in Brussels by Elisabeth was merely an onerous duty. King, Queen, bridegroom, and bride were waiting to greet her on the station platform. Once again Marie Festetics hymned the beauty of the Empress, at that time forty-three years old, and the veneration Rudolf showed toward her: "he literally threw his arms around her neck—kissed her hands over and over, and then came the bride—young, sparkling, unformed, a badly dressed child. . . . The Empress bent forward, embraced her—kissed the little one, and that one looked up to her beautiful mother-in-law with undisguised admiration, and her bright-red little face looked happy and merry!"

Even at this first meeting, the Empress managed to get the better of her daughter-in-law.

Marie Festetics: "I was so proud and could not help staring at the Crown Prince!— he looked at his mother, then his bride. I was sorry, for *that* could hardly be to her advantage! but I think he looks more contented than happy!"

The visit to Brussels lasted exactly four hours—from the arrival at eight o'clock in the morning to the equally ceremonial departure at noon. The time was spent with a breakfast in the Palais de Bruxelles. Marie Festetics felt just as ill at ease as did her mistress: "to me every thing seemed so theatrical—parvenu?? . . . I did not like it. Everything so banal, so hackneyed, and everything so borrowed." The kingdom of the Belgians, in spite of its enormous wealth, was considered an upstart. "We Austrians are not so favorably disposed to the Belgians," Marie Festetics wrote, chiming in with her mistress.[73] The relationship between Elisabeth and her son was hardly improved by the fact of the new daughter-in-law.

Elisabeth prepared herself for still another hunting trip in 1881. She trained as usual but increasingly suffered from attacks of rheumatism, the first sign of age. Her mood became increasingly somber. She also underwent more frequent nervous collapses, which frightened those around her, including little Valerie. On January 1, 1881, for example, Valerie noted in her diary, "Mama had a very strong bath, and when I went in to her, she could not stop laughing, the bath had made her completely nervous. I was afraid, but fortunately she is already well again today."

Beyond all measure Elisabeth worried about Middleton, who had suffered a skull fracture in a fall but who was back in the saddle after only a month. It was arranged that he would be guiding the Empress soon again.

This time, however, Elisabeth could not get her way. A new trip to Ireland was no longer politically feasible. For better or worse, she had to deign to hunt in England if she was going to hunt at all. A suitable mansion was found in Cheshire: Comermere Abbey, whose owner was traveling in the West Indies at the time. Austrian workmen were sent there as before all the Empress's trips, to make structural changes. Most importantly, a chapel and an exercise room had to be added, and electric bells had to be installed all over the house.

Elisabeth's living room was provided with a new spiral staircase, which allowed her to descend unnoticed to her own kitchen; there, undisturbed, she could take her scanty meals alone. The little railroad station at Wrenbury was given an additional waiting room, for this was where the hunting party took the special trains that carried them to the races. An additional siding was required for the horse-transports. Since the expectation of going to Ireland after all had not been abandoned, at the same time expensive preparations were made in Summerhill. Finally, however, England was settled on, and all the horses were taken there from Vienna, from Gödöllö, and from Ireland. Count Rudolf Liechtenstein, who was once again among Elisabeth's companions, brought an additional eight horses from his stables; Middleton contributed ten.

The Empress rode out on twenty-two hunting days of a total of twenty-eight; two were omitted because of snow.[74] Middleton was always at her side. The Empress was exceptionally well prepared; but the strenuous hunts at the side of Bay, only thirty-five years old, took their toll on her far more than they used to. Middleton, for his part, had personal problems: His fiancée of many years, a daughter of the landed gentry, was jealous. After the long engagement, she was eager to be married, and she had no intention of continuing to tolerate Bay's adoration of the Empress. The English press published numerous highly critical articles concerning the Austrian Empress, who responded in high dudgeon, "I am surprised all the more when someone writes or speaks well of me."[75]

Only one more time, in 1882, did Elisabeth go hunting in England. But Middleton was no longer her guide. And with someone else, Elisabeth no longer enjoyed hunting. She abruptly gave up hunting and sold all the horses from the English stables. A phase of her life had come to an end.

Instead, the Empress gave in to the Austrian army's request to appear tall in the saddle at a military review on the Schmelz, at the side of the Emperor, the Crown Prince, and the Crown Princess.

Oddly enough, the horse she rode, one of her favorites, was named Nihilist. Marie Festetics could hardly contain her pride: "It was so solemn and splendid that it filled one's heart;—from every direction drumming, trumpeting, national anthem, lowering of flags, and the thunder of the

'Attention,' the chief! It was such a beautiful picture, this beautiful, beautiful Empress who, with her horse, seemed like a statue and with majestic grace and indescribable charm lowered her head in thanks—I shall *never* forget the day."[76]

Elisabeth's critical view of the military was well known in Vienna, and even Countess Festetics "heard a great deal of talk that *She* did not love the army." At official receptions in the Hofburg, therefore, the Empress avoided the higher military officers (especially her principal antagonist, Archduke Albrecht) and did not dignify them by addressing them. Given the extremely important position of the army in the imperial and royal monarchy, such an attitude also meant opposition to the Emperor. On the other hand, according to Marie Festetics, "during recent weeks, the generals [drew] back almost ostentatiously" whenever the Empress appeared.[77]

There can be no doubt of Elisabeth's dislike of the army. In her poems, she confessed a clear belief in pacifism, praising, for instance, the politics of Sweden.

> *Schweden, o, da geht's schon besser!*
> *Sieht man ordentlich mit Neid,*
> *Wie, dort über dem Gewässer,*
> *Glücklich sind die braven Leut'.*
>
> *Konnt' ihr Herrscher stolz gestehen,*
> *Dass Millionen er erspart,*
> *Freilich fehlen dort Armeen,*
> *Und Kanonen aller Art.*[78]

[Sweden—oh, life is better there! / We cannot help but feel envy as we see / How, across the waters, / The good people are happy. / / Their ruler could admit with pride / That he saved the lives of millions, / True, armies are lacking there, / As are cannons of every sort.]

On another occasion, during the time of the Bulgarian crisis in the mid-1880s, she was even more outspoken.

> *Das arme Landvolk schwitzet,*
> *Bebaut mühsam sein Feld.*
> *Umsonst! Gleich wird stibitzet*
> *Ihm wiederum das Geld.*

Kanonen sind sehr teuer,
Wir brauchen deren viel,
Besonders aber heuer,
Wo Ernst wird aus dem Spiel.

Wer weiss! gäb's keine Fürsten,
Gäb' es auch keinen Krieg;
Aus wär' das teure Dürsten
Nach Schlachten und nach Sieg.[79]

[The poor farmfolk sweat, / Working their fields with toil. / In vain! At once they are deprived / In turn of their money. / / Cannons are most expensive, / We need many of them, / And most especially today, / When the game is turning serious. / / Who knows! If there were no princes, / There would be no war; / There'd be an end to the costly thirsting / For battles and for victory.]

It is beyond question that all public appearances, but especially presence at military exercises, cost the Empress considerable effort. But by being present on this particular occasion, she silenced her critics.

Once more that same year, the Empress showed her good will. In September 1882, she accompanied the Emperor on an official trip to Trieste, to attend the celebration of the five-hundredth anniversary of Trieste's inclusion in Austria. Fourteen-year-old Archduchess Marie Valerie confided her fears to her diary. "I'm so terribly afraid. . . . It is awfully dangerous. For the Italians want Trieste for themselves and hate Austria. When Uncle Karl [Ludwig] was there, they threw a bomb at an Austrian general, and now there is concern. . . . Oh! No! I cannot even think of it."[80] Her fears were justified; two Italians were found carrying bombs "to welcome the Emperor of Austria."

Countess Festetics was in the entourage. Her diary records the excitement of those days. For example, "then we still have the theater *paré*—very unpleasant, since an assassination attempt was feared or expected?—on arrival at the theater?—inside?—or on leaving it?—Only one of these assigned to do the deed could be captured—outside the theater!—The people, the ones in charge, tried to cover it up, but were themselves so agitated that they were unable to; Their Majesties were splendid!" The Emperor ordered that only the essential retinues were to be taken along to the various public functions: "It is more than one can ask of anyone!"[81]

During this trip, Elisabeth showed considerable courage. She would not be stopped from accompanying her husband on all formal visits. Elisabeth told her daughter, "In the carriage I insisted on sitting on the land side [where armed assassins were supposed to be more likely] and let the Emperor sit on the ocean side, it could not have done much good, but perhaps a little." Valerie could hardly contain her pride in her mother: "Oh, when I have a husband, I shall also endeavor to sacrifice myself like Mama. That his life should be dearer to me than my own."

According to Valerie, Elisabeth was "so angry at the false Italians. I barely nod to them," she said. "They keep shouting, 'Evviva, evviva,' and stab us in the back." Marie Valerie: "I have never seen Mama like this. There were tears in her eyes, and she was still very angry at this terrible riffraff."[82]

Elisabeth's decision to give up hunting was a great relief to those who worried about her reputation. When she appeared at the opera with her husband, daughter, and daughter-in-law on New Year's Day of 1882, to hear Weber's *Oberon* from the box where she could make a quick getaway, Count Hübner noted, "It is an event to see the Empress other than on horseback, and the public expresses its gratitude for this rare spectacle."[83]

The sudden end of hunting and daily riding left a vacuum in the Empress's life. For almost ten years, she had led the life of a champion sportswoman, had lived for little but her horses. Now, when this activity abruptly came to an end, her body had difficulty adapting to a quiet, "imperial" life. She began to satisfy her extraordinary need for exercise in a different way: by daily walks, lasting for hours and at extreme speeds, to the point of exhaustion of the ladies-in-waiting who went with her, in every sort of weather, over mountains and meadows in the most scenic areas of Austria, Bavaria, and Hungary, as well as along dusty country roads. In order not to overtax the ladies-in-waiting, who were not in training, a carriage frequently followed them, so that the "ladies" could find refuge in it when their feet would no longer carry them. But the Empress could march on for hours. Neither rain showers nor snowstorms could keep her from her walks.

She wore sturdy hiking shoes, a practical dark skirt of a heavy material, and with it a close-fitting jacket. (She had adapted this practical outfit from her riding costume and thus became one of the first advocates of the new "tailored suit.") She protected herself against the sun (and more importantly, against the glances of the curious) with large, very unwieldy umbrellas made of leather. It goes without saying that she did everything even remotely possible to safeguard her anonymity and to avoid being recognized. Whenever she encountered strangers, she darted past shyly. When she stopped at a country inn, she invariably chose a seat in the most remote corner, where she felt safer from curious glances. Nothing pleased her so much as when she could drink her glass of milk and leave again unrecognized.

By now the ladies-in-waiting were no longer selected according to the customary aristocratic rankings, for the position had stopped being considered desirable. Sound feet and an excellent physical and mental constitution had become the most important prerequisite for this honor, at one time considered such a plum.

Especially Countess Festetics, who had had no other occupation during the English hunts than to wait for hours in inns for the Empress, had a very difficult time with this new craze. She was short and tended to stoutness, and she panted after the long-legged, wiry Empress; furthermore, she was always ravenous. For during these forced marches, Elisabeth allowed no time for eating. After all, she was constantly on a diet and had little tolerance for her companions' needs. After one such outing, of almost six hours, the Emperor greeted the lady-in-waiting with the compassionate words, "And are you still alive, Countess? Really, it is going too far."[84]

But Franz Joseph accepted his wife's new quirk with his usual patience and indulgent humor, even when Elisabeth, who felt bothered by sightseers, more and more frequently chose the nights for her wanderings—not unlike the nighttime excursions of Ludwig II. In the summer of 1885, for example, she set out at one o'clock in the morning from Zell am See for the Schmittenhöhe, accompanied by a lady-in-waiting and several mountain guides carrying lanterns.[85]

Not infrequently, odd scenes occurred. Ladies rushing along in double time were an unusual sight and gave rise to misinterpretations. During the way back from one of these extensive hikes, a policeman was convinced that the two running ladies (the Empress and Countess Festetics) were being pursued by an evildoer and was anxious to offer his protection. Marie Festetics: "Then he realized that it was the Empress and stopped his interference, but followed us, panting as far as the castle."[86]

Another way to work off her need for movement during the 1880s was fencing. This activity was also soon turned into hard work. For a time, Elisabeth took two fencing lessons a day, in addition to daily fencing practice—on top of her usual gymnastics.

During the 1880s, Elisabeth traveled to England several times, but only for the ocean swimming. In this, too, she went too far and was ridiculed. Emperor Wilhelm I also "laughed at her eccentric way of life, and voiced the opinion that few people could tolerate bathing three times in the same day for half an hour at a time in the ocean."[87]

Bay Middleton's marriage took place in late 1882. A secret correspondence with the Empress apparently continued. The two also met several more times. Marie Larisch mentions a "surprising" meeting in Amsterdam, where both the Empress and Middleton were taking a course of massages by Professor Metzger, popular at the time, Elisabeth for her sciatica and Bay in order to alleviate the consequences of a fall. The walk à quatre in Amsterdam resembled, as Marie Larisch reports, a "sort of funeral march." Ruefully Elisabeth referred to herself and Bay as "the Cripple Guard."[88] And Elisabeth's chief chamberlain, Baron Nopcsa, complained, "Her Majesty is unfortunately so nervous . . . that Metzger is delighted to see us leave and said that he hoped we would never return."[89]

One final time—on March 20, 1888—Archduchess Marie Valerie mentions a visit by Bay Middleton to Gödöllö. "It recalled old but not good times," she commented disapprovingly. In 1892, Middleton broke his neck during a horse race. His wife destroyed all letters from the Empress. Only a few of her presents were preserved: a ring, cuff links, a medallion.

CHAPTER NINE

TITANIA, QUEEN OF THE FAIRIES

"I was . . . certainly not raised to be an empress, and I know that a great deal is lacking in my upbringing—but I have never done anything improper, as God is my witness. I had opportunity. They would have liked to separate me from the Emperor," Elisabeth told her lady-in-waiting in 1872[1]—and said much the same thing to other intimates at other times in similar words. There is no reason to doubt the truth of her statements, even if the gossip in Vienna dealt at length with alleged affairs of Elisabeth with other men, and even if, in her book, Elisabeth's niece, Marie Wallersee, who became Countess Larisch by marriage, mentioned such alleged affairs, though always only in obscure hints. In examining all these allegations, it turns out that no solid proof underlies any of the gossip.

Empress Elisabeth was one of the most beautiful women of the day, unhappy in her marriage, unfulfilled and without an occupation. Furthermore, she was almost always away from home, shy and unsociable, and surrounded by an aura of mystery. All these circumstances were calculated to quicken the imagination. Wherever she was, she was under the watchful eye of a great many people, from the chambermaid through the footmen to the ladies-in-waiting and members of the family.

Given these circumstances, secrets were impossible. Thus, everyone at court knew all about the imperial marriage. Quarrels and reconciliations were noted and commented on. Since the Emperor and the Empress had separate quarters, any time the two were with each other had to be won by a veritable running of the gauntlet (or so, at least, it was felt to be by Elisabeth).

Of the many gossipy stories, only one example is given here. It is particularly telling because even the Empress's closest confidants, her chief chamberlain, Baron Nopcsa, and Valerie's governess, Miss Throckmorton, were involved. Marie Festetics could hardly contain her outrage when Miss Throckmorton—without Baron Nopcsa, who was also present, objecting—asked the lady-in-waiting "whether my night's rest had not been disrupted?" Marie Festetics: "Of course I asked why, and now, with a sweet-sour expression, she told me that Their Imperial and Royal Majesties had quarreled, and the Empress would not open the door to him and barricaded *le passage!*" A gardener was said to have related the story. "These people are paid to know everything that happens to Their Supreme Majesties."[2]

Many at court who were engaged in shady dealings formed parties and stirred up dissension even in the imperial family for their own profit. Countess Festetics was not the only one to bemoan such behavior, and she repeatedly stressed how difficult it was for any individual at court to steer clear of all the intrigues or even to find out the truth. Her diary was the only place where the Countess could confide what annoyed her. "The beehive is the monarchic principle, the only difference being that there the worker bees kill the useless drones and cast them out—here it is otherwise—the drones kill the worker bees and live off what those have amassed."[3]

On their travels, conditions were not very different from those in Vienna—though, of course, there were differences of degree. While traveling, at least, the Empress could choose whom to take along, and her worst enemies were left behind in Vienna. But the size of the entourage was considerable each time: chief chamberlain, ladies-in-waiting, lady's maids, secretaries, hairdressers, bathing women, cooks, a pastry chef, coachmen, stablehands, and "dog boys." Usually, little Valerie was of the party, and with her came governesses and tutors. A doctor and a clergyman were usually also in the party. Of course, all of the more high-ranking servitors brought their own staffs (maids and valets). Thus, the Empress's traveling retinue consisted of fifty to sixty people, who were always quartered in the same building or nearby. It is quite unthinkable that, under these circumstances, the Empress would have been able to keep an affair secret.

Nevertheless, Elisabeth's unusual way of life provided plenty of food for gossip. Her shyness and the measures she took because of it gave her "almost a *ridicule*," as Marie Festetics wrote—that is, made her a figure of fun. Furthermore—and probably the most serious consequence—her strange behavior aroused suspicion. In an effort to penetrate the game of hide and seek, the most fantastic stories were invented. Marie Festetics: "one looks for other reasons, or at least one hands the reins over to those who are quick to think the worst."[4]

Given the circumstances, the truth that the marriage of the Emperor and Empress was not harmonious could not be concealed. Their reconciliation at the time of the Hungarian coronation and Valerie's birth remained an isolated episode. Quarrels erupted time and again. Most of the time, the discussions ended in Elisabeth's departure, wherever the flight might take her.

In her diaries, Marie Festetics was discretion itself. The reader has to supply the backgrounds that incited her to entries, such as one from 1874: "Yesterday it was questionable for a moment whether she would remain here. She wanted to get away. How and why I am not allowed to say. But her good angel won out, and she remained!"[5]

Everyone at court also knew how strong Elisabeth's influence on her husband was, how much she dominated him—and how humbly he courted her favor. She was the adored one, in whose moods he acquiesced—and she was extremely frugal with proofs of her favors. When the Emperor was close by, she usually suffered from some indisposition—headache, toothache, stomachache, and the like—so that he, always considerate, did not dare to make any demands. Two excerpts from Elisabeth's letters of 1869 may serve as examples. "I miss you very much, my little one, the last few days I have again trained you so nicely. Now I will have to start educating you all over again when you come back."[6] And two weeks later, "I miss you very much, my little one, but when we are alone even more. You know me and my habits and *extinction de roi* [approximately, "extinguishing the king"]. But if you do not like me the way I am, I will simply go into retirement."[7]

Repeatedly, she responded to Franz Joseph's jealousy with teasing. For example, she wrote him from Zurich in 1867, "One other thing is famous here, and that is such neat students from every nation, all of whom greet your loving wife so very politely."[8]

And from Hungary in 1868: "came home late from the theater, where, you will be reassured to learn, handsome Bela was not in attendance."[9]

From Possenhofen in the same year: "Bellegarde has arrived. Calm down, I do not flirt with him, any more than with anyone else!"[10]

From Rome in 1870: "My great favorite here is Count Malatesta. You cannot imagine what a nice, pleasant person he is. What a pity that I cannot bring him back to you."[11]

On the other hand, she left no doubt that she knew all about Franz Joseph's weakness for the female sex. After the spectacular crisis in their marriage and her flight from Vienna, she never again gave signs of jealousy. Rather, she cultivated a mocking understanding. "Last night I was . . . at the Red Mill, where we ate Schmarren [shredded sweet pancakes] and I saw a very pretty person. A good thing that you were not there. You would have run after her." Or: "You must have some very entertaining audiences, since you constantly receive beautiful girls. . . . I know why Agatha Ebergenyi was with you, how do you like her? Do not forget to tell Andrássy to come to Paris with me."[12]

This generosity was also a sign that, for Elisabeth (though by no means for Franz Joseph), the love of the early years of the marriage was irrevocably over. She recorded her hurt in many poems.

Elisabeth—an excessively sensitive, highly cultured woman given over to fantasy—was tied to a man who was practical and industrious but had no understanding for her complicated emotional life. As husband and wife grew older, abysses opened to separate them, chasms that could be bridged only precariously by outward cordiality and formal politeness. The more eccentric Elisabeth grew, the more pedantic and sober, taciturn and impersonal grew Franz Joseph. More than ever, Elisabeth complained of his obstinacy and lack of sensitivity.

Marie Festetics was extremely close to the Empress for more than twenty years but did not witness the early days of the marriage. She gave her impression of Elisabeth's relation to the Emperor. "The Empress valued her husband and was deeply devoted to him. No . . . he did not bore her, that is not the right word. But she felt it to be natural that he took no part in her spiritual life and was unable to follow her flight to higher things, her 'eccentricities' [sky-scraping]. . . . On the whole, I must say that she respected him and liked him, but I doubt that she loved him."[13]

It was Gyula Andrássy who was considered by contemporaries to be the

Empress's great love. Without a doubt, to the end of his life, he held a special place in Elisabeth's affections. The events surrounding the coronation of Franz Joseph as King of Hungary speak for themselves. But it can be considered quite certain (as far as a biographer can make such a statement after careful examination of the sources) that even this deepest feeling that united Elisabeth with a man was a platonic one. In later years, Elisabeth emphatically and proudly told various people, "Yes, it was a true friendship, and it was not poisoned by love."[14] By this word she meant physical love; all her life, the Empress was unable to find anything good in it.

None of the other men in Elisabeth's life got beyond the stage of unsuccessful suitor. Elisabeth accepted their homage as a tribute to her beauty, enjoyed their veneration, but remained the unapproachable sovereign. Marie Larisch described Elisabeth's position very accurately.

> Elisabeth was in love with love, because to her it was the spark of life. She regarded the sensation of being worshiped as a tribute offered to her beauty. But her enthusiasms never lasted long, apparently because her artistic feelings would not allow her senses to be captured. . . .
>
> She should have been enthroned among the gods, she should have been courted on the hills of Parnassus or singled out, like Leda and Semele, by a triumphant Zeus. The coarseness of life repelled the Empress to the same degree that its beauty attracted her.[15]

In spite of her sense of being one of the elect and of her sovereign position, Elisabeth nevertheless never lost her desire to know the life of the common people. Life outside court protocol held a powerful attraction. There she sought simplicity, straightforwardness, and truth. This pleasure in playing Harun al-Rashid and finding out everything that did not reach the select circles of the imperial court also played a part in the biggest adventure the Empress allowed herself: Once, masked and disguised, she secretly attended a costume ball, the Rudolfina Ball held in the Musikvereinsaal on Mardi Gras of 1874. Only a few were privy to the adventure—Ida Ferenczy, who accompanied the Empress; Fanny Feifalik, the hairdresser; and Schmidl, the lady's maid, who got the Empress ready for the big event.

Many documents have allowed this story to survive. Elisabeth, for one, considered the outing so important that she composed several long poems on the subject. Her beau of the evening, Friedrich Pacher von Theinburg, preserved the ensuing correspondence (with letters written by Elisabeth herself in a disguised handwriting); he also gave a detailed report to Elisabeth's biographer, Corti. Marie Larisch and Marie Valerie also recorded the adventure, which they heard about from the Empress herself.

The significance the Empress gave to this outing surely justifies the conclusion that it was the only one of its kind and that it made perhaps too strong an impression on her. It happened the winter after the Vienna World Exhibition, before she traveled to England to hunt, when she was thirty-six years old and had just become a grandmother for the first time.

Fritz Pacher, at the time a twenty-six-year-old government employee and a bachelor, related that at the ball, he had been drawn into conversation by an unknown woman in a red mask. (It concealed Ida Ferenczy. Elisabeth was much too shy to take the initiative.) Elisabeth and Ida had already spent some time on the gallery, watching the comings and goings of the ball below, but they had not yet met anyone. Finally, around eleven o'clock, when they grew tired of watching, Ida proposed that Elisabeth select a young man, and then she, Ida, would act as go-between: "At a ball, one must speak to people and plot." The man Elisabeth chose was Fritz Pacher.[16]

Ida first made sure that the young man was not a member of the aristocracy nor was personally acquainted with the leaders of society. Then she talked a little more without coming to the point, until finally she mentioned her friend "who is sitting up there in the gallery, all alone, and is bored to death." She led the way upstairs to a box. There sat a lady in "unusually elegant dress" of the heaviest yellow brocade equipped with a "train that was most impractical for such purposes." Her mask was so large that Pacher could not see either her features or her hair. "My mysterious lady was disguised to the point of unrecognizability and must have suffered a great deal from the heat."

The woman in red disappeared discreetly, and (according to Pacher) a "pretty dull" conversation began. They stepped to the railing and watched the carnival bustle.

Pacher: "And while, during these totally indifferent conversations, I was tortured by the thought: Who can this be? she suddenly came out with the unexpected question: 'I am a stranger here in Vienna, tell me, do you know the Empress, how do they like her, and what do they say, what do they think about her?' "

Elisabeth could not have introduced the subject more awkwardly. The question made Pacher leery. Cautiously he replied, "The Empress, well, of course I know her only by sight, when she drives to the Prater in order to go riding there. What they think of her? Actually, they do not talk about her much, because she does not like to be conspicuous in public, does not like to show herself, and busies herself primarily with her horses and dogs. I would not know anything more to say, perhaps they are not being fair to her. In any case, she is a beautiful woman."

The woman in yellow then asked her cavalier how old he thought she was. But when Pacher guessed Elisabeth's true age—thirty-six—she became surly, and shortly afterward she said abruptly, "All right, you can leave now." She addressed him in the familiar form. But the sort of treatment any courtier had to accept from an empress, Fritz Pacher refused to accept from a strange masked woman. Irritated, he countered, "How gracious you are. First you send for me to join you here, pump me for information, and then send me packing." (In speaking to her, he, too, used the familiar form of address.) Elisabeth, who was not used to such an attitude—even the Emperor responded humbly when she expressed her wishes!—relented. Pacher thought he noticed some astonishment. In any case, she said, "All right, you can stay. Sit down, and later take me down to the dance floor."

Pacher:

> From that moment on, the invisible barriers between us seemed torn down. My yellow domino, until then stiff and formal, seemed transformed, and our conversation, which touched on the most diverse topics, never came to a halt again. She took my arm, gently linking hers in mine, and, chatting steadily, we strolled through the crowded ballroom and the adjacent rooms, it must have been at least two hours. I anxiously avoided paying more insistent court to her, avoided every suggestive word, just as her conversation also bore the stamp of a "lady."

The couple did not dance. Pacher noticed how ill at ease the woman in yellow felt in the crowd. "She trembled all over her body if people did not step out of her way. Clearly, she was not used to these conditions." Her slender, tall, and extraordinarily elegant appearance caused a sensation and "visible interest among the aristocrats." Pacher: "In particular it was the well-known sportsman Niki Esterházy, the constant companion and leader of the fox hunts, in which at the time the Empress participated enthusiastically, who did not take his eyes off her and seemed to pierce her with his looks whenever we passed him. Even at the time, I felt that he suspected or perhaps even knew who was hidden behind this mask."

The conversation between the woman in yellow and Fritz Pacher turned to personal matters—Pacher's life, their shared love of dogs, finally Heinrich Heine, a topic Elisabeth found inexhaustible. Elisabeth was open about her partisanship without giving herself away by so much as a word. She paid Pacher compliments and complained, "Oh, yes, people! Whoever has come to know them as I have can only despise them, the flatterers." She put him off when he wanted to see at least her hand without a glove, fobbing him off with the possibility of a tryst at some later time in Stuttgart or Munich: "For you must know that I have no home and am constantly traveling."

Pacher's suspicion that the Empress was hidden behind the yellow mask grew stronger. He also felt that his companion was "an intelligent, cultured, and interesting woman, with a touch of originality, to whom everything ordinary was completely foreign."

Long after midnight, the woman in red (Ida Ferenczy) came back; according to Pacher, she had "been hovering around us somewhat anxiously." The three descended the large staircase to the principal approach, where they had to wait a few minutes for a carriage. When they said good-bye, Pacher boldly tried to unmask at least his companion's chin. The disguise was so tight-fitting that he was foiled, but his attempt caused the woman in red to utter "a bone-chilling scream in her ultimate alarm, which to me spoke volumes."

The adventure was not yet at an end. A few days later, the woman in yellow, who called herself Gabriele, sent a letter to her cavalier, postmarked Munich. It was Elisabeth's own handwriting, though it was disguised. She continued to toy with him and was not very modest as regarded her supposed effect. "You have talked with thousands of women and girls, you have even thought yourself amused, but your spirit never encountered a kindred soul. Finally, in a lively dream, you found what for years you had searched for, perhaps to lose it again forever."

Gabriele's next letter arrived a month later from London. She apologized for the long delay.

> My spirit was weary unto death, my thoughts did not take wing. Many a day I sat at the window for hours staring at the desolate fog, then again I was wild with joy and rushed from one diversion to the next. . . . You want to know about my doings and my life. It is not interesting. A couple of old aunts, a vicious pug, many complaints about my extravagance, for recreation a drive each afternoon in Hyde Park. In the evenings,

a party after the theater, and there you have my life, with all
its desolation and vapidity and boredom to the point of despair."

This was just as unmistakably Elisabeth's style as were the sarcastic
sentences, "Are you dreaming of me at this moment, or are you launching
yearning songs on the still night air? For the sake of those who live near
you, I hope for the former."

A third and final letter followed, this one also from London, containing
the familiar teasing allusions, the deceptions. Between them flashed a
glimpse of truth. "So you want to know what I read. I read a great deal,
quite unsystematically, just as my whole life is unsystematic—from one
day to the next."

After this letter, the only messages were from a masked woman named
Henriette, who (unsuccessfully) demanded the return of Gabriele's letters
—two years later.

In his tales, Pacher mentioned that he saw the Empress once, years later,
in the Prater. He was on horseback and she in her carriage. He was certain
that she recognized him. This impression was confirmed in Elisabeth's
verses.

> *Ich seh' dich reiten, ernst und traurig,*
> *In Winternacht im tiefen Schnee;*
> *Es bläst der Wind so eisig schaurig,*
> *Mir ist so schwer zumut, so weh!*
>
> *Im dunkeln Osten, fahl verschwommen,*
> *Da dämmert jetzt ein blasser Tag,*
> *Mit Centnerlast das Herz beklommen,*
> *Trägst heimwärts du die bitt're Klag'.*[17]

[I see you riding, sad and serious, / In the winter night, in
deepest snow; / The wind is blowing so icily eerie, / I feel so
heavy, so aching! / / In the dark east, pallid-lurid and blurred, /
A pale day is now dawning, / Your heart weighed down by
tons, / You carry homeward the bitter lament.]

Fritz Pacher's report in no way indicates, however, that he had felt any
"bitter lament." He was chiefly curious whether, as he suspected, it really
had been the Empress who was concealed behind the yellow mask. Not

a hint that he was pining away because of a great lost love, as Elisabeth's poem claimed.

Pacher's surprise was great when, in 1885—that is, eleven years after the event—he received another letter from the lady in yellow with the request that he send his address and a photograph of himself to a post-office box. Pacher replied, ". . . I have become a bald, respectable, but *happily* married man, I have a wife who resembles you in height and stature, and an adorable little girl." He did not enclose a photograph. Four months later, a second request arrived for a photograph of the "paternal bald head." Pacher grew annoyed and replied with some irritation. "I am truly sorry that after eleven years you still find it necessary to play hide-and-seek with me. Unmasking after so long a time would have been a pleasant lark and a fine ending to Mardi Gras of 1874, an anonymous correspondence loses its charm after so long a time."[18]

Elisabeth had expected quite a different outcome. Now she was so angry that the lines she wrote about Pacher held little imperial dignity. She railed at him.

> *Ein ganz gemeines Beast;*
> *Kahl war er auch, dazu noch schiech,*
> *Gehört nur auf den Mist.*[19]

[An altogether common beast; / And bald he was, and ugly to boot, / Belonging only on the dungheap.]

Of course, Pacher did not know that the lines existed. Two years later, as a coda to the Carnival adventure, he received a letter from Brazil. Lacking a return address or signature, it contained a printed poem.

> *Das Lied des gelben Domino*
> *Long, long ago*
>
> *Denkst du der Nacht noch im leuchtenden Saal?*
> *Lang, lang ist's her, lang ist's her,*
> *Wo sich zwei Seelen getroffen einmal,*
> *Lang, lang ist's her, lang ist's her.**
> *Wo unsre seltsame Freundschaft begann.*
> *Denkst du, mein Freund, wohl noch manchmal daran?*

* This refrain alternates with every one of the following lines.

Denkst du der Worte, so innig vertraut,
Die wir getauscht bei der Tanzweisen Laut?
Ein Druck der Hand noch, und ich musste fliehn,
Mein Antlitz enthüllen durft' ich dir nicht,
Doch dafür gab ich der Seele Licht.
Freund, das war mehr, das war mehr!
Jahre vergingen und zogen vorbei,
Doch sie vereinten nie wieder uns zwei.
Forschend bei Nacht fragt die Sterne mein Blick,
Auskunft noch Antwort gibt keiner zurück.
Bald wähnt' ich nahe dich, bald wieder fern.
Weilst du vielleicht schon auf anderem Stern?
Lebst du, so gib mir ein Zeichen bei Tag,
Das ich kaum hoffen, erwarten vermag.
So lang ist's her, so lang ist's her!
Lass mich warten nicht mehr,
Warten nicht mehr![20]

[Do you remember the night in the glittering ballroom? /
Long, long ago, long ago, / Where once two souls met, / Long
long ago, long ago. / / Where our strange friendship began, /
Do you, my friend, think of it at times? / Think you of the
words, so deeply intimate, / That we exchanged as the dance
music played? / Once more we pressed hands, and I had to
fly, / Nor was I allowed to disclose my features to you, / But
instead I lighted up my soul, / Friend, that was more, that was
more! / Years passed and disappeared, / But never again did
they unite us two. / Searching at night, my gaze questions the
stars, / No answer or news comes back from any of them. /
Sometimes I think you near, and then again far. / Dwell you
perhaps on another star? / If you live, give me a sign by day /
That I can hardly hope for or expect. / Long, long ago, long
ago! / Keep me waiting no more, / waiting no more!]

When Elisabeth's niece, Marie Wallersee-Larisch, published her book
Meine Vergengenheit (My Past) in 1913 and included the story of the
Empress's masked adventure, Fritz Pacher had proof of what the yellow
mask had concealed. But in no uncertain terms he contradicted Marie's
account, which made a richly amorous affair of this episode. "If the
Empress's other adventures were as innocent as the Carnival jest she played

with me à la Harun al-Rashid, she truly has nothing to reproach herself with."

When Elisabeth was a girl, in Munich, even Duchess Ludovika had looked forward to secretly visiting such balls. And in Paris, Empress Eugénie and Pauline Metternich attended such functions, concealed behind masks. The problem was the motives and consequences of such leisure diversions: the Empress of Austria was so unfulfilled that in her case, this kind of amusement not only was a diverting pastime (as it was for Empress Eugénie), but grew into dreams that papered over raw reality.

Court society could not keep up with the Empress's fantasies. Gossip occupied itself with something that was not unusual for beautiful, idle, and unhappy rich women—affairs. It was said, for instance, that "it was an open secret in the Hofburg that Her Majesty was having an affair with Niky Esterházy, and that everyone knew that, disguised as a man of the cloth, he came up through the garden and that the meetings took place in Countess Festetics's apartments."[21]

Countess Festetics was excessively puritanical and herself above all suspicion. When she learned of this gossip, her anger took on absolutely frightening proportions.

The gossip about Bay Middleton (see pages 277ff) ran along very similar lines. Here, too, examination of the sources yields no concrete proof. Even Marie Larisch merely describes a rendezvous the Empress and Middleton had in London—the highlight of the amorous adventure, as it were. Under the pretext of visiting a beauty salon, she wrote, Elisabeth had gone to London using the strictest incognito. She was accompanied by Count Heinrich Larisch, her niece Marie, and two servants. "My aunt gave the impression of a boarding-school pupil who for once had gone on vacation all on her own."[22]

Arrived in London, the Empress decided to pass up the beauty salon in favor of the Crystal Palace. Two carriages were hired, and suddenly Bay Middleton seemed to be one of the party. Elisabeth lowered her veil over her face and, at Bay's side, disappeared into the crowd. For a short time, she was (what shocking behavior for an empress!) alone with a man who was not of the aristocracy, in the midst of the booths with trained monkeys, fortune tellers, shooting galleries, in a world of jugglers and magicians, which she had loved as a child but which, because she was an empress, had been forbidden to her ever since. It is hard to find anything in this episode —or in the adventure at the masked ball—that could be criticized.

Having had this taste of disappearing into the life outside the court, the Empress dared one more sidestep: She allowed herself to visit a small restaurant. Marie Larisch: "I could hardly believe it, Aunt Sissi with her fanatical diets and timetables wanted to go to a restaurant!" Heinrich Larisch calmed the excited young lady, explaining "that surely one should not begrudge the Empress the innocent pleasure of enjoying her freedom for once." To Marie Larisch's astonishment, Elisabeth ate "at this late hour, not only roast chicken, but also Italian salad, drank champagne, and devoured a considerable amount of delicate pastry, things she usually despised." Never in Vienna had the Empress eaten so much at table.

During the return trip—without Bay—the Empress was "extremely cheerful, and said that it really was wonderfully amusing for a change to pass a day without trailing a comet's tail." Marie Larisch was nevertheless astonished when Middleton, who had taken the evening train to Brighton, stood ready to welcome the Empress, wearing an innocent expression, bowing respectfully, and saying, "I hope your Majesty had a good time."

One can hardly deny that Elisabeth showed a sense of humor during her escapades. She amused herself, for example, by leading the ever daring Prince of Wales (later, King Edward VII) up the garden path. A poem (probably exaggerated with her usual flights of fancy) records the scene.

"There is somebody coming upstairs"

Wir sassen im Drawing-room gemütlich beisammen
Prince Eduard und ich.
Er raspelte Süssholz und schwärmte,
Er sagte, er liebte mich.
Er rückte sehr nah und nahm meine Hand,
Und lispelte: Dear cousin, wie wär's?
Ich lachte von Herzen und drohte:
"There is somebody coming upstairs."
Wir lauschten, es war aber nichts,
Und weiter ging das lustige Spiel.
Sir Eduard ward mutig,
Ja, er wagte auch viel.
Ich wehrte mich nicht, es war interessant,
Ich lachte: "Dear cousin, wie wär's?"
Da ward er verlegen und flüsterte leis:
"There is somebody coming upstairs."[23]

[We were sitting cosily together in the drawing room, / Prince Edward and I. / He whispered sweet nothings and raved on, / He said that he loved me. / He drew very close and took my hand, / And whispered, Dear cousin, how about it? / I laughed with all my heart and warned him, / "There is somebody coming upstairs." We listened, but it was nothing, / And the merry game went on. / Sir Edward grew bold, / Yes, and very daring. / I did not protest, it was interesting, / I laughed, "Dear cousin, how about it?" / At that he grew embarrassed and whispered softly, / "There is somebody coming upstairs."]

A man as well informed as Count Charles Bombelles, chamberlain to Crown Prince Rudolf, declared all the sensationalist gossip around the Empress to be untrue—and he was anything but a supporter of Elisabeth. In 1876, he mentioned "the extravagances of the Empress, but very innocent ones," as Hübner noted in his diary. He, too, attributed a major part of Sisi's behavior to the effects of her early very unhappy life in Vienna and the excessive severity of Archduchess Sophie. "One has placed one chain after another around this bottle of champagne, and finally the cork blew. It is a lucky thing that this explosion had no consequences other than the ones we see: unfettered preference for horses, hunting, and sports, as well as a secluded life, which is not easy to reconcile with the obligations of an empress."[24]

The older Elisabeth grew and the more her shyness increased, the more she became trapped in her fantasies and her dream world. It was specifically in this area that her inhibited relations with men became evident.

Among the myths and legends that particularly caught the Empress's fancy was the story of a legendary Egyptian queen who never grew old and who lived, veiled, in a mysterious place. Her name had long ago been forgotten. "She" retained her power not to age, but only so long as she did not give herself in love to a man.[25] Elisabeth, too, was unapproachable, with the deep fear that love might rob her of her power and aura.

In her poems, she saw herself most often as Titania, Queen of the Fairies. The unsuccessful suitors were represented as donkeys. Every castle where the Empress lived boasted a painting of Titania with the donkey. Elisabeth to Christomanos: "That is the ass's head of our illusions, which we caress ceaselessly. . . . I never get tired of looking at it."[26]

In almost all her poems, Franz Joseph is depicted as Oberon, King of the Fairies, standing by Titania's side. Occasionally, however, Elisabeth included even her husband in the ranks of her admirers, which was probably a realistic view of the attitude he demonstrated toward her for the world to see.

In all these poems, the influence of Heinrich Heine is all too plain: His laments about false love, about lies and disappointments also appear in Elisabeth's verses. After she had stopped riding so abruptly, she lived in total seclusion, remained far away from Vienna, sought solitude and nature, and did not miss the company of men.

Her poems also dealt with the dead and with heroes of legend, such as Heine and her favorite Achilles. It is hard to distinguish where, in her feelings, infatuation stops and the yearning for death begins. Both are quite certainly evident in Elisabeth's dabbling with spiritualism. She no longer found anyone among the living who understood her. She was too sensitive, too vulnerable for a real, "normal" relationship with a man. She therefore took refuge in fantasy relations with dead heroes, who could not hurt her.

No matter how florid some of these poems and fantasies might be, reality was much more ordinary. Many of Elisabeth's statements and poems give indications of an extreme tension when it comes to sexuality. Only in her poems did Titania lower herself to the ass. In reality, she loathed love.

> *Für mich keine Liebe,*
> *Für mich keinen Wein;*
> *Die eine macht übel,*
> *Der andere macht spei'n!*
>
> *Die Liebe wird sauer,*
> *Die Liebe wird herb;*
> *Der Wein wird gefälschet*
> *Zu schnödem Erwerb.*
>
> *Doch falscher als Weine*
> *Ist oft noch die Lieb';*
> *Man küsst sich zum Scheine*
> *Und fühlt sich ein Dieb!*
>
> *Für mich keine Liebe,*
> *Für mich keinen Wein;*
> *Die eine macht übel,*
> *Der andre macht spei'n!*[27]

[For me no love, / For me no wine; / The one makes you
ache, / The other makes you ill! / / Love grows sour, / Love
grows bitter; / The wine is doctored / For base gain. / / But
more false than wine / Often is love; / We pretend to be kissing / And feel like thieves! / / For me no love, / For me no
wine; / The one makes you ache, / The other makes you ill!]

There are more examples of this sort. As has been seen, Elisabeth may
be retrospectively diagnosed as a victim of anorexia nervosa. Psychologists
now believe that this disorder is caused by a deep revulsion against everything that is physical and voluptuous, but most especially against sexuality.

Even when her favorite daughter, Marie Valerie, married and became
pregnant, Elisabeth could not conceal her distaste. She knew nothing to
say to the extremely young wife and prospective mother except that she
"sighed for 'the good old times, when I was still an innocent virgin'
. . . yes sometimes, joking in her peculiar way, she said that looking at my
changed figure made her altogether impatient and that she was 'ashamed
of me.' "[28]

At times, Elisabeth's tried-and-true game—unapproachable goddess and
infatuated ass—turned into a real jest. In the late 1880s—the Empress was
at least fifty years old—a young man from Saxony named Alfred Gurniak
Lord Schreibendorf began to dog her footsteps. He followed her as far as
Romania, pursuing her with endlessly long, florid love letters and urgent
pleas for proof of her favor. Elisabeth remained aloof. But she saved
Alfred's letters and made them the basis of a cynical poem, "Titania and
Alfred," which she never completed.

There is no doubt that for the Empress, this overwrought young man
was merely a figure of ridicule. Nevertheless, her thoughts dealt so in-
tensely with the matter that she composed many pages of poetry about it.
Surely she also kept the "enchanted stag" Alfred in thrall by offering now
and again tiny proofs of her favor (such as flowers deliberately left behind
on a park bench). She saw the episode not only as a cause for merriment,
but also as a welcome distraction in her empty life.

Among the many lines about her admirer Alfred, however, we also find
the revealing lines:

> *Besitzest du den kecken Mut,*
> *Mich jemals zu erreichen?*
> *Doch tödted meine kalte Glut,*
> *Ich tanze gern auf Leichen.*

[Are you so bold and brave / As to reach me ever? / But my cold fire kills, / And I will stop at nothing.]

And in another poem, "Titania's Spinnlied" (Titania's Spinning Song), some very similar lines occur.

Du willst ein Spiel der Minne,
Verrückter Erdensohn?
Mit goldnen Fäden spinne
Dein Leichentuch ich schon. . . .

In meiner schönen Mache
Verzapple dich zu Tod,
Ich schaue zu und lache
Von jetzt bis Morgenrot.

[You want a game of love, / Mad mortal? / With golden threads I am already / Spinning your shroud. . . . / / In my handsome net / Enmesh yourself until you die, / I stand by and laugh / From now until dawn.]

But in spite of threats of suicide, Alfred had no real intention of becoming a corpse. Instead, he demanded money from his idol. For this, too, Elisabeth had only scorn.

Ich glaube nicht an die Liebe,
Was dir dein Leben vergällt,
Das sind ganz andere Triebe,
Ich ahne wohl was dir fehlt.
Mein Jüngling, du hast wohl Schulden
Und wähnst in schlauem Sinn:
Die Liebe mit goldenen Gulden
Lohnt mir meine Königin.[29]

[I do not believe in love, / What is souring your life / Are quite different urges, / I truly sense what you need. / My boy, surely you have debts / And imagine slyly: / My queen will repay me / My love with golden guldens.]

This farce of "Titania and Alfred" is not as trivial as it may at first glance seem in the context of a biography. It characterized Elisabeth's relations with her admirers, as well as her inability to separate reality from fantasy. The fact that she spent many hours composing the Alfred poems shows the extent of her isolation.

The episode with Alfred Gurniak took place in 1887–1888, a time of crises in the Balkans and the constant threat of war, a time when the European system of alliances was changing in fundamental ways through the Reinsurance Treaty between Germany and Russia, concluded behind the back of Austria-Hungary. During this time, two men politically close to the Empress—Gyula Andrássy and Crown Prince Rudolf—voiced opposition to the Emperor's foreign policy. Both expected and hoped for backing from the only person whose word could have gained the Emperor's ear—the Empress. Elisabeth evaded all expectations and all hopes. She abandoned both Andrássy and Rudolf, just as for decades she had abandoned her husband with his problems. She showed the world her contempt—and concentrated on the jest of infatuated Alfred from Dresden.

The tragedy of Crown Prince Rudolf was coming to a head. Elisabeth was so caught up in her reveries of Titania, Queen of the Fairies, and various besotted asses that she did not even acknowledge her son's unhappiness, though repeatedly, with extreme shyness and caution, he asked for her help.

The seductiveness of Elisabeth's personality outlived even her beauty. In the 1890s, when her skin had long since become wrinkled and her sight had grown blurred, she still, when she made the effort, exerted her usual magic. The young Greek readers who accompanied her during these years fell in love with the solitary, melancholy woman, and for the rest of their lives they raved about the hours they had been allowed to spend in her company. Konstantin Christomanos, for one, wrote gushy and lyrical books about her. The people around Elisabeth, however, felt sorry for these young men. Chief Chamberlain Nopcsa wrote to Ida Ferenczy that 'the Empress was spoiling the Greeks "in a way I have never yet witnessed in Her Majesty. Pity the young man, since he will be made unhappy."[30]

Even Alexander von Warsberg, who at the outset had been very critical of the Empress, gave clear signs of love after only a short time of traveling in Greece with her.

It hardly needs repeating that Emperor Franz Joseph's love for his wife remained constant through all the years, in spite of everything.

CHAPTER TEN

EAGLE AND SEAGULL

The more Elisabeth's tendency to withdraw from the world and her fear of people increased, the more closely she became attached to her cousin King Ludwig II of Bavaria, who had turned out very like her. The relationship between the two had not begun as a particularly close one. There had been significant quarrels, rooted in family relations; the rivalry between the royal and the ducal Bavarian lines was generations old. The kinship was not very close: Ludwig's grandfather, King Ludwig I, and Sisi's mother, Ludovika, were brother and sister, making Sisi the cousin of Ludwig's father, King Max II. The eight-year difference in their ages played a large part in their early years; when Elisabeth left Bavaria in 1854 at the age of sixteen, the then Crown Prince Ludwig was only eight years old.

Ten years later, Ludwig became King. From approximately this time on—Ludwig was eighteen, Elisabeth twenty-six—they grew closer. Shortly after his accession in 1864, the young King visited his imperial cousin in Bad Kissingen, where he remained for some time, going on walks with her and talking with her so intimately and in such detail that Sisi told her family, "delighted by their being in unison, of many shared hours"— making her favorite brother, Karl Theodor ("Gackel") jealous.[1]

Elisabeth and Ludwig attracted attention wherever they went. The young King was exquisitely beautiful, tall, serious, with a romantic flair; beside him, his Wittelsbach cousin, in full bloom, tall and slender, slightly sickly and melancholy. Ludwig's effect on the court at Munich was much like Sisi's in Vienna. According to Prince Philipp zu Eulenburg, he strutted, "handsome as a golden pheasant, among all the domestic hens."[2]

Both Ludwig and Sisi felt contempt for their world and indulged themselves in ever new eccentricities to shock those around them. Both made their likes and dislikes extremely plain, especially Ludwig. When, for example, he had a guest whom he did not like, he had huge bouquets of flowers placed on the table, so as not to have to look at the miserable wretch.[3] The guest, for his part, had to make desperate efforts to make himself heard.

Both loved solitude and hated court constraints. The following sentences by Ludwig II could just as easily have come from Elisabeth's pen, except that Munich, and not Vienna, was meant. "Shut up in my golden cage . . . Can barely wait for the arrival of those blessed days in May to leave for a long time the hated, accursed city to which nothing ties me, which I inhabit with insurmountable loathing."[4]

Elisabeth, too, liked to act unconventionally and irritated the rigidly conformist people around her with unusual expressions, often to such an extent that some concluded that she, too, was at the very least "peculiar," like her Bavarian cousin. Marie Larisch:

> In many things the Empress was very like Ludwig II, but unlike him, had the mental and physical strength not to fall prey to eccentric ideas. She was wont to say, half seriously, half joking: "I know that sometimes I am considered mad." As she spoke, she wore a mocking smile, and her golden-brown eyes flashed like heat lightning in restrained mischievousness. Everyone who knew Elisabeth well wrote about her pleasure in teasing innocents. Thus, with the straightest face, she could sometimes say the most outrageous things or, with an enchanting smile, throw

an elegant indiscretion at someone, in order, as she put it, to enjoy her listener's gape. Unless you knew Elisabeth through and through, it was sometimes hard to decide if she was saying something seriously or was only joking.[5]

Prince Eulenberg also pointed out shared traits.

The Empress, who had a tendency to be somewhat eccentric and who was very talented, always had more understanding for her cousin than other mortals. Considering that she would work for hours in her salon at the trapeze, wearing a kind of circus costume, or would suddenly—attired only in a long rain skirt over jersey clothing—walk from Feldafing to Munich, a distance of about 50 kilometers (I encountered her once so attired), it is understandable why she found her cousin's extravagances 'reasonable'; his worst excesses surely never reached her ears.[6]

Both Elisabeth and Ludwig loved learning and read a great deal, especially classical literature. Both were admirers of Schopenhauer. Both were antimilitarist. Both also had felt great assurance in their feelings about the church; Ludwig to Crown Prince Rudolf: "Let the people keep their good Catholic faith, with its soothing promise of a hereafter, its miracles and sacraments; but as you correctly put it, the educated man cannot possibly be satisfied with these antiquated views."[7] Sisi could not talk so well about her mother-in-law, Archduchess Sophie, with anyone else as with her "royal cousin," who considered Sophie an "Ultramontane, deluded woman."[8]

No matter how many puzzles the relationship between Ludwig and Elisabeth presented, one thing was certain: sexuality had no part in it. Ludwig, who liked calling himself "the virgin king," had homosexual tendencies, though he struggled against them with all his might, always striving for the ideal of chivalric purity. Since, "thank God," he knew nothing of desire for the female sex, he once wrote, his "adoration for the purity of women" was "all the more deeply felt."[9]

To picture the strange relationship of these two Bavarian relatives, we must always recall Ludwig's total absence of sexual response to women. It was (in Ludwig's sense) a "pure"—that is, completely nonerotic—love between the handsome King, who crossed the boundary between normality and madness as early as the 1870s, and the Empress, who, at least as an aging woman, increasingly cultivated odd habits.

Elisabeth and Ludwig were close, but in a manner that differed from the closeness of a man and a woman. It was the intimacy of two fairy-tale characters who have left reality and "normal people" behind.

During the 1860s, however, the older and more highly placed Elisabeth was still a person the young King must respect—as she knew only too well. She could afford to scold him in no uncertain terms in 1865, when Bavaria recognized the Kingdom of Italy. In her opinion, Ludwig showed too little Wittelsbach solidarity with the Italian rulers, especially with the King and Queen of the Two Sicilies. Elisabeth to Ludwig II: "I cannot conceal from you that I was very surprised by the recognition of Italy particularly on the part of Bavaria, for each of the banished princely families includes members of the Bavarian royal family, though I imagine that the reasons that have persuaded you to this inexplicable step must be so weighty that my simple view of your attitude cannot even be considered, given the important interests and sacred duties you must espouse." After these outspoken words, however, she assured the King of the "fervent love with which I cling to my home," and the "cordial, honest friendship I feel especially for you."[10]

But these were surely the usual court clichés. Sisi's comments on the appearances of her highly theatrical cousin were usually sarcastic, as when she wrote from Bavaria to Rudolf, sixteen years old at the time, "Yesterday the King paid me a long visit, and if Grandmama had not eventually joined us, he would still be here. He is quite reconciled, I was very well behaved, he kissed my hand so much that Aunt Sofie, who was looking through the door, afterward asked me whether I still had it! Once again he was wearing an Austrian uniform and was heavily perfumed."[11]

The Aunt Sophie mentioned in this letter was Elisabeth's youngest sister. Because of her beauty and her highly placed relatives in Vienna, there were many aspirants for her hand, and she handed out refusals right and left. In 1867, Sophie became engaged to King Ludwig II. It was love in Ludwig's style: impassioned, unworldly, without the "sensuality" Ludwig hated. Sophie, who adored Wagner, was extremely musical. She had a beautiful voice and could sing to the King for hours. Most important, she was Elisabeth's sister and very like her. Even during the brief period the engagement lasted, Ludwig's letters to the Empress were far more ardent that those to the young bride, whom he always addressed as Elsa. Characteristically, however, Ludwig did not see himself as the loving Lohengrin; his letters to Elsa were always signed Heinrich—that is, he assumed the role of King Henry the Fowler.

The King spoke less and less of marriage, even though a splendid wedding coach was ready and waiting. Finally, Duke Max laid down the law and gave the vacillating bridegroom an ultimatum. Ludwig, offended in his sense of majestic grandeur, took this as the welcome excuse to break the engagement and to assure his "beloved Elsa" that he loved her "like a precious sister." "Now I have had time to examine my feelings, to reflect seriously, and I see that now as before, my true, fond brotherly love for you is rooted deep in my soul, but not the love that is necessary to a wedded union."[12]

Relieved, he wrote in his diary, "Sophie written off. The somber picture scattered; I long for freedom, I thirst for freedom, for a return from the tormenting nightmare."[13] He took the sculpted bust of his beautiful bride and threw it out the window. (After only a few months, Sophie was consoled and became engaged to the equally good-looking Duke of Alençon. Ludwig made no further attempts to find a queen.)

Ludwig's admiration of Elisabeth, however, was unchanged by the embarrassing incident of the failed engagement. Beginning in 1872, every time Elisabeth stayed in Possenhofen, Ludwig paid her a visit. His arrival always occasioned a great fuss, because the King was unwilling to see anyone except the Empress—not her siblings (not even his former fiancée), not her parents, not the servants. Countess Festetics: "quickly he replaced the cap, which rode precariously atop the beautiful wavy hair, with the shako. He was wearing Austrian uniform and sported aslant across his chest the ribbon of the Great Cross of St. Stephen and over it, going in the opposite direction, the field ribbon. He alighted from the carriage—a handsome man with the mannerisms of a stage king or like Lohengrin in the wedding processions."

Contrary to Ludwig's wish, Elisabeth introduced her lady-in-waiting to the King. In her diary the attendant described Ludwig's "wonderful dark eyes, which quickly changed expression; dreamily soft, then again, like lightning, a flash of spiteful amusement—and to say it all—the glowing, sparkling eyes grow cold, and a glance, a glow more like cruelty flashes in them!! Then again, he looks melancholy and gentle; what he says shows intelligence; he speaks well and self-confidently."[14] This was the time when Ludwig's younger brother Otto was already mad; in Ludwig, too, certain character traits became increasingly evident that no longer conformed to normal standards. Even during this visit of 1872, Marie Festetics reacted with compassion to the strange behavior of the Bavarian King.

The friendship between Ludwig and Elisabeth was not without its tensions. Several times, Elisabeth insisted on bringing along her "only child," little Valerie, to a meeting. Her excessive maternal love set Ludwig's teeth on edge. "I really do not know what the Empress is constantly telling me about her Valerie, she wants to see me, but I do not want to see her,"[15] Ludwig complained to one of his confidants. Sisi, for her part, wrote her husband in 1874, "If only the King of Bavaria would leave me alone,"[16] and she complained to her ladies-in-waiting about Ludwig's exhausting visits.

Elisabeth, too, felt "immeasurable compassion" (Festetics) for Ludwig, because "he is not mad enough to be locked up but too abnormal to manage comfortably in the world with reasonable people." The King's long and generally taciturn visits tired her, but (to the consternation of Countess Festetics) she kept finding new traits they had in common. "And since he loves solitude and, as he says, 'is unappreciated,' she believes that there are similarities between them, and the trace of melancholia in him is another thread!—God forbid that this similarity is real!"

The Countess comforted herself with one thought: "That is just one of her ideas, like an excuse, to explain why she too likes to seclude herself. It would be a family trait, which one does not have to account for."[17]

In the early 1870s, it was Crown Prince Rudolf who kept the relationship between Ludwig and Elisabeth alive. The King liked the fifteen-year-old boy, who was lively and very well-read, immensely. He discussed Grillparzer's plays and Richard Wagner with him. He sent many rhapsodic letters filled with assurances of friendship and many hymns of praise for Elisabeth.

Though Ludwig's ties to Rudolf loosened as Rudolf's intellectual independence grew, the links with the Empress became closer than ever during the 1880s. Both felt unappreciated, felt that they were among the elect, not subject to any human laws and obligations. As a young woman, at the time of her greatest triumphs, Elisabeth had still made fun of the King because of his buffoonery. Now, twenty years later, she too withdrew into herself, was extremely shy of company, and almost reveled in her problems and fears. She rediscovered the advantages of her Bavarian royal cousin. The increasingly close relationship with the mentally ill King proved an enormous risk to the aging Empress.

All the encounters of the two cousins during this time seem bizarre. In 1881, Sisi took a boat across Lake Starnberg to the Rose Island, where Ludwig II had fled from the affairs of government. She brought along only Rustimo, the blackamoor. On the return trip, the King accompanied her. As they crossed the lake, Rustimo sang foreign folk songs to the guitar, and as a reward, Ludwig placed a ring on his finger. Elisabeth made the scene the occasion for a poem in which she presented herself as a northern seagull (she happened to be traveling through Holland while writing these lines) and Ludwig as an eagle. In her usual way, she did not mail these verses but left them in Ludwig's castle on the Rose Island when she paid a return visit in June 1885, while the King was away.

It was not until September 1885 that Ludwig II found Sisi's poem. In return, he wrote a poem in an elegiac tone. He attached a letter of explanation. "For years I have not visited the Rose Island, only a few days ago I learned what joy was awaiting me there. At this news, I flew hurriedly to the idyllic island and there found the precious greeting from my seagull! Deepest, most fervent thanks!"[18]

Encounters between Elisabeth and Ludwig were nevertheless infrequent. By this time, Ludwig II was living sequestered from the world in his fairy-tale castles, sleeping through the days and spending the nights on solitary horseback rides through the mountains. It was especially during this time, when Ludwig was living a totally isolated fantasy life and no longer found support even among his family, that Elisabeth defended her royal cousin. After all, she had always been interested in mental illness, which claimed so many victims in the Wittelsbach family during this period. She felt almost magically attracted to people who had stepped over the boundary between "normality" and "madness." In 1874, in the company of Queen Marie of Bavaria, the mother of Ludwig II and the mad Otto, Elisabeth visited an insane asylum in Munich. Countess Festetics, who was also present at this visit, reported, "The Empress was pale and somber, but the Queen—God have mercy—who has two mad sons, she was amused and laughed."

On the other hand, Elisabeth was so fascinated by this visit that she replicated it as soon as possible—six months later, in London. Marie Festetics cautiously expressed her fears of what was to become of Elisabeth. "Who can say where the dividing line between madness and reason lies? Where order stops in the human mind? Where sense, what is right— between imagined and real woes—between real joy and fictive imaginings, stops and begins?"[19]

Elisabeth must have realized the hereditary taint to which she was subject. Ludwig's and Otto's disorder presumably came from the maternal line (Queen Marie was a Hohenzollern), to which the ducal branch of the Wittelsbachs was not related. But Elisabeth's grandfather, Duke Pius of Bavaria, was also mentally disturbed and spent the final years of his life as a recluse, completely cut off from human society. Some of Elisabeth's brothers and sisters were at the very least unstable; in any case, they gave signs of a strong tendency to melancholia. Her sister Helene, for example, had severe mental disturbances after the death of a son in 1885, and according to Archduchess Valerie, she "often seemed mad in her terrible passion"[20]—not unlike the youngest sister, Sophie. The "Italian" sisters, Marie and Mathilde, were also depressive as they grew older.

Elisabeth also assured her Greek reader Konstantin Christomanos of her belief. "Have you not noticed that in Shakespeare the madmen are the only sensible ones. In the same way, in real life we do not know where reason and where madness are to be found, just as we do not know whether reality is the dream or the dream is reality. I tend to consider anyone reasonable who is called mad. What is actually reason is considered to be 'dangerous madness.' "[21]

When events concerning the increasingly strange King came to a head in June 1886, when he was declared insane and removed from government, Elisabeth happened to be in Bavaria, living in Feldafing on the other shore of Lake Starnberg, where Ludwig II met his death by drowning. It was said that the Empress had wanted to help the King to flee and had a carriage made ready for him in Feldafing. These rumors are not confirmed by any of the sources, and in themselves sound unlikely. For Elisabeth hardly had the energy required for such a spectacular abduction under such complicated conditions. It is true that she made an attempt to speak with the interned King, but she abandoned her plan when she was advised against it.[22]

She took Ludwig's death in her own way: laments about the sorrows of the world, despair and heated expressions of feeling, frightening to those around her. Archduchess Valerie's diary gives an account of the evening of the day the news of Ludwig's death was received.

> When I was with Mama in the evening for prayers, she threw herself headlong on the ground—I screamed aloud, for I thought she had seen something, and I grasped her so tightly that finally we could not help laughing. Mama said that she wanted only to beg God's forgiveness in repentance and humility for her rebellious thoughts, she had cudgeled her brains about unfathomable God's unfathomable decree of retribution in the hereafter through time and eternity—and weary of her fruitless, sinful brooding, she was now determined, whenever doubts arose, humbly to say, "Jehovah, You are great, You are the God of vengeance, of mercy, of wisdom."[23]

As an unusually well-informed correspondent of the Berlin *Tageblatt* later wrote, Elisabeth fell into a deep swoon at Ludwig's catafalque. "But when she opened her eyes and regained her speech, she categorically demanded that the king be taken from the chapel—that he was not dead at all but 'was only pretending, so as to be left in peace forever by the world and the insufferable people.' " This newspaper report is entirely plausible, as is the statement, "But from then on, the Empress's ailment took a sudden and very grave step forward."[24]

Elisabeth's chamberlain, Baron Nopcsa, even informed Andrássy about the Empress's alarming mental state. Though she was, "thank God, in good health, unfortunately her mental state is not as I would like to see it. Though there is no reason for it, she is nevertheless emotionally disturbed. Since she lives so utterly alone, she talks herself into it more and more."[25]

Even the Wittelsbachs—that is, Sisi's closest relations—felt (justifiable) worry about Elisabeth's mental state during this time. The daughter of Duke Karl Theodor, Amélie, wrote in her diary after Ludwig's death, "Aunt Sisi is stricken. Often I fear, after her own statements and Valerie's words about her, that everything is not right with her. It would be so terrible!!!" At a later time, Amélie wrote of Sisi's "bewildered glance, her gloomy, disturbed expression during these days."[26]

Crown Prince Rudolf came to Munich for Ludwig's funeral. He sounded worried when he told Valerie that "he found Mama disturbed beyond his expectations and questioned me a great deal."[27]

Only slowly did Elisabeth recover to the point where she could return to writing poetry; it goes without saying that her lines dealt with the death of her cousin. The reproaches the Empress leveled at the Bavarian government for having driven the King to his death were merciless. She demanded revenge and retribution. By laying the principal blame for Ludwig's death (and she never doubted that it was suicide) on Prince Regent Luitpold, Elisabeth was in agreement with popular opinion in Bavaria at the time. For in spite of his eccentricities, Ludwig II was very popular with the common people, and—in spite of undisputed personal loyalty—Prince Regent Luitpold was reputed for years to have unnecessarily interned Ludwig II and therefore to have driven him to his death. (Luitpold never became King of Bavaria but was called Prince Regent all his life because Ludwig's official successor, his brother Otto, was too mad to rule.) Nor was Elisabeth ever reconciled with Luitpold—a situation that led to some embarrassing moments, for Luitpold was her daughter Gisela's father-in-law.

Unlike Elisabeth, Duchess Ludovika took the part of the Prince Regent, causing serious differences between mother and daughter. In Ludovika's opinion, it was necessary to hope that Ludwig II was mad, "so as not to have to accuse him of the horrifying and sadly neglected responsibility for having brought his blooming land and almost unbelievably loyal subjects so low."[28]

Sisi's favorite brother, Duke Karl Theodor, who knew Ludwig II very well, and who, as a doctor, had diagnosed some madness in the King as early as the 1860s, was also entirely on the side of the "reason of state" and Prince Regent Luitpold. According to Archduchess Valerie, Karl Theodor continued to assert that "there could be no doubt about the complete madness of the King and attempted to calm Mama [that is, Elisabeth], who is terribly disturbed and in an emotional state that makes me very sad."[29] His attempts were in vain. Quite the contrary; now Elisabeth was seriously at odds not only with the rest of her Bavarian family, but even with her favorite brother.

Even years later, Elisabeth lamented the death of her royal cousin; she went so far as to work herself into a melancholy quite out of proportion with the extent of her friendship with Ludwig. She, who had seen the living Ludwig only on the rarest of occasions, now made an idol of the memory of the dead "eagle." In his memory, Elisabeth even went to Bayreuth in 1888 (for the first and last time in her life) to attend a performance of *Parsifal*. Her response to the music was extremely sentimental. "Since then, I feel homesick for it as I do for the North Sea. It is something of which we wish that it would never end, that it continue forever."[30] Archduchess Valerie: "Mama was so ravished that she wished to see the conductor, Mottl, and the singers [who took the parts] of Parsifal and Amfortas . . . their unpoetical appearance diminished the illusion somewhat."[31]

The Empress also had a long conversation with Cosima Wagner; they spoke especially about Ludwig. Cosima Wagner later told Elisabeth's niece Amélie that "she had never yet seen anyone so affected as Aunt Sisi after the *Parsifal*."[32] Cosima Wagner, too, mentioned the resemblance between Ludwig II and Elisabeth.

As Elisabeth's spiritualist tendencies increased in the late 1880s, Ludwig's figure assumed greater importance in her imagination. She repeatedly mentioned that he had "appeared" to her and had spoken. In her growing isolation, Ludwig's destiny seemed to her almost enviable.

Und dennoch, ja dennoch beneide ich dich,
Du lebtest den Menschen so ferne,
Und, jetzt, da die göttliche Sonne dir wich,
Beweinen dich oben die Sterne.[33]

[And yet, and yet I envy you, / You lived so distant from men, / And now that the divine sun has evaded you, / The stars above weep for you.]

The Empress drew consolation and even a kind of piety from these spiritualist encounters, as Valerie described in her diary in 1887.

Thank God Mama has struggled through her weltschmerz and her doubts of last year more successfully than I—her faith in Jehovah, into Whose arms she threw herself after the King's death in order to find rest from the torments that persecuted her, is absolute; she attributes everything to His disposition and guidance, she leaves everything in His hands. I have never known Mama to be so devout as [she has been] since that time —it leads me to believe that her spiritual dealings with Heine and the King are countenanced by God. . . . Mama's piety is, however, different from other people's . . . extravagant and abstract as her death cult.[34]

And shortly thereafter, Valerie wrote, "Since her intense spiritual dealings Mama really is . . . calmer and happier, and in meditating and composing poetry . . . she has found a satisfying lifework."[35] Elisabeth's poems also confirm the fact that her spiritual congress with her dead "royal cousin" brought her comfort and relief.

In this, the Empress was supported by one of the friends of her youth, Countess Irene Paumgarten, in Munich. In a "very confidential" report to Bismarck, Prince Eulenburg revealed what only "a few initiates" knew. "Countess Paumgarten is a so-called 'writing medium.' She has the ability of writing 'automatically,' which is to say: her hand is guided by 'spirits' while she falls into a dreamlike somnambulistic state. When asked questions, she writes down the answers given by the 'spirits.' The Empress has been in touch with this medium for years. She uses her stays in Munich for 'sessions,' but she also sends written inquiries to the Countess when she encounters problems in her life."[36]

Naturally, Elisabeth was not alone in her interest in spiritualism. Séances with table tilting and the most diverse mediums had become the rage among high society. The famous mediums did a thriving business, though now and then one of them was unmasked as a fraud—the medium Bastian, for example, was found out by none other than Elisabeth's son, Crown Prince Rudolf, during a sensational session in 1884. Rudolf was among the most active opponents of the spiritualist fad, even writing a pamphlet, *Einige Worte über den Spiritismus* (A Few Words About Spiritualism), which was published anonymously in 1882. These activities of the Crown Prince's were indirectly aimed at his mother, though she was, of course, as unaware of Rudolf's antispiritualist pamphlet as she was of his other writings.

Prince Eulenburg also found nothing unusual in the fact that Empress Elisabeth was a spiritualist. For him (and for the person to whom the report was addressed, Prince Bismarck), the only significant question was whether or not Countess Paumgarten was exerting political influence on the Empress. And in this regard, Eulenburg could reassure the chancellor. "I am unable to call the Countess's automatic writing mischief because she is acting bone fide and her character guarantees her honesty. Nor does the Countess use her influential connections in any way for personal purposes. But that Her Majesty's belief in the messages from the spirit world can under certain circumstances have great significance can surely not be in doubt."

Sisi even took Marie Valerie along on one such visit. The practical fifteen-year-old, however, was anything but pleased with the spiritualist conversations and, astonished, wrote in her diary the following exchange between Elisabeth and Irene Paumgarten: Elisabeth begged her friend, "Tonight lay Empress Marianne at our feet" (Empress Maria Anna was the wife of Emperor Ferdinand I; she had died in 1884). Whereupon Irene Paumgarten replied, "Oh, she is still wandering along dark paths."[37]

In her diary (not found to this day but quoted by Marie Larisch), the Empress explained her tendencies.

> I do not belong to those whose spiritual senses are closed off. And that is why I hear—or, rather, feel—the thoughts and the will concerning me of my spirit. That is why I see blonde Else of the Rhine and Bubi [her nephew Taxis, who died young], once I also saw Max [Emperor Maximilian of Mexico], but he did not have the strength to tell me what he clearly wished to tell me. . . . These images come to me in a waking state, just

as memory arouses "phantoms" while we sleep. But what I see in the waking state are not phantoms, not hallucinations, as some people, who lack understanding, claim, and so give a meaningless word instead of a logical explanation. . . . It gives me great satisfaction and deep reassurance in many an hour that I can make a connection with spirits from the beyond. But with very few exceptions, people do not understand that. And whatever ignorant people do not understand, they declare to be nonsense.[38]

The Empress tried to receive messages from the other world by every conceivable method. She also tried to fathom the future, and she was highly superstitious. Marie Larisch: "Sometimes . . . she beat the white of an egg in a glass of water, and together we tried to read portents in the shapes it assumed. Whenever Elisabeth saw a magpie, she bowed to it three times, and when the moon was new, she begged that long-harbored wishes might come true. The Empress firmly believed in the protective power of cold steel and never passed nails or cast horseshoes without picking them up. She had a boundless fear of the evil eye and was afraid of the baneful influence of those who had it."[39]

Elisabeth also believed all prophecies, such as the one about the legendary Monk of the Tegernsee, whose damned soul would be released only along with that of the last survivor of the ducal line in Bavaria. Repeatedly the Empress related that the monk had prophesied to her, "Before a hundred years have passed, our line will have died out!"[40] In view of the considerable number of young princes, these words sounded unlikely. (The hundred years have since passed, and the line of the dukes in Bavaria is, in fact, extinct. The current head of the house, Duke Max of Bavaria, comes from the royal line, having been adopted by the last male representative of the ducal house and appointed his heir.)

Elisabeth told not only her daughter Valerie, but also Marie Larisch about the "apparitions" of Ludwig II. Once, she said, she had heard a noise like the gurgling of water while she lay in bed.

Gradually this soft trickle filled the whole room, and I experienced the entire plight of drowning. I wheezed and choked and struggled for air, then the horror disappeared, with my last strength I sat up in bed and could breathe freely again. The moon had risen, and its glow turned the room bright as day. Then I saw the door slowly opening, and Ludwig entered. His clothing was soaked with water, which ran down and formed small puddles on the parquet floor. His damp hair was sticking to his white face, but it was Ludwig, looking just as he did in life.

Then, Elisabeth continued, a conversation with Ludwig's spirit took place, and he spoke of a woman who was burning: "I know that it is a woman who loved me, and until her destiny is fulfilled, I shall never be free. But afterward you will meet us, and the three of us will be happy together in Paradise." It is not surprising that in her book, published in 1913, Marie Larisch interpreted these prophecies as referring to the death of Ludwig's one-time fiancée, Sophie Alençon, in 1897 in a fire, and to the Empress's death, which occurred a year later. Elisabeth to Marie Larisch: "But while I spoke, the apparition vanished; once again I heard the dripping of unseen water and the gurgle of the lake against the shore. I was seized with horror, for I felt the nearness of the shades from that other world who were holding out their ghostly arms, seeking the comfort of the living."[41]

Beginning in the mid-1880s, the Empress repeatedly spoke of suicide. The waters of Lake Starnberg, where Ludwig II had perished, held a particularly strong attraction for her.

Marie Valerie was one of the few people who clearly understood Elisabeth's poor emotional state. Her diary records her concern at the vehemence and despair with which the forty-eight-year-old Empress reacted, for example, to an attack of sciatica. "Much worse than the ailment is Mama's indescribable despair and hopelessness. She says that it is a torment to be alive, and she indicates that she wants to kill herself. 'Then you will go to hell,' Papa said. And Mama replied, 'But we already have hell on earth!' " And the distressed seventeen-year-old reassured herself: "That Mama will never kill herself—of that I am confident; that she feels her life to be a burden and that to know this makes Papa just as unhappy as it makes me—about that I could weep for hours."[42]

CHAPTER ELEVEN

HEINE'S DISCIPLE

Emperor Franz Joseph did his utmost to make life in Vienna as agreeable as possible for his wife and to fulfill her wishes. Since she was not comfortable either in the Hofburg or in Schönbrunn, Laxenburg, or Hetzendorf, in the mid-1880s he built her a summer residence of her own at the center of the deer park in Lainz, where she would be entirely free from court life. Designed by Karl Hasenauer, the architect of the Ringstrasse, the mansion turned into a little castle altogether to her taste. In front of the building stands a statue of Elisabeth's favorite Greek god, Hermes (which also gave the house its name, Hermes Villa), on the balcony a bust of Heinrich Heine, in the entrance hall a statue of the dying Achilles. The walls and ceilings of Elisabeth's bedroom were covered with frescoes depicting scenes from *A Midsummer Night's Dream*

(painted by the young, then still unknown, Gustav Klimt after drawings by Makart). The centerpiece, at Elisabeth's bed of state, depicted Titania with the ass—a joke that can hardly have pleased the Emperor. The walls of the exercise room were covered with frescoes showing antique gladiatorial battles, just as much an expression of Elisabeth's love of Greece as were the numerous small Greek sculptures.

What Elisabeth valued most of all about the mansion in Lainz—"Titania's dream castle," as she called it—was the solitude at the heart of an unspoiled forest, home to a great many deer. The Lainz deer park was surrounded by a wall. Guards kept watch on the gates. No outsider was allowed to glimpse the mansion when Elisabeth was in residence. She could go walking for hours, observing the deer (she always carried wooden rattles with her to protect her from wild boars, who were afraid of the noise) or composing poems.

At first, the Empress had misgivings about the modern sanitary arrangements, such as the built-in bathroom (the other imperial castles did not yet sport such modern fashions). For under these circumstances, "so and so many bathing women, whose job it was to set up and fill the tubs," would "be deprived of their occupation." Another innovation to which she was unaccustomed were the sinks in the corridors. Once the architect, Hasenauer, saw the Empress with evident pleasure turning the faucets on and off again and again, because she had never encountered such a thing before.[1]

When, in May 1887, the imperial family spent the night in Lainz for the first time, Marie Valerie moaned with homesickness for Bad Ischl. "Sadly I lay down on my white bed, which stands in a strange alcove and from which a most affected chubby-faced cherub stares down at me." Nor did Valerie approve of the Empress's state rooms. "Mama's rooms have the best will in the world to be enormously friendly, but I detest their mannered rococo. Oh—if only we were home again!"[2]

Valerie found the Hermes Villa "actually uninvitingly handsome and modern, and it is not at all like us and what we have been used to so far."[3] For his part, Emperor Franz Joseph once again responded with helplessness, as he did when faced with so many ideas his wife got in her head: "I shall always be afraid that I will spoil everything."

But now that she owned her own secluded castle, Elisabeth had no intention whatever of spending more time in Vienna. She stayed in her sinfully expensive villa for only a few days each year before setting out on her travels once more. Though she no longer went hunting, she took long sight-seeing trips, preferably abroad.

At this time, Elisabeth was quite unmistakably in a serious crisis. She was nearly fifty. The splendor of her beauty had faded. She hid her wrinkles behind fans and umbrellas. The "Queen Riding to Hounds," once so energetic and zestful, was suffering from sciatica and deep nervous disorders. In spite of her outstanding intellectual gifts, Elisabeth was without influence. One last time, she pulled herself together and tried to give some meaning to her life—though not, of course, within the framework of her imperial position or her family. Rather, she began to write poetry with a matchless intensity, and she wrested a bitter balance from her life.

Verlassen (Gödöllö 1886)

In meiner grossen Einsamkeit
Mach' ich die kleinen Lieder;
Das Herz, voll Gram und Traurigkeit,
Drückt mir den Geist darnieder.

Wie war ich einst so jung und reich
An Lebenslust und Hoffen;
Ich wähnte nichts an Kraft mir gleich,
Die Welt stand mir noch offen.

Ich hab' geliebt, ich hab' gelebt,
Ich hab' die Welt durchzogen;
Doch nie erreicht, was ich erstrebt.—
Ich hab' und ward betrogen![4]

[Abandoned (Gödöllö 1886): In my great loneliness, / I make tiny songs; / My heart, filled with grief and sadness, / Weighs down my spirit. / / Once I was so young and rich / In love of life and hope; / I thought nothing could match my strength, / The whole world was open to me. / / I loved, I lived, / I wandered through the world; / But never reached what I strove for.— / I deceived and was deceived.]

Elisabeth had given up all hope of finding understanding among her contemporaries. More than ever, she frequented the company of spirits and placed all her hopes in the "souls of the future," for whom she wrote her poems. She decided that, unlike the poems she had written when she was young, her verses from the 1880s should see publication. She chose 1950 as the date of printing—a time, that is, when none of her contemporaries, any more than herself, would still be alive. Elisabeth wanted, at least posthumously, to gain what her contemporaries denied her: justification, understanding, lasting fame. The often confused hymns to liberty in many of these poems were modeled on Heine's. They were also intended as comfort for the oppressed in future times.

Elisabeth gave extraordinary care to safeguarding her poetry for posterity. During the winter of 1886 and 1887, she had copies made under the seal of the strictest secrecy and with the help of two family members who came from Bavaria for the purpose: Marie Larisch and Marie's (nonaristocratic) cousin Henny Pecz. Countess Larisch's claim that these copies were intended to serve as manuscripts for a secret printing of the poems[5] at first sounded fantastic; but by now her statements can no longer be so easily dismissed. The Empress's literary estate in the Swiss Federal Archives actually includes, along with the manuscript originals, anonymous printings, until now unknown, of two volumes of poems (*Winterlieder* [Winter Songs] and *Nordseelieder* [Songs of the North Sea]), which are identical with the manuscripts.

In 1890, Elisabeth deposited a sealed casket containing both the originals and the printed versions in the Hofburg, with instructions that after her death, it be given to her brother Duke Karl Theodor. She requested that he, in turn, keep the box and, after a period of sixty years, pass it on to the Swiss federal president. This request was honored in 1951. The same instructions also provided that some of her closest friends—such as "beautiful prince" Rudolf Liechtenstein—be given printed copies of the poems. Prince Liechtenstein's estate in Brno and the Austrian Academy of Sciences in Vienna made available an additional copy of each volume to Switzerland.

(How many copies were in other hands and have been lost we cannot know. Elisabeth did not herself deal with the printer—as her son Rudolf did in similar situations—but remained entirely anonymous.)

To the casket meant for her brother, the Empress added a letter in her own hand, addressed to the recipient she had destined to sort and publish the poems in the future.

> Dear Future Soul!
> To you I pass on these writings. The Master dictated them to me, and he has determined their purpose—that is, sixty years

from 1890, they are to be published to benefit political prisoners
and their needy families. For in sixty years no more than today
will happiness and peace—I mean liberty—be established on
our little star. Perhaps on another one? Today I am unable to
tell you this, perhaps by the time you read these lines—Cordially, for I sense that you wish me well,

Titania

written in midsummer of the year 1890 in a rapidly speeding
special train.[6]

These complicated provisions indicate how deeply persecuted she felt,
how suspicious she was of the Austrian authorities and of the Habsburg
family, whom she did not trust to have sufficient loyalty to safeguard her
poems. Even Emperor Franz Joseph, we must conclude from all these secret
actions, knew nothing of the arcane dispositions his wife made for the
"future souls."

Nor did Elisabeth show faith in the stability of the monarchy. Just as
she transferred a large part of her wealth (without the Emperor's knowledge) to the banking House of Rothschild in Switzerland, so as to be secure
in case of forced emigration, she also assigned the most valuable asset she
had to leave to posterity—her writings—to Switzerland. She praised that
nation in several poems as the "bulwark of liberty," and she considered its
republican form of government safer for the future than a monarchy.

In a short covering letter to the president of Switzerland, the Empress
repeated the intended purpose of the money to be brought in by publication. "After sixty years, the profits are to be used exclusively for helpless
children of political prisoners of the Austro-Hungarian monarchy."[7]

To this day, the "future souls" cannot easily fulfill the Empress's explicit
request. For though it is fairly plain that she wanted to express criticism
of the political conditions in the Danube monarchy, it is still completely
uncertain what sort of political prisoners she had in mind. Who were the
political prisoners of 1890? Socialists, anarchists, German nationalists; but
Elisabeth cannot have meant these. Might she, as so often, have been
thinking of the families of the Hungarian revolutionaries who rose against
the Austrian central government of 1848–1849? And how can their de-
scendants be found today?

Elisabeth's arrangements, however, show that she was convinced of the
quality of her poems. She was totally unaware that her writing was little
more than dilettante rhyming.

For almost ten years, Elisabeth concentrated on her poetry. During this time, Empress Elisabeth of Austria, Queen of Hungary and Bohemia, turned into the self-styled Titania, Queen of the Fairies. Her husband the Emperor, unsuitable as it might have been to his personality, became Oberon, King of the Fairies. Fairies and sprites, but especially the figure of the "Master," Heinrich Heine, began to fill Elisabeth's life. The real people of her empire were as foreign to her as the problems of her family, including those of her son, whose sad fate fulfilled itself during this same decade—without his mother's acknowledging or even having an inkling of his difficulties.

Only a very few intimates knew about the Empress's versifying. Archduchess Marie Valerie, who probably was the most involved in listening to and reciting her mother's poems, considered Elisabeth a major poet. Nevertheless, occasionally she made fun of Sisi's urgent need to communicate at once to the "future souls" every little disagreement, every annoyance, couching it in poetic form. It was, she noted, a "shared family trait to leave everything to posterity. Surely one day posterity will call us a funny family."[8] Valerie complained: "strange life, my mother's—her thoughts are occupied by the past, her activities deal with the distant future. The present is, to her, an insubstantial shadow, her greatest pride that no one suspects she is a poet."[9]

For at first, Elisabeth did not tell the Emperor about her writing. She showed him only the childish rhymes of Archduchess Valerie, whom she talked into believing herself to be an equally gifted poet. The young girl, who is more likely to have inherited her father's practical cast of mind than her mother's dreamy temperament, was reluctant. Somewhat at a loss, she wrote in her diary, "Mama wants me to give my poems to Papa tomorrow, which makes me unhappy, for I am convinced that Papa thinks it affected to write poetry."[10] Countess Festetics also cautiously noted, concerning the Emperor, "The poetic vein is not very strongly developed in him."[11]

Gyula Andrássy was another of the few who were initiated into the secret. He took the Empress's poems as the welcome occasion for compliments, in 1889 writing to Sisi's chamberlain, Baron Nopcsa, "You know what a high opinion I have always had of her mind and her heart, but since reading a few of her poems, this opinion has grown into the highest admiration, and the fact that in her being, so much feeling is united with so much intellect, which would do honor even to the greatest man, I can only say briefly that no other such woman exists on earth. One thing saddens me, however, and that is that so few people know what she is. I would wish that the whole world were informed about it and admired her as such a rare personality deserves."[12]

Elisabeth's brother, the ophthalmologist Karl Theodor, saw this new preoccupation with a far more sober and worried eye. He found the poems that were shown him very beautiful but warned Elisabeth against "burrowing so deeply into the extravagant ideas in which she lives, for he thinks that this imaginary spiritual intercourse with Heine might so overly strain her nerves that in the end, she might 'crack up.' "[13] Within the family, Karl Theodor spoke bluntly about Sisi, "who is intelligent but has a 'definite kink.' "[14]

Elisabeth's father, Duke Max, had always taken a highly critical view of his daughters, including Elisabeth. On the occasion of his diamond wedding anniversary in September 1888, he read to the assembled family his favorite passage from a newly published book, *Das Nervöse Jahrhundert* (The Nervous Century) by Paolo Mantegazza: "The nervousness of those who do no work can be cured only gradually—not until, that is, the dukes, counts, and barons teach their children that work is the best occupation for the nobility and at the same time the surest road to a long and happy life."[15] This quotation was soon afterward reprinted in a celebratory article on the anniversary in the Vienna *Fremdenblatt*—coming close to public criticism of the Empress. The relationship between Elisabeth and her father, who was quite ill by this time, was so bad that she did not even attend his funeral in Munich in November 1888—officially because of her own precarious health.

Elisabeth's poems from the 1880s (after Rudolf's death in 1889, she abruptly stopped writing poetry) cover about six hundred printed pages. They constitute one long hymn to the extravagantly idolized Heine. Her adoration went far beyond the usual appreciation of a literary being, the Empress knew long passages by heart and intensively studied the poet's life. She believed herself closely linked to Heine, who had died in Paris in 1856, considered herself his disciple, was even convinced that he was dictating the verses for her pen to record. "Every word, every letter, anything by Heine is a jewel," Elisabeth wrote to Valerie, confessing that the poet "is with me always and everywhere."[16]

This close link with her beloved dead Master was another form of flight, no different from riding or traveling.

Elisabeth was firmly convinced of her spiritual dealings with Heine. For example, she described to Valerie one such apparition in all its details. One evening in bed, she related, she had suddenly seen before her Heine's profile, as it was known to her from one of his portraits. She had the strange . . . but pleasant sensation as if this soul wished to separate hers from her body. This struggle lasted a few seconds, but Jehovah did not permit her soul to leave the body. The apparition disappeared and, in spite of her disappointment at having to go on living, Mama was left for a long time with a happy strengthening of faith, a greater love for Jehovah, and the conviction that Heine's soul was with Him and that He permitted it to maintain its connection with Mama's soul. And Mama affirms the story even today and says she could swear any oath that this is true and that she saw the apparition while she was fully awake and with her actual eyes.[17]

The Empress collected editions of Heine's works and portraits of the poet. She surrounded herself with busts of Heine. She called on Heine's aged sister, Charlotte von Embden, in Hamburg and visited Heine's grave in Paris.

Elisabeth also shared the Master's likes and dislikes. For example, she took an interest in the Hebrew poet Jehuda ben Halevy, whom Heine had praised in "Romanzero." At that time, one of the foremost Halevy scholars, Professor Seligmann Heller, was living in Vienna. Unannounced and without having exchanged so much as a line with the scholar beforehand, Elisabeth appeared at Heller's home one day. Heller was standing "at the window in his comfortable house jacket, looking out at the street, when he saw an equipage drive up to his house and stop. Since he was shortsighted, he could not make out that it was a court coach; he only joked to his son about an elegant carriage stopping before the old suburban house and whether he might be the intended recipient of the visit. A few moments later, there was a knock at the door, and the Empress stood before the surprised writer and scholar. In her own simple way, which immediately banished embarrassment, she explained the purpose of her visit. She spoke about Jehuda ben Halevy, whom she knew only from Heine's verses, but whose own writings she was eager to learn with Heller's help."

Seligmann Heller delivered an improvised lecture on the life and work of the Hebrew poet, explaining also the difficulty of putting oneself into so entirely alien an intellectual world. The Empress, he suggested, would do well to stick to Heine's "openly laudatory judgment."[18]

Elisabeth's reputation as a Heine expert was so great that occasionally she was asked for advice, for example by one literary historian from Berlin. He turned to the Empress with three unpublished Heine poems and asked for her opinion as to whether the somewhat problematic verses should be published. Elisabeth replied in a long letter in her own hand, declaring one of the poems to be spurious (and she was right, as subsequent examination proved) and advocating publication of the other two, "for Heine's public are the peoples of the earth, and they have a right to know him completely, especially as the poet himself, unlike the majority of other poets, scorned all dissimulation and always liked to present himself as he was, with all his virtues and human failings."[19]

Elisabeth's veneration for Heine did not rule out absorption in other poets. She continued enthusiastically to read Shakespeare's plays, and she had committed most of *A Midsummer Night's Dream* to memory. With Marie Valerie she read *Faust* (unabridged, something considered unsuitable for a young girl of the period, because of the "immoral" tragedy of Gretchen). In the late 1880s, she began to study ancient Greek, so as to be able to read Homer in the original, but subsequently she concentrated on modern Greek. For practice, for example, she translated *Hamlet* from English into modern Greek. In 1892 she also tackled some passages by Schopenhauer but complained, "If only each day were twice as long; I cannot learn and read as much as I would like."[20] She gave a reason for spending hours a day studying Greek, not stopping until she mastered the language: "It is so beneficial to have to struggle with something difficult, so as to forget one's own thoughts."[21]

As with Hungarian, Elisabeth also favored the demotic Greek the people spoke. She explained this preference to one of her readers very much in Heine's manner. "The only reason for my preference for the popular language is that I wish to speak the language spoken by ninety percent of the population, and not that of the professors and politicians. If there is anything I abhor, it is pretence in thought, writing, or anything else."[22]

On her walks, she was accompanied by a Greek student, who was made not only to speak Greek with her, but also to read to her as they walked. This was a difficult endeavor, given the Empress's rapid pace, and elicited many astonished glances from passersby. When Elisabeth asked her brother Karl Theodor why he, too, did not make use of walks to have foreign languages read to him, he answered, "Because they would think I had gone mad." To which Elisabeth replied, "Does that matter? Is it not enough that we ourselves know that we are not?" Marie von Redwitz, a Bavarian lady-in-waiting, who overheard this conversation, commented, "With this she explained so much in her own life. She did what gave her pleasure, and she left it to others to believe whatever they chose. With all her peculiarities, as a person she had remained simple and entirely natural."[23]

The love of Greece was a Wittelsbach family tradition. Elisabeth's uncle, King Ludwig I, had also loved Greece, as did his son Otto, who was King of Greece from 1832 to 1862. During that time, many Bavarians made their way to Greece and gave personal and financial aid to develop the country impoverished by the long Turkish occupation. Elisabeth's father, Duke Max, also knew Greece intimately, not only from his travels, but also through his preoccupation with Greek history and literature.

Elisabeth's love for Greece was well grounded in knowledge of the country's language, mythology, and history. One of her favorite poets was Lord Byron, probably the best-known foreign participant in the Greek wars of liberty. Elisabeth translated many of Byron's poems into German, here, too, imitating Heine.

Probably the greatest German-speaking expert on Greece during the 1880s was the Austrian consul on Corfu, Alexander von Warsberg, who was known to the Empress through his books, especially his *Odysseische Landschaften* (The Landscape of the Odyssey). In 1885, she asked him to be her scholarly guide on her travels in Greece. Before Warsberg's first audience, Elisabeth's chief chamberlain advised the writer a little fearfully "that I should keep my statements brief, concentrated; that the Empress could not tolerate much talking. So I was brought before her. She purred at me, curtly, not discourteously; I thought she looked ugly, old, thin as a rail, badly dressed, and I felt that I was looking, not at a foolish woman, but at a mad one, so that I grew truly sad."

But it was not long before the critical Warsberg changed his mind. For while sightseeing,

> the Empress was a changed woman: talkative, informal, clever, quite outstanding, familiar, open-minded—in short, one of the most enchanting creatures I ever met. For four hours I walked next to her or—when the path was too narrow—immediately behind her, and she made me talk ceaselessly, so that by evening my throat was inflamed, and she made the strangest, most honest remarks to me. In any case, an intellectually very advanced nature, which interests me to the utmost degree. She seems aware of her stature and to feel that it justifies her lack of embarrassment. Otherwise it would make no sense for the Emperor to be so considerate to her.[24]

Nor did it take long for Alexander von Warsberg to exhibit all the usual signs of infatuation. "She is enchantingly cordial. Cannot resist the woman. . . . I care only about her, the woman," his diary records in 1888.[25]

Wherever Elisabeth appeared in those parts that had not yet seen tourists, she caused a sensation: a tall, excessively thin, foreign woman dressed in dark colors, striding manfully along even the worst paths, behind her the always ailing scholar Warsberg and the panting, stout Countess Festetics. According to Warsberg, people called her "the railroad train"[26]—and it was meant absolutely as an expression of profound respect, for this new nineteenth-century invention was just being introduced to Greece and was admired for its unbelievable speeds.

Time and again, Elisabeth's companions caused problems, as when the party climbed Sappho's Cliff. Warsberg had planned everything so beautifully. Twenty years earlier, he had climbed the rock and visited a hermit who lived at the top in a ramshackle hut. Since Warsberg's visit, the hermit had not seen another stranger. "And now the second visitor was—the Empress of Austria!" Warsberg wrote proudly. "I invited the monk, whose hair had turned snow-white and who had grown a long beard, once again, as on a previous occasion, to lead the way to the site of the temple of Apollo and the spot where Sappho had made her leap. At the time, I thought it the most beautiful sight in the world, I never had a happier day." Because the rock is also interesting from the point of view of navigation, the Empress allowed several naval cadets from the yacht *Miramar* to come along. Warsberg: "Now this pack of young people chattered so much, and about matters so unsuitable to the location, that any kind of poetic atmosphere was destroyed. While we stood on Sappho's Cliff, the Empress whispered to me that she felt as if she were in a railroad-station restaurant." Warsberg "had long ago grown quite melancholy and silent, because I saw that I would be robbed of the pleasure of being able to lead the Empress around in a mood of sacred solemnity."[27]

Nor is there much mention of a mood in Countess Festetics's report. "By the time we got to the top after three hours, it had turned very cloudy, and then it poured, the path was slippery and hard, we therefore inspected only the spot from which she [Sappho] jumped. On the climb up, we saw nothing, since we were running as if we were in Gödöllö, and we had to watch out so as not to break our arms and legs."[28] There are dozens of such letters.

Elisabeth tirelessly followed the traces of her Greek heroes. From Ithaca, she sent her daughter Valerie cyclamens with a note to say that in the morning she had been at the spot "where Odysseus landed, and there I picked the two cyclamens for you. Just as on Corfu, here too there are flowers everywhere. I read Warsberg's Ithaca on the way, I converse a great deal with him, it is a real grand tour."[29]

Emperor Franz Joseph nevertheless could not "imagine what you find to do for so many days in Ithaca," and, "I am glad that you like Ithaca so infinitely much. That it is nerve-calming and quiet I can well believe, but that it is supposed to be more beautiful than Hallstatt seems impossible to me, especially given the sparse southern vegetation."

Almost gleefully, Franz Joseph returned to the subject of Hallstatt in his next letter. He could reconcile himself neither to Ithaca nor to Odysseus. "I was right after all that Ithaca cannot compare to Hallstatt, for the Hereditary Prince of Meiningen, who has traveled all through Greece and has admired Greece for a long time, assures me that the island is completely bare and is anything but beautiful."[30]

In 1888, the Empress announced to her husband that she "was considering" Greece "a home for the future." She made long sea voyages in the Aegean, even had an anchor tattooed on her shoulder—an act the Emperor called "a dreadful surprise."[31] Elisabeth intended the gesture to prove her undying love for the sea.

We do not know what the Empress thought of modern literature. We only know about her close ties to such contemporary Hungarian writers as Moriz Jókai and Josef Eötvös. Nothing is known of an equal interest in contemporary German-speaking writers—with one exception: Carmen Sylva. This poet's outpourings, however, are literature only in the most qualified sense.

Carmen Sylva (as previously mentioned) was the pen name of Queen Elisabeth of Romania, the wife of Carol I, born Princess zu Wied, six years younger than Elisabeth. During the 1880s, she had a great success with her plays in French, her poems in German, and her fairy tales, novels, and lay sermons in Romanian. All shared a sentimental, feverish style. Carmen Sylva became Elisabeth's ideal. With her "poet friend," Elisabeth, usually so shy, thawed and left no doubt that she preferred her above all other royalty. Sixteen-year-old Marie Valerie shared Sisi's admiration. Writing about Carmen Sylva's visit to Vienna in 1884, she noted, "And they call *her* a bluestocking, I thought to myself as I looked at the laughing large green eyes, the cheeks still colored with youthful freshness, the snow-white, conspicuously handsome teeth. O Carmen Sylva, if you can see into human hearts, you must know that ours were yours from that hour on— wholeheartedly yours."

Valerie described Carmen Sylva's appearance. "Her way of dressing was a little peculiar. Under the voluminous fur coat, the Queen wore a loose, almost dressing-gownlike garment of very dark red velvet adorned with colorful embroidery and fastened around the waist with a ropelike silk cord. She wore a closed hat . . . and had a veil, on top of which she had placed her pince-nez."[32] The Romanian Queen was a figure of fun in Viennese society—an additional reason for Elisabeth to rally to her.

Many poems give evidence of Elisabeth's veneration for Carmen Sylva, her "sister," her "friend." Because the Romanian Queen was often homesick for the Rhine, when Elisabeth visited Heidelberg in 1884, she wrote "Rheinlied" (Song of the Rhine) expressly for Carmen Sylva. (The same year, Sylva's collection of poems, *Mein Rhein* [My Rhine] was published.)

Several times, Elisabeth undertook the long journey to Romania to visit Carmen Sylva.

> *Nicht den Hof wollt' ich besuchen,*
> *Auch zur Königin nicht gehn,*
> *Nur die Dichterin zu sehen*
> *Kam ich, Carmen Sylva suchen.*[33]

[It was not the court I wanted to visit, / Nor to go to the Queen, / Only to see the poet, / I came seeking Carmen Sylva.]

The two friends had much in common: spiritualism, a love for the Greek poet Sappho (about whom Carmen Sylva wrote a poetic tale), and finally, their distance from worldly honors and monarchic governments. Carmen Sylva in her diary: "I must sympathize with the Social Democrats, especially in view of the inaction and corruption of the nobles; these 'little people,' after all, want only what nature confers: equality. The republican form of government is the only rational one; I can never understand the foolish people, the fact that they continue to tolerate us."[34]

Carmen Sylva was also one of the few who not only accepted but also understood Elisabeth's love for Heine. After Elisabeth's death, she wrote:

It was very natural that of all poets she would have had to love Heine best, simply because he is also so despairing about all the falseness in the world and cannot find enough words to lash out at all that is empty! What she could not forgive in our position was that we have so much to do with appearances and falseness and have such difficulty penetrating to the core. She could not get over the fact that people want to see us as Olympians and do not like us to weep and sigh as they do. They have placed us on high, so that we should always smile and fill them with the certain belief that it is possible to be happy on this earth. But it is just this that contains the implacable, cruel lie. . . . It was in Heine that she found her contempt for all outward appearances, which she felt so deeply; she found the bitterness with which her harsh, solitary destiny fulfilled itself, and the mischievousness that was part of her as well and elicited from her such original and startling statements.[35]

As sovereigns, the two women had little in common. Elisabeth of Romania fully realized the responsibilities that went with her position. She was energetic and eager—though she, too, had some traits that were not entirely realistic, and she, too, was criticized for them. In Romania, she gained status through her collection of folk songs and legends and her encouragement of Romanian folklore—though she continued to write principally in German.

Carmen Sylva did not, however, encourage Elisabeth's strivings to dedicate herself entirely to fantasy and to writing poetry in solitude. Sylva very practically expected that the obligations of a queen be met. But in this regard, Elisabeth would not be influenced even by her "poet friend." Bluntly she wrote her daughter Valerie, "Carmen Sylva is very dear, entertaining, interesting, but her feet are firmly planted in this world; she can never understand me, though I her, I love her. She enjoys spinning tales, it gives her pleasure, and the King [Carol] is so prosaic that an emotional abyss yawns between them. Of course, she never says so openly, but I got it out of her."[36]

Both "poet queens" were unfulfilled and unhappy in their marriages—sufficient reason for Carmen Sylva to decide, after a long conversation with her friend, to write "about the absurdity of marriage."[37]

Whenever the opportunity presented itself, Elisabeth showed her sympathies for self-confident, cultured women who did not feel that their life was complete within the family, contrary to the view of the nineteenth-century middle class. The Emperor, on the other hand, was utterly disconcerted by this preference on the part of his wife. Once he openly admitted to Frau Katharina Schratt that Carmen Sylva "got on my nerves. . . . Of course, I kept growing colder, almost discourteous."[38]

Elisabeth's thirst for culture, her interest in philosophy, literature, and history put her at an even greater distance from her husband and the court in Vienna—a situation very similar to the one the Crown Prince had to face. At this time, Viennese society was not only uneducated, but openly

29

Sisi put great emphasis on a truly Hungarian court. Seated from the left: Franz
Joseph with Gyula Andrássy, the Hungarian nurse with Marie Valerie, Sisi, and
Rudolf. Standing from the left: Sisi's dear friend and reader, Ida Ferenczy;
Gisela; and lady-in-waiting Countess Marie Festetics with Sisi's chamberlain,
Baron Franz Nopcsa.

32

30

ABOVE: Sisi's "cavaliers"; from the left: Imre
Hunyady, Rudolf Liechtenstein, and László
Szápáry. RIGHT: Count Nikolaus Esterházy,
Sisi's riding friend. ABOVE RIGHT: Esterházy's
rival, Bay Middleton

31

Elisabeth's passion for riding (she was one of the finest horsewomen of her day) was a favorite subject of the artists and photographers who recorded her life.

As a young bride in Bad Ischl with her husband and his adjutant Graf Grünne

33a

33b

1870 (Photograph by Angerer of Vienna)

33c

Elisabeth built a riding school at Gödöllö in Hungary, where she trained with the famous circus riders of the time. (Painting by Wilhelm Richter, 1876)

Hunting with the Emperor
(Painting by Julius von Blaas, 1860)

33d

33e

A cartoon of Sisi being piloted
by Captain Bay Middleton
when hunting in the English
shires with the Earl of
Harrington's Hounds
(Reproduced by gracious
permission of Her Majesty
the Queen)

Even when hunting, Sisi shielded
herself from curious bystanders.

33f

34

During the World Exhibition in Vienna in 1873, the Imperial couple
were hosts to the Shah of Persia (seated right). Behind him are the
Russian foreign minister Count Gorchakov, the German Crown Prince,
Bismarck, and Gyula Andrássy, the foreign minister. Kaiser Wilhelm of
Germany stands between the Emperor and Crown Prince Rudolf.

·1854· ·1879·

A Silver Wedding portrait, with Crown Prince Rudolf

LEFT: Gisela's engagement to Prince Leopold of Bavaria. BELOW: Rudolf's engagement to Princess Stephanie of Belgium; second from left: King Leopold I of the Belgians; far right: his wife, Queen Marie Henriette

FRANZ JOSEPH I.
KAISER VON ÖSTERREICH.

ELISABETH,
KAISERIN VON ÖSTERREICH.

GISELA. MARIA VALERIA.

RUDOLPH.
KRONPRINZ.

ELISABETH.

STEPHANIE,
KRONPRINZESSIN.

The Imperial Family in 1888, with Rudolf's only child, Elisabeth (Photographs by Erssi)

39

This idyllic picture of Imperial life at Laxenburg Castle is deceiving. There was almost no contact whatever between father, mother, son, or daughter-in-law.

40

As Elisabeth grew older and refused to be photographed, photographers would touch up prints of her from earlier years, in order to suggest more recent sittings.

41

An imaginary portrait by Gyula Benczur, circa 1898

In Sisi's hands, one of her books of poetry 42

Sisi was often depicted as Mater Dolorosa in the 1890s. 43

Katharina Schratt posing as "Lady Truth" 44

Persistent photographers pursued Sisi on her increasingly lonely journeys. LEFT: With her lady-in-waiting Irma Sztaray in Territet. BELOW: Walking with former Empress Eugenie in Mentone

45

46

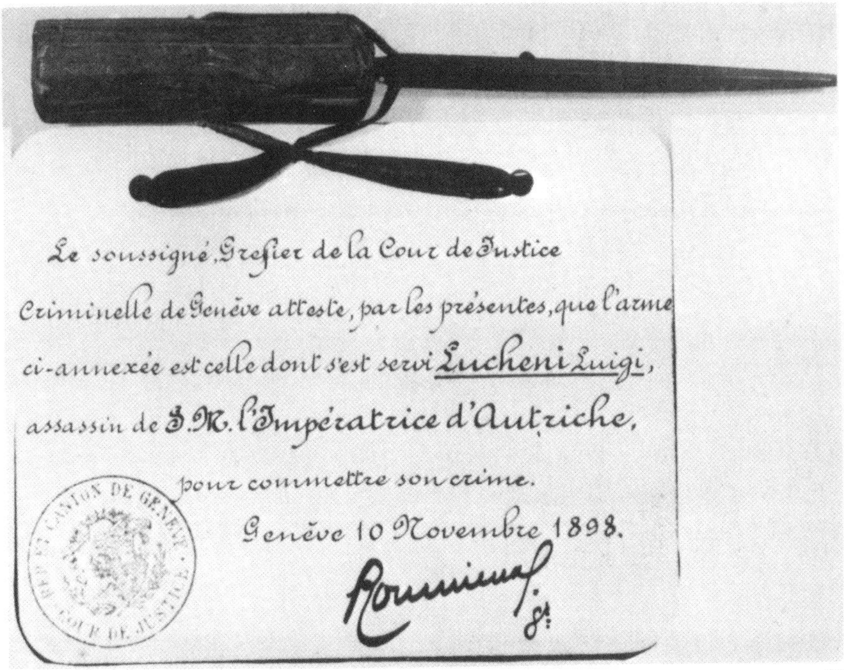
Le soussigné, Grefier de la Cour de Justice
Criminelle de Genève atteste, par les présentes, que l'arme
ci-annexée est celle dont s'est servi Lucheni Luigi,
assassin de S.M. l'Impératrice d'Autriche,
pour commettre son crime.
Genève 10 Novembre 1898.
REP. ET CANTON DE GENEVE
COUR DE JUSTICE

47

The dagger used by the anarchist Luccheni to assassinate Elisabeth on the shore of Lake Geneva on September 10, 1898

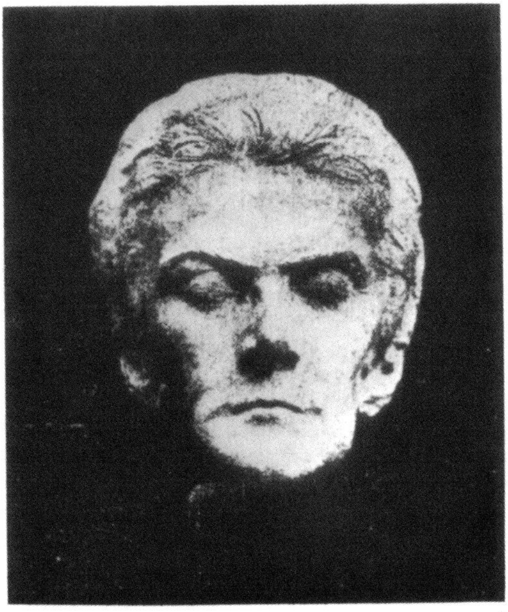

48

Elisabeth's death mask

49

Franz Joseph outlived his beloved wife by eighteen years. Her portrait hung over his desk, both in the Hofburg in Vienna and at Schönbrunn. (Painting by Franz von Matsch)

hostile to education. Foreign observers all had their little anecdotes. One such was Hugo, Count Lerchenfeld. "More than once I was transfixed in Vienna, when I heard adult, perfectly intelligent people spend hours talking with the deepest seriousness about absolutely childish matters. To a certain degree, I explained this lack of earnestness in their view of life by their alienation from public life, which the government forces on the nobility."[39] In this atmosphere, a well-educated and cultivated woman such as Elisabeth was more than a curiosity. She was an irritant.

In 1893, Elisabeth embellished her New Year's wishes to the Emperor with a quotation from Schopenhauer. In response, the Emperor, though granting that the philosopher "was correct in this case," reasserted his earlier opinion. "Otherwise, as you have correctly noted, I do not think much of such philosophical works that only serve to confuse us."[40] Franz Joseph continued his long letter with his usual inquiries about the weather.

There were fewer and fewer common topics of conversation. Even the few days and weeks of the year the Emperor and Empress spent under the same roof—in separate suites, located far from each other—brought no closeness; instead, the time together demonstrated their differences.

In many of her poems, Elisabeth tried to revenge herself on those around her. She caricatured the failings of all those who were her enemies—real or imagined—especially the Viennese aristocracy and all the Habsburgs. Posterity was to come to know the Habsburgs not only through the official histories written by courtiers but also with the eyes of a critic from deep inside. Elisabeth gives no evidence that she had any sense of belonging to aristocratic and court society. She proves herself an opponent of her own class, always passing the judgments of an outsider—somewhat like judgments Heine might have written if he had been observing these particular people.

Thus, the Empress of Austria herself presents us with the most unsparing descriptions of the Habsburg family at the end of the nineteenth century, the *fin de siècle* (the period in Austria that Hermann Broch called the "cheerful apocalypse"). She placed "fools' caps" with bells on the heads of those by whom she felt persecuted (and that, in fact, included everyone around her in Vienna); the poems were intended to make these people ridiculous, long after her death.

Modeling herself on Heine, Elisabeth criticized the human follies of hypocrisy, artificiality, pretentiousness, addiction to medals and distinctions, and arrogance. Like Heine—and like her father and her son—she looked for and found these despised traits particularly in evidence among the aristocracy. She contrasted the life of these idle pleasure-seekers, as she characterized them, with the harsh lives of the workers and the poor.

In a long poem, "Was mir der Tegernsee erzählt" (What the Tegernsee Tells Me), for example, Elisabeth lamented the despoiling of the natural landscape by new mansions along the lakeshore. This, too, became an occasion for praising workers and scorning the aristocrats.

What troubled Elisabeth most were the scandals within the Habsburg family. During the 1880s, Archduke Karl Ludwig's two oldest sons, Franz Ferdinand and Otto, supplied her with ample material by engaging in tasteless pranks, which did irreparable harm to the reputation of the dynasty. Archduke Otto (father of the future King Karl), for example, during one drinking spree threw the pictures of the Emperor and Empress out of the window. Another time, in an equally drunken state, he tried to lead his cronies into his very pious wife's bedroom (in order, he said, to show them a "nun"), but was prevented from carrying out his intention by his adjutant. Elisabeth combined these two scandals into one poem, "Eine wahre Geschichte: Geschehen zu Klagenfurt im Jahre 1886" (A True History Which Occurred in Klagenfurt in the Year 1886), with the moral:

> *Ihr lieben Völker im weiten Reich,*
> *So ganz im geheimen bewundre ich euch:*
> *Da nährt ihr mit eurem Schweisse und Blut*
> *Gutmütig dies verkommene Brut!*[41]

[You good people all through the realm, / So very secretly I admire you: / With your sweat and blood you support, / Good-naturedly, this depraved brood!]

In 1886, one of the two archdukes (according to some witnesses, it was Franz Ferdinand; according to others, his younger brother Otto) caused a scandal that quickly became public knowledge when he jumped his horse over a coffin being carried to the cemetery. This, too, served Elisabeth as the occasion for a long poem, "Eine wahre Begebenheit, geschehen zu Enns" (A True Occurrence, Which Happened at Enns).

Time and again the Empress contrasted the Habsburgs' sense of being among the elect with the middle-class virtues of the age of liberalism.

Also like Heinrich Heine, Elisabeth questioned monarchy as a form of government, proving herself a committed republican. The entries from Elisabeth's diary quoted by Marie Larisch are totally in accord with the testimony of the poems and are convincing.

The beautiful phrases about the King or Emperor and his sub-jects! I have a strange feeling. Why should the people—I mean the poor, lowly people—love us, who live in excess, in the light, while the others, with all their hard work, barely have their daily bread and live in want? Our children in velvet and silks—theirs often in rags!

Surely, one cannot help everyone, no matter how much is done to alleviate the need. The abyss remains! Our gracious smile cannot bridge it.

An uncanny feeling overcomes me at the sight of the people. I want to help each and every one, yes, often I wish to change places with the poorest woman. But I fear the "people" in the mass. Why? I do not know. And our "clan"! This I despise, as I despise all the frippery around us.

I would so much like to tell the Emperor:

> *Das beste wäre, Du bliebst zu Haus,*
> *Hier im alten Kyffhäuser.*
> *Bedenk ich die Sache ganz genau,*
> *So brauchen wir keinen Kaiser!"*[42]

[It would be best if you stayed at home, / Here in the old Kyffhäuser. / If I think it through very carefully, / We do not need an Emperor!]

(These lines are taken from Heine's well-known satire on royalty, "Kobes I.")

Elisabeth's views made a lasting impression on her children. Not only Crown Prince Rudolf, but also the "only child," Archduchess Valerie, believed that the "republic is the best form of government"—and ascribed their statements to their mother.[43]

Even the first poem in *Winterlieder* utterly destroys the legend of the nonpolitical Empress. Elisabeth unmistakably allows her imperial consort to speak—though in a dream—and characterizes him and his policies mercilessly. It is improbable that Franz Joseph ever saw these lines. Elisabeth's closing couplet—to the effect that she would be incarcerated in Bründlfeld (Vienna's renowned insane asylum) should her poem become common knowledge—clearly shows that she had no illusions about the discrepancy offered by an empress and queen's admitting to being a republican.

Another long poem, equally political and relating to the Emperor, "Neujahrsnacht 1887" (New Year's Night 1887), found at the end of the second volume, *Nordseelieder,* is placed in a similarly prominent position. This poem, too, was conceived at the time of the Bulgarian crisis, when the Danube monarchy—that venerable old oak—once again saw its survival threatened. To the west, a new German-French war loomed; it could not leave Austria-Hungary, the ally of the German Reich, untouched. The Judgment Day mood of the poem has clear parallels in Crown Prince Rudolf's political pamphlets written at the same time. What is remarkable is that even in this context, Elisabeth presents her husband as "unlucky" *(Pechvogel),* a word he sometimes applied to himself.

Ich sah im Traume Gauen,
So weit, so reich und schön,
Umspült vom Meer, dem blauen,
Bekränzt von Bergeshöh'n.

Und mitten in den Gauen
Ein hoher Eichbaum stand,
Ehrwürdig anzuschauen,
So alt fast wie sein Land.

Es hatten Sturm und Wetter
Ihm arg schon zugesetzt;
Fast bar war er der Blätter,
Die Rinde rauh, zerfetzt.

Nur seine Krone oben
War noch nicht weggeweht.
Aus dürrem Reis gewoben,
Vergang'ner Pracht Skelett!

Ein Vogel sass dort unten,
"Pechvogel" nennt man ihn,
Wohl, weil sich manche Wunden
Durch seine Schwingen zieh'n.

In Ostnordost da türmte
Die schwarze Wolkenwand,
Von Westen aber stürmte
Ein roter Feuerbrand.

Wie Schwefel schien der Süden,
Denn dort im fahlen Licht
Urplötzlich Blitze glühten
Als naht das Endgericht.

Ich hört den Eichbaum krachen
Bis in sein tiefstes Mark,
Als würde er zerschlagen
Zu seinem eignen Sarg.

Der Baum muss endlich fallen,
Er hat sich überlebt;
Doch für den armen Vogel
Da hat mein Herz gebebt![44]

[In a dream I saw territories, / So broad, so rich and hand-some, / Lapped by the blue sea, / Rimmed by mountains' crests. / / And at the center of the territories / Stood a tall oak tree, / Of venerable appearance, / Almost as old as its country. / / Storms and weather / Had already taken their toll; / Almost bare of leaves it was, / Its bark rough and shaggy. / / Only its crown on high / Had not been blown away, / Woven of parched twigs, / Skeleton of former splendor! / / A bird sat there, / "Unlucky" it was called, / Perhaps because many a wound / Has scarred its wings. / / To the east-northeast rose/ The black wall of clouds, / But from the west approached / A red firebrand. / / Like sulfur glowed the south, / For there in the pale light / Lightning flashed abrupt-ly, / As if Judgment Day were drawing nigh. / / I heard the oak tree crack / Down to its deepest marrow, / As if it were being slashed / Into its own coffin. / / The tree must fall at last, / It has outlived its usefulness; / But for the poor bird— / For him my heart trembled!]

Elisabeth saw only too clearly her husband's bitterness, his "anxious grieving" about the state of the empire in the late 1880s. But she was also the one who consoled him, once again by reassurances about posterity, which would surely mete out justice.

So werden, wenn die Jahre längst entschwunden,
Noch leben Deine Thaten fort und fort;

Dass Du einst warst, wird dankbar nachempfunden,
Und segnen wird Dich noch manch' betend' Wort.[45]

[Thus, when the years have long since vanished, will / Your
deeds live on and on still; / That you once lived will be felt
with gratitude, / And many a prayer's word will bless you still.]

To someone who was totally uninvolved, M. C. Marinaki, one of her
Greek readers, she confessed during the 1890s, "When I think of him [the
Emperor], I am distressed that it is not in my power to help him. But I
abhor modern politics and I think it full of deception. It is only a contest
in which the most crafty gets the lion's share, to the detriment of the one
who hesitates to act against his conscience. Nowadays nations and individuals can advance only if they are unscrupulous."[46]

She expressed herself in a similar vein to another Greek, Konstantin
Christomanos. "And I have too little respect for politics and do not
consider it worthy of interest." She was scathing about the ministers. "Oh,
they exist in order to fall; then others take their place," she said, according
to Christomanos, "with a strange tone in her voice that was an inner
laugh." "Anyway, all of it is such self-deception! The politicians believe
that they control events and are always surprised by them. Each ministry
contains its own fall, from the very first moment. Diplomacy exists only
in order to grasp some booty or other from the neighboring states. But
whatever happens happens by itself, from internal necessity and ripeness,
and the diplomats do no more than take note of the fact."[47]

With great circumspection, Elisabeth excepted her husband from her
criticism of the Viennese court. She respected him, pitied him, and never
included him in the ranks of the Habsburg family and the courtiers. In
Elisabeth's poems, Franz Joseph was also shown for what he truly was: a
sovereign of personal integrity, always well intentioned, and dutiful. Even
Elisabeth, who knew him better than anyone, could never say anything
pejorative of him—nor did she want to.

The imperial office, on the other hand, seemed to Elisabeth nothing but
a burden—and a meaningless one at that. For she plainly believed that the
imperial and royal monarchy (like every other monarchy) was now little
more than "a skeleton of former splendor," belonging to a time long past
and no longer suited to the people of the nineteenth century.

Elisabeth could not wrest anything good even from the technical progress of the age. "People believe that they rule nature and the elements with
their ships and express trains. On the contrary—now nature has enslaved

mankind. In earlier times, living in secluded valleys which one never left, one felt as a god. Now, globe-trotters, we roll like drops of water in the sea, and in the end we will realize that we are no more than these."[48]

Her poems, too, reflect Elisabeth's feeling for nature, her rejection of all that is artificial, all artifacts. By far the majority of the poems are devoted to nature. Even the titles of the two printed volumes—*Nordseelieder* and *Winterlieder*—indicate the overwhelming Heine model. Elisabeth wrote that the Master had initiated her into "the mysteries of nature." Nature became her friend and comforter. There are long poems about Tegernsee and Lake Starnberg within her own borders, the isles of Greece, the North Sea, the forests, the ocean, and the stars, as well as poetic descriptions of an excursion in the mountains near Bad Ischl. Marie Valerie: "the Jainzen really is Mama's magic mountain, where she writes and dreams and where even I would find it hard to be astonished by anything."[49]

The more Elisabeth withdrew into her fantasy life, the more impossible she found it to stay in Vienna. The Hermes Villa in Lainz offered only fleeting respite. More than ever, she sought out solitude, more than ever she felt the pull to Greece. On Corfu, she looked for the peace of mind she could not find in Vienna.

On Corfu, Elisabeth built a castle on a hill by the sea, facing the Albanian mountains. It was completely secluded and invisible from outside, with its own landing stage at the water and its own electrical generator.

An architect from Naples planned the building according to precise instructions from Alexander von Warsberg. It was to be in the Pompeiian style, and the relics from Pompeii and Troy in the Museum of Naples were to serve as models.

Elisabeth dedicated her new castle to Achilles, naming it the Achilleion, "because for me he personifies the Greek soul and the beauty of the landscape and the people. I love him also because he was so fleet of foot. He was strong and willful, despised all kings and traditions, and considered the masses to be unimportant, just good enough to be cut down by death like blades of grass. His own will was the only thing he held sacred, and he lived only for his dreams, and his grief meant more to him than all of life."[50]

In the Achilleion, Elisabeth surrounded herself with the busts of the writers and philosophers she worshiped: Homer, Plato, Euripides, Demosthenes, Periander, Lysias, Epicurus, Zeno, Byron, Shakespeare. Apollo and the Muses—copies of statues in museums—were also assigned a place in

Elisabeth's "museum garden." The walls of the white-marble colonnade were covered with frescoes depicting Greek legends; more statues adorned it. Some of them came from the collection of Prince Borghese. Elisabeth to Christomanos: "he went bankrupt, and so he had to dispose of his gods. You see how terrible it is, nowadays even gods are marketable slaves of money."[51] This remark, too, is drawn from Heine's essay "Die Götter im Exil" (The Gods in Exile).

Franz Matsch, a Viennese painter and student of Makart, painted *Achilles Triumphant* for the Achilleion. The painting was huge—eight meters long and four meters wide—to fit the stairwell. In his preliminary discussions with the Empress, the painter was astonished at Elisabeth's thorough knowledge of Schliemann's excavations of Troy.[52] Elisabeth laid down the specifics for the picture in great detail; she wished to have Achilles depicted in a gesture of victory, riding a chariot drawn by horses, dragging behind it the body of Hector, outside the walls of Troy. Matsch also painted the altarpiece for the castle chapel. It represented the Virgin Mary as the patron saint of sailors, on the model of the *Stella Maris* in Marseilles. The imperial yacht *Miramar* is also featured in the painting.

Most of the statues were copies of classical works. The furniture, copies of Pompeiian models, was made by Neapolitan craftsmen. Only Franz Joseph's living quarters made any acknowledgment of the present; here the pieces were modern. "The Emperor does not like Greek furniture," Elisabeth explained to Countess Sztaray. "He thinks it is uncomfortable, which it really is. But I very much like seeing these nobly shaped objects around me, and since I rarely sit, it does not matter to me whether the chairs are comfortable or uncomfortable."[53]

Once again, Elisabeth refused to consider the Austrian economy. She further angered the Viennese by having all these Neapolitan pieces of furniture intended for Greece shipped first (and at further considerable cost) to Vienna and exhibited in the Austrian Museum of Crafts—as models for local crafts, though these had reached a much greater sophistication. The museum director, Eduard Leisching, recalled, "So we were forced to empty out an exhibition hall and show . . . these unwelcome things, causing consternation and displeasure in the circles of industry and crafts, which were not, at the time, faring very well."

In Vienna, Elisabeth had never been a zealous museumgoer. But now she came (unannounced, as was her habit), "rapidly crossed the rooms until she arrived at the furniture, praised the pieces, but quickly departed again, remarking that the building was too warm, which she could not tolerate; she would return before long, which, however, she never did."[54]

Even before the Achilleion was finished, Elisabeth invited Valerie and her husband, Franz, to Corfu. Valerie was enchanted by the island's physical charm: "A marvelous spot, and if one knows Mama and knows what she needs in the way of beauty, wonderful climate, and quiet serenity for body and soul, one can only be happy about wonderful Gasturi and this spot [outside it]! From the terrace, Mama showed me the view through two tall, dark cypresses to the open sea, this is the very place where she wants to be buried."[55]

Proudly Elisabeth led the young couple to her favorite places. She showed them Ithaca and "the small picturesque bay where Telemachus, greeting the rising sun, washed his hands." She next took them to Corinth and to Athens, of course, to show them the Acropolis by moonlight.

More than anything, however, she liked being alone in the Achilleion. She greeted each dawn in the colonnade and in the castle garden with her statues of classical deities, dreaming and composing verses. Once when Christomanos also came there around five o'clock in the morning, "she approached rapidly like a black angel charged with defending a paradise" and courteously sent him away. Christomanos: "I left silently; I was startled and as if lost in a dream: I felt as if I had lived the fairy tale of the fair Melusina."[56]

Starting in the late 1880s, she no longer allowed her ladies-in-waiting to accompany her on her excursions; generally she chose the company of her Greek readers. Whether traveling in Austria, Hungary, France, Holland, Italy, Switzerland, or elsewhere, she spoke Greek with her companion and had him read to her in Greek. If anyone asked where she came from (for only a very few recognized her), she pretended to be Greek. She justified this answer to Marinaky: "Looked at in the proper light, it is not a lie, for I own property in Greece and could be naturalized."[57] An astonishing remark to come from the Empress of Austria and Queen of Hungary and Bohemia!

Without wishing it, at the end of the 1880s, Elisabeth found herself trapped in a current political quarrel. It concerned the erection of a memorial to Heine in Düsseldorf. Of course, the Empress promised the committee her support. She donated the major part of the funds needed for the planned memorial, which was to take the form of a Lorelei fountain. According to the statement of accounts, she contributed 12,950 marks to the Berlin sculptor Ernst Herter (who also made the large statue of Hermes in Lainz and the *Dying Achilles* for Corfu, at a cost of 24,000 marks each).[58]

Elisabeth's open commitment to Heine turned into a public scandal and a huge public commotion at a time when anti-Semitism was in virulent eruption. For the decision to erect a monument to Heine, a Jew, the creator of the *Wintermärchen* (A Winter's Tale) and critic of German princes, was considered an outrage by both the anti-Semites and the German nationalists and monarchists. There were newspaper campaigns and public demonstrations against the memorial. Elisabeth found herself linked to the "slaves of the Jews" and attacked along with them.

At an anti-Semitic meeting ("Jews Forbidden Entry"), for example, the leader of the All-German Party, Georg Ritter von Schönerer, denounced the "subversion of pure German essence, German traits, and German customs" and included both Crown Prince Rudolf (because of his connections with the "Jewish press") and Empress Elisabeth in his tirade. He did not, of course, name names, but it was plain enough who was meant when he spoke of the "most decisive factors eager to dedicate a monument to the memory of the Jewish author of printed abominations and obscenities."[59]

Unverfälschte deutsche Worte (Pure German Words), the newspaper of the All-German Party, excoriated Heine and Heine's admirers. "Let Jews and those who are enslaved by the Jews rave about this shameless Jew; we Germans turn from him with loathing and call out to all our racial comrades: Here you see how the Jew thinks, how all of Jewry takes his part, how they beat the drums for him and how, sadly, some Germans also march to the beat of this Jewish drum."

Because of press censorship, the newspaper could not attack the Empress directly. It printed an editorial vituperating against the "liberal Jewish press," for "drawing even a most highly placed lady into its agitation." Thus, though in roundabout ways (which every newspaper reader of the day understood), Elisabeth was ranked among those "enslaved by the Jews."[60]

Even without mentioning names, the following sentence amounted to a reprimand of the Empress. "Is there not enough hardship and misery in Vienna, in Austria, not enough people who are hungry and cold through no fault of their own, and is caring for them not our first duty as citizens?"[61]

The French anti-Semite Édouard Drumont, in his *La Fin d'un monde*, also attacked both Crown Prince Rudolf and Empress Elisabeth for their pro-Semitic attitude. He sharply criticized Elisabeth's visit to Heine's sister in Hamburg and quoted at length Heine's macabre satire of Marie Antoinette, a Habsburg. "Sovereigns and noble lords love the Jews . . . they have drunk of the secret love potion, they love those who mock them, defame them, and betray them, and they feel nothing but indifference for those who defend them!"[62]

The liberal newspapers of the monarchy (called "Jewish papers" in anti-Semitic jargon) expressed their gratification at the Empress's allegedly pro-Semitic attitude. They praised Elisabeth in every way; the chorus included the Vienna *Tageblatt,* whose editor-in-chief, Moritz Szeps, was one of Crown Prince Rudolf's closest friends (a fact unknown to the Empress).

But Elisabeth had no intention of actively intervening in the quarrel and joining the battle for tolerance, as Rudolf thought. She avoided all political partisanship, remaining untouched by both the praise and the abuse handed out by the newspapers. She simply did not care what the public thought about the Heine memorial or how her own position was judged. Her relationship to Heine, whatever its form, was a purely personal matter. "The journalists think highly of me for being an admirer of Heine," she told Christomanos. "They are proud of the fact that I love Heine, but what I love in him is his boundless contempt for his own humanity and the sadness worldly matters inspired in him."[63]

Elisabeth withdrew without a struggle. In 1889, she gave up her support of the Heine memorial in Düsseldorf and retired in disgust.

Later, the anti-Semitic newspapers claimed that a strongly worded letter from Bismarck to the Austrian foreign minister had persuaded the Empress to this step. In this letter, Bismarck was said to have pointed out, "courteously but nevertheless very plainly, what an unpleasant impression must have been made on the imperial family by the enthusiasm of Empress Elisabeth for a poet who never had anything but mockery, insults, and scorn for the House of Hohenzollern and the German people."[64] There is no proof for this statement in the diplomatic correspondence, but it does show how much Elisabeth's private interests were given a political interpretation. Herter's Heine memorial, intended for the Hofgarten in Düsseldorf, was subsequently erected by German-Americans in New York. It still stands in a small park at 161st Street and Mott Avenue.[65]

The Empress now ordered her own Heine memorial on Corfu, on the grounds of the Achilleion. She carefully examined all extant portraits of Heine; she also invited Heine's nephew Gustav Heine-Geldern to visit her, so that he could advise her which of the portraits was the best likeness.

Then she decided on a statue by the Danish sculptor Hasselriis; it represented the ailing Heine during the last years of his life, tired, his head drooping, and his hand holding a piece of paper with the lines:

> *Was will die einsame Träne?*
> *Sie trübt mir ja den Blick—*
> *Sie blieb aus alten Zeiten*
> *In meinem Auge zurück.*
> *Du alte, einsame Träne,*
> *Zerfliesse*
> *jetzunder auch. . . .*

[What use the solitary tear? / It merely dims my sight— / A remnant of the olden times, / Left behind in my eyes. / You ancient, solitary tear, / Dissolve / now, too. . . .]

The Empress had the figure placed in a special small temple on a rise in the gardens. Even her chief chamberlain, Baron Nopcsa, was horrified. He found it unsuitable that "the poor man is dressed only in a shirt (which amuses Her Majesty greatly)," wrote Countess Festetics. Tested by adversity, she added, "I think that it is still better than if he were in the costume of a Greek deity—that is, naked."⁶⁶

When she first inspected the installation, the Empress told the sculptor, "Heine himself would be pleased with this spot. . . . For here is everything he loved! The beauties of nature, a laughing sky above, splendid surroundings, palms, cypresses, and pines. Over there, the mountains and down here, the sea he loved so much, such a singular, refreshing peace."⁶⁷ This was to mean primarily that the monument had been taken away from those people of whom Heine thought as little as did his disciple Elisabeth. Nature alone, distance from humanity, was the proper frame for a monument to Heine such as Elisabeth envisaged.

(The fate of this private Heine memorial after Elisabeth's death is worthy of note. The Emperor's older daughter, Gisela, inherited the Achilleion and sold the highly impractical castle to the Imperial Family Fund, which in 1907 sold it at far below its construction cost to Emperor Wilhelm II. The first thing Wilhelm did was to have the Heine monument removed—with the approval of the anti-Semitic press. It announced mockingly to "the Israelite people" that the " 'Man with the solitary tear' " had spent most of its time staring at the Blue Adriatic."⁶⁸

(The statue was offered to the city of Düsseldorf as well as to Hamburg

—in vain. Finally it was acquired by a café owner, who used it to advertise his premises by placing it between the two doors of his Heine Coffeehouse. Today the statue has found a more dignified home in the Jardin de Mourillon in Toulon. The little temple, however, which Elisabeth built specifically for her "Master" Heinrich Heine, still stands on Corfu; instead of Heine, the Empress herself is now honored by a monument under the temple roof.)

CHAPTER TWELVE

KATHARINA SCHRATT, "THE FRIEND"

I t was at a gala performance of the Vienna municipal theater on
the occasion of the twenty-fifth anniversary of Franz Joseph's
assumption of the throne, in December 1873, that the Emperor
Franz Joseph, with the Empress by his side, first saw Katharina Schratt, at
that time twenty years old; she was playing the popular part of Katherina
in *The Taming of the Shrew.*

He did not see the actress again for ten years. In that time, she worked
in Berlin and St. Petersburg. In 1879, she married Nikolaus von Kiss von
Ittebe, a Hungarian estate owner and subsequent consul; she had a son,
Anton (Toni); and eventually she separated from her husband, who was
never out of debt, but did not divorce him.

In 1883, Schratt, the daughter of a baker in Baden near Vienna, had reached the high point of her acting career: She was engaged for the Imperial and Royal Hofburgtheater. Even her debut was a huge success. She played the ingenue, Lorle, in the play *Dorf und Stadt* (Village and Town) by Birch-Pfeiffer, now lost. Valerie, on November 27, 1883: "A new one by the name of Schratt played Lorle, she is very beautiful but not as charming as Wessely."

It was the custom for a new actress to thank the Emperor personally for her engagement. The Burgtheater, after all, was part of the court and was subsidized by private imperial funds. Several anecdotes are told about this first meeting between the fifty-three-year-old Emperor and the thirty-year-old Katharina Schratt. According to Heinrich Benedikt, Katharina Schratt had been extremely shy and unsure of herself; before the audience with the Emperor, she had asked one of her friends, Paul Schulz, for advice on how to comport herself. In the patent office, of which Paul Schulz was president, she painstakingly rehearsed her performance. She sat down in an armchair and recited the words she had memorized. "Your Majesty is so gracious. . . ."

Schulz interrupted. "You must not cross your legs, you may not even sit down. You must stand and say your piece after you make your court courtsey."

Thus prepared, Schratt set off for her imperial audience.

Katharina: "Your Majesty is so gracious—"

The Emperor: "My dear lady, won't you have a seat?"

Katharina: "I thank Your Majesty. Your Majesty is so gracious—"

The Emperor: "But why won't you be seated?"

Katharina: "Paul Schulz won't let me."

The Emperor's laughter is said to have rung out all the way to the antechamber, to the utter astonishment of the adjutants, footmen, and many of those waiting for their audiences, all of whom were totally unaccustomed to such sounds from their Emperor.[1]

This anecdote may or may not be absolutely truthful; whatever the case, Schratt made an impression on Franz Joseph. She lost her shyness and a short time later reported for another audience. This time she came as her husband's emissary, on a financial matter. It was the first of many, many requests for money in the decades that followed—but probably the only one that was refused. Frau von Kiss, née Schratt, came to beg the Emperor for indemnification for the Hungarian estates of the Kiss family. After the Revolution of 1848, the estates had been confiscated and not returned until 1867. Now the family wished the income lost during the years of confiscation to be restored. Franz Joseph was unable to grant this request, like others of the same sort. Instead, he referred Frau von Kiss to the Hungarian Prime Minister, Count Koloman Tisza.[2]

It was soon noticed that the Emperor attended the Burgtheater more frequently than had been his habit—more particularly, that he did not miss a single play in which Schratt appeared. She became something like his favorite actress. Visits to the Burgtheater had always been one of the few pleasures the Emperor allowed himself—often attending several times a week. He did not have to use a carriage, for the old Burgtheater was connected to the Hofburg. (It stood on what is today St. Michael's Square.) Whenever he felt the need for entertainment, he simply walked the short distance. Nor did he have to keep to a rigid timetable, for he could enter the imperial box at any time, without being seen by the audience, and leave again the same way.

A further personal encounter between the Emperor and his favorite actress did not take place for a long time. At the Industrialists' Ball of 1885 the Emperor first engaged Schratt in conversation at some length. He therefore said more to her than his usual brief courtesies—a situation that was immediately noted and provided food for gossip.

In August 1885, Schratt was one of four performers summoned to entertain at the highly political meeting at Kremsier with the Czar and Czarina of Russia (see page 329). Defying all court customs, after their performance the artists were invited to an intimate dinner with the Emperor, the Empress, the Czar, the Czarina, both crown princes, and all ministers present. On this occasion, Katharina Schratt was presented to the Empress for the first time. It is quite possible that it was Elisabeth who instigated this highly unorthodox invitation in order to meet Schratt. Crown Prince Rudolf, in any case, found the situation unusual enough to write to his wife about it in somewhat circumspect and cautious tones: "at eight o'clock the theater, then supper with Wolter, Schratt, and Fräulein Wessely; it was strange."[3]

One thing was certain: The Emperor had fallen in love. The Empress, far from being jealous, promoted the potential relationship. It is even probable that the Emperor's infatuation, so far quite innocent, with the married woman more than twenty years his junior might never have grown into anything more without Elisabeth's very active support.

The Emperor's constant solitude, even isolation, was evident. As we know from her poems, Elisabeth suffered pangs of guilt on this account. On the other hand, the marriage was shattered. The Emperor and Empress no longer had anything to say to each other. The embarrassing tedium of family meetings was confirmed by all witnesses, including Countess Festetics and Countess Fürstenburg as well as Marie Valerie.

Elisabeth was determined to live for her own interests. But first she wanted to make certain that the two people she cared about—her husband and her favorite daughter—were safe and to know that they were not alone. During this time, she looked hard for a husband for Valerie, and she sought a companion or friend for Emperor Franz Joseph.

Ladies of the aristocracy were out of the question. First, any of these might eventually pose a serious danger to the Empress; second, most of them were related to so many members of the court that political insinuation and influence might easily result, an outcome no one—the Emperor least of all—could want.

Katharina Schratt was selected after long and careful consideration—by none other than the Empress herself. In the past, Franz Joseph had become involved with a number of other women without the Empress's coming to his aid and smoothing the path. Whatever her reasons, in May 1886, Elisabeth took the initiative and decided to give the Emperor a portrait of Katharina Schratt—a fairly straightforward gesture. Heinrich von Angeli was commissioned to do the painting, and the Empress arranged a meeting in his studio.

The Emperor wrote to Angeli, "With the permission of the Empress, I should like to come to your studio tomorrow at one o'clock to see the painting of Frau Schratt, which you are painting for me on her commission."[4]

Elisabeth did one thing more: She, who always shied away from all meetings with strangers, accompanied the Emperor to the studio. There they came upon the unsuspecting Schratt posing for Angeli.

Elisabeth's presence robbed this crucial meeting of any embarrassment. In this way, she made herself into the guardian of her husband's love.

Two days later, the Emperor sent Schratt an emerald ring to thank her "for having gone to the trouble of posing for Angeli. Once again, I must assure you that I would not have allowed myself to request this sacrifice from you and that my joy at this dear gift is therefore all the greater. Your devoted admirer."[5]

Franz Joseph was a very shy, somewhat helpless suitor, always finding reasons to apologize for some trifle. Schratt, for her part, was a woman of experience who knew her way around men, especially men in high places, and who learned in an astonishingly short time how to treat the Emperor: with respect, but quite without formality. Franz Joseph to

Katharina Schratt: "If one has so much work, so many cares, so much heartache as I do, a casual, frank, and cheerful talk is a true joy, and that is why the moments I am allowed to spend with you are so infinitely precious to me."[6]

In July 1886, the Emperor called on Schratt for the first time in her home, Villa Frauenstein near St. Wolfgang. Elisabeth knew of the visit. Scarcely a week later, she herself drove out to Lake Wolfgang. She took along Archduchess Marie Valerie, who knew nothing of the circumstances. Valerie captured this visit in her diary, writing about the actress, "she showed us the pretty house she has rented ... darling and natural, and spoke very untheatrically, awfully Viennese. We came back by steamboat with money we borrowed from Frau Schratt."[7]

Obviously, Elisabeth's discretion was such that she did not take a lady-in-waiting on this visit. This highly unusual situation left her in the difficult position of suddenly finding herself without the fare for the steamer. The ladies-in-waiting always did all the paying, and Elisabeth never carried money.

Katharina Schratt received a few more imperial visits that summer, some paid by the Emperor and Empress jointly. In this way, Schratt officially advanced to the position of "friend of the Empress."

Small courtesies followed: Marie Valerie gave her father photographs of Katharina Schratt to put in the villa in Lainz. Elisabeth commissioned another portrait of Schratt; Franz Matsch painted the actress in Franz Joseph's favorite role, Frau Wahrheit, in a very light, popular comedy.[8] It became a Christmas gift to the Emperor, intended for his rooms in Elisabeth's Hermes Villa. In one of her poems, Elisabeth lightly mocked her husband's—"Oberon's"—besotted eagerness because he looked at this portrait as often as possible.

Schratt gave the Emperor a four-leaf clover, and on March 1, 1887, she brought violets to Schönbrunn for the Empress and Marie Valerie, meant to bring good luck. She repeated the gesture every subsequent year. Marie Valerie wrote in her diary, "1st act of the *Hüttenbesitzer* [The Hut Owner], and from our bench we winked at the beautiful Claire [the role played by Schratt]."[9] ("From our bench" indicates that Elisabeth had chosen to sit on a bench in the furthermost corner of the imperial box in the Burgtheater, where she could follow the performance without being seen by the audience. This was Elisabeth's usual manner of visiting the Burgtheater, generally only for one act.

The Emperor thanked Schratt for the violets in his own way: On every possible occasion, no matter how trivial, he sent his idol jewels that formed the basis for one of the richest jewelry collections in the Old Monarchy. Very cautiously he begged her for the favor of allowing him again and again to give her money—for new dresses, for her household expenses, strained by the imperial friendship. Franz Joseph: "I can reassure you further that the birthday and name-day presents I give my children are in the form of money."[10]

For the present, the only difficulty was how to meet. Every public encounter became a test of nerves. At the Concordia Ball of 1887, for example, the Emperor did not come near Schratt. It was only by letter that he could confess to her his anger because "I did not have the courage to address you at the ball. But I would have had to break through the people surrounding you, while one is observed from all sides through opera glasses, and everywhere stand the press hyenas, snapping up every word one says. I just did not dare, much as everything drew me to you."[11]

Once again, the Empress helped her husband out of his troubles. She repeatedly invited Katharina Schratt to Schönbrunn. It was also Elisabeth's idea that the couple should meet in Ida Ferenczy's apartment. For though Ida lived inside the Hofburg complex, her rooms had a private entrance, away from the watchful eyes of servants. Thus, while Schratt officially called on the Empress's reader and friend, Ida Ferenczy, she met Emperor Franz Joseph, who made his way to her along the winding corridors of the Hofburg. In this way, the trysts remained private. Because of protocol and the many servants, meetings in the Hofburg imperial apartments were hardly possible. On the other hand, a visit from the Emperor to the (still very modest) living quarters of the actress would have caused a scandal.

In order to see the imperial private rooms, Schratt needed Elisabeth's intervention. It was the Empress herself who took her "friend" to her husband's quarters for the first time. Franz Joseph to Schratt: "How happy I am to show you my rooms and show you the inside of that certain window on which you have so often been gracious enough to direct your glance from the outside."[12]

To see each other at all, the couple had agreed on specific times when Schratt was to walk across the Burgplatz. On those occasions, she would always look up at the window behind which the Emperor stood and greeted her politely. For a long time, this was the only opportunity, aside from performances at the Burgtheater, for the Emperor to see his beloved.

If we recall how jealously, with what deep disappointment, the young Elisabeth greeted the escapades of the young Emperor, how she had let herself be carried away by almost hysterical attacks and precipitately fled the family circle, we will realize how fundamentally the situation had changed. What linked the two had long ago ceased to be love. Elisabeth felt compassion for the lonely man with whom she no longer wished to live or could live. She proved to be a good and generous friend, acting in extremely tactful ways. On Schratt's name day in November 1887, for example, Franz Joseph wrote to his friend, "This day I dined alone with the Empress and Valerie and was astonished to see champagne glasses on the table, since normally we do not allow ourselves the luxury of this wine. The Empress explained that she had ordered the champagne so that we could drink to your good health, which then occurred most sincerely. This was a successful and charming surprise."[13]

Thus, the love story between the Emperor and the actress could unfold. In February 1888, a mutual declaration was made, and the Emperor issued an assurance to Frau Schatt: "You say that you will control yourself, so will I, though it will not always be easy for me, for I do not wish to do anything that is not right, I love my wife and do not wish to abuse her trust and her friendship for you."[14]

With a clear conscience, Franz Joseph dispelled all Schratt's fears that the Empress might hold something against her. "The Empress has . . . repeatedly expressed herself in the most favorable and gracious terms about you, and I can assure you that she is very fond of you. If you knew this wonderful woman better, you would, I am certain, be filled with the same sentiments."[15]

Elisabeth did everything in her power to show her sympathies, as when Schratt suffered from some indisposition. Franz Joseph to Frau Schratt: "The Empress is very worried about you, she even claims more than I am, but that is positively untrue. Whenever I go to her room, she asks me for the latest news of you, and I cannot always oblige her, since I cannot be so brash and importunate as to constantly send for news of you."[16] On another occasion, he wrote, "The Empress, too, was shocked at your ride yesterday, and keeps admonishing me that I alone will have to bear the blame should you fall seriously ill."[17] And again, "The Empress would urge you not to take any cold sea baths at this time of year, instead she recommends baths of warm sea water and then rinsing with cold."[18]

Elisabeth's strong support of her husband's love affair did not mean that she found Katharina Schratt as likable and lovable as Franz Joseph assured Schratt. In her poems, Elisabeth struck up a richly complacent tone. If her husband's infatuation did not rouse her to jealousy, it nevertheless gave rise to mockery. Franz Joseph's frequent infatuated questions about the whereabouts of his friend at any particular time occasionally strained Elisabeth's nerves. Franz Joseph to Katharina Schratt: "The Empress thinks that it may be an honor to be my friend, but *assomant* [sic; immensely boring] because of my constant inquiries about your whereabouts."[19]

When Prince Albert of Thurn und Taxis was visiting the imperial family at the Hermes Villa, he saw, in the Emperor's apartments, a portrait of Schratt, whom he did not know.

Elisabeth, lightly: "How do you like this one?"

Taxis: "She looks horribly common."

Bright laughter from the Empress greeted this declaration, and even the Emperor could not help joining in, whether he felt like it or not.[20]

From this time on, Elisabeth's poems no longer referred to Emperor Franz Joseph only by the name of Oberon (the counterpart to her Titania; she also called him King Visvamitra. This was the name of a legendary Indian king who loved a cow (Sabala), and as such the name also occurs in Heine.

As early as August 1888, Katharina Schratt came to Bad Ischl to join the Emperor and Empress. Twenty-year-old Archduchess Marie Valerie recorded her disapproval in her diary. "In the afternoon, Mama, Papa, and I showed Frau Schratt the garden . . . she is truly simple and likable, nevertheless I bear her a kind of grudge, although it is not her fault that Papa has this friendship with her, but wicked people talk about it and cannot believe the childlike view Papa takes of the matter, how touching he is even in this. But he is someone one should never talk about—I feel bad about it, and I think for this reason, Mama should not have encouraged this acquaintance so much."[21]

But even Marie Valerie clearly saw how much good the friendship with Katharina Schratt did the Emperor. "She is so easygoing that finally one cannot help feeling comfortable—I understand that her calm, very natural ways are attractive to Papa."[22]

After the tragedy at Mayerling, Franz Joseph's friendship with Katharina Schratt proved to be a true blessing, especially for Elisabeth, who now attempted to get away from Vienna entirely. Schratt relieved the Empress of her feelings of guilt and her worry about the deeply afflicted Emperor. Schratt had become the only bright spot in his sad life. Elisabeth to her sister-in-law Marie José: "I must get away. But to leave Franz alone— impossible. And yet—he has Schratt—she looks after him as no one else does and watches over him." And: "With Schratt he can relax."[23]

Harmless chatter in Schratt's increasingly elegant parlor, a little warmth and human feeling, of which the Emperor had had so little until then; no philosophical discourses, no spiritualism and no poetry; instead, extremely worldly, uncomplicated, and undemanding topics, over breakfast with coffee and croissants. These are what gave the Emperor comfort and provided him with distraction during the next few years.

In 1889, Schratt settled in Vienna in a house next to the park at Schönbrunn, and she bought a villa in Bad Ischl adjacent to the imperial summer residence. According to Franz Joseph, this had "the advantage of nearness, which makes it possible, with your permission, for me to visit you much more often, the Empress also wishes to give to you the key to the little door through which you can arrive in our garden without having to go through the streets of Ischl."[24]

By this time, Marie Valerie understood the true situation. She held it very much against her mother that the Empress promoted the relationship. "Oh, why did Mama herself go so far! . . . but of course, now one cannot and may not change anything, I must, although it embarrasses Franz [her fiancé], meet with her [Schratt] again and not give away my feelings."[25] The very religious and puritanical young Archduchess looked on with disapproval as her own mother over and over invited the actress to visit and appeared in public with her—with and without the Emperor's company—in order to present the relationship as innocent and honorable.

Katharina Schratt was even granted the great privilege of dining rather frequently at the Hofburg with the most immediate family—that is, with only the Emperor, the Empress, and Archduchess Marie Valerie. The Empress, who refused more than ever to take part in the official court dinners, and who, above all, contemptuously ignored the court nobility, thus left herself wide open to criticism. An actress at a Habsburg family table—such a thing had never before been seen. The fact that Katharina Schratt was not a single woman but was married further fed the gossip at this Catholic court.

Archduchess Marie Valerie suffered true torments during these dinners. "Frau Schratt dined with us (we were four), took a walk with us, and remained until evening. I cannot say how embarrassing such afternoons are for me, how incomprehensible that Mama finds them rather cozy."[26]

Singular as it may sound, to Elisabeth, her husband's love for Katharina Schratt was a reassurance—even, on occasion, a pleasure. In late 1890, for example, she wrote to Valerie, "One must not look forward to anything nor expect anything good. Life has enough bitter pain. But Poka [the Hungarian word for "turkey," a code name for Franz Joseph] is happy tonight, I have invited his friend for 6:30 to Ida's to tell her a few travel memories. And today we went for a walk in Schönbrunn. It is so good finally to see a happy face in this dark, sad, and abandoned castle, and tonight Poka is truly merry as a lark."[27]

Then, too, the couple had something to talk about with one another at last, and Elisabeth could reassure her daughter on the subject of marital harmony. "It works, since almost always we talk only about the friend or the theater."[28]

On the other hand, Franz Joseph and Frau Schratt also found much to say to each other about Elisabeth. The Emperor was constantly concerned and often did not even know where his wife, away on one of her far-ranging travels, happened to be. Franz Joseph to Katharina Schratt in 1890: "How happy I would be if I could talk over my fears for the Empress with you and find comfort with you."[29] Elisabeth regularly sent her regards to Schratt, as she did, for example, from Arcachon. Franz Joseph wrote to Frau Schratt that the Empress "desires me to send you the enclosed card, since she thinks the sight of it might tempt you to go to Arcachon—but not just now, I hasten to add."[30] The Emperor had noticed how much his friend imitated his wife, and he correctly feared that Katharina Schratt, too, would now want to travel, hardly ever returning to Vienna.

The friendship with Schratt created some problems as well. The actress's huge gambling debts and her other enormous expenses were not the trouble. Franz Joseph paid up gladly, just as he was used to doing for his wife. But Katharina Schratt's friends kept asking her to intercede for them with the Emperor. And most of the time, she did not wait to be asked. The management of the Burgtheater ran into no end of trouble, too; for unless Schratt was agreeable, few parts could be assigned or plays chosen.

The German ambassador, Prince Eulenburg (who was smart enough to maintain a good, even friendly relationship with Schratt, promptly arousing the Emperor's jealousy), wrote to Emperor Wilhelm II in 1896: "Of course, she is the absolute monarch of the theater, and when she arrives, all of them, not excluding the manager, fall to their knees." Stella Hohenfels, a highly regarded actress, was eager to leave Vienna to escape the constant slights offered by Schratt—as was her husband, Alfred Berger, the Burgtheater's director. Eulenburg: "It is an extremely odd situation! As I have heard, old friends of Frau Kathi push themselves forward more and more, and this influence makes itself unpleasantly felt among the court administration." But then he pointed out the principal problem. "Baron Kiss—Kathi's husband—is a further inconvenience. He was sent to Venezuela, where he is terribly bored. He urgently wishes to return to

Europe, which is all the more understandable as all his debts have been paid up. It would have been smarter to omit that step."[31]

In 1892, Toni Kiss, Schratt's son, who was twelve years old at the time, received an anonymous letter with defamatory statements about his mother and her relations with the Emperor. The police were unable to identify the author. Everyone was upset. Once again, the Empress interceded; she invited little Toni to visit her in the imperial residence in Bad Ischl, walked with him in the garden, and spoke "most lovingly of his mother, how fond she was of her, how well she thought of her, and how he must love and respect her, and that only evil people could think up such lies." For years, she had the court bakery send pastries and sweets to the boy, in still another effort to prove her affection for mother and son, as a further precaution against gossip.[32]

In spite of extreme caution and good will on the part of the Empress, such a love affair could not go wholly unnoticed. In 1889, Count Hübner wrote:

> All the great and small evils seem to converge over the imperial family and to descend on our poor Austria as well. The Emperor continues to be under the spell of an actress at the Burgtheater, Schratt, pretty and stupid, who, as is claimed, lives respectably within the Emperor's immediate family. The Empress, who, they say, arranged this liaison, which they call platonic but which is by no means so considered by the public, and which in any case is ridiculous—and young Archduchess Valerie. This silly business does the Emperor considerable damage in the opinion the bourgeoisie and the people have of him.[33]

Eulenburg: "The local imperial family is admittedly interesting from a psychological point of view. Anyone who does not know the personalities, with all their oddities, will be unable to understand the singular relationship among the Emperor, the Empress, the actress, and the daughter."[34]

Valerie admitted in her diary that she "has a groundless resentment to overcome against Frau Schratt—because she is an actress???" Valerie's fiancé told her, "No, whether she is an actress, a ballet dancer, or Princess XY makes no difference if she is a decent person—I believe that, too— and there is nothing to it—but—but if they talk to me about it, I cannot say: no!—And one should not talk about the Emperor."[35]

When it was a matter of Franz Joseph's relationship with Katharina Schratt, the otherwise dutiful daughter dared to be critical, confessing to her diary "how embarrassing to me are Papa's often rough, contradictory way with Mama, his curt replies. . . . Though I do know that he means no harm by it, I nevertheless understand that Mama's view of the future is bleak." The thought that Franz Joseph might deal less roughly with the actress deeply distressed Marie Valerie. "I wish I need never be with the good woman again and that Papa had never seen her." Given the circumstances, it was almost a humiliation for the Emperor's daughter to kiss Schratt on meeting and leave-taking, as was also Elisabeth's custom: "but I am afraid of offending Papa if I omit it even once."[36]

Valerie's complaints mounted. "The fact that I can no longer always think Papa right in my innermost heart, as once I did, that is the most bitter thing for me—even though the matter is so innocent. Oh, why did Mama bring about this acquaintance, and how can she say to boot that it is a reassurance to her! . . . How can it be that two such noble natures as my parents can be so mistaken and can so often make each other unhappy."[37]

And after a desolate Christmas in 1889 in the Hofburg, Marie Valerie wrote, "O dear God, how sad is our family life, which seems so wonderful to outsiders, so that Mama and I are glad when we can be peacefully alone. I do not know why, but this has increased to a frightening extent this year. —Papa has such few interests anymore and has—shall I say it—grown so much more dull and petty. . . . Encounters with my parents made up of small but unbelievably irritating embarrassments—Mama constantly tells me her troubles. And I no longer look at Papa with eyes of fervent admiration."[38]

Prince Leopold of Bavaria, Gisela's husband, tried to reassure his sister-in-law. He thought the Schratt affair "very natural," he explained to the overwrought Valerie, adding, "It's just that Franz [Archduke Franz Salvator, Valerie's fiancé] is still so very innocent."[39]

The closer the Emperor's relationship with the actress became, the less the Empress felt obliged to spend time in Vienna. Marie Valerie: "Mama more and more in low spirits. Her lot is hardest when she is with Papa. The sacrifice of being with him diminishes in necessity to the degree that the unfortunate friendship with Schratt increases."[40]

We can easily imagine Valerie's deep embarrassment when, in 1890, the Empress asked her, "should she die . . . to encourage Papa to marry Schratt."[41]

Elisabeth pleaded for circumspection only abroad—for example, when the Emperor, the Empress, and Schratt were all staying at Cap Martin simultaneously in 1894. Franz Joseph to Frau Schratt: "When the Empress wrote you of her wish to see you here, that was not an empty phrase or an expression of pity, as you thought, but a genuine longing for you, which she felt throughout the journey." Nevertheless, Elisabeth did not think that a meeting in Cap Martin would be advisable. "Of course, there can be no thought of an incognito here, one is constantly under observation by a crowd of people, the place teems with the curious and the highly placed, and we fear that our relationship with you could be subject to malicious criticism. At home, almost everyone has learned to understand the manner of our friendship, here abroad, and in this place, which, unfortunately, is not quiet but very trafficked and busy, it is different. The Empress, whose judgment is always right, thinks that none of this would harm us old people, but she is thinking first of all about you and Toni."[42]

Furthermore, Elisabeth was increasingly convinced that it must be a hardship for the actress to spend time with the ever less lively Emperor and Empress. Franz Joseph from Cap Martin to Frau Schratt in Monte Carlo in 1897: "I hinted gently to the Empress that you might after all come to visit us, whereupon she replied: The poor thing! You must know that she always thinks that it must be very uncomfortable and unpleasant for you to interrupt your amusements in Monte Carlo to be bored with us old people here."[43]

A few times, differences of opinion arose between Franz Joseph and Katharina Schratt. Each time it was the Empress who was conciliatory and soothed the ruffled feathers, who jollied angry Schratt out of her sulks. The Emperor was so downcast by these quarrels that dealing with him at these times was difficult; everyone around him always longed for Schratt's return. With her, Franz Joseph behaved exactly as he did with Elisabeth: He was the one who begged, the one who was abject, the one who gave in. Prince Eulenburg dutifully sent detailed reports on these events to Emperor Wilhelm II. "He missed Frau Kathi's merry chatter about the large and small miseries of the world of the stage, about her puppies and birdies and domestic doings. . . . He also needs the charm of Frau Kathi's beautiful femininity, which he commands with the utmost innocence. In short: Matters could not go on without her. Even the Empress seems to have thought so, having already on two previous occasions smoothed over differences of a sort similar to the present situation."[44]

However, even Elisabeth at times could not entirely conceal the fact that, in spite of everything, she felt neglected. During one of the last walks before her death with Franz Joseph and their "friend," she showed her feelings with the macabre wit peculiar to her. They were speaking, as so often during this period, about death, and specifically of Elisabeth's death. Elisabeth indicated her attitude by quoting an old verse, *"Ach, da wäre niemand so, als der Ritter Blaubart froh"*—literally, "In the event, Bluebeard would be happiest of all," and obviously meaning that her death would gladden Franz Joseph most. The Emperor grew annoyed and said defensively, "Go on, don't talk that way." (Katharina Schratt related the story after Elisabeth's death to Prince Eulenburg.)[45]

Nevertheless, Elisabeth's steadfast advocacy of the unevenly matched couple managed to keep the gossip within bounds. So perfect were Elisabeth's discretion and her protection that, to this day, it is impossible to find concrete proof of an affair. The question of whether the imperial family's reputation suffered as a result of this unusual relationship must, at least for the most part, be answered in the negative. Plainly, this outcome is Elisabeth's achievement.

The crucial importance of the Empress to the relationship between Emperor and actress could be fully realized only after Elisabeth's death. For when Schratt could no longer frequent the court as the official "friend of the Empress," her position became all but untenable. A marriage, which would have legitimized the relationship, was impossible, since Schratt was still (according to Catholic canon law, which was decisive in this case) legally married. Valerie in 1899: "He will never, never renounce her, and unfortunately he cannot marry her, for she is very lawfully married."[46]

Two years after Elisabeth's death, a serious disagreement, lasting several months, broke out between Franz Joseph and Katharina Schratt. The Emperor explained to Valerie "almost in tears, that she [Schratt] has been working since Mama's death on this decision [to leave the Emperor], because since that time, she no longer felt highly regarded, her position not being a proper one."[47]

In response to the Emperor's sadness, many intermediaries tried to effect a reconciliation and to bring Schratt back to Vienna from Switzerland, where she had gone to sulk. The *Neue Freie Presse* printed a bold advertisement that caused a great stir: "Kathi, come back—all in order—to your unhappy, abandoned Franzl." Burgtheater Director Berger wrote to the German ambassador, "since the death of a sovereign lady [Elisabeth], a subtlety has been missing which until then gave to everything a different, more elegant form," which was completely true.[48]

The enormous embarrassment surrounding Katharina Schratt after Elisabeth's death damaged the Emperor's standing. Now, too, the actress did exactly what her great model, the Empress, had done whenever she was offended: Time and again she left Vienna for significant periods of time, and she let herself be implored in vain for a long time before resuming the customary walks in Schönbrunn. One of these serious and long quarrels was ended only by Franz Joseph's appeal to their "love for her [Elisabeth], the last thing that still unites us."[49] Valerie's well-meant attempt to persuade her father to marry Aunt Sparrow—that is, Elisabeth's sister, the widowed Countess Mathilde Trani—so that Schratt could return to being "the friend of Papa's wife,"[50] demonstrates the muddle that prevailed after Elisabeth's protective hand no longer rested on this, her husband's late love.

When Nikolaus von Kiss died in May 1909, the Emperor was seventy-eight and Schratt almost fifty-six years old. By that time—as Franz Joseph's letters, preserved in their entirety, show—the relationship was still a friendly one but much less ardent than it had been in Elisabeth's day.

Nevertheless, time and again (of course, only after 1909, when such an event became a possibility), Vienna gossiped about a secret marriage. But there is no proof, nor do the letters and diaries of the families give any indication of such an occurrence. Whatever the case, until Franz Joseph's death, the two used the polite form of address to each other and met only rarely.

CHAPTER THIRTEEN

RUDOLF AND VALERIE

For all practical purposes, Gisela and Rudolf grew up without a mother. Elisabeth was so preoccupied with her own worries and cares that she devoted little time to the children and offered them neither warmth nor security. She considered them the foster children of Archduchess Sophie, and that was enough to permanently impair the relationship.

Nevertheless, whenever Elisabeth turned up at the Viennese court for one of her sudden, short stays, she showed herself to be a strong (though extremely self-willed) personality, with such a power of attraction that even the little Crown Prince idolized her—not like a mother, but rather like a beautiful apparition out of a fairy tale, bringing life into his gray, duty-bound days.

More than either of his sisters, Rudolf was his mother's child. Temperament and talents, imagination, liveliness, sensibility, wit, a quick understanding—all these he shared with Elisabeth. Marie Festetics on the fifteen-year-old boy: "The Crown Prince's eyes glowed. He was thrilled to be with his mother, whom he worships . . . he is very like his mother, in particular, he has her charm as well as her brown eyes."[1]

All his life, Rudolf gratefully remembered that in 1865, when he had been tested so severely mentally and physically, it was his mother who had taken his part with such fervor (see page 121). Even the little Crown Prince was fully aware that she had been able to bring about the change only at the cost of real family rifts and only against strong court opposition. Latour, the tutor Elisabeth selected, became a deeply beloved father substitute to the little boy. And Latour taught the boy the same liberal views Elisabeth herself developed. Latour brought mother and son very close, even if they had little direct contact with each other.

His markedly bourgeois—even anticourt—education distanced the Crown Prince from his aristocratic surroundings. It erected barriers that subsequently proved insurmountable. From childhood on, Rudolf had to live with the heavy burden of being Elisabeth's son—and of being so very like her. All the Empress's antagonists saw Rudolf as a potential danger —specifically, they scented the danger that eventually they would be living under a "revolutionary," "bourgeois," "anticlerical," "antiaristocratic" emperor, someone rather like Elisabeth. And this danger (seen, conversely, as a hope by large groups of the population) did indeed exist.

During Elisabeth's most politically active period, after the defeat of Königgrätz and during the negotiations in Budapest, Rudolf, aged eight, was with his mother in Hungary. Here, the Crown Prince met Gyula Andrássy, whom he revered all his life and who was as influential to the boy's political world view as he was to Elisabeth's. Those few weeks in Budapest with his mother and Andrássy—Franz Joseph was in Vienna— were, for Rudolf, the best time he ever spent with his mother (see pages 156ff.).

But Elisabeth's support of her son in 1865 and the time in Budapest remained isolated episodes. In 1868, Marie Valerie was born—Elisabeth's "coronation gift" to Hungary. The Crown Prince, who was nine years old, was shunted aside.

Gisela married at sixteen and moved to Bavaria. Her relations with her mother were chilly. Though the Crown Prince remained in Vienna, he was practically abandoned to his teachers and tutors. The beautiful mother he worshiped paid no attention to him. Her thoughts were concentrated on

Valerie, and Rudolf grew extremely jealous. He treated the little girl roughly and unkindly. Valerie, for her part, was afraid of her big brother. In this situation, Elisabeth, like a brood hen, went over entirely to her youngest child and rejected her son even more.

It rarely happened that all the members of the imperial family were in one place at the same time. Each member of the imperial family had his own household; petty jealousies and dissensions raged between the various staffs. Given the circumstances, it was almost never possible to create a feeling of family intimacy. They were strangers to each other, and as Archduchess Valerie noted, their meetings were marked by awkwardness and embarrassment. Elisabeth would have had to take the initiative even to begin approaching her son. But she did not take the first step, nor did Emperor Franz Joseph.

Thus, Rudolf remained isolated not only at court, but also within the immediate family. No one was aware that he had problems. The successor to the throne was regarded with respectful timidity and with distrust. Valerie once confessed to one of her Bavarian relatives that, though she lived under the same roof with Rudolf, she might not see him for months on end.[2] Gisela, who was closest to her brother, noted with surprise during a visit to Vienna, "actually the whole family regards him as a person to be treated with caution." To which Valerie replied, "The poor man! Unfortunately, it's only too true."[3] The kind of trusting and confidential relationship that existed between Elisabeth and Valerie was out of the question for Rudolf and his mother.

Rudolf's marriage to Stephanie, daughter of the King of the Belgians, placed an additional strain on family relations. Elisabeth in particular stubbornly maintained her dislike of her daughter-in-law. But when young Stephanie showed an interest in making obligatory public appearances— since she felt at ease in public and enjoyed attracting attention—Elisabeth saw her chance simply to pass on to her daughter-in-law (who was only seventeen) the major part of these tasks. In her memoirs, Stephanie recalled Elisabeth's words. "This drudgery, this torture, as she called the duties of her position, were hateful to her. . . . She espoused the view that freedom was everyone's right. Her picture of life resembled a beautiful fairy-tale dream of a world without sorrow or constraint."[4]

Elisabeth's poems expressed great dislike of Stephanie, who valued outward appearances and social forms above all (which was not good for her marriage to the unconventional Crown Prince). Elisabeth felt great scorn for the "mighty bumpkin" with her "long, fake tresses" and her "cunningly watchful" eyes.[5]

Young Stephanie's frequent public appearances several times put the Empress in the shade, just as had happened many years before in connection with Stephanie's aunt Carlotta of Mexico (now dreaming the rest of her poor, disturbed life away in a castle in Belgium). Whenever Elisabeth wanted to hurt Stephanie's feelings, she alluded to this sister-in-law, whom at one time she had so cordially abhorred. The fact that Stephanie proved herself a committed friend to the high aristocracy and for her part criticized Elisabeth's lack of a sense of duty was enough to cool the relationship between mother-in-law and daughter-in-law forever.

Nor did the Crown Prince and his wife receive support from the Emperor. The generations were alienated from each other, and there was no familiarity. Valerie, in 1884: "How different, how courteous but self-conscious Papa is with them [Rudolf and Stephanie] as compared with [his behavior to] me! Surely that is the reason for Rudolf's jealousy."[6]

Rudolf all but courted his mother's favor, imitating her preferences and dislikes down to the last detail. Elisabeth, for example, was fond of large dogs, who followed her into the most precious salons—to the Emperor's perpetual consternation. The Crown Prince, too, surrounded himself with dogs; around 1880, in Prague, he even opened a dog-breeding establishment, where he specialized in wolfhounds. In the Crown Prince, Elisabeth's love of animals grew into a thorough and serious preoccupation with zoology—more particularly, with ornithology. Rudolf made long sea voyages for research, traveling most particularly with his older friend, Alfred Brehm (on whose *Tierleben* he collaborated). He honored the scholar to such an extent that the ship's officers made fun of his attitude[7] —not unlike the ridicule the crew of the *Greif* heaped on the Empress because she overwhelmed Alexander von Warsberg, her archeological guide through Greece, with gratitude and favor.

The Emperor very generously allowed his wife to pursue her interests. But he refused to grant the Crown Prince's dearest wish—to attend the university and study the natural sciences. At that time, university study was out of the question for a Habsburg, considered out of keeping with the standing of the dynasty. This stance was in contrast to that of the House of Hohenzollern. Prince Wilhelm (later Wilhelm II), who was Rudolf's coeval, was practically forced by his liberal parents to study at the University of Bonn. The young man complied with their wishes with less than moderate enthusiasm and without taking a degree. The Wittelsbach family also did not consider an involvement in the sciences out of place. Elisabeth's brother, Karl Theodor, the head of the ducal branch, was an ophthalmologist, recognized even in professional circles. But Emperor

Franz Joseph insisted that his son become a soldier. As for Rudolf's propensity for science and literature—the Emperor regarded these interests as mere "notions"—very like his comments on Elisabeth's predilections.

Rudolf had to content himself with remaining a self-taught ornithologist; and yet he managed to complete an amazing body of work, respected by professionals to this day.[8] His parents took no cognizance of it. His career as a soldier was less distinguished, to his father's great disappointment. The Crown Prince also worked on political memoranda and wrote clandestine political editorials for the "democratic organ," *Neues Wiener Tagblatt*, under his friend Moritz Szeps. The common interests of Rudolf and Elisabeth went so far that both Empress and Crown Prince had their writings printed at about the same time by the state printing office, both in very small editions. And yet neither knew of the other's work. Rudolf composed "Reisebilder" (Travel Images); unfinished, preserved only in manuscript, while Elisabeth wrote her two volumes of poetry. All three works were indebted to Heine.

As a nineteen-year-old, Rudolf wrote his first anonymous pamphlet, *Der Österreichische Adel und sein constitutioneller Beruf* (The Austrian Nobility and Its Constitutional Calling), in which he lashed out at the privileges of the nobility, which were not earned by work and achievements—his principal accusations differing little from his mother's.[9] Elisabeth was not familiar with her son's forty-eight-page pamphlet any more than was the Emperor. Rudolf was so shy of his parents—even afraid of them—that he did not dare to show them his writings.

Elisabeth's anticlericalism, her very independent position on the dogmas of the Catholic church, are also found in Rudolf. Even her enthusiasm for republicanism was passed on—without her knowledge—to the Crown Prince. Prince Karl Khevenhüller on the twenty-year-old Rudolf: "He talked a lot of incongruous nonsense about freedom and equality, railed at the nobility as an outmoded idea, and said that the best position he could wish for himself was to be the president of a republic."[10]

And if Elisabeth took seriously the possibility of exile in Switzerland (even considering such "retirement" desirable), Rudolf, too, toyed with the thought of a potential bourgeois life. "If I am chased away from here, I will enter the service of a republic, probably the service of France," he confessed to his confidant, the journalist Berthold Frischauer.[11]

Elisabeth's political views were also passed on to her son in their entirety. Elisabeth and Rudolf both saw in Andrássy the great man who could lead Austria-Hungary out of the calamities of the old times into a new, modern, liberal world. At the age of nineteen, for example, Rudolf told Marie Festetics that "every day he thanked God for Andrássy's being in the world. For only as long as he was there would everything go well."[12] The first political memorandum the twenty-two-year-old Crown Prince wrote was an unmitigated paean of praise to Andrássy.[13]

With the same unanimity with which they defended the person and policies of Andrássy, Elisabeth and Rudolf condemned Count Eduard Taaffe, the prime minister. A childhood friend of the Emperor, Taaffe took office after the fiasco of the Liberals in 1879. There was no possible area of agreement between Taaffe and Andrássy. Shortly after Taaffe joined the government, Andrássy tendered his resignation on grounds of poor health. It was granted at once—which he had not expected. He had wanted to be asked to stay on as foreign minister. In that way, he would have strengthened his position vis-à-vis Taaffe, his archenemy, and would have had a chance to win the power struggle.

In this situation, everyone at court assumed that now, when Andrássy was in trouble, the Empress would abandon her reservations about politics and would intervene. In June 1879, Franz Joseph's younger brother, Archduke Karl Ludwig mentioned to Count Hübner "that the Empress was wholly uninterested in politics and that the riding academy absorbed her wholly. Nevertheless, those around her, all of whom are devoted to Andrássy, continue their efforts to serve him through intervention in his favor by the Empress when the occasion offered."[14]

Elisabeth showed her opposition to Taaffe's government by accompanying the Emperor when, in 1879, he called on the ailing Andrássy. Hübner: "This is a demonstration on the part of the empress which naturally disheartened Taaffe." His physicians advised Andrássy to take the cure in Bad Gleichenberg, "but the Empress (!!), his last but powerful support, suggested Bad Ischl, where he intends to go," Hübner wrote.[15] The hidden motivation was that in Bad Ischl, a meeting between the Emperor and Andrássy in a relaxed atmosphere could be arranged, and Andrássy would have a chance to withdraw his resignation. Andrássy followed Elisabeth's advice. A meeting with the Emperor did take place in Bad Ischl, but there was no question of recalling the foreign minister. Andrássy's term as imperial and royal foreign minister came to an end in late 1879.

To demonstrate his friendship with Andrássy and to sign their joint accomplishment, the Austro-German Alliance, Bismarck came to Vienna in the autumn of 1879. Hübner's cutting comment on the brilliant success of Bismarck's visit: "This is the huge fireworks that Andrássy set off at the end of his ministry in the style of a melodrama, or rather, a Franconi circus." Nevertheless, even on this friendly occasion, the German Nationalists staged demonstrations outside Bismarck's quarters at the Hotel Imperial. Hübner did not forget to mention in his diary "that the Emperor was annoyed by the public ovations offered to Bismarck."[16]

Baron Heinrich Haymerle, who succeeded Andrássy, died after only a brief period in office. Now that a new foreign minister had to be chosen and Andrássy's health had improved, the Empress brought his name back into the deliberations. Of course, there had not been enough time to make preparations for winning a new term for Andrássy. The most powerful statesman, the one who could count on the Emperor's trust, was more than ever Prime Minister Count Eduard Taaffe, and he had no use in his cabinet for Andrássy. The time of liberalism, which Andrássy embodied, was over in Austria. Taaffe ruled with the support of the farmers, the clergy, and the Czechs (the so-called Iron Ring) and neither could nor wanted to put up with a liberal foreign minister—one who was a Hungarian and a Freemason besides.

The nonappointment of Andrássy (Count Gusztáv Kálnoky was named foreign minister) was a defeat for the Empress as well. The imperial family split over Taaffe's new policy. Emperor Franz Joseph supported Taaffe with the full authority of the crown; Empress Elisabeth and Crown Prince Rudolf—the two liberals—were opposed to him.

Rudolf's political pamphlets and his private letters are full of statements unfavorable to Taaffe and his policies. "The good Count Taaffe is and remains the same as he always was, a reckless swindler who can still cause great harm," Rudolf wrote, for example, in October 1879 to his former tutor, Latour.[17] And over and over he lamented the "anticonstitutionalism" and the reversal of liberal achievements under Taaffe. "In Germany and among us, reaction and ultramontanism are mightily on the move. . . . What was won in long struggles, the concept of a modern civilized state, is endangered here." Rudolf was almost as blunt as his mother. "A repellent trend now prevails in central Europe, a time in which parsons and highly placed numbskulls wallow in their own idiocy."[18]

Elisabeth used similar expressions, even though hers were couched in verse. She accused Taaffe of unscrupulously exploiting the Emperor, who, in her opinion, was too good-natured. Franz Joseph, she thought, was losing his popularity on Taaffe's account. Elisabeth complained to Countess Festetics, "The Emperor was popular as few sovereigns are. . . . He was irreproachable—standing above everyone in sublime dignity, which was a part of his 'self' and now? now—'He' stands at the edge of great complications and is a mere tool in the hands of a reckless acrobat who wants to stay on top and uses him as a balancing rod!" And Elisabeth wished: "If I were a man—I would step forward and tell the truth. He could still do as he wished—but he would have to know what games are being played with his sovereign dignity."[19]

These statements clearly show how times had changed since 1867. By now, the situation was one in which Elisabeth no longer dared to express her political opinion openly. If even she was so afraid of plain speaking, how much more difficult would it have been for the young Crown Prince to discuss basic questions of Austrian policy with the Emperor!

After Andrássy's resignation, neither Elisabeth nor Rudolf could find anything positive to say about Austro-Hungarian foreign policy. Rudolf: "Never was Austria as strong, happy, and respected as during the years when Andrássy stood at the helm of politics, and yet this outstanding man had to fall; for the struggle against impalpable, invisible opponents is an impossible one."[20]

At about the same time, without knowing her son's views, the Empress expressed an even more drastic judgment about "the fat little donkey," the new imperial and royal foreign minister, Count Kálnoky, and the "noble steed," Andrássy.

An meinen Ehgemal

Sag' an, mein trauter Ehgemal,
Was willst Du wohl bezwecken?
Mir däucht, zur allgemeinen Qual
Bleibt schier Dein Fuhrwerk stecken.

Das Es'lein, das Du vorgespannt,
Es kann schon nimmer weiter,
Zu tief hat sich's im Dreck verrant;
O, wär' es nicht gescheidter,

Du fingest jenen edlen Gaul
Dort, auf der freien Weide,
Und zwängest ihm den Zaum in's Maul,'
Nicht morgen, nein noch heute.

Schon einmal riss er aus dem Dreck
Dir den verfahr'nen Karren,
D'rum jag' Dein dickes Es'lein weg
Eh' man Dich hält zum Narren.[21]

[To My Husband: Tell me, my beloved husband, / What is it you are trying to achieve? / It seems to me that to everyone's torment, / Your cart is mired. / / The little donkey you put in the harness, / It cannot go on, / It is stuck too deep in the mud; / Oh, would it not be smarter / / If you were to capture the noble steed / There, on the open meadow, / And force the bridle between its teeth, / Not tomorrow, but this very day. / / Once before, it pulled out of the mud / Your mired carriage for you, / So chase away your fat little donkey / Before you make a fool of yourself.]

Elisabeth's and Rudolf's opinion of the imperial and royal foreign policy was also expressed in 1885, at Kremsier, at the friendly conference between Emperor Franz Joseph and the Russian Czar Alexander III on the subject of Balkan policies. Both Empress Elisabeth and Crown Prince Rudolf were present, and both had nothing but scorn for the demonstrations of Austro-Russian friendship—behaving not at all unlike that traditional Russophobe, Andrássy.

Elisabeth depicted the Czar's family in one of her poems as monkeys.[22] Rudolf gained a similarly poor impression. From Kremsier he wrote Stephanie, his wife, "The Emperor of Russia has grown colossally fat, Grand Duke Vladimir and his wife as well as the Empress look old and feeble. The entourages, and especially the servants, are awful; the new uniforms have made them quite Asian again. At the time of the late Emperor [Czar Alexander II], the Russians were at least elegant, and a few of the gentlemen of the retinue looked quite refined. Now it is an awfully common company."[23]

But most of all, the Empress and the Crown Prince mistrusted the Russian assurances of peace and friendship (in contrast to the Emperor and Foreign Minister Kálnoky). Rudolf wrote Latour, "In the Balkans, matters are once again on the boil; . . . at the Ballplatz, little is known about all this, and matters are being handled with sovereign stupidity. Russia exploits Kálnoky's shortsighted ministry and the so-called rapprochement with Austria to form committees, send money, arms, etc., etc. to Bulgaria, Rumelia, Macedonia, Serbia, and even Bosnia with the greatest aplomb."[24]

The skepticism the Empress and the Crown Prince felt about the Russian assurances of peace soon proved only too well founded. In the Bulgarian crisis of the subsequent years, Russia and Austria faced each other as enemies.

The Empress and the Crown Prince accused Foreign Minister Kálnoky of having acted with too little assurance, of having been almost humble toward both Russia and the German Reich and, all unsuspecting, of having fallen into the traps set by Bismarck and the Czar. (The fact that in 1887, Austria's supposed ally Germany made common cause with the Czar behind Austria's back through the most secret Reinsurance Treaty in retrospect confirmed Elisabeth and Rudolf's suspicions.)

Even Gyula Andrássy, the creator of the Austro-German Alliance and a well-known admirer of Bismarck, clearly moved away from Bismarck's policies during the Balkan crisis and began quite sharply to criticize Austria-Hungary's concessions to the German Reich, which he felt had gone much too far.

Elisabeth and Rudolf (as well as Andrássy) were also unanimous in their attitude toward the third partner in the Triple Alliance, Italy.

In some situations, even Crown Prince Rudolf expressed criticism of his mother. He especially resented her idleness. As early as 1881, Rudolf wrote to Latour, his former tutor and a fervent admirer of Elisabeth, "there was a time when the Empress often—whether successfully, I leave as an open question—concerned herself with politics and had serious discussions with the Emperor based on views diametrically opposed to his. Those times are past. The sovereign lady only concerns herself with sports; now even this opening to the outside world and to her . . . rather liberal views is closed off."[25]

The Crown Prince reacted with disappointment, anger, and jealousy to Elisabeth's excessive enthusiasm for riding. Several times he expressed this anger, causing serious conflicts with his mother, and especially when the quarrel centered on Bay Middleton (see pages 228ff.). Rudolf also criticized Elisabeth's tendency to spiritualism. One of the anonymous pamphlets he wrote and published was the antispiritualist polemic *Einige Worte über den Spiritismus* (A Few Words About Spiritualism) of 1882. In it, he used the methodology of the natural sciences to refute the spectral apparitions, the table rapping, clairvoyance, and similar spiritual enterprises very much the fashion in aristocratic society of the day. In 1884, the Austrian press printed reports that it was Crown Prince Rudolf himself who, in the course of a séance, had unmasked and exposed to ridicule one of the most famous mediums of the day, Bastian.[26]

This very circumspect opposition, of which Elisabeth was probably unaware, grew out of Rudolf's disappointed love for his mother. Especially during the 1880s—the time of the Taaffe government and a growing new conservatism—he was driven into increasing isolation both personally and politically. By this time, Emperor Franz Joseph was limiting his conversations with his increasingly self-confident son to the specific topics of hunting, the military, and family matters. Politics was never mentioned —a circumstance that caused Rudolf to complain repeatedly. Never once did Elisabeth mediate between the Emperor, over whom she continued to wield a great influence, and the heir to the throne, who was so extremely close to her in political questions. There are no documents to indicate that she ever spoke with Rudolf about his problems.

The tense family relations were common knowledge in diplomatic circles as well. According to a confidential report, "the personal relations between the monarch and his son lack that trait of cordiality which normally prevails in sovereign families. His Majesty Emperor Franz Joseph, unlike his usual custom, observes a certain outward sternness toward the Crown Prince, in order always to keep before his eyes the limits which the Archduke is inclined to overstep in word and judgment. It is significant that both Their Majesties are agreed in their judgment of their only son."[27]

Only with Rudolf's daughter Erzsi, born in 1883, did the Emperor come out of his shell—in contrast to Elisabeth, who spent practically no time with her granddaughter and showed no grandmotherly pride. During a visit to Laxenburg, where the Crown Prince and Crown Princess lived, Franz Joseph allowed little Erzsi to tousle his beard; she was even allowed to play with his medals, as Marie Valerie's diary noted with admiration for her father.[28]

The few official family gatherings were overshadowed by quarrels and jealous spite. On Elisabeth's fiftieth birthday at Christmas 1887, for example, Valerie's diary lamented the "embarrassing discomfort" aroused by the smoldering family dissension. She held Rudolf responsible for the situation.[29]

The difficulties which began to show themselves in 1886 in the Crown Prince's marriage were soon known to all Vienna—to all, that is, except the Emperor and Empress. Countess Festetics: "But in these circles, one is always the last to learn of the important things. That is what is so sad about the lives of the well-born." But when Elisabeth finally learned of the discord—and she heard about it from Marie Festetics—it never crossed her mind to intervene, to mediate, or to placate. Instead, once more she shifted the blame to her long-dead mother-in-law, Archduchess Sophie. "I myself feel that Rudolf is not happy," she told Countess Festetics. "Sometimes I have wondered what I could do. But I am reluctant to interfere, for I myself suffered so unspeakably under my mother-in-law that I do not wish to incur the reproach of a similar fault."[30] Elisabeth did not consider that the circumstances were very different in this case. And Countess Festetics was so considerate and so cautious that she did not dare to press further.

Nor did Rudolf's severe illness in the spring of 1887 give Elisabeth cause for particular worry. (According to the official version, the Crown Prince was suffering from a bladder ailment and rheumatism, but he may have had a severe case of gonorrhea, which continued to spread, affecting the joints and eyes and casting him into a deep depression).[31] No one dared to enlighten the imperial mother and father about their son's increasingly unstable way of life. Only a few people knew the details of his dangerous political dealings during the past two years anyhow.

The paradox was that the son to whom Elisabeth paid so little attention was so like her, whereas the effusively beloved daughter, Marie Valerie, took a very different direction. She had inherited more of her father's temperament, was calm in judgment, devout, and rational, and like her sister Gisela, she was helpless in the face of her mother's flights of imagination. Most significantly, however, this "Hungarian" child, born in the royal castle in Budapest, raised by Hungarian tutors, developed a strong aversion to Hungary when she was still a very young girl. When she was fifteen, for example, she timidly asked her father occasionally to speak with her, not only in Hungarian (as Elisabeth wished), but also in German. She was overjoyed at Franz Joseph's good-natured compliance.[32] Valerie's dislike of Hungary culminated in her dislike of Gyula Andrássy. The gossip about the relationship between him and the Empress, the many suggestive remarks about the "Hungarian child," could not go unnoticed and of necessity left their mark. Repeatedly, Valerie unburdened her heart to her diary about her feelings toward Andrássy; in 1883, for example, she wrote, "Dinner in honor of Andrássy, it pained me to grant him the triumph of hearing me speak Hungarian."[33] And in 1884, "I held out my hand to him with great brusqueness. . . . His detestable familiarity makes me so sick that almost involuntarily my voice turns cold, almost scornful. . . . Surely he hates me as much as I do him, at least I hope so."[34]

Of course, Marie Valerie did not dare to reveal her dislike of Hungary and all things Hungarian in the presence of her mother. She continued to speak nothing but Hungarian with the Empress. Her correspondence was carried on in Hungarian as well.

Valerie's hatred of Hungary and of all Slavic concerns grew over time into an almost militant German nationalism, which went so far as to include some anti-Austrian strains, strange as that might seem for the daughter of a Habsburg emperor.

Valerie's diary entries sometimes create the impression that Elisabeth agreed with her attitude. But Elisabeth's poems in no way support such hints. Elisabeth viewed the German problem from the Bavarian and Austrian standpoints, with a strong aversion to "the Prussians." If she was pro-German (but never pro-Prussian), it was only in the sense of 1848— quite unlike Valerie, who longed for a unification of all German nations under the leadership of Berlin and in total disregard of the "Austrian idea." This view was the opposite of the stance taken by the openly "Austrian" and "anti-Prussian" Crown Prince Rudolf. The young Archduchess used the concepts "Prussian" and "German" almost interchangeably, and she saw the power center of a greater German nation in the new German Empire under Wilhelm II.

To the same extent that Elisabeth and Rudolf were of one mind on ideology, the young Archduchess was of quite another. She was a deeply devout Catholic—in contrast to Rudolf—and all her life remained zealously committed to the tenets and dogmas of the Catholic church in every detail. She abhorred any kind of liberalism and worried a great deal about the eternal salvation of the Empress, who boldly developed her own religious views without consideration of church rules—in this, too, the perfect model to her son.

Elisabeth's excessive maternal love for Marie Valerie, at times approaching hysteria, began not only to arouse considerable ridicule among the court society and the Crown Prince's ardent jealousy, but sometimes also became burdensome to the young Archduchess, especially when it caused conflicts with her deeply beloved father. After one painful scene between her parents concerning her welfare (the Emperor had, as he did in most instances, given in), Valerie wrote, "What I most wanted to do was fall at his feet and kiss his paternal imperial hands, even as I felt—God forgive me—a momentary anger at Mama, since her unbridled love and exaggerated, groundless concern place me in such an embarrassing and false position."[35]

The fifteen-year-old worshiped her father and was overjoyed when she was allowed to sit silently by while he went over his papers at his desk. Marie Valerie:

> For more than an hour I sat next to him, quiet as a mouse, while he worked and smoked. It must have been important, for he looked up only once, and that was to remark, "But you must be terribly bored," to which, of course, I answered impetuously, "Oh, no, Papa, it is good to be sitting here. . . ." "A pretty

pleasure," he said and continued working. The poor man! As I saw him sitting so patiently before this pile of papers, without a word of complaint . . . how every man in the state always pushes the cares and sorrows away, always higher and higher, until finally everything comes to the Emperor—and he, who cannot send it higher, accepts everything and works everything through patiently, personally caring for the welfare of each and every one. How wonderful it is to have such a father."[36]

The Empress's return shortly thereafter broke up this warm relationship: "The ideal coziness of those unforgettable days in Schönbrunn is over— now that Mama is here, I do not dare to cheer him up and to show my love half-furtively, as before."[37]

Although the Empress never left any doubt that only her love for Marie Valerie still kept her at the Viennese court, she was nevertheless understanding when her daughter came of marriageable age and the suitors arrived—among them Friedrich August, Crown Prince of Saxony, and Prince Miguel of Braganza. Marie Valerie was a most reasonable girl, who could clearly distinguish between a purely dynastic match, which she flatly rejected (with Elisabeth's energetic support), and a marriage for love, which—once again, supported by her mother—she ardently wished for.

In this situation, Valerie had a friend and confidante in her mother. Together they appraised the suitors for Valerie's hand. Prince Alfons of Bavaria also came to visit in Vienna, and Valerie immediately sensed that he was checking her out "like a cow at the cattle market." He kept up his part in the conversation by talking about horses, especially about the various ways to harness them, endlessly boring both mother and daughter in his heavy Bavarian dialect. Finally, Elisabeth seized the initiative and set out to trip him up. "Surely you go only to operettas and fall asleep at classical works? But I'm sure you're always awake at the circus? Don't you prefer the city to the country? You must think the country is too isolated and boring, isn't that true?"

Valerie observed this conversation sharply and in her diary made fun of the admirer who was unable to withstand the Empress's irony. "All unsuspecting, he heartily agreed to all her questions and fell into the trap so completely that it was all . . . I could do not to burst out laughing. He seems very kind-hearted but does not impress me."[38]

Even when there was an end to the games and Valerie fell in love, Elisabeth remained her daughter's ally. The man Valerie chose was Arch-

duke Franz Salvator from the Tuscan branch of the family—a choice that
at first made the Emperor uncomfortable, primarily because of the close
degree of kinship. Franz was inexperienced, very young, and extremely
shy. It was the Empress who brought the couple together, arranging an
"accidental" meeting at the Burgtheater.

Franz was too shy to come to the imperial box, but a second attempt,
the following night, to bring about the planned meeting succeeded. Marie
Valerie captured the scene in her diary.

> Ten minutes after seven, Mama and I went down. How jittery
> I was. . . . Now Mama quietly sneaks to the archway [of the
> box] and opens the door. There sits Franz, alone, pressed into
> a corner, but does not recognize Mama until, beckoning with
> her finger, she softly says: "Come." He jumps up—I am stand-
> ing outside behind Mama . . . he answers all her questions
> without so much as a glance at me—quite the same as before.
> . . . Finally Mama turns to me: "Isn't that right? Valerie has
> grown?" "Yes, grown some more," and shakes hands with me
> with such a blissful expression that my heart leaps up and I feel
> that everything is good, terribly good.[39]

Two more years passed before the young couple became engaged at
Christmas of 1888. Elisabeth insisted that Valerie not act hastily: "Once in
the lives of most women there comes a moment when they fall in love.
That is why I owe it to Franz and myself," Valerie told her diary, "to get
to know other young men, so that I will not encounter the 'right' one when
it is too late."[40]

The Emperor's reservations about this alliance could be easily countered,
since Elisabeth took Valerie's part wholeheartedly. The Crown Prince, on
the other hand, long continued to object to the Archduke, whom he
considered too insignificant. It may be that Valerie tended to exaggerate
her brother's qualms. Whatever the case, the relationship between brother
and sister was extremely strained during this period. Since for her part
Elisabeth was intent on sparing her youngest child every grief and reacted
hysterically to every complication, her relationship with her son suffered
now irreparable damage. She saw him as the enemy of her darling, and
that was the worst that could happen to him. The Empress did not know
that during this time, Rudolf had problems quite other than his youngest
sister's affairs of the heart.

Even on the rare occasions when mother and son met, the only topic

was Valerie's future. One of these encounters occurred at the unveiling of
the Maria Theresia Memorial in Vienna on May 13, 1888, which both the
Empress and the Crown Prince attended. On the eve of the ceremony,
there had been riots against the House of Habsburg and in favor of
affiliation of German Austria with the German Reich. The Crown Prince's
carriage happened to become trapped at the center of the demonstration,
leaving Rudolf deeply depressed and shaken in his faith for Austria's
future.[41] Even the Empress noticed how ill he looked, but her only
question was, "Are you unwell?" To which he replied, not mentioning his
entanglements, "No, just tired and nervous."

By this time, the Crown Prince must have realized that his mother was
quite unable to help him out of his troubles, or even to understand them.
Once again (as happened every time they happened to meet at official
events) she spoke to him in her dreamy, unrealistic way of his younger
sister's well-being: "I am Sunday's child, I have links with the other world,
and I can bring good or bad fortune," she told the seriously ill and severely
depressed Rudolf, without paying any attention to him. Rudolf could
hardly make any other answer but "I shall never harm Valerie, Mama."[42]
The destiny of the Crown Prince, who soon after began to plan his suicide,
ran its course unchecked.

Because she did not concern herself with anything but her favorite
daughter's welfare, Elisabeth usually interpreted Rudolf's seriousness and
remoteness as hostility toward Valerie. Mother and daughter worked each
other up into a fear of the Crown Prince—and this at a time when Rudolf's
faith in the future of the Danube monarchy and in himself was already long
dead.

Valerie even confided to her diary how unbearable it was to know
that "beloved Ischl"—that is, the imperial villa—would eventually be
Rudolf and Stephanie's possession. She found the idea "so terrible that I
would like to put the beloved villa to the torch." Elisabeth reassured her
by hinting that she had long ago discussed the matter with the Emperor
and that not Rudolf but Valerie would inherit the house (as was eventually the case).[43]

The Empress did everything to secure her daughter's future even beyond
Franz Joseph's death, demonstrating a great distrust, even dislike, of Rudolf. Valerie: "During a walk in Schönbrunn, Mama and I talk about
Rudolf as a person, as the next Emperor, as possible brother-in-law to
Franz [Valerie's fiancé]. Mama thinks that he would hold Franz down,
hinder him in his military career." As a solution, Elisabeth proposed, "If
he [Franz] has the character I wish for you . . . he will not stand for such

suppression but will develop his capabilities in German service"—that is, leave Austria. "Mama would like to suggest to Franz the idea that if the war between Germany and France breaks out before ours with Russia, to enter the German army as a volunteer until duty calls him back here. That way he would gain glory. . . . That would show whether he is a man or merely an archduke."[44]

Elisabeth, who never carried on a political conversation with her highly talented only son, asked her daughter's bridegroom-elect for his political opinion. Valerie's diary records the following discussion between Elisabeth and the twenty-year-old Archduke Franz Salvator. Elisabeth began by asking "whom he would prefer to take the field against—Germans, Russians, Italians?"

> "No matter."
> Mama: "If it goes against the Germans, so sad . . . brothers. . . ."
> Franz: "But one cannot rely on their friendship, I cannot stand the Prussians, calculating, unreliable."
> Mama: "If they seek the advantage for their country and are capable of gaining it, one cannot really blame them for it . . . and not all Germans are Prussians. . . ."
> And then Mama explained how devout and hardworking the Westphalians were, how bright and cultured the Rhinelanders, Badensians, Württembergers, how they learn and discuss things so very differently from us, where conditions are lax and without unity and firm order.

Elisabeth added that it was "such a pleasure to fight the Russians, for I hate them and the Italians as well. . . . The Italians are false and cowardly"[45]—a remark hardly calculated to please the Italian-born Franz.

Elisabeth also told the Crown Prince about the young couple's plans to emigrate. Rudolf was horrified at the idea that the son-in-law of the Austrian Emperor might enter the service of Germany because the Empress of Austria felt conditions in her own country to be too unfavorable. Rudolf to Valerie: "Papa will never allow it, and it would have the most disastrous effect on the whole army." If study abroad was considered absolutely necessary, then he, Rudolf, would recommend the artillery college in Woolwich.[46] At this suggestion, however, the bridegroom-elect fell into real despair, since he could not speak English.

Elisabeth's mind became set on Valerie's emigration. The logic of this fixed idea is difficult to reconstruct today. It serves to show, however, the depth of Elisabeth's antipathies for Austria. On May 5, 1888, Archduchess Marie Valerie's diary captured one of Elisabeth's typical reactions. "Franz talked about the deterioration of conditions here," it reads. "Of course, this made Mama very happy."

Marie Valerie, who drifted more and more into German Nationalist waters, interpreted Elisabeth's ideas in her own way and urged the irresolute bridegroom on with the following arguments, astonishing in the daughter of a Habsburg emperor. "First we are Germans, then Austrians, and only in third place Habsburgs. The welfare of the German fatherland must be the first thing in our hearts—so long as it flourishes, it does not matter whether under Habsburgs or Hohenzollerns. . . . That is why you are wrong to say that in the service of Emperor Wilhelm, you would be in foreign service.—German is German, and the fatherland comes before family."[47] Given these views, any last chance of arriving at an understanding with her brother was gone; he was an emphatic, even fanatical Austrian, and to him Wilhelm II was the archenemy.

But the Empress did not make Valerie's life easy once the engagement was announced. Now she complained that "she hated people in general, and men in particular, more than ever," wrote Marie Valerie. And shortly thereafter: "Mama said, if I ever marry she will never be glad to see me again, she is like some animals who abandon their young as soon as someone touches them."[48]

In her conversations with her future son-in-law, Elisabeth repeatedly expressed thoughts of death. "You must not believe, as many people do, that I want to see Valerie married to you so as to keep her near me. When she marries, it does not matter whether she goes to China or remains in Austria—she is lost to me in any case. But I trust you, your character, your love for her, and if I were to die today, I could die in peace only because I entrust Valerie to you."[49]

All fears based on Rudolf's supposed hostility vanished when Elisabeth brought him the news of Valerie's engagement in December 1888. As Valerie described it:

> he was not at all unfriendly, and so I felt encouraged for the first time in my life to throw my arms about his neck. . . . Poor brother, so he does have a warm heart in need of love, for he embraced me and kissed me with the full fervor of true brotherly affection—again and again he drew me to his heart, and

one could feel that he was pleased at my showing him the love
that for so long had been almost stifled by fear and timidity.
Mama begged him always to be good to me, to us, once we are
dependent on him, and he solemnly swore it, simply and
warmly. At that she made the sign of the cross on his forehead
and said God would bless him for it and bring him good luck
—she assured him of her love, and he fervently kissed her hand,
deeply moved. I thanked him and enfolded him and Mama in
a single embrace, while I said almost instinctively: "We should
be this way always!"[50]

Countess Festetics described still another emotional scene, which took
place on Christmas Eve of 1888. The Crown Prince threw his arms about
his mother's neck "and broke out in long sobbing, which would not stop,
and which frightened her deeply." The ladies-in-waiting and adjutants,
who were invited to join the family at the Christmas tree immediately
afterward, "found the members of the imperial house still tear-stained and
emotional."[51]

At this, the final Christmas celebration of his life, the Crown Prince gave
renewed proof of his great veneration of his mother. The public outcry
attending the plans for a Heine memorial in Düsseldorf (see pages 301ff.)
had erupted. Rudolf—who, like Elisabeth, was attacked by the anti-
Semites—believed that in the mother he loved so passionately he had now
found an ally, a fellow fighter in the cause of liberalism against German
Nationalism and anti-Semitism. Furthermore, in this affair, too, he felt
himself to be the opposite number of the hated young Wilhelm II, who
sided with the anti-Heine faction.

In order to prove that he revered his mother, Rudolf paid an outrageous
price in Paris for eleven Heine autographs and placed them under the
Christmas tree for the Empress. Elisabeth, however, was so preoccupied
with her daughter's engagement that she did not pay Rudolf's gift the
attention he had expected.

No one took very seriously the thirty-year-old Crown Prince's frequent
mentions of his imminent death. Significantly, he spoke of his feelings not
to family members, but to Marie Festetics. She, in turn, was too sparing
of the Empress to give her even the slightest hint of them.

When the historian Heinrich Friedjung interviewed the Countess in
1909 and heard the many excuses she was quick to make for Elisabeth, he
raised the same objection that must occur to anyone who thinks about the
tragedy of Mayerling. Friedjung:

I could not refrain from telling the Countess that, no matter how deeply her statements moved me and filled me with sympathy for the Empress, I could not comprehend how a mother as deeply sensitive as the Empress could remain ignorant of what was disturbing the Crown Prince and how she could not know how far he had strayed. The Countess then repeated emphatically a remark she made several times: You must never forget that persons of high rank live quite differently from other people, that they find out less and that actually they may be called very unhappy because the truth reaches them only rarely and never completely.[52]

The family was wholly unprepared for the tragedy that struck on January 30, 1889. It was the Empress who was the first to be told. Count Joseph Hoyos, Rudolf's hunting companion from Mayerling, interrupted Elisabeth as she was reading Homer with the news of her son's death. Hoyos also mentioned a second victim: a young girl named Mary Vetsera. He said that she had given the Crown Prince poison before taking it herself.

The control and composure the otherwise overly sensitive Empress showed in this situation is astonishing. She did not run from any of the obligations awaiting her. It was she who gave the news to the Emperor. Then Elisabeth went to Ida Ferenczy's apartments, where she knew that Katharina Schratt was waiting for the Emperor. She herself took the actress to Franz Joseph, because she knew that his friend was the only person who could comfort the stricken man.

The Empress continued on to her favorite daughter, Marie Valerie. Elisabeth was shocked when the young woman's first assumption was that Rudolf had taken his own life. Elisabeth said, "No, no, I will not believe that, it is so likely, so certain that the girl poisoned him."[53] The confusion persisted.

Next Valerie brought Rudolf's widow, Stephanie, to the Emperor and Empress. Stephanie described the scene in her memoirs. "The Emperor sat at the center of the room, the Empress, dressed in dark clothes, her face white and rigid, was with him. In my bewildered, shaken state, I believed that I was being looked at like an unfaithful wife. A crossfire of questions, some of which I could not answer, some of which I was not permitted to answer, descended on me."[54]

In the meantime, Baroness Helene Vetsera, in her desperate search for her daughter, had also made her way to Ida Ferenczy's antechamber and would not be turned away when she requested to speak to the Empress.

"I have lost my child, she is the only one who can give her back to me," she sobbed, unaware that her daughter was already dead. Ida first requested Baron Nopcsa to give the news to the Empress. Then the Empress went to Helene Vetsera, whom she knew from more pleasant times of horse racing in Hungary, Bohemia, and England at the center of a merry, shallow crowd. Helene Vetsera had always gathered admirers around her, among them, at times, the same men who surrounded Elisabeth, especially Count Nikolaus Esterházy. During the 1870s, Helene Vetsera had also made clear advances to the Crown Prince, barely out of his teens—with every appearance of success.[55] Her reputation was far from impeccable. Now, hysterical with fear, a desperate mother, she stood before the Empress.

The scene that followed was described later by Ida Ferenczy, who was present, to Archduchess Valerie, who recorded it in her diary.

> Her Majesty, full of grandeur, stands before the agitated woman who demands her child, and speaks to her softly. She tells her that the girl is dead. At that, Vetsera breaks out in loud weeping: My child, my beautiful child!
>
> But do you know, says Her Majesty, raising her voice, that Rudolf is dead as well? Vetsera staggered, fell to her knees before Her Majesty, and clasped her knees. My unhappy child, what has she done? This is what she has done!! So she, too, saw the matter in that light and believed, as did Her Majesty, that the girl had poisoned him. A few words more, then Her Majesty leaves Vetsera with the words, "And now remember that Rudolf died of a heart attack!"[56]

It was not until the following day that the Emperor and Empress learned from their personal physician, Dr. Hermann Widerhofer, how the lovers had really died. According to Valerie's notes, Widerhofer saw the "girl stretched out in bed, hair loose over her shoulders, a rose between her folded hands—and Rudolf in a half-sitting position, the revolver on the ground, fallen from his stiffened hand, nothing but cognac in the glass. He laid down the corpse, long ago turned cold, the skull cracked, the bullet in one temple, out the other. Same wound in the girl. Both bullets found in the room.[57] Elisabeth's comment: "Great Jehovah is terrible as He marches onward sowing destruction like the storm."[58]

For the moment, the Crown Prince was laid out in state in his Hofburg apartments. Elisabeth visited her dead son on the morning of January 31 and kissed his lips. Archduchess Valerie: "He was so handsome and lay there so peacefully, the white sheet pulled up to his chest and flowers strewn all around. The narrow bandage on his head did not disfigure him—his cheeks and ears were stilll rosy with the healthy glow of youth—the restless, often bitter, scornful expression that was often characteristic of him in life had given way to a peaceful smile—he never seemed so beautiful to me before —he seemed to be asleep and calm, happy."

At dinner in the same room where the unusually warm family scene had occurred as recently as Christmas, the Empress lost her composure ("for the first time," as Valerie reported) and began to weep bitterly. Rudolf's widow and his five-year-old daughter were also of the party. Shared misfortune did not ease the strain between Elisabeth and Stephanie. On the contrary; both Elisabeth and Valerie placed a share of the blame for Rudolf's death at the Crown Princess's door. Stephanie, for her part, "kept asking all of us again and again for forgiveness, for she must surely have felt that her lack of devotion contributed to driving Rudolf to this horror."

The Empress gave free rein to her abhorrence of her daughter-in-law, saying "she was ashamed of her before the people. If one comes to know this woman properly, one must excuse Rudolf for looking elsewhere for distraction and a narcotic to ease the emptiness of the heart in his own home. It is certain: Things would have been otherwise had he had a different wife, one who understood him."

Two years after the tragedy of Mayerling, the Empress flung harsh words at Stephanie: "You hated your father, you did not love your husband, and you do not love your daughter!"[59] Elisabeth's accusations may have been true. As usual, she saw only the faults of others, never her own. For in setting up this balance sheet of blame, Elisabeth did not consider that the unhappy Rudolf had lacked love, not only from his wife, but also from his mother.

Rudolf left behind several farewell letters, but they did not give the reason for his suicide. The longest of the letters was to Elisabeth. In it, Rudolf confessed himself "not worthy of writing to his father," as Archduchess Valerie reported. It also described Mary as a "pure angel . . . , who accompanies him into the hereafter" and stated his wish "to be buried next to her in Heiligenkreuz"[60]—a wish that was not honored.

Ida Ferenczy, one of the few who was familiar with the letter, related that Rudolf had "taken the girl along as companion on the gruesome journey only out of fear of the gruesome unknown, she gave him courage, without her he might not have dared, he did not do it because of her."[61] (The exact wording of the letter was never made public. The letter itself was among the papers Ida Ferenczy destroyed on the Empress's instructions after Elisabeth's death. Nor did Archduchess Valerie's notes record the exact wording.)

Rudolf wrote a short letter to his younger sister. "On the day Papa closes his eyes forever, things will grow very uncomfortable in Austria. I know all too well what will follow, and I advise you to emigrate."[62] He, who had so markedly defended the value of Austria-Hungary to his mother and sister, agreed at the end with their somber prognosis. Marie Valerie commented in her diary, "It is odd that only the other day he told Mama that if Franzi [that is, the next heir to the throne, Franz Ferdinand, the Archduke whose assassination led to World War I] ever assumes the throne, things could not go on." Like Elisabeth, it seems, Rudolf had given up hope in a future for the Danube monarchy—surely one of the many reasons why his life ended in despair and guilt.

Elisabeth expressed herself even more clearly. As Marie Valerie wrote in her diary, "Mama believes that Austria will no longer be able to assert herself after Papa, who unites all contradictions by sheer force of impeccable character and self-sacrificing goodness. . . . Only the love for Papa, she says, holds the peoples of Austria back from confessing openly how much they long to be back with the great German fatherland, from which they are banished."[63]

Within the imperial family, an apocalyptic mood prevailed. With Rudolf's death, Austria-Hungary's future seemed to have died. As a heavy storm raged the night after the Crown Prince's body was brought to the Hofburg, shaking the windows "so that the old castle creaked and groaned at every joint," twenty-year-old Marie Valerie noted, "Mama is right— it has outlived itself"—by which she meant not only the Hofburg, but also the entire Danube monarchy.

Marie Valerie's diary captured the Emperor's and Empress's different responses to Rudolf's death. "Papa's resignation—unearthly, devout, without complaint, Mama's rigid anguish, with her belief in predestination, her grief that it was her Bavarian blood that rose to Rudolf's head, all this is so unspeakably bitter to watch."[64] A church funeral for the suicide required an affidavit from the doctor that Rudolf was mentally unbalanced. This certificate was a consolation to Emperor Franz Joseph but a source of new pain for Elisabeth. For her, the risk of insanity was always near; she had to feel personally affected. When she met Karl Theodor before Rudolf's interment, she heaped reproaches on herself: "If only the Emperor had never set foot in her family home, if only he had never seen her! What would he and she not have been spared!"[65]

On the other hand, the rationalization that Rudolf had not been in his right mind when he committed the terrible act reassured the Emperor because it lessened Rudolf's guilt. The imperial family physician, Dr. Widerhofer, who saw both bodies in Mayerling, did everything to reinforce this version. Marie Valerie: "Widerhofer says that he [Rudolf] simply died of insanity, as someone else dies of a disease. It is this thought, I believe, that keeps Papa from collapsing." But even Marie Valerie doubted this explanation, comfortable though it was. "I do not believe that this is the whole truth about the entire misfortune."[66]

Rudolf's death was followed by serious differences with the Bavarian family. For it turned out that Elisabeth's favorite niece, Countess Marie Larisch (the daughter of her brother Ludwig) had acted as go-between for the Crown Prince and Mary Vetsera. There were scenes in Vienna between the Empress and her brothers. Marie Larisch was banished from court. In spite of her fervent pleas to be allowed to explain herself, she was no longer received.

It was Andrássy, already seriously ill, who loyally stood by the Empress. At her request, he visited Countess Larisch to learn the circumstances of the tragedy. Elisabeth could not believe that love was all there was to it. Though a political reason was suspected (and Andrássy questioned the Countess about this as well), no one could provide facts.[67] The Crown Prince's political activities had been absolutely covert, and then again Elisabeth had never—literally, not once—taken an interest in the problems of her son after his childhood. Rudolf had been a stranger in the imperial family, a solitary figure, desperate in his complete isolation. The only explanation, and the simplest one, for his devastating end was the doctors' statement that in a condition of mental confusion he had done away with the girl and with himself.

Though Elisabeth had comported herself with remarkable courage in the first few days after the news of the death, her bearing deteriorated in the spring of 1889. The German ambassador reported to Berlin that Elisabeth "abandons herself to incessant brooding, reproaches herself, and attributes to the inherited Wittelsbach blood the mental confusion of her poor son."[68] She felt born to misfortune.

Rudolf's death thus receded more and more into the background. The suicide—of which Elisabeth never learned the true motives—became still another occasion for her to brood about her own life, and to despair.

The circumstance that a different Habsburg line now became heir to the throne was seen by Elisabeth as a further, even the greatest, triumph of the world of Vienna, which she hated so passionately. Elisabeth to Valerie after Rudolf's interment: "And now, all these people who, from the hour of my arrival here, have said so many bad things about me will have the satisfaction after all of seeing me pass on without leaving a mark on Austria."[69]

Nor can it have remained a secret from the Empress that both the court and diplomatic circles found new reasons to criticize her. Countess de Jonghe: "This time, the first lady of the land bears the principal blame. If she had thought less of herself and more of her obligations, this recent catastrophe would not have occurred."[70]

Count Alexander Hübner's diary probably correctly pinpointed the general attitude: "there is not the least doubt that the public is deeply concerned for the Emperor's grief, caring little for the tears of the Empress and nothing at all for those of Archduchess Stephanie."[71] As if to invalidate these accusations, Emperor Franz Joseph chivalrously made a public declaration of his gratitude to Elisabeth. "How much I owe to my dearly beloved wife, the Empress, during these difficult days, what a great support she has been to me, I cannot describe nor express warmly enough. I cannot thank Heaven enough for having given me such a helpmate," he wrote in acknowledgment of the declaration of condolence from the national diet.[72] And five days after Rudolf's death, Franz Joseph wrote to Katharina Schratt, "How can I think of the sublime sufferer, the truly great woman, other than with a prayer of thanks to God, Who has granted me such great fortune."[73]

After Rudolf's death, Elisabeth's spritualist tendencies hardened. Only a few days after his interment, she tried to establish contact with him. One evening, she secretly went to the Kapuzinergruft—the family crypt. Archduchess Valerie:

> She dislikes the crypt, and she was not at all eager to descend to it, but she had a sense that an inner voice was calling her, and she did it in the hope that Rudolf would appear to her and tell her whether he was unwilling to be buried there. For this same reason, she sent away the friar who had unlocked it for her, shut the iron door to the crypt, which was lit only by some torches around Rudolf's coffin, and knelt down by it. The wind groaned, and the flowers that had fallen off the wilted wreaths rustled like soft footsteps, so that she kept glancing around— but nothing appeared to her.

Elisabeth's comment on the spirits that did not materialize in the crypt: "They can only come when great Jehovah permits it."[74]

Elisabeth continued her efforts to establish spiritual communications with her son so that she might learn from him the reasons for his deed. These attempts remained no secret in Viennese society and caused still more gossip. As late as 1896 (according to Bertha von Suttner), Vienna was saying "various things about Empress Elisabeth. Among others: Spirit messages (presumably in spiritualist séances) had been received that the place where Crown Prince Rudolf resides is worse than hell and that no praying can help him; about this, the Empress in despair."[75]

In the critical situation after Rudolf's death, it became clear how far the Empress had departed from the Catholic faith. Marie Valerie was deeply worried on this account. "Mama is actually merely deistic. She prays to great Jehovah in His destructive power and greatness; but that He hears the pleas of His creatures she does not believe because—she says— from the beginning of time, everything is predestined and man is powerless against eternal predestination, which is based, simply, on Jehovah's inscrutable will. In His sight, she is equal to the most insignificant gnat—how could He care anything about her."[76]

One night, the Empress and her daughter visited the observatory in Vienna and philosophized about man's puniness and insignificance in the face of the universe. Marie Valerie: "Understand Mama's view that the individual is nothing in the eyes of the Lord, who has created these countless worlds . . . but she is too bleak and too different from Christianity."[77] Elisabeth to Valerie: "Rudolf's bullet killed my faith."[78]

According to Valerie, the Empress "from childhood on, had felt, and now it has become a certainty for her, that great Jehovah wanted to lead her into the wilderness, where she should spend her last days wholly dedicated to Him, in contemplation and worship of His divine majesty."[79]

Elisabeth also declared to Amélie, her niece, that she could not "believe according to the Church. If she did, she would have to think that Rudolf was damned. . . . The happiest person, she said, was the one who had the most illusions." Amélie replied that "happiness lies in actions which benefit one's fellow man." Elisabeth's response to this remark was characteristic of her: "Aunt Sisi thinks this is all very well, but people interest her too little for her to find happiness in this. That may be the key to many things that otherwise seem puzzling in Aunt Sisi."[80]

Elisabeth's feelings about Rudolf's death varied. Once she told Amélie that Rudolf "was the greatest philosopher after all. He had everything, youth, riches, and good health, and he gave it all up." At other times, she saw his suicide "as such a disgrace that she would have liked to hide her face from all the world."[81]

Elisabeth's mood grew increasingly disconsolate, her nerves stretched to the breaking point. Valerie: "I often worry about Mama now. . . . She says that Papa is over it and her ever-increasing sorrow was becoming a burden to him, he does not understand her and rues the day when she first saw him, to his misfortune. No power in the world can dissuade Mama from such ideas."[82]

On the other hand, even such distant acquaintances as Countess de Jonghe remarked on the Emperor's unusual cheerfulness. "The Emperor's gaiety has been noticed by everyone; in addition: lively gaze, energetic behavior, more talkative than ever before. Was his posture forced? One could think so, could in any case hope so."[83] The Emperor regained his spirits in his love for Katharina Schratt, grew more relaxed, at times even humorous, and came to terms more easily with the catastrophe of his son's death.

During a visit the Emperor and Empress paid to Munich in December 1885, the lack of harmony between them was evident. Amélie: "As so often in earlier times, I had occasion to notice once again that, without intending to, Aunt Sisi and Franz Joseph hurt each other so easily. He cannot understand her extraordinary, fiery nature, while she lacks all understanding for his simple character and practical turn of mind. And yet he loves her so much."[84]

Marie Valerie, by now twenty-one years old, stood by helplessly as the daily friction continued. Though increasingly incensed with her father because of the ever more important position given to Katharina Schratt, she was able to write in her diary in the autumn of 1889, "If it was always difficult to keep up a conversation with Papa even halfway, it has become almost impossible since he was struck by the deep sorrow of this winter. . . . I understand that being with him, without any point of contact except their pain—and even this of such different sorts—oppresses Mama. On those occasions, she is even more desolate than when we are alone . . . when she thinks ahead and sees years of this life stretching before her."[85]

Valerie longed to get "out of this sad atmosphere into a more healthy sphere of action."[86] Her parents' unhappiness in their marriage was a heavy burden on her. "I tell myself in deepest sorrow that this heavy suffering, instead of bringing . . . my parents closer together, has separated them even more (because neither understands the pain of the other)."[87]

It was in this very period of abysmal despair that the disturbing news arrived of the hopeless state of Gyula Andrássy's health. In February 1890, he died. Elisabeth visited his widow in Budapest; she told Valerie "that it was not until now that she knew what she had in Andrássy; for the 1st time she felt completely abandoned, without adviser or friend."[88]

Three months later—in May 1890—Elisabeth rushed to the deathbed of her sister Helene Thurn und Taxis in Regensburg. Valerie recorded the sisters' last conversation.

> Aunt Néné, did not believe in death at all, was glad to see Mama and said to her, "Old Sisi"—she and Mama almost always spoke English together.
> "We two have hard puffs in our lives," said Mama.
> "Yes, but we had hearts," replied Aunt Néné.[89]

Thirty-seven years had passed since the summer in Bad Ischl that had determined their lives. Both sisters had been surrounded by splendor and glitter, immense material wealth and an enormous inner void. After a short, happy marriage, Helene had been a widow for over twenty years. Her spirits were darkened by depression and melancholy. Helene's last words made a deep impression on the Empress: "Ah, yes, but life is a sorrow and a misery."

Elisabeth's increasing longing for death saddened all those close to her. Valerie: "Mama will probably never again be as she was at one time; she envies Rudolf his death, and day and night she longs for her own."[90] A month later: "Mama says that she is too old and too tired to struggle, her wings are singed, and the only thing she wants is rest. It would be the noblest deed if all parents would immediately kill every newborn child."[91]

In October 1889, a circular was sent to all the Austrian representatives abroad informing them of the Empress's wish that any felicitations on her name days and birthdays be omitted, "not only in the immediate future but for all time." At the end of 1889, when the official year of mourning was coming to an end, the Empress gave away all her light-colored gowns, umbrellas, shoes, scarves, purses, and all accessories to Gisela and Valerie. She kept only the plain mourning outfits; for the rest of her days she did not wear colored dresses again.[92] Her only concession was a simple pearl gray dress at Valerie's wedding and at the christening of Valerie's first child, little Elisabeth (Ella).

She also gave away her jewelry—the wealth of pearls, emeralds, diamonds. Most of these pieces went to her two daughters and to her granddaughter Erzsi. But she also remembered such relatives as her Bavarian sister-in-law Marie José, who was given a brooch with the remark, "It is a remembrance of the time when I was alive."[93] The Empress was determined to spend the years that were left her as a *mater dolorosa,* always dressed in black, far from all court splendor. The German ambassador in Vienna commented, "The Emperor puts up with even these regrettable oddities with great resignation and patience."[94]

Elisabeth felt the marriage of her favorite daughter, Valerie, as a further blow of fate. "Mama seems dazed by deep melancholy, and all the more so because she can never understand why anyone would want to be married and would expect any good from a marriage."[95] Elisabeth left no doubt that she "finds marriage unnatural," as the young bride confided to her diary.[96] For Valerie, who had inherited her father's practical cast of mind and who was looking forward to marriage, this melancholy, overwrought mother was a great emotional burden.

Marie Valerie's wedding to Archduke Franz Salvator took place at the end of July 1890 in the parish church of Bad Ischl. Elisabeth as well as Valerie had forbidden all court ceremonial of the sort that had been taken for granted at Gisela's and Rudolf's weddings in Vienna. There was not even a nuptial mass—only a quiet mass for the immediate families preceding the wedding ceremony. This, too, was at the express wish of the Empress, who considered the usual solemn nuptial mass "too long." Among the flower girls was little Erzsi, the Crown Prince's daughter, barely seven years old. Anton Bruckner, whom the young Archduchess admired extravagantly and whom she sponsored, played the organ.

Valerie's happiness was evident to see. She was the only child of the Emperor and Empress who married without court considerations and for love. Elisabeth, disconsolate at the loss of her favorite daughter, cautioned Valerie's mother-in-law, Archduchess Marie Immaculata, even on the wedding day, not to visit the young couple during the honeymoon period "and not to interfere in anything."[97]

Elisabeth's visits to her daughter were infrequent and short. Time and again, she pointed out that a mother-in-law could only interfere with a young couple's happiness. To Valerie, who always urged her mother to stay longer at Lichtenegg, she said, "precisely because she liked it so much here, she should not let herself get used to it. A seagull did not fit in a swallow's nest, and a serene, happy family life was not her fate!"[98]

The Empress persisted in her conviction that now she had lost all her children.

CHAPTER FOURTEEN

THE ODYSSEY

The marriage of her favorite daughter marked the beginning of a period for which Elisabeth had been preparing for a long time. "Once I no longer have any responsibilities to my Valerie, and once she is taken care of and is a happy wife with a great many children, which is what my *kedvesem* [Hungarian for "darling"] always wanted, then I am free and my 'seagull flight' can begin." And again, "I shall travel the whole world over, Ahasuerus shall be a stay-at-home compared to me. I want to cross the seven seas on a ship, a female 'Flying Dutchman,' until I drown and am forgotten."[1]

Her only son was dead. Her only friend in the outside world, Andrássy, was dead. The Emperor was happy in his friendship with Katharina

Schratt, her daughter Valerie was happy in her home, enriched by an increasing number of children. Empress Elisabeth was in her fifties. Her beauty was a thing of the past. "As soon as I feel myself aging, I shall retire from the world altogether. There is nothing more 'horrendous' than gradually becoming mummified and unwilling to say farewell to youth. To go about as a rouged larva—dreadful! Perhaps later, I shall always wear a veil, and even those closest to me will no longer see my face."[2]

Elisabeth made good on her prediction. Never again did she allow herself to be portrayed—either by painters or photographers. Never again did she go out without fan or umbrella, behind which to hide her wrinkled, weather-beaten, emaciated face. The black fan and the white umbrella became, as Elisabeth's Greek reader Christomanos wrote, "the loyal companions of her outward existence"; they could even be said to be "almost constituent parts of her physical appearance." "In her hands, they are not what they mean to other women, but only emblems, weapons and shields in the service of her true self. . . . She wishes to use them only to ward off the external life of human beings, not to let it have any validity for herself, not to bow to the 'herd laws of evolved animals'; she is eager to preserve her inner silence unprofaned; she is not willing to leave the locked gardens of grief she carries within herself."[3]

Elisabeth left Austria as often and for as long as she could, and her journeys became ever more purposeless. The Emperor had always dared to voice only the most circumspect objections to her long, repeated absences: "If you think that it is necessary for your health, I shall keep silent, although this year we have not spent more than a few days together since spring," he wrote in October 1887.[4] During the 1890s the Empress spent at most a few weeks out of every year in Vienna, and even these she passed not in social activity or at public functions, but in total isolation in the Hermes Villa in Lainz.

It had been years since Elisabeth had tried to take a hand in political matters. Nor did she leave the slightest doubt that she no longer wished to be bothered with these affairs. Archduchess Valerie complained that Elisabeth's "general way of life can be brought into harmony less and less with that of other people. . . . When will the time finally come when Mama will realize that she should live differently in order to give God an accounting of her talents?"[5]

Franz Joseph's servants gained the impression that Elisabeth was deliberately offending her husband. Eugen Ketterl, the valet de chambre, for example, recorded the situation as he saw it.

In Gödöllö, the Emperor was only rarely allowed to see his wife, even though they were living under the same roof. If Franz Joseph wished to visit her of a morning and went to her apartments without having made an appointment, the spirits on duty explained to His Majesty that the Empress was still sleeping! Sometimes the sovereign lady was already in the mountains, from where she returned in the evening with her unhappy lady-in-waiting, and now, exhausted, she certainly would not receive the Emperor. So it could happen that the Emperor might try to see her in vain for ten days running. How embarrassing that was in front of the staff, anyone can imagine; I often felt endless pity for my sovereign lord.[6]

By this time, many people viewed Franz Joseph's relationship with Katharina Schratt with approval, gladly granting the old, ever more resigned gentleman the cozy hours spent with his friend.

On her travels, too, the Empress's behavior became increasingly odd. Even Countess Marie Festetics expressed her complaints in a letter from Corfu to Ida Ferenczy, who had remained behind (and this was in November 1888—that is, before the great emotional shock of the tragedy of Mayerling). "It bothers me, dear Ida, what I see and hear here. Her Majesty is always nice when we are together, and she speaks as she always did. But she is not the same—a shadow darkens her soul. I can use no other expression; in speaking of a person who suppresses or denies all handsome and noble feelings out of convenience or for amusement, one can only say that it is bitterness or cynicism! Believe me, my heart weeps bloody tears!" And then Marie Festetics cited a few examples of Elisabeth's behavior.

And yet she does things that make not only your heart but also your understanding stop. Yesterday morning the weather was bad, nevertheless she went out in the sailboat. At nine it began to pour, and the terrible rainstorm, along with thunder, lasted until three in the afternoon. All this time she sailed around us, sat on the deck—held the umbrella over her head and was soaked to the skin. Then she went ashore somewhere, ordered her car to come for her, and decided to spend the night in some strange villa. You can imagine how far we have come—fortunately, the physician goes everywhere with her. But even more outrageous things happen.[7]

This habit of simply going to strange houses—without saying a word or explaining what she had in mind—became a mania during the 1890s. Even the Emperor knew about this oddity of his wife's; in 1894, after an incident in Nice, when an old woman chased away the stranger who seemed to want to enter her house, he wrote to Elisabeth, "I am glad that your Nice indigestion has passed so quickly and that you did not also get a beating from the old witch, but sooner or later that is exactly what will happen, for one does not simply push one's way uninvited into people's houses."[8]

Uninvited and unannounced, she also turned up at various European courts, in order to fulfill her official obligations in a very strange and extremely uncourtlike manner. In 1891, for example, she drove directly from the railroad station to the royal palace in Athens and (in Greek) asked the first servant she encountered whether Their Majesties were at home. She was in traveling costume, and her only companion was her daughter. The servant, who did not recognize them, declared that if they wished an audience, they would have to call on the chamberlain. At that point Elisabeth revealed her identity. Valerie: "But it was true that they [King George I and his wife] really were not at home, and so we drove to the Crown Prince's palace, in order to burst in on his family in the same way." They were received by poor Crown Princess Sophie, who was unfamiliar with the local language and could not follow Elisabeth's Greek conversation.[9] In order to teach her a lesson, Elisabeth did not switch to German but continued to speak in modern Greek.

Other crowned heads had to endure similar raids, among them the King of the Netherlands and Empress Friedrich. The latter, the mother of Wilhelm II, had retired to a castle near Bad Homburg. Elisabeth had a great liking for the very intelligent but embittered widow of the "Ninety-nine Day Emperor," Friedrich III, and wished to honor her with a visit —on a hot summer's day, naturally unannounced, and unaccompanied by a lady-in-waiting. The sentry, of course, stopped the strange woman who claimed to be the Empress of Austria. Empress Friedrich was roused with the alarming news that Empress Elisabeth was being held in the guard-room. The incident seemed to amuse Elisabeth, for she did not appear at all angry when the distraught chamberlain released her; she took the episode as an occasion for laughter.[10]

On the other hand, she paid her respects very formally to a faded glory of yesteryear, the former Empress Eugénie of France. The widowed Eugénie lived in retirement at Cap Martin on the Riviera. Elisabeth ordered her companions to show the ex-Empress all the respect formerly due her.

Archduchess Valerie was impressed, praising Eugénie's "charm, although there are hardly any traces left of her former beauty. Her demeanor extremely plain. One would hardly recognize her eventful past, she makes so little show of pain or toppled greatness."[11]

The two ladies shared drives and excursions in the countryside surrounding Cap Martin. Eugénie on Elisabeth: "It was as if one were going driving with a ghost, for her spirit seems to dwell in another world. She was rarely aware of what was happening around her, nor did she take notice when she was greeted by people who recognized her. When she did, she answered the greeting with a singular toss of the head instead of the customary bow."[12]

On her travels, the Empress gave ample demonstration of her utter contempt for any kind of etiquette. Marie Festetics to Ida Ferenczy from Genoa: "*Entre nous,* yesterday Her Majesty received the simple commandant of the German training ship, although before this, she has turned away admirals, high dignitaries (military, civilian, and clerical) from Spain, France, and Italy. This disturbs me, since I am afraid of the newspapers."[13]

The Austrian diplomats were unsuccessful in their proposals that the Empress take part in official functions. "The Empress, however, was gracious enough to allow me to offer her an introduction to Arab snake charmers, conjurors, and soothsayers." So wrote the Austrian chargé d'affaires in Cairo to the foreign minister in 1891. He added that Elisabeth's "average march capacity per day is ca. 8 hours"[14]—and this in Egypt!

Her attempt, in 1891, to attend a ball one more time was a failure. Archduchess Valerie: "Many ladies are said to have sobbed, and in spite of diamonds and bright feathers, the whole resembled a funeral more than it did a carnival. Mama herself was in deepest mourning crepe."[15]

In 1893, Elisabeth made a final appearance at the "ball at court." The geologist Eduard Suess described the party.

> All the old imperial splendor. Every candelabrum seemed to want to tell its experiences. Close to the door to the inner salon, in his red hussar's uniform, stands the master of ceremonies, Count Hunyady, with the long white staff, and . . . a Milky Way of youthful beauties streamed past him, the swarm of the whole new female generation of the nobility, who are eager to honor their Empress, know everything, and are without any adornment beyond their own charms. In the middle of the salon, however, two black figures, the perpetually mourning Empress and her chatelaine, and it was as if all

the glittering diamonds with which the mothers standing on the sidelines adorned themselves were extinguished by this deep, dull sorrow, and as if each of the bowing young creatures were told how much magnificence and how much grief can be combined in one life.[16]

The presence of the Empress at court balls was crucial for social reasons. Before being introduced to society, the young girls of the aristocracy had to be introduced to the Empress. That was the tradition of the court of Vienna. By her refusal to participate in social occasions, the Empress brought a good deal of disorder into the strictly regulated structure of Viennese society.

The question of which archduchess was to represent the Empress on ceremonial occasions soon set quarrels and jealousies in motion. Rudolf's widow, Stephanie, was very unpopular. Franz Joseph's younger brother Karl Ludwig claimed that his wife, the beautiful Archduchess Maria Theresia, was the legitimate first (deputy) lady of the court.

Elisabeth's position at court was thus given away in her lifetime. The court no longer counted on her—quite correctly, since she left no doubt that she despised such obligations.

Those familiar with life at the court could not fail to suspect that Rudolf's death was not the true reason for Elisabeth's absences from Vienna. It served merely as the pretext, a justification to the world.

Elisabeth's aimless wanderings through Europe, in her own parlor car or on the imperial yachts *Greif* and *Miramar,* were a genuine martyrdom for her ladies-in-waiting, most especially Countess Festetics, whose health was no longer the best. Marie Festetics's complaints were frequently voiced in letters. "Here I sit on the rolling ship in the alien world—alone. This too shall pass, but it is hard to watch with a cheerful countenance. I am homesick."[17] Her letters make much mention of bad weather—"Thunder, storm, and rain as if it were Judgment Day"—and of endless inspection tours.

The Empress paid no attention at all to the weather. She loved the forces of nature and had no understanding for the sensitivities of her companions. There were almost grotesque scenes; once the traveling party had to go aboard the *Miramar* at Corfu during a "powerful northeaster." "In their mortal terror," as Alexander von Warsberg reported, two of the chamberwomen fled into a corner. Elisabeth, unaffected by storm and rough seas, was intent on forcing the two of them, in this unsettling situation, "to admire the magnificent sunset, the colors on the mountains behind Patras, until the poor creatures broke out in wretched cries, saying that they could see nothing at all but the terrible waves."[18]

Countess Festetics, who was always seasick, found it particularly difficult to walk up and down alongside her mistress on the ship, in any weather, because Elisabeth could not sit still. After one such ocean voyage in the Aegean in November, Marie Festetics stated, "To roam for two weeks on the open sea, at this time of year, is no pleasure."[19]

The same Elisabeth who, in Vienna, sighed at every cool breeze, proved, on her travels, to be totally indifferent to bad weather. Countess Festetics: "Her Majesty left Vienna because she cannot endure the cold, and we are spending the very worst six weeks in the coldest places, she goes out even in weather so bad that the wind twice turned her umbrella inside out and blew her hat off her head."[20]

During stormy seas, she even had herself tied to a chair on deck. "I do this like Odysseus, because the waves tempt me," she explained to Christomanos.[21]

Sometimes Elisabeth spared her ladies-in-waiting when she went on her excursions in storm and rain and took along whoever happened to be her Greek reader at the time. Konstantin Christomanos—the short, hunchbacked philosophy student—once walked with her in the park at Schönbrunn in December during a wet snowstorm. They were forced to keep jumping over large puddles of water. "Like frogs, we go hunting in the pools," said the Empress. "We are like two damned souls wandering through the underworld. For many people, this would be hell. . . . I like this sort of weather most of all. For it is not for other people. I am allowed to enjoy it all by myself. Actually, it exists only for me, like those plays poor King Ludwig had performed for himself alone. Except that out here, it is even more splendid. It could even be a wilder storm, then one feels so close to all things, as in conversation."[22]

Elisabeth's hectic restlessness also cast its shadows on the construction of the Achilleion on Corfu. Countess Festetics complained, "Her Majesty grows more willful and more self-indulgent by the day and is ever more demanding—she is trying to give herself heaven on earth. . . . Her Majesty tells herself that for money one can have even a garden like a castle's, she is in despair because the trees are still not green. In her mind's eye, she sees the garden of Miramar, which was truly magnificent this year, and that is the cause of her discontent."[23]

But even her Greek property did not inspire Elisabeth to settle down. Hardly had the castle been completed than she set out again, not unlike the way she had behaved about the Hermes Villa, which she no longer especially liked. Much as she longed for a home, serenity in it escaped her.

Abruptly she persuaded herself that she needed money for Valerie and that she therefore had to sell the Achilleion. "I shall even sell my private silver service engraved with my dolphin; perhaps some American will take it. I have an agent in America who advised me to do this," she explained to the astonished Christomanos.[24]

The Emperor could not accept Elisabeth's proposal to use the monies realized from a sale for Valerie.

> Valerie and what will probably be her numerous children will not starve even without the profit from your house, and it will surely seem very strange and give rise to unpleasant comment if you try to get rid of the entire property immediately after having built the villa with so much effort, so much care, and at such great expense, have had so many things brought there, after you most recently bought additional property adjoining it. Do not forget how accommodating the Greek government has been in serving you, how everyone on every side cooperated to smooth the path for you and give you pleasure, and now it was all in vain.

A commensurate price, he added, could not be expected in any case, since the house already needed repairs, "and yet it will cause quite a scandal." Elisabeth should really give the matter some more thought.

"For me," Franz Joseph's letter continued, "your plan also has its sad side. I had quietly hoped that, after you built Gasturi with so much joy, so much eagerness, that you would pass in your new creation at least the greater part of the time you unfortunately spend in the south. Now this, too, is to be stopped, and you will travel even more and roam the world." He was looking forward to a reunion "with infinite impatience."[25]

But in spite of these serious objections, once again, what Elisabeth wanted was what Elisabeth got; as soon as the Achilleion had been fully furnished, it was emptied out again. The expensive copies of antique furniture were shipped to Vienna and stored in the various castles and warehouses because the Empress was no longer interested in them. No buyer was found.

One other time the Empress had a plan to build herself a house—this time in San Remo—but she quickly abandoned it. From this time on, she preferred hotels. But here, too, her excessive demands created perpetual problems. All too often she would arrive unannounced at the height of the season, bringing a sizable entourage, demanding a great many rooms—at times the entire hotel—with a private entrance and hundreds of complicated security precautions to protect herself from curiosity seekers. Soon, therefore, her arrival became a matter of dread. "Her Majesty grows more demanding by the year, and with the best will in the world, it is not possible to satisfy her; the people are so astonished at us that I blush," Marie Festetics wrote from Interlaken to Ida Ferenczy in Hungary in 1892.[26]

Ida Ferenczy went along on none of the trips because of her precarious health. By the early 1890s, Countess Festetics had also become ill and tired. "Where we shall be in 2–3 days, we do not know. I understand that man seeks warmth, but that one spends three months on board ship in the winter probably requires a special gusto. Where we are headed, not even Her Majesty really knows."[27] After more than twenty years of hard work as a lady-in-waiting to the Empress, Marie Festetics was finally replaced by the much younger and more athletic Countess Irma Sztaray, also a Hungarian. Accompanied by Irma, the Empress spent her final years wandering through Europe and around the Mediterranean. In 1890, for example, she traveled to Bad Ischl, Feldafing, Paris, Lisbon, Algiers, Florence, and Corfu. Often she changed her destination on short notice, causing considerable confusion. Her mail was sent to her in care of general delivery wherever her ship was scheduled to dock (according to information in Vienna, which was frequently incorrect). The name to which letters were directed was almost always a pseudonym. For example, in October 1890, the imperial adjutant general, Count Eduard Paar, sent Emperor Franz Joseph's letters to a "Mrs. Elizabetha Nicholson—*Chazalie*" (*Chazalie* being the name of the ship Elisabeth was using on this trip) to general delivery in "Arcachon, La Coruña, Oporto, Oran, Algiers, Toulon, Gibraltar, San Remo, Marseilles, Monaco, Cannes, Mentone, and Livorno . . . and finally a small chest . . . to Gibraltar." Elisabeth's chief chamberlain, Baron Nopcsa, was required to find out from the consulates in question "whether mail had been left at one of these places and to send it back."[28]

The Empress's retinue came to see a great deal of the world in this way. Thus, one of the Greek readers, M. C. Marinaky, was in Elisabeth's service for ten months in 1895–1896; this time was spent in the Hermes Villa outside Vienna (May and June), the Hungarian spa of Bartfeld (July), Bad Ischl (August), Aix-les-Bains and Territet on Lake Geneva (September), Gödöllö (October), Vienna (November), Cap Martin (December to February), and Cannes, Naples, Sorrento, and Corfu (March).

The itineraries for other years were not very different. Some of her destinations were chosen on a sudden whim and were irreconcilable with

Austrian politics. For example, the German ambassador, reporting on Elisabeth's trip to Florence, wrote that "Emperor Franz Joseph did not wish his wife to set foot anywhere on Italian soil. Nor was this place part of her itinerary, but the sovereign lady's decisions are not always known ahead of time."[29]

Two years later, after an audience with Emperor Franz Joseph, the German ambassador informed Berlin, "But it is clear from all his statements how little he himself knows about the plans of Her Majesty his wife, and he has little influence on her travel decisions. . . . I am not stating anything new if I most humbly remark that these long absences from home on the part of the Empress are not gratifying to the Emperor, and that they are seen with displeasure in the country and unfortunately are judged harshly."[30]

And time and again, Elisabeth traveled to Munich, the site of her childhood. Countess Sztaray reported, "Walking slowly, we traversed the city; we did not wish to see anything new, anything surprising; this visit was entirely dedicated to the past, to memories. Now we stopped before an old-fashioned palace, then again before an old building, at a stand of trees whose branches had spread wide since then, at a bed of flowers that had been blooming even then. The Empress . . . had something to tell about each one, something lovely from the good old days." She never left Munich without a visit to the Hofbräuhaus—incognito of course, and behaving "like the best of the bourgeois," as she said. Each time she ordered a small pitcher of beer for herself and her lady-in-waiting.[31]

On all these travels, Elisabeth refused police protection. But in view of the growing danger of anarchists, some governments insisted on having her followed by police agents—even against her express wishes. One of these tormented agents, Anton Hammer from Karlsbad, recounted, "Empress Elisabeth made a tremendous lot of work for us. No one was allowed to look at her. In one hand she held an umbrella, in the other her fan. To this were added her sudden walks, once at three o'clock at night, then again in the mornings she would go to the woods. One had to be on the alert at all times. And with all this, I had been given strict orders to watch the Empress's every step in such a way that she would not notice." Often enough, when Elisabeth became aware of one of these agents, she fled across fences or along untrodden paths to shake off her watchers. These escapades were the cause of great unpleasantness for the agents, because they had failed to comply with their orders to accompany the Empress. Hammer: "We had to stalk after the Empress for five hours. Always at a distance of about two hundred meters, using trees or rocks to hide behind."[32] The curiosity to catch a glimpse of what had been the most beautiful woman in the world was great everywhere. Many observers noted the great disparity between legend and reality. One of these was Prince Alfons Clary-Aldringen, who saw the Empress in Territet when he was a small boy in 1896–1897. He and his sister were in the hills behind the hotel where both the Clary family and the Empress were staying. When they saw the black, slender figure of the Empress, the children blocked her path, "and lo and behold, because no adult was nearby, this time the Empress did not open her fan! My sister curtseyed, and I made my best bow; she smiled at us in a friendly way—but I was stunned, for I saw a face full of wrinkles, looking as old as the hills."

When the children spoke to their grandmother of the encounter, she solemnly told them, "Children, do not forget this day, when you saw the most beautiful woman in the world!" Alfons Clary: "In response to my smart-aleck answer, 'But, Grandmama, her face is all wrinkled!' I received a hefty slap."[33]

Even today we do not know what Elisabeth's face looked like in age —there are no pictures. In the memories of her contemporaries as well as for posterity, she remains the woman the pictures show: beautiful and young. This legend, which she herself encouraged, cast a shadow over her last years. For now she had one more reason to fear other people: They might see her real face.

Only very, very few still knew the Empress during her final years. To accidental observers, encounters with her during this time were deeply disappointing. For example, the actress Rosa Albach-Retty saw the Empress and her lady-in-waiting, Countess Sztaray, in 1898 in a small country inn in Bad Ischl. Since Elisabeth's true appearance was nowhere pictured, Retty did not recognize the ladies at once. One was "clearly in mourning, for with her black, high-necked dress she wore black laced boots and a black hat, its thick veil turned back over a broad brim." It was the Empress. The other lady, younger and in light clothing, Countess Sztaray, briefly went into the inn, leaving Elisabeth alone at the table. Rosa Albach-Retty: "For seconds Elisabeth stared downward, then with her left hand she took out her dentures, held them sideways over the edge of the table, and rinsed them off by pouring a glass of water over them. Then she put them back in her mouth. All this was done with such graceful nonchalance, but most particularly at such lightning speed, that at first I could not believe my eyes."[34]

Of all the gossip about Elisabeth's restlessness, which seems pathological, only one example need be cited here, recorded by Bertha von Suttner.

Countess Ernestine Crenneville, she stated, had told her, "I still remember our sitting together one day after a small dinner at the Empress's, a very few of us. Archduchess Valerie, the Duke of Cumberland, and I. A few ladies-in-waiting to one side. The Empress was very silent and sad. Suddenly she calls out, 'Oh, out! Out into the country, far away. . . .' Archduchess Valerie jumps to her feet: 'For heaven's sake, Mama. . . .' The Duke of Cumberland interrupts in an attempt to mollify. 'You are right, Your Majesty!' and quietly to the daughter, 'But never leave her alone, never alone!' "[35]

As early as three months after Rudolf's death, the news made its way through the European press that the Austrian Empress had succumbed to madness. In a surprisingly well-informed article, the Berlin *Tageblatt* described the course of this disease honorably (and probably correctly, in contrast to the other reports, which simply indicated insanity) as an "extreme nervous disorder."

> For those familiar with conditions at the Austrian court, there is nothing surprising in this news. The extravagances of the unhappy Empress, her ever more strongly expressed reluctance to appear in public, her shy nature, which so resembles that of the unhappy Ludwig, King of Bavaria, has long since given rise to the fear of a catastrophic occurrence sooner or later. It would, accordingly, be an error if one were to present the dreadful end of Crown Prince Rudolf as the cause of the disorder; it has long existed and has slowly and steadily been spreading.[36]

Of course, these reports of the Empress's illness, circulated by all the major European papers, were countered with energetic denials in the Austrian press: The Empress was merely suffering from painful neuralgia. The neurologist Professor Richard Krafft-Ebing (the same doctor who had treated and committed Elisabeth's sister Sophie Alençon) had not—as the Austrian papers emphasized—been called.[37]

Over and over, during the 1890s, the international press brought up the subject of Elisabeth's supposed insanity. In 1893, the Milan newspaper *Il Secolo* wrote, "Empress and Queen Elisabeth is suffering from the onset of insanity. Every night, she is plagued by hallucinations. Her obsession is touching. She believes that Crown Prince Rudolf is still a child and is with her. To calm her, it was necessary to have a wax doll made, and this she incessantly covers with kisses and tears."[38]

These lurid reports, however, were highly exaggerated. Quite the contrary: At the very time when these stories appeared and when Emperor Franz Joseph was visiting his allegedly mad wife in Territet, Elisabeth's frame of mind was good. Writing about this meeting between the Emperor and the Empress, Marie Festetics noted, "Her Majesty is in particularly good humor, and he too glows with happiness. Her Majesty has really been looking forward to his visit and [I] can say only that she has the master entirely in her pocket."[39]

The Emperor and Empress relaxed with long walks and shopping, constantly besieged by journalists. The Swiss paper *Der Bund* gave a detailed list of the purchases they made in Territet. "The Emperor ordered a considerable quantity of Villeneuve wine, which he particularly enjoys, and 10,000 Grandson and Vevey cigars; the Empress put in an order for cookies from Viviser and Villeneuve."[40]

Elisabeth's letters to Bavaria from this period also attest to an untroubled frame of mind. "I am glad that the Emperor can take a little vacation at last, and nowhere could he enjoy it more than in a republic. He is in good humor, enjoys his freedom, the beautiful surroundings, and the excellent cuisine."[41] Valerie, for her part, found her father's stay "in a republic" by no means worth the risk. After Franz Joseph's departure, she noted in her diary, "It was not without worry that we saw him set out without any entourage or almost any security measures to the country notorious as the residence of nihilists and socialists."[42]

But the continuing news reports about the Empress's supposed madness were not pure speculation. For on her travels she behaved so oddly, her shyness had taken on such proportions, that innocent observers who encountered her on her constant escape routes or who tried to follow her (which invariably prompted Elisabeth to extremely odd responses) could easily think they were dealing with a lunatic. Countess Festetics: "With us, everything is extraordinary. Her Majesty is simple, it is only that she begins from the back what others begin from the front, begins from the left what others begin from the right. It is from this that the difficulties arise."[43]

Her Bavarian family also noted Elisabeth's idiosyncrasies, but they rejected the rumors of mental illness. Marie von Redwitz, one of the Bavarian ladies-in-waiting, summed up the family's opinion when she wrote that Elisabeth "has always been strange and has followed only her whims and wishes, and now shyness and melancholia have been added. Who among gifted people who enjoy unlimited freedom is entirely normal? The Empress is, as we all are, the product of conditions."[44]

When Elisabeth spoke, it was, according to Valerie, about "only the saddest things." She complained of her unhappy fate and was so inconsolable that religious Valerie feared for her eternal salvation and prayed earnestly for her mother's "conversion."[45] When Valerie's deepest wish came true and she became pregnant, the Empress expressed bitterness. Valerie: "She sighed about my condition, it was difficult for her to feel with me the happiness which, strangely, in spite of her motherlove for me, she cannot understand at all.—For the rest, I found Mama in a disconsolate frame of mind, more closed off and embittered than ever. . . . She told me . . . that the birth of every new human being seemed to her a misfortune, since one can fulfill one's destiny only in suffering." At Valerie's suggestion that she consult a doctor, Elisabeth replied only, "Oh, doctors and priests are such donkeys"—a statement that deeply offended her devout daughter.[46]

Even the Emperor repeatedly complained. For example, he spoke to his chief of the general staff, Baron Beck, about the Empress's poor health, "her overstressed nerves, her increasing restlessness, her extravagances, her very sick heart." But Franz Joseph's complaints always contained "tones of deep concern."[47]

During these final years, Elisabeth's chief attention was given to her waning health. She still put herself through her starvation diets. She still complained of every little weight gain. Dr. Viktor Eisenmenger examined the Empress in Territet during the 1890s. "In the otherwise healthy woman I found fairly pronounced swelling, especially in the ankles. A condition physicians saw rarely in those days and which did not become regrettably notorious until the war. Edema of hunger!" Elisabeth totally rejected all suggestions pertaining to diet.[48]

Marie Henike, one of the Empress's servants, listed the tortures Elisabeth voluntarily underwent, such as "steam baths followed by 7-degree [Celsius = 45 degrees Fahrenheit] full baths, it would put many people into a faint, bring on death. Her Majesty also admits to having had a ringing in her ears after this." Then there were "sweat cures—every evening dressed very warmly quickly walking up the mountain several times. . . . This was also to prevent getting fat—Her Majesty always looked so exhausted!!" Elisabeth's weight was given as 93.2 pounds—that is, 46.6 kilos (= 102.7 U.S. pounds): "In Cap Martin two years ago after decongestion of her leg, 87 [pounds = 95 U.S. pounds]!!" It is well to remember her height—172 centimeters (= 5 ft., 7.7 in.).[49]

The Emperor, too, suffered from Elisabeth's constant complaints about her weight, and repeatedly he expressed his discontent to Katharina Schratt (who, though she also constantly dieted along the same lines as Elisabeth, never managed to reduce her chubby figure). In 1894, for example, he mentioned that the Empress was "worried that she would grow too heavy again, because, since she has been drinking Karlsbad water and lives only on black coffee, cold meat, and eggs, she has gained quite a bit of weight. But that is pure craziness!"[50] His "sweet, beloved soul"—as he still addressed his wife in his letters—implored the Emperor not to communicate her dieting whims to Katharina. Around 1897, Elisabeth hatched a plan "to have installed two bathing cubicles in the Hermes Villa, one for you and one for our friend, in which you are to be roasted or burned away. It would be so terrible if, after the sad experiences you had with steam baths, you were to undertake another, similar cure and drag your friend, who goes along with every medical mischief, down with you into ruin!"[51] And in 1897, before an encounter with Elisabeth, Franz Joseph wrote Frau Schratt, to be on the safe side, "Should you be frightened at her quite bad appearance, I beg you not to let it show, nor to speak very much with the Empress about health, but if that is unavoidable, to cheer her up, but especially not recommend to her any new cure and new system. You will find the Empress very dull, very sickly, and in an especially depressed mood. You can imagine how worried I am."[52]

Though she ate very little now, Elisabeth was extremely fussy about what she did eat. Her daily quota of milk presented a special problem. Even in Vienna, it was difficult to obtain good milk. The Empress therefore repeatedly sent cows to Vienna for the Emperor from her travels. In April 1896, for example, two cows arrived in Vienna at the same time, one from Brittany and the other from Corfu—a further indication as well of Elisabeth's hectic travel schedule.[53] The Empress kept her own dairies, both in Schönbrunn and in the deer park at Lainz, where her favorite cows were kept, and when she traveled—at least when she traveled by ship—she usually took along two milk cows and a goat, to guarantee a steady supply of fresh, healthy milk. Caring for these animals—hardly seasoned sailors —was an additional burden on Elisabeth's entourage. The Empress's health depended on the animals' well-being, since she nourished herself almost entirely on milk and eggs.

It must be remembered that the Empress's principal destinations, the Greek islands and southern Italy, were not yet organized for tourism, and there were none of the hotels that would have catered to it; and the Empress always preferred the most out-of-the-way places. Stores of food therefore had to be brought along from Vienna. And though the entourage had long since grown much smaller than it was at the time of the English hunts, it still amounted to at least twenty people, not counting the ship's crew. All of them had to be provided for. Only in the last two years of her life did the Empress restrict herself to railway travel and to hotels in such regions as Switzerland and the Riviera, which were open to tourism.

Only once during these final years of her life did the Empress appear in public in her official role—at Hungary's Millennial Celebration of 1896. Hardly anyone recognized her, she had changed so much: "a black, female head, a new, an infinitely sorrowing face, with a smile that seemed no more than a shallow reflex. Her greeting is cordial but mechanical. . . . This face holds itself completely aloof, as it were," the Hungarian newspaper *Magyar Hirlap* reported.[54] In her usual way, on this occasion, too, Elisabeth kept her face hidden behind a black fan.

During the 1897 Badeni crisis, ugly nationalist struggles shook the monarchy; the Empress took no stand. At the beginning of the Jubilee Year of 1898, the fiftieth anniversary of Franz Joseph's reign, martial law had to be declared in Prague because the nationalist struggles had grown to uncontrollable proportions; the Empress remained disinterested. Social hardship ravaged the great cities as well as the villages of the monarchy; the Empress took no notice. Her daughter Valerie looked on her mother's apathy with concern. "How differently Mama would view life's joys and sorrows if only once she could realize the value of time and action."[55]

The Empress, now sixty years old, spent the winter of 1897–1898—her last one on earth—on the French Riviera, steeped in illness and melancholy. Once again, Franz Joseph visited his wife for two weeks, but later he told the German ambassador that, because of his worry about the Empress's health, "the whole stay in Cap Martin had been spoiled. . . . Further, intercourse with the sovereign lady seems to be more than usually disturbed because of her great nervousness."[56] In February 1898, Elisabeth wrote her husband "that she is alive and feels as if she were 80 years old."[57]

Archduchess Valerie did not see her mother again until May 1898, when they met in Bad Kissingen. "Mama looks terribly ill. But everyone here says she is better. . . . According to everything I am told here, Mama's winter was even worse than we knew . . . all the grief of this poor, desolate life, now aggravated by age and sickliness, and still without that comforting light which alone can help to overcome all the misery." Valerie was, of course, once again referring to the religious faith Elisabeth continued to lack.[58]

Elisabeth's steps, once almost floating, had grown slow and heavy. She could no longer take her long walks. She was restricted mostly to rounds through such spas as Bad Kissingen, Bad Gastein, Karlsbad, and Bad

Nauheim, and to shopping expeditions to purchase mainly toys for her numerous grandchildren.

In the summer of 1898, the Emperor and Empress met for two weeks in Bad Ischl, where Archduchess Valerie joined them. Elisabeth was "in low spirits, as always," and Valerie criticized "the melancholic effect of court life, this exclusion from all natural situations, which one must become accustomed to all over again even if one has grown up in it oneself. What must Papa's usual life be like for him to find life here comfortable and enjoyable?"[59]

After Elisabeth's departure for Bad Nauheim, Valerie remained her father's guest in Bad Ischl for a few more weeks and felt strong pangs of conscience. "It makes me so sad, and yet I am unable to change the fact that being with Papa places a constraint on me as if I were with a stranger."[60] She understood very well why overly sensitive Elisabeth could not endure being with her husband for long, though she laid the blame for all the family misery on Archduchess Sophie (who had been dead for twenty-six years). "This year more than ever I felt the fossilized court life to be oppressive . . . since it seeps suffocatingly between the most intimate family relationships, turning them from spontaneous pleasure only to indescribable constraint. If that is the result of Grandmama Sophie's system, it may well prepare a bitter Purgatory for her . . . this awful court life, which artificially robbed Papa of the ability to enjoy simple, unforced relations."[61]

The cure in Bad Nauheim did not improve Elisabeth's outlook one whit. "I am in bad humor and sad, and the family can be glad that they are away from me. I have a sense that I will not rally again," she wrote her daughter in late July.[62]

From Bad Nauheim she traveled to Switzerland. Valerie: "She felt drawn to Switzerland all summer long, she wanted to enjoy her beloved mountains, warmth and sunshine, and she did enjoy them, with a sense of improved health."[63] Elisabeth loved Lake Geneva: "It is altogether the color of the ocean, altogether like the ocean." Of all Swiss cities, she had always preferred Geneva. "It is my favorite place to stay, because there I am quite lost among the cosmopolites: it confers an illusion of the true human condition," she once told Christomanos, who diligently wrote down her every word.[64]

Elisabeth's preference for Switzerland developed only during her last years. In the 1880s, she had still written quite chilly lines referring to Switzerland's generous right of asylum for anarchists. In the final years of her life, however, even the danger of anarchists was unable to frighten her: She longed for death. Danger began to attract the Empress, who was weary of life. In spite of urgent recommendations from the Swiss police, she still refused the protection of security agents.[65]

Elisabeth was staying, as she had several times before, in Territet, outside Montreux, where she intended to take a four-weeks' cure. From here, she and Countess Sztaray set out on September 9, 1898, for an excursion to Pregny. They were going to visit Baroness Julie Rothschild the wife of Adolphe Rothschild from Paris and the sister of the Vienna Rothschilds Nathaniel and Albert. (There could, of course, be no real friendship with Julie Rothschild. Elisabeth's sister, ex-Queen Marie of Naples, defrayed her high cost of living with Rothschild funds, in return honoring the socially ambitious family with her royal company. Elisabeth's visit in Pregny, the first in decades, was a service done for her sister.) The three ladies had lunch, walked around the splendid old park, visited the orchid nursery, and engaged in very animated conversation in French. As Countess Sztaray confirmed, Elisabeth felt well during the visit.

Of course, even on this occasion the Empress preserved her incognito. (She was traveling under the name of Countess von Hohenembs.) The fact that at the time of the largest groundswell of anti-Semitism, aroused by the Dreyfus trial, in Paris, the Empress and Queen of Austria-Hungary was calling on a member of the Rothschild family would surely have occasioned headlines.

After a three-hour visit, Elisabeth and her lady-in-waiting continued on to Geneva, where they planned to spend the night before returning to Montreux the following day. Here in Geneva, which she knew very well, the Empress visited her favorite pastry shop, bought toys for her grandchildren, and, as always, retired very early. In the hotel, too, she was registered as Countess von Hohenembs. But the hotel manager was aware, from her previous stays, of the prominence of the guest who graced his establishment.

The following morning, a Geneva newspaper carried a news item to the effect that Empress Elisabeth of Austria was staying at the Hotel Beau Rivage. It was never established who had informed the newspaper. This report sealed Elisabeth's fate.

A member of the "Regicide Squad," the Italian anarchist Luigi Luccheni, had been preparing himself for a "great deed." He had purchased the murder instrument—a file he had ground to a triangular shape and given a knife edge. But his intended victim, Prince Henri of Orleans, pretender to the throne of France, had not, as planned, come to Geneva.

Nor did Luccheni have money for the fare to travel to Italy and stab his preferred victim, King Umberto of Italy. The newspaper item came as a godsend—Luccheni had found his target. For Elisabeth fulfilled the chief prerequisites for Luccheni's victim: She was an aristocrat (Luccheni hated all aristocrats) and of sufficient prominence to assure that the deed would cause a sensation.

The twenty-five-year-old anarchist bided his time. On September 10, he observed the comings and goings outside the hotel, the file concealed in his right sleeve. The Empress intended to return to Montreux from Geneva by the lake steamer scheduled to leave at one forty in the afternoon. Her servant had already gone ahead with the luggage, watched by Luccheni.

Accompanied by Irma Sztaray, as always dressed in black, her fan in one hand and the parasol in the other, "Countess von Hohenembs" walked to the landing stage, only a few hundred meters from the hotel. And it was along this path that Luccheni was lying in wait. When the two ladies came abreast of him, he threw himself at them, cast a swift glance under the parasol to make certain, and stabbed. He had earlier consulted an anatomical atlas to learn the precise location of the heart. His aim was accurate.

Elisabeth fell on her back. But the force of the fall was broken by the weight of her heavy, pinned-up hair. The assassin fled, was captured by passersby, and taken to the police station. At first it was not realized that he was a murderer; for the foreign lady got to her feet immediately after the fall and thanked all those who had helped her, speaking in German, French, and English. Her clothes were dusted off. The hotel porter, who was a witness to the deed, begged the two ladies to return to the hotel, but Elisabeth refused. She wanted to get to the boat.

Walking quickly, because little time was left before the ship's departure, the ladies went to the landing stage. Elisabeth, in Hungarian, to Countess Sztaray: "What did that man actually want?"

Countess Sztaray: "The porter?"

Elisabeth: "No, the other one, that dreadful person."

"I do not know, Your Majesty, surely he is a vicious criminal."

"Perhaps he wanted to take my watch?" the Empress conjectured.[66]

The ladies walked about a hundred meters from the site to the ship. It was not until they were on board the steamer, just departing, that Elisabeth collapsed. It was thought that she had fainted as a result of the fright she had endured. It was only when her bodice was unbuttoned so that her chest could be rubbed that a tiny brownish spot and a hole in her batiste camisole became apparent. Only then was the extent of the tragedy evident.

The ship's captain was informed—he was unaware that the Empress of

Austria was one of his passengers. The boat turned around and sped back to Geneva. A litter was improvised from oars and velvet chairs; the Empress was bedded on it and returned to the hotel as quickly as possible. There the doctor could do nothing but pronounce her dead.

Elisabeth died without pain. Heart specialists explained the fact that she was not even aware of her fatal wound and could still walk a hundred meters at a rapid pace by the smallness of the wound: The blood trickled so slowly into the pericardium that the heart's action stopped very gradually. Only a single drop of blood escaped. That is also why some of the witnesses thought it was a leech bite.

In the meantime, the murderer was subjected to a preliminary interrogation. He was elated, filled with pride at his deed, which he was unwilling to share with anyone: He insisted that he had acted alone and that he alone could lay claim to the "fame" that attended it. He saw the assassination as the culmination of his life, and he asked for the death sentence. Each time he was questioned about his motive, he repeated the same sentence: "Only those who work are entitled to eat!"

Lucheni had had several previous arrests for vagrancy, and he had led a wretched life: Abandoned at the foundling home by his unmarried mother, taken from institution to institution, pushed from one foster family to another. At one time, he was an unskilled laborer working on the railroad. His military service with the Italian cavalry in North Africa had been the best time in his life. Then, for a few months, he worked as a servant in the home of an Italian duke, who dismissed him. Then he lived by roving from place to place, picking up odd jobs along the way.

Only a few days of Lucheni's life had been spent in the Austro-Hungarian monarchy—in Fiume, Trieste, Budapest, and Vienna. But this sojourn had no influence on his political ideology; the problems of the Italian nationalities in the monarchy played no part in his motive. It was entirely rooted in the ideas of international anarchism, which he had picked up in Switzerland. Nor was there a special link with Empress Elisabeth. All he knew about her was from the newspapers. She was a crowned head; assassinating her would make headlines and confer fame on the name of Lucheni.

Lucheni gave one more command performance, at his trial. His name was in the newspapers: He was sentenced to life imprisonment. Then there was silence. In 1910, after eleven years in prison, Luigi Lucheni killed himself in his cell by hanging himself with his belt. Almost no one paid any attention.[67]

This sensational act of violence in Geneva was a deliverance for a deeply unhappy, emotionally disturbed, and physically debilitated woman whose parting left hardly a gap. Though the shock of the news of Elisabeth's death was terrible enough for the immediate family, Archduchess Marie Valerie, for one, found grounds for consolation. "Now it has happened as she always wished it to happen, quickly, painlessly, without medical treatment, without long, fearful days of worry for her dear ones." Valerie remembered Elisabeth's lines, "And when it is time for me to die, lay me down at the ocean's shore," and the Empress's repeated remark to Countess Sztaray that Lake Geneva was "altogether the color of the ocean, altogether like the ocean."[68]

Elisabeth's friend, the poet Carmen Sylva, found suitable words when she pointed out that this death was terrible "only for the world," but that for Elisabeth it was "beautiful and calm and great in the sight of beloved great nature, painless and peaceful." She continued:

> Not everyone finds it pleasant to give up the spirit in the midst of a large circle of mourners and to be attended by all possible ceremonies even in dying. Some like to perform their death handsomely for the world, but that would not have been at all like her. She had no wish to be anything for the world, not even in her death. She wanted to be solitary and to remain just as unnoticed in her leaving of the world through which she had so often wandered in search of repose in her restless striving to something higher and more ideal."[69]

The Emperor's reaction to his wife's sudden death was also less dramatic than the newspapers made it seem. Archduchess Valerie wrote about her reunion with her father immediately after the news of her mother's death was received. She noted that he had wept. "But even then he did not lose his composure, and he quickly regained the calm he had shown after Rudolf's death. Together we went to Sunday mass, and then I was allowed to spend this whole first day almost uninterruptedly with him, sitting next to his desk while he worked as usual, reading along with him the more detailed reports arriving from Geneva, helping him to receive the family condolence calls." And three days later: "He works all day every day as always, himself deciding everything, what is to be done according to traditional ceremonial." He repeatedly said, "How can you kill a woman who has never hurt anyone."[70] But no one doubted the words Franz Joseph spoke to his daughter and her husband: "You do not know how much I loved this woman."[71]

On September 15, the body arrived at the Hofburg in Vienna, surrounded by all the pomp of the empire. Of course, there was no question of meeting Elisabeth's wishes to be buried "at the ocean, preferably on Corfu," any more than Crown Prince Rudolf's final wish for eternal rest in Heiligenkreuz at Mary's side was respected. As had been done for Rudolf, Elisabeth was also laid out in the castle chapel, though (unlike Rudolf) in a closed coffin.

Arguments broke out over the body as it lay in state, because a prominently displayed coat of arms bore the inscription, "Elisabeth, Empress of Austria." The protest from Hungary was prompt: Why was "Queen of Hungary" omitted? Was that not the only title Elisabeth had cherished? That same evening, the office of ceremonies ordered the desired addition made. Now there was a protest from Bohemia: Had Elisabeth not also been Queen of Bohemia (though uncrowned)? Then there were very similar complications over the limited amount of seating in the Kapuzinerkirche. Because there were not enough pews to accommodate everyone, the delegation of the Hungarian parliament, of all groups, had not been assigned seats and now suspected still another deliberate slight on the part of the Viennese to the Hungarians.

The shock and sorrow felt in Vienna could not compare to the expressions of grief for the death of the Crown Prince. Count Erich Kielmannsegg: "Not many tears were shed for her."[72] The mourning was not for the Empress but for the new blow of fate that had struck the Emperor, now sixty-eight years old. A wave of affection welled up when, on September 14, the Emperor's proclamation of thanks "To All My Peoples!" was published.

The following weeks brought the ordering of the Empress's estate. No one, least of all the Emperor, had suspected that the Empress was in possession of a substantial fortune—not counting real estate, more than 10 million guldens, invested in gilt-edged securities. It turned out that "each year, she had invested her annual allowance and pin monies profitably, while the Emperor was made to defray her extravagances."[73]

In her will, Elisabeth disposed of her unexpectedly, even "shockingly large fortune," as Valerie put it in her diary.[74] She left each of her daughters two-fifths of the whole, with one-fifth going to her granddaughter Elisabeth (Rudolf's daughter).

In addition to the large money gifts Elisabeth had made to Valerie during the Empress's lifetime, Valerie was now also favored over her older sister, Gisela. She received a preliminary bequest of a million guldens as well as the Hermes Villa, while Gisela had to content herself with the

Achilleion, which stood empty and stripped. According to the statement of the division of the estate, the Hermes Villa was assessed at 185,000 guldens (it had cost several million), being livable and situated close to the capital. The Achilleion, conversely, was far away, in need of repairs, and unfit for habitation. Its book value was only 60,000 guldens, although the building costs had far exceeded 2 million. The yearly maintenance alone ran to 50,000 guldens.[75]

The contemporary papers reported at length on the Empress's fabulous jewelry collection. These private jewels—gifts from the Emperor as well as from many friendly sovereigns, such as the Sultan of Turkey and the Shah of Persia—were estimated to be worth 4 to 5 million guldens. It can now be seen from the statement of accounts of her estate, however, that the Empress had long since given away most of this legendary jewelry, keeping hardly anything for herself. The total value of the pieces she left behind amounted to a mere 45,950 guldens.[76]

Neither the valuable wedding presents—three diamond tiaras alone— nor the famous triple strand of pearls—the Emperor's gift on the occasion of Rudolf's birth—was still in her possession. Elisabeth had parted with everything, even her famous emeralds and the diamond stars for her hair, which had become so well known through Winterhalter's portrait. The most valuable piece in her estate was the Order of the Star Cross (valued at 12,000 guldens), which had to be returned, and a tiara set with black pearls valued at 4,500 guldens—the only remaining tiara. Black pearls had been a symbol of bad luck to the highly superstitious Elisabeth; now they represented the only jewelry of value in her possession. There were 184 other jeweled trinkets—combs, mourning jewelry, many cheap brooches, buttons, crosses, and watches. The jewelry box left by the Empress of Austria and Queen of Hungary clearly shows Elisabeth's contempt for worldly goods as well as the extent of her resignation.

Relatively few letters were found among her papers. "Most of the important letters Mama burned or—as, unfortunately, Rudolf's last letter —ordered to be burned." Her agent in this was her closest confidante of many years, Ida Ferenczy. Only a few letters from the 1860s and all the letters from about 1891 remained of those Franz Joseph had written to her through the tens of years of separation. Valerie was "deeply moved" by this fact, seeing in it "how the relationship between my parents became better, increasingly intimate, how in the final years, there were no more instances of even passing ill feelings."[77] In other words, the couple got along better from the moment they were separated and when Franz Joseph's relationship with Katharina Schratt was regularized, with Elisabeth's approval.

Even a few days after his wife's interment, Franz Joseph resumed his usual walks with Schratt. Expressing her embarrassment in her diary, Archduchess Valerie wrote, "Every morning Papa takes his walk with Schratt, whom I was also repeatedly forced to see and embrace—not with my heart—and yet I think her in herself—that is, aside from the people who cling to her—a harmless, loyal soul.—With fear I think of Mama's wish, expressed to me so often, when I die Papa should marry Schratt. In any case, I wish to remain passive, cannot act coldly to her in view of Papa's true friendship with her, would find it unjust and cruel to sour this comfort for Papa—but do not consider it my duty to abet him."[78] Soon, the dislike of the Emperor's daughter for his friend was known throughout the court.

But the Emperor found neither comfort nor relaxation in the bosom of Valerie's family. His visits were marked by awkwardness and embarrassment, from which Valerie suffered deeply, complaining,

> not to know whether one should talk about our misfortune or about distracting things, to try in vain to find subjects of conversation of the latter kind, to wish the children to act natural . . . and yet tremble that their shouting might irritate Papa— to see him now sink into dull unhappiness, now being nervous. . . . How well I understand now that being in Papa's company almost crushed Mama. Yes, it is difficult to be with Papa, since he has never known a real exchange of views. I know how deep his feelings go and how deeply he suffers and stand powerless before all this woe, with no other weapon than the traditional routines.[79]

Adjutant General Count Paar also found fault with the family circle in Wallersee. "It is barely possible to endure the boredom, for no one dares to say a word, and so conversation at table and in the evenings dries up almost completely."[80] Even surrounded by his grandchildren, Franz Joseph was the unapproachable sovereign, a figure of fear. Not even here did he have the ability or the need to carry on a casual, informal conversation.

In earlier years, Valerie had repeatedly accused her mother (of course only in her thoughts, she did not dare to speak aloud) of not having treated her father well enough, of having neglected her wifely duties. Now she deeply regretted her earlier feelings. For now she, too, found dealing with

Franz Joseph anything but easy. "The trial it is to me now to be in Papa's company is my punishment for my former harshness," she wrote in her diary, as an expression of remorse toward her mother.[81]

The "nasty court" got on her nerves now just as much as in former days it had annoyed her mother. Family life among the Habsburgs, with the many archducal rivalries and privileges, embittered her. She "realized very clearly once again that a nature like Mama's can experience this sort of family life only as an unbearable obligation to an empty comedy."[82]

In December 1898, the fifty-year jubilee of Franz Joseph's reign was celebrated with restraint and subdued by mourning, overshadowed by severe nationalist riots. Valerie about her father: "And in the midst of all this, he still stands upright, *vir simplex et justus* [a simple and just man], concerned only with fulfilling his difficult duties day after day, loyal and untiring, forgetting self and caring only about others."[83]

But the Emperor's daughter quarreled with the future of the monarchy. Elisabeth had turned her into a "republican," as she had Crown Prince Rudolf. Now, after Elisabeth's death, Valerie recalled her mother's example. "There is, then, my perhaps highly treasonable lack of belief in Austria's survival and its only salvation in the House of Habsburg. That is the real reason why I cannot become excited about a cause which I simply consider lost. I admit that these are views I have taken over from Mama —but every new experience always convinces me more and more of their correctness. . . . After him [Franz Joseph], let come what is most likely to bring about new and better conditions."[84]

For almost fifty years—from 1854 to 1898—Elisabeth was Empress and Queen of an empire riddled with problems in a time of decline. She did nothing to slow the decline. She was not a woman of action, like her successor, Zita, whose fate it was to live through the collapse. Self-surrender, retreat into private life, even into poetry, finally into solitude —this was Elisabeth's answer to the demand for the fulfillment of duties such as her imperial husband so indefatigably demonstrated to his subjects.

Madness? Wisdom? An understanding of the inevitable? Or simply convenience and whim? The *fin de siècle* of the Danube monarchy is personified in Elisabeth, who refused to live as an empress.

NOTES

INDEX

NOTES

The principal sources are cited with the following abbreviations:

Albrecht   Hungarian State Archives, Budapest. Papers of Archduke Albrecht. Quoted from the microfilm in Haus-, Hof- und Staatsarchiv, Vienna, by reel number.

Amélie D.   Sexau Papers. Diary of Duchess Amélie von Urach. Partial copy.

Amélie M.   Sexau Papers. Memoirs of Duchess Amélie von Urach to her grandmother Ludovika. Copy.

Bern   Swiss Federal Archives, Bern. Political Reports of the Swiss Envoy in Vienna: E 2300 Wien.

Bourgoing   Jean de Bourgoing, ed., *Briefe Kaiser Franz Josephs an Frau Katharina Schratt* (Vienna, 1949).

Braun Papers   Haus-, Hof- und Staatsarchiv, Vienna. Papers of Court Councillor Baron Adolf von Braun.

Corti Papers   Haus-, Hof- und Staatsarchiv, Vienna. Papers of Egon Caesar Conte Corti, materials for biography of Elisabeth.

Crenneville   Haus-, Hof- und Staatsarchiv, Vienna. Papers of Count Franz Folliot de Crenneville.

Elisabeth   Swiss Federal Archives, Bern. Literary Bequest of Empress Elisabeth of Austria: J I. 64.

Festetics   Széchenyi Library, Budapest. Manuscript Collection. Diary of Countess Marie Festetics.

Fürstenberg   Fürstenberg Family Archives in Weitra/Waldviertel. Letters from Landgravine Therese to her family.

Grünne   Grünne Family Archives in Dobersberg/Waldviertel. Letters from Empress Elisabeth to Karl Count Grünne.

Hübner   Historical Institute, University of Padua. Diary of Count Alexander von Hübner.

Khevenhüller Haus-, Hof- und Staatsarchiv, Vienna. Depot Khevenhüller. Diary of Prince Carl Khevenhüller-Metsch.

Nostitz   Georg Nostitz-Rieneck, *Briefe Kaiser Franz Joseph an Kaiserin Elisabeth,* 2 vols. (Vienna, 1966).

Rudolf   Haus-, Hof- und Staatsarchiv, Vienna. Family Archives, Papers of Crown Prince Rudolf.

Scharding   Carlo Scharding, *Das Schicksal der Kaiserin Elisabeth* (privately printed, n.p., n.d.), with letters from Countess de Jonghe to her family.

Schnürer   Franz Schnürer, ed., *Briefe Kaiser Franz Josephs I. an seine Mutter 1838–1872* (Munich, 1930).

Sexau Papers Bayerische Staatsbibliothek, Munich. Manuscript Collection. Papers of Richard Sexau. Materials for the biography of Duke Karl Theodor of Bavaria.

Sophie Haus-, Hof- und Staatsarchiv, Vienna. Papers of Archduchess Sophie. Diary.

Valerie Sexau Papers. Diary of Archduchess Marie Valerie. Partial copy.

In addition, the following abbreviations are used throughout the notes:

AA	Archiv des Auswärtigen Amtes (Foreign Office Archives), Bonn
BAB	Schweizer Bundesarchiv (Swiss Federal Archives), Bern
BStB	Bayerische Staatsbibliothek (Bavarian State Library), Munich
DStB	Deutsche Staatsbibliothek (German State Library), Berlin
FA	Familienarchiv (Family Archives)
GHA	Geheimes Hausarchiv (Secret Family Archives), Munich
HHStA	Haus-, Hof- und Staatsarchiv, Vienna
I.B.	Informationsbüro
NFP	*Neue Freie Presse*
NWT	*Neues Wiener Tagblatt*
OMeA	Obersthofmeisteramt (Office of Chief Chamberlain)
SStA	Sächsisches Staatsarchiv (Saxon State Archives), Dresden
StbW	Stadtbibliothek (Municipal Library), Vienna

CHAPTER I

1. Sexau Papers, Ludovika to Marie of Saxony, April 7, 1853.
2. Ad. Schmidl, W. F. Warhanek, *Das Kaiserthum Österreich* (Vienna, 1857), VI.
3. *Österreichische Rundschau*, September 15, 1910.
4. Corti Papers. To Princess Metternich.
5. GHA. Max II Papers. Schönbrunn, July 12, 1849.
6. Heinrich Friedjung, *Österreich von 1848 bis 1860* (Berlin, 1912), vol. II, p. 257.
7. Egon Caesar Conte Corti, *Mensch und Herrscher* (Vienna, 1952), p. 102.
8. Ibid., p. 103.
9. Amélie M.
10. Aloys Dreyer, *Herzog Maximilian in Bayern* (Munich, 1909), p. 32. All facts in this section about Max are from the same source.
11. Sexau Papers, Conversation with Prince Thurn und Taxis, July 27, 1938.

The quotation that follows is from the same source.
12. Schnürer, p. 207.
13. Sophie's detailed letter was published in the *Reichspost*, April 22, 1934. The quotations that follow are from the same source.
14. Corti, *Mensch*, p. 121.
15. Amélie M.
16. *Von Marie Theresia zu Franz Joseph*, Part II, *Selbstbiographie des Feldmarschall Leutnant Hugo Freiherr von Weckbecker* (Berlin, 1929), p. 195.
17. Amélie M. The information that follows concerning Ludovika and Sophie is taken from the same source.
18. Hans Flesch-Bruningen, ed., *Die letzten Habsburger in Augenzeugenberichten* (Düsseldorf, 1967), p. 33.
19. Sexau Papers, Ludovika to Auguste of Bavaria, from Bad Ischl, August 19, 1853.
20. Valerie, August 21, 1889.

21. Hübner, Summary for 1853.
22. Egon Caesar Conte Corti, *Elisabeth: Die Seltsame Frau* (Vienna, 1934), p. 30.
23. *Weckbecker*, p. 196.
24. Sophie, August 19, 1853.
25. Ibid., August 21, 1853.
26. Ibid.
27. Sexau Papers, Ludovika to Auguste of Bavaria, from Bad Ischl, August 26, 1853.
28. Corti, *Mensch*, p. 126.
29. Hermann von Witzleben and Ilka von Vignau, *Die Herzöge in Bayern* (Munich, 1976), pp. 197ff.
30. Festetics, from Possenhofen, September 19 and 17, 1872.
31. Schnürer, pp. 208ff.
32. Sexau Papers, Ludovika to Marie of Saxony, December 10, 1853.
33. Ibid., December 3, 1853.
34. Max Falk, "Erinnerungen," *Pester Lloyd*, September 12, 1898.
35. Scharding, "Report 55," September 9, 1853.
36. Sexau Papers, to Marie of Saxony, December 16, 1853.
37. Schnürer, p. 213, from Vienna, September 20, 1853.
38. Ibid., p. 210, from Schönbrunn, September 15, 1853.
39. GHA, papers of Therese of Bavaria, to Auguste of Bavaria, October 8, 1853.
40. Schnürer, pp. 215f., from Munich, October 17, 1853.
41. Ibid., p. 216.
42. Amélie M.
43. Scharding, p. 96.
44. Sophie, December 14, 1853.
45. Schnürer, p. 219, from Munich, December 27, 1853.
46. Schnürer, p. 221, from Munich, March 13, 1854.
47. Richard Kühn, ed., *Hofdamen-Briefe um Habsburg und Wittelsbach* (Berlin, 1942), pp. 341ff.
48. Friedrich Walter, ed., *Aus dem*

Nachlass des Freiherrn Carl Friedrich Kübeck von Kübau (Graz, 1960), p. 134, January 18, 1854.
49. HHStA, FA, March 4, 1854.
50. HHStA, OMeA, Franz Joseph to Liechtenstein, April 21, 1854.
51. Schnürer, p. 222.
52. Ibid., p. 223, from Munich, March 16, 1854.
53. Sophie, April 8, 1854.
54. HHStA, OMeA 134/8.
55. SStA, Letters from Queen Marie of Saxony to Fanny von Ow, from Dresden, October 1, 1853.
56. Richard Sexau, *Fürst und Arzt* (Graz, 1963), p. 54.
57. Schnürer, p. 217, from Munich, October 17, 1853.
58. Elisabeth, *Winterlieder*, p. 243.

CHAPTER 2

1. Anton Langer, *Dies Buch gehört der Kaiserin. Eine Volksstimme aus Österreich* (Vienna, 1854), pp. 8 and 11.
2. Ibid., p. 21.
3. Tschudy von Glarus, *Illustriertes Gedenkbuch* (Vienna, 1854), p. 28. This volume also contains a detailed description of the festivities.
4. HHStA, OMeA, 1854, 140/24.
5. *Weckbecker*, p. 204.
6. Tschudy, p. 43.
7. Konstantin von Wurzbach, *Biographisches Lexikon des Kaiserthums Österreich.*
8. *Österreichs Jubeltage* (Vienna, 1854), No. 3, p. 9.
9. Scharding, pp. 52f., Report of April 25, 1854.
10. Eugen d'Albon, *Unsere Kaiserin* (Vienna, 1890), pp. 36–39.
11. Tschudy, p. 51.
12. Jean de Bourgoing, Elisabeth, p. 6.

13. Amélie M.

14. *Österreichs Jubeltage*, p. 12.

15. Friedrich Walter, ed., *Aus dem Nachlass des Freiherrn Carl Friedrich Kübeck von Kübau* (Graz, 1960), p. 141.

16. Sophie, April 24, 1854 (in French).

17. Hellmuth Kretzschmer, *Lebenserinnerungen des Königs Johann von Sachsen* (Göttingen, 1958), p. 71.

18. Sophie, April 27, 1854.

19. Festetics, from Bad Ischl, October 15, 1872.

20. Sophie, April 27, 1854.

21. Sexau Papers, Ludovika to Auguste of Bavaria, from Vienna, April 27, 1854.

22. Hübner, April 27, 1854.

23. Sexau Papers, from Possenhofen, June 18, [1854].

24. Egon Caesar Conte Corti, *Elisabeth: Die seltsame Frau* (Vienna, 1934), p. 53.

25. Ibid., pp. 54f.

26. Festetics, October 15, 1872.

27. Sophie, November 5, 1855, and others.

28. Amélie M.

29. Festetics, October 15, 1872.

30. SStA, Marie of Saxony to Fanny von Ow, May 6, 1854.

31. GHA, Papers of Max II, from Schönbrunn, May 22, 1854.

32. Valerie, May 30, 1881.

33. Festetics, June 14, 1873 (in Hungarian).

34. *Weckbecker*, p. 204.

35. *Wiener Zeitung*, June 19, 1854.

36. Ibid., June 8, 1854.

37. Ibid., June 11, 1854.

38. Fürstenberg, Diary of Therese Fürstenberg.

39. *Wiener Zeitung*, June 17, 1854.

40. Recollections of the Court Chaplain Dr. Hasel, in *Wiener Tageblatt*, September 15, 1898.

41. Sophie, June 15, 1854.

42. Valerie, June 3, 1898.

43. Corti, *Elisabeth*, p. 56.

44. Schnürer, pp. 227f., from Laxenburg, July 17, 1854.

45. Sexau Papers.

46. Ibid., from Possenhofen, June 30, 1854.

47. Richard Sexau, *Fürst und Arzt. Dr. med. Herzog Carl Theodor in Bayern* (Vienna, 1963), p. 63.

48. Sexau Papers, to Marie of Saxony.

49. Ibid., to Auguste of Bavaria, from Bad Ischl, September 8, 1854.

50. Egon Caesar Conte Corti, *Mensch und Herrscher* (Vienna, 1952), p. 149.

51. Festetics, June 14, 1873 (in Hungarian).

52. Schnürer, p. 232, October 8, 1854.

53. Ibid.

54. Walter, *Kübeck*, pp. 155 and 153.

55. Richard Charmatz, *Minister Freiherr von Bruck* (Leipzig, 1916), p. 113.

56. The definitive source for these financial transactions is Harm-Hinrich Brandt, *Der österreichische Neoabsolutismus, Staatsfinanzen und Politik* (Göttingen, 1978).

57. Valerie, December 26, 1887.

58. Schnürer, p. 232, from Schönbrunn, October 8, 1854.

59. Ibid., p. 233.

60. *Weckbecker*, p. 204.

61. Corti Papers.

62. *The Correspondence of John Lothrop Motley*, vol. I.

CHAPTER 3

1. Sophie, March 5, 1855 (in French).

2. Sexau Papers, to Therese of Bavaria, from Vienna, March 22, 1855.

3. Festetics, June 26, 1872 (in Hungarian).

4. Eugen d'Albon, *Unsere Kaiserin* (Vienna, 1890), p. 176.

5. *Wiener Tageblatt*, September 15, 1898.

6. Schnürer, p. 256, September 18, 1856.
7. Festetics, June 2, 1872.
8. Ernst II of Saxe-Coburg-Gotha, *Aus meinem Leben und aus meiner Zeit* (Berlin, 1888), Vol. II, p. 174.
9. Bern, December 21, 1860.
10. Corti, *Elisabeth*, p. 74.
11. Ibid., p. 68.
12. Schnürer, p. 259, December 4, 1856.
13. Daniel Freiherr von Salis-Soglio, *Mein Leben* (Stuttgart, 1908), Vol. I, p. 79.
14. Schnürer, p. 259, December 4, 1856.
15. Ibid., p. 264, March 2, 1857.
16. Richard Sexau, *Fürst und Arzt* (Graz, 1963), pp. 79f.
17. Schnürer, p. 267, from Budapest, May 19, 1857.
18. Crenneville, from Budapest, May 9, 1857.
19. Schnürer, p. 267, from Budapest, May 19, 1857.
20. Ibid., p. 270.
21. Sexau Papers, to Auguste of Bavaria, July 23, 1857.
22. Schnürer, p. 280, from Vienna, November 3, 1857.
23. Sophie, August 4, 1857 (in French).
24. Sexau Papers, from Munich, December 30 and 31, 1857.
25. Ibid., July 27, 1858.
26. Ibid., to Marie of Saxony, November 21, 1857.
27. Ibid., from "Possi," August 5, 1857.
28. Ibid., to Sophie, May 15, 1858.
29. *Wiener Zeitung*, August 23, 1858.
30. Ibid., August 26, 1858.
31. Sauer, ed., *Sämtliche Werke* (Vienna, 1937), Sec. 1, Vol. 12, Pt. I, p. 92.
32. Sexau Papers, from Munich, March 12, 1859.
33. Sophie, January 13, 1859 (in French).
34. Sexau Papers, January 23, 1859.
35. Marie Louise von Wallersee, *Die Heldin von Gaeta* (Leipzig, 1936), p. 16.
36. Sexau Papers, to Marie of Saxony,

January 27, 1859.
37. Wallersee, pp. 17f.
38. Sexau Papers, to Marie of Saxony, March 2, 1860.
39. *Wiener Zeitung*, April 29, 1859.
40. Bern, May 19, 1859.
41. Ibid., Enclosure with the above report.
42. Sophie, May 9, 1859 (in French).
43. Sophie, May 28, 1859 (in French).
44. Khevenhüller, Summary for 1859.
45. Schnürer, p. 292, from Verona, June 16, 1859.
46. Joseph Redlich, *Kaiser Franz Joseph von Österreich* (Berlin, 1929), p. 243.
47. FA, Nischer-Falkenhof, Diary of Leopoldine Nischer.
48. Grünne, n.d., 1859.
49. Sexau Papers, to Marie of Saxony, June 3, 1859.
50. Nostitz, Vol. I, pp. 10f., from Verona, June 2, 1859.
51. Ibid., p. 11.
52. Sexau Papers.
53. Joseph Karl Mayr, ed., *Das Tagebuch des Polizeiministers Kempen von 1848 bis 1859* (Vienna, 1931), p. 515, June 6, 1859.
54. Ibid., pp. 532f., September 4, 1859.
55. Roger Fulford, ed., *Dearest Child* (London, 1964), p. 286. The first note on this page in source, concerning the Queen of Naples, must be corrected to refer to Marie (and not Therese).
56. Nostitz, Vol. I, p. 14, from Verona, June 7, 1859.
57. Ibid., p. 16, from Verona, June 7, 1859.
58. Redlich, p. 245.
59. Ernst II, Vol. II, p. 499.
60. Heinrich Laube, *Nachträge zu den Erinnerungen. Ausgewählte Werke*, Vol. IX (Leipzig, 1909), p. 433.
61. "Die Schlacht bei Solferino," *Das Volk*, June 25, 1859.
62. Nostitz, Vol. I, p. 26, from Verona, June 26, 1859.

63. Ernst II, Vol. II, pp. 500f.
64. Sexau Papers, from Possenhofen, July 1, 1859.
65. Nostitz, Vol. I, p. 33, from Verona, July 5, 1859.
66. *Weckbecker,* p. 216.
67. Nostitz, Vol. I, p. 30.
68. Ibid., p. 28, from Verona, June 27, 1859.
69. Ibid., p. 25, from Villafrancca, June 23, 1859.
70. Ibid., p. 35, from Verona, July 8, 1859.
71. Sexau Papers, October 20, 1859.
72. Nostitz, Vol. I, p. 35, from Verona, July 8, 1859.
73. Bern, July 13, 1859.
74. Joseph Karl Mayr, "Das Tagebuch des Polizeiministers Kempen (September bis Dezember 1859)," *Historische Blätter,* 1931, no. 4, p. 88.
75. Ibid., p. 106, December 22, 1859.
76. Sexau Papers, from Possenhofen, November 11, 1859.
77. Schnürer, pp. 294f., from Laxenburg, September 1, 1859.
78. Sexau Papers, from Possenhofen, November 11, 1859.
79. *NWT,* November 6, 1875.
80. Grünne, from Schönbrunn, November 2, 1859.
81. BStB, manuscript collection, to Amalie von Thiersch. March 1, 1860.

CHAPTER 4

1. Crenneville, January 29, 1860.
2. Fürstenberg, Diary.
3. Grünne, from Possenhofen, August 3, 1860.
4. Egon Caesar Conte Corti, *Anonyme Briefe an drei Kaiser* (Salzburg, 1939), p. 132.

5. Schnürer, p. 300, from Schönbrunn, October 2, 1860.
6. Ibid.
7. Sophie, December 31, 1860 (in French).
8. The distance amounts to roughly twenty kilometers.
9. Albrecht, reel 32, from Vienna, November 11 [1860].
10. Ibid., November 4, 1860.
11. Ibid., November 6, 1860.
12. Sophie, October 31, 1860 (in French).
13. Sexau Papers, from Possenhofen, November 11, 1860.
14. Albrecht, reel 32, from Vienna, November 18, 1860.
15. Sexau Papers, to Marie of Saxony, November 19, 1860.
16. Corti Papers.
17. Sexau Papers, January 5, March 17, and 16, 1861.
18. Albrecht, reel 42, February 21, 1861.
19. Grünne, from Funchal, December 19, 1860.
20. Ibid., from Funchal, February 25, 1861.
21. Ibid., from Funchal, April 1, 1861.
22. Sophie, February 15, 1861 (in French).
23. Sexau Papers, May 21, 1861.
24. Corti Papers, from Vienna, June 21, 1861.
25. Sexau Papers, June 17, 1861.
26. Ibid., from Possenhofen, June 24, 1861.
27. Sophie, June 18, 21, and 22, 1861 (in French).
28. Albrecht, reel 42, June 24, 1861.
29. Crenneville, June 25, 1861.
30. Festetics, November 3, 1872.
31. Ibid., October 1872 (in Hungarian).
32. Sexau Papers, from Possenhofen, August 10, 1861.

33. Grünne, from Corfu, August 22, 1861.
34. Sexau Papers, to Marie of Saxony, August 10, 1861.
35. Ibid.
36. Ibid., from Possenhofen, September 13, 1861.
37. Schnürer, p. 206, from Laxenburg, September 30, 1861.
38. Albrecht, reel 32, from Weilburg, September 3, 1861.
39. Sexau Papers, Possenhofen, August 22, 1861.
40. Schnürer, p. 305, from Laxenburg, September 30, 1861.
41. Schnürer, pp. 308f., from Corfu, October 16, 1861.
42. Sophie, October 27, 1861.
43. Sexau Papers, from Munich, February 27, 1862.
44. Corti Papers, Report of January 28, 1862.
45. Ibid.
46. Sexau Papers, to Archduchess Sophie, from Venice, April 25, 1862.
47. Ibid., from Venice, May 3, 1862.
48. Excerpts from Sisi's collection of photographs are published in: *Sisis Familienalbum* (Bibliophile Taschenbücher, No. 199) and *Sisis Schönheitsalbum* (No. 206) (both, Dortmund, 1980). Also: *Sisis Künstleralbum* (No. 266; Dortmund, 1981), selected and with an introduction by Brigitte Hamann.
49. *Die Presse,* July 1, 1862.
50. Ibid., July 10, 1862.
51. Fürstenberg, August 30 and September 1, 1867.
52. Ibid., December 8, 1865.
53. SStA, to Fanny von Ow, February 7, 1863.
54. Sexau Papers, to Auguste of Bavaria, from "Possi," September 5, 1862.
55. Marie Louise von Wallersee, *Die*

Heldin von Gaeta (Leipzig, 1936), pp. 88 and 93.
56. *Morgen-Post,* October 14, 1862.
57. Crenneville, July 14, 1862.
58. SStA, to Fanny von Ow, December 31, 1862.
59. Crenneville, from Possenhofen, July 18, 1862.
60. Schnürer, p. 313, August 25, 1862.
61. *Morgen-Post,* August 15, 1862.
62. Corti, *Elisabeth,* p. 113.
63. Albrecht, reel 32, from Weilburg, August 16, 1862.
64. Corti, *Elisabeth,* p. 114.
65. Fürstenberg, August 30, 1867.
66. Crenneville, *Grosse Korrespondenz,* p. 3 (n.p., n.d.).
67. Sexau Papers, Ludovika to Sophie, March 6, 1863.
68. Corti, *Elisabeth,* p. 115.
69. Corti Papers, September 28, 1862.
70. Egon Caesar Conte Corti, *Wenn* (Vienna, 1954), p. 160.
71. Valerie, October 31, 1889.
72. Sophie, March 24, 1864.
73. Schnürer, pp. 333f., from Schönbrunn, August 2, 1864.
74. Crenneville to his wife, August 26, 1864.
75. Dr. Konstantin Christomanos, "Aufzeichnungen über die Kaiserin," in *Die Wage,* September 17, 1898.
76. Brigitte Hamann, *Rudolf Kronprinz und Rebell* (Vienna, 1978), p. 27.
77. Festetics, June 30, 1882.
78. Sexau Papers. (Also quoted, in a slightly different version, in Corti, *Elisabeth.*)
79. Sophie, April 22, 1865 (in French).
80. StBW, manuscript collection, Friedjung Papers, Interview with Marie Festetics, December 29, 1910.
81. Crenneville, from Salzburg, August 5, 1865.
82. Ibid., from Vienna, October 9, 1865.

83. AA, from "Österreich Wien," December 28, 1865.

84. Valerie, October 25, 1889.

CHAPTER 5

1. Private communication from Princess Ghislaine Windisch-Graetz, based on the Empress's notebook of weight and measurements, meticulously kept over a number of years.

2. Sophie, May 1, 1855 (in French).

3. Ibid., April 6, 1860 (in French).

4. Joseph Karl Mayr, ed., *Das Tagebuch des Polizeiministers Kempen von 1848 bis 1859* (Vienna, 1931).

5. Crenneville, October 17, 1861.

6. Rudolf, box 18, from Zurich, September 1, 1867 (in Hungarian).

7. *Die Presse,* June 11, 1868.

8. Corti, *Elisabeth,* p. 111.

9. Brigitte Hamann, *Sisis Schönheitsalbum* (Dortmund, 1980), Foreword, p. 7.

10. Ibid., p. 8.

11. Sophie, from Dresden, February 10 and 11, 1864.

12. SStA, Marie of Saxony to Fanny von Ow, February 18, 1864.

13. *The Correspondence of John Lothrop Motley.*

14. Ibid., p. 199.

15. Roger Fulford, ed., *Dearest Mama* (London, 1968), p. 266, from Berlin, September 8, 1863.

16. Scharding, p. 93.

17. Festetics, March 5 and 25, 1874.

18. *Wiener Tageblatt,* September 14 and 17, 1898.

19. *Morgen-Post,* April 27, 1863.

20. Sophie, April 28, 1863.

21. Konstantin Christomanos, *Tagebuchblätter* (Vienna, 1899), p. 84.

22. Corti, *Elisabeth,* pp. 356f.

23. Irma Countess Sztaray, *Aus den letzten Jahren der Kaiserin Elisabeth* (Vienna, 1909), pp. 40f.

24. Christomanos, pp. 58–62.

25. Maria Freiin von Wallersee, *Meine Vergangenheit* (Berlin, 1913), p. 27.

26. Ibid., p. 53.

27. *Fremdenblatt,* December 8, 1864.

28. Crenneville, Franz Joseph to Crenneville, December 8, 1864.

29. Christomanos, pp. 90f. and 108.

30. Marie Louise von Wallersee, *Kaiserin Elisabeth und ich* (Leipzig, 1935), p. 204.

31. Hübner, October 31, 1881.

32. Valerie, October 15, 1882.

33. Emperor Wilhelm II, *Aus meinem Leben 1859–1888* (Berlin, 1929), p. 87.

34. Festetics, from Bad Ischl, June 21, 1872.

35. Carmen Sylva, "Die Kaiserin Elisabeth in Sinaia," *Neue Freie Presse,* December 25, 1908.

36. Festetics, September 14, 1879.

CHAPTER 6

1. Amélie M.

2. Schnürer, p. 328, from Schönbrunn, October 20, 1863.

3. Max Falk, "Erinnerungen," *Pester Lloyd,* September 12, 1898.

4. Corti, *Elisabeth,* p. 125.

5. Ibid., p. 130.

6. Corti Papers, November 15, 1864.

7. Ibid., from Vienna, June 3, 1866.

8. Kakay Aranyos II, *Graf Julius Andrássy* (Leipzig, 1879), p. 74.

9. Ibid., p. 109.

10. Hübner, August 21, 1878.

11. Eduard von Wertheimer, *Graf Julius Andrássy. Sein Leben und seine Zeit,* Vol. I (Stuttgart, 1910), pp. 214 and passim.

12. Crenneville, to his wife, February 4, 1866.

13. Ibid., January 31, 1866.

14. Schnürer, p. 351, from Budapest, February 17, 1866.
15. HHStA, Braun Papers, Diary, February 2, 1866.
16. Schnürer, p. 350, from Budapest, February 17, 1866.
17. Crenneville, from Vienna, February 9, 1866.
18. Ibid., from Budapest, February 15, 1866.
19. Ibid., from Budapest, February 27, 1866.
20. Budapest, Orszagos Leveltar, n.d.
21. Corti Papers, from Schönbrunn, June 2, 1866.
22. Schnürer, p. 351.
23. Corti, *Elisabeth*, p. 147.
24. Ibid.
25. Rudolf, box 18, June 29, 1866.
26. Ibid.
27. Ibid., box 1, July 1, 1866.
28. Ibid., July 4, 1866.
29. Fürstenberg, July 6, 1866.
30. Gordon Craig, *Königgrätz* (Vienna, 1966), p. 11.
31. Fürstenberg, July 8, 1866.
32. Bern, Report from Vienna, July 20, 1866.
33. Sophie, July 11, 1866.
34. Fritz Reinöhl, "Die Panik nach Königgrätz," *NWT*, Weekend edition, March 4, 1933.
35. Manr. Konyi, *Die Reden des Franz Deák*, Vol. VIII, p. 763.
36. Corti, *Elisabeth*, pp. 154ff.
37. Nostitz, Vol. I, p. 41, from Vienna, July 18, 1866.
38. Ibid., pp. 44f., from Vienna, July 20, 1866.
39. Sophie, July 11, 1866.
40. Ibid., July 14, 1866.
41. Nostitz, Vol. I, pp. 45f., from Vienna, July 21, 1866.
42. Ibid., p. 49, from Vienna, July 23, 1866.
43. Sophie, July 29, 1866.

44. Nostitz, Vol. I, p. 53, from Vienna, July 27, 1866.
45. Ibid., p. 54, from Schönbrunn, July 28, 1866.
46. Ibid., p. 53, July 28, 1866.
47. Wertheimer, Vol. I, p. 222.
48. Ibid., p. 223.
49. Nostitz, Vol. I, p. 55, from Schönbrunn, August 4, 1866.
50. Ibid., p. 56, from Schönbrunn, August 6, 1866.
51. Ibid., pp. 57f., from Schönbrunn, August 7, 1866.
52. Ibid., p. 54, from Schönbrunn, July 28, 1866.
53. Ibid., p. 58, from Schönbrunn, August 9, 1866.
54. Ibid., p. 60, from Schönbrunn, August 10, 1866.
55. Ibid.
56. Fürstenberg, from Bad Ischl, August 18, 1866.
57. Nostitz, Vol. I, p. 61, from Schönbrunn, August 20, 1866.
58. Ibid., p. 63, from Schönbrunn, August 22, 1866.
59. This and the following from Max Falk's recollections, *Pester Lloyd*, September 12, 1898.
60. Sophie, January 12, 1867.
61. Fürstenberg, from Bad Ischl, November 1, 1866.
62. Sophie, October 1866.
63. Wallersee, *Elisabeth*, p. 256.
64. HHStA, I. B., 1867, Register under Archduke Albrecht, No. 443, 1016, 1080, 1755, 1831, 2350, passim. On Archduke Albrecht, see: Brigitte Hamann, "Erzherzog Albrecht—die graue Eminenz des Habsburgerhofes," in *Festschrift für Rudolf Neck* (Vienna, 1981), pp. 32–43.
65. Wertheimer, Vol. I, p. 271.
66. Sophie, February 7, 1867.
67. HHStA, cabinet A, secret files 17, February 1, 1867.

68. "Fragmente aus dem Nachlasse des ehemaligen Staatsministers Grafen Richard Belcredi," in *Die Kultur*, 1905, p. 413.

69. Wertheimer, Vol. I, p. 273.

70. Sophie, February 6, 1867.

71. Ibid., March 11, 1867.

72. Falk recollections.

73. Juliana Zsigray, *Königin Elisabeth* (Budapest, 1908; in Hungarian).

74. Corti, *Elisabeth*, May 16, 1867.

75. *Pester Lloyd*, May 23, 1867.

76. Ibid., June 8, 1867.

77. Ibid., June 13, 1867.

78. Przibram, p. 187.

79. Ibid., p. 180.

80. Bern, June 9, 1867.

81. Przibram, pp. 187f.

82. Scharding, p. 293.

83. Przibram, pp. 184f.

84. Bern, Report of June 14, 1867.

85. Crenneville, to his wife, June 11, 1867.

86. Bern, Report of April 22, 1868.

87. Ibid.

88. Festetics, March 8, 1874.

89. *Pester Lloyd*, April 28, 1868.

90. Albrecht, reel 33, from Vienna, April 28, 1868.

91. Crenneville, to his wife, from Vienna, June 20, 1868.

92. Festetics, June 2, 1872.

93. Ibid., April 30, 1874.

94. Fürstenberg, from Bad Ischl, August 20, 1869.

95. Corti Papers, April 30, 1869.

96. Orszagos Leveltar Budapest, n.d.

97. Corti Papers, July 31, 1869 (in Hungarian).

98. Festetics, October 15, 1872.

99. HHStA, Braun Papers, Letter of October 3, 1876.

100. From the extensive literature, we need cite only three anthologies, all under the same title, *Der*

österreichisch-ungarische Ausgleich von 1867: (1) Ed. by the Forschungsinstitut für den Donauraum (Vienna, 1967); (2) Vol. XX, Buchreie der Süddeutschen Historischen Kommission (Munich, 1968); and (3) by Ludovit Holotik (Bratislava, 1971).

CHAPTER 7

1. Fürstenberg, July 3, 1867.

2. BStB, manuscript collection, Sophie to Oskar von Redwitz, from Vienna, February 15, [18]69.

3. Corti, *Elisabeth*, p. 184.

4. Fürstenberg, from Bad Ischl, August 19, 1867.

5. *Hans Wilczek erzählt seinen Enkeln Erinnerungen aus seinem Leben* (Vienna, 1933), p. 76.

6. Ibid., p. 74.

7. Prince Kraft zu Hohenlohe-Ingelfingen, *Aus meinem Leben*, Vol. I (Berlin, 1906), p. 369.

8. Rudolf, box 18, March 31, 1865.

9. Ibid.

10. Festetics, March 13, 1872.

11. Ibid., September 19, 1872.

12. Fürstenberg, from Bad Ischl, August 23, 1867.

13. Ibid., from Vienna, March 9, 1868.

14. Ibid., from Bad Ischl, August 1, 1869.

15. Festetics, February 14, 1872 (in French).

16. Ibid., September 17 and 19, 1872.

17. Crenneville, March 25, 1869.

18. Hans Christoph Hoffmann, Walter Krause, and Werner Kitlitschka, *Das Wiener Opernhaus* (Wiesbaden, 1972) pp. 410ff. The Empress's parlor was burned out in 1945 and could not be restored.

19. Scharding, p. 106.

20. Festetics, February 2, 1883.
21. Ibid., January 13, 1874.
22. Corti Papers, from Merano, November 18, 1871.
23. William Unger, *Aus meinem Leben* (Vienna, 1929), p. 152.
24. Corti Papers, from Bad Ischl, July 16, 1870.
25. Ibid., from Neuberg, August 10, 1870.
26. Sophie, September 25, 1870.
27. Ibid., October 5, 1870.
28. Festetics, July 4, 1871.
29. Ibid., February 2, 1872.
30. *Meraner Zeitung,* April 12, 1903.
31. Festetics, February 23, 1872 (in Hungarian).
32. Ibid., March 17, 1872.
33. Ibid., April 2, 1873.
34. Ibid., September 27, 1878.
35. Elisabeth, manuscript.
36. Most recently, Heinrich Lutz, *Österreich-Ungarn und die Gründung des Deutschen Reiches* (Frankfurt, 1979).
37. Sophie, December 31, 1871.
38. Corti Papers, from Vienna, March 12, 1874.
39. Ibid., from Vienna, April 24, 1872.
40. GHA, Papers of Leopold of Bavaria, from Merano, February 17 [1872].
41. Festetics, April 8, 1872.
42. Schnürer, p. 385, from Budapest, April 8, 1872.
43. Sophie, April 7, 1872.
44. Leopold Papers, from Budapest, April 7, 1872.
45. Sophie, April 23, 1872.
46. Festetics, May 25, 1875.
47. Richard Sexau, *Fürst und Arzt* (Graz, 1963), p. 242.
48. Festetics, April 17, 1872.
49. Ibid., May 28, 1872.
50. Bern, May 29, 1872.
51. Hübner, May 28, 1872.
52. Festetics, June 2, 1872.

53. Sexau, March 19, 1862.
54. Festetics, June 2, 1872.
55. Ibid., October 15, 1872.
56. Ibid., December 9, 1872.
57. Ibid., December 28, 1873.
58. Valerie, December 24, 1890.
59. Fürstenberg, May 3, 1882.
60. Festetics, April 21, 1873.
61. Ibid.
62. Ibid., April 23, 1873.
63. *NWT,* April 21, 1873.
64. Corti Papers, from Munich, January 12, 1874.
65. Rudolf, box 18, Bad Ischl, 24.
66. GHA, Papers of Leopold of Bavaria, from Budapest, January 9, 1874.
67. Festetics, May 21, 1873.
68. Ibid., May 4, 1873.
69. Ibid., May 21, 1873.
70. Ibid., May 29, 1873.
71. Ibid., June 4, 1873.
72. Crenneville, June 3, 1873.
73. Ibid., to his wife, June 5, 4, and 7, 1873.
74. Ibid., May 9, 1873.
75. Ibid., June 25, 1873.
76. Ibid., June 26, 1873.
77. Ibid., July 6, 1873.
78. Festetics, July 14, 1873.
79. Ibid., June 8, 1873.
80. Corti, *Elisabeth,* p. 245.
81. Crenneville, July 28, 1873.
82. *NWT,* August 3 and 2, 1873.
83. Ibid., July 31, 1873.
84. Ibid., August 8, 1873.
85. Ibid., August 9, 1873.
86. Festetics, August 9, 1873.
87. *NWT,* August 9, 1876.
88. Crenneville, September 21, 1873.
89. Festetics, September 23, 1873.
90. Bern, December 7, 1873.
91. *Fremdenblatt,* November 30, 1873.
92. Festetics, December 3, 1873.
93. *Fremdenblatt,* December 2, 1873.
94. *NWT,* December 3, 1873.

95. Festetics, March 3, 1874.
96. Ibid., March 4, 1875.
97. Ibid., August 14, 1873.

CHAPTER 8

1. Corti Papers.
2. Scharding, p. 140.
3. Maria Freiin von Wallersee, *Meine Vergangenheit* (Berlin, 1913), pp. 43, 49, and 40.
4. Sexau Papers, conversation with Privy Councillor von Müller, September 23, 1938.
5. Ketterl, p. 39.
6. Corti Papers, from Gödöllö, January 26, 1875.
7. Both letters in Roger Fulford, ed., *Darling Child* (London, 1976), p. 145, from Osborne, August 2, 1874; and from Sandown, August 3, 1874.
8. Corti Papers, from Ventnor, August 2, 1874.
9. Ibid., from Steephill Castle, August 15, 1874.
10. Ibid., from Claridge's Hotel, August 22, 1874.
11. Ibid., from Steephill Castle, August 28, 1874.
12. Corti, *Elisabeth*, p. 270, from Ventnor, September 13, [18]74.
13. Corti Papers, from Isle of Wight, August 18, 1874.
14. Festetics, August 26, 1874.
15. Ibid., January 15, 1874.
16. Ibid., January 18, 1874.
17. Ibid., December 15, 1872.
18. Crenneville, July 3, 1875.
19. HHStA, Imperial and Royal General Direction of the Family Fund, Reserve Files, 1892.
20. Corti Papers, from Sassetôt, August 4, 1875.
21. Ibid., August 27, 1875.

22. Corti, *Elisabeth*, p. 279.
23. Festetics, August 8, 1875.
24. Corti Papers, September 16 and 22, 1875. A Countess Zanardi Landi (*The Secret of an Empress*, London, 1914) tried to profit from the Empress's accident by claiming that in Sassetôt Elisabeth secretly gave birth to a child; Countess Marie Larisch (who was not along in Sassetôt) picked up this story, in: Marie Louise von Wallersee, *Kaiserin Elisabeth und ich* (Leipzig, 1935), pp. 303ff.

The diaries of Countess Festetics and Archduchess Valerie—both kept meticulously—as well as the memoirs of Bishop Hyazinth Rónay (who was also present in Sassetôt) leave no doubt that this story is pure myth. The contemporary French newspapers allow us to examine the course of the Empress's day from hour to hour. Thousands saw her daily while she was bathing in the ocean and witnessed her horseback stunts. How, then, can she have been in her ninth month of pregnancy? The imperial family physician, Dr. Widerhofer, was along on the trip at the express wish of the Emperor, since Elisabeth's daredeviltry made the risk of an accident very real, and it was not desirable to depend on strange physicians. The sources documenting the stay in Sassetôt are voluminous and give no hint of any gaps nor any attempts at concealment. The riding accident is beyond question. See also Corti, *Elisabeth*, p. 282.
25. In King James version, Ps. 91.1–2, 10–11. Private communication from Dr. Michael Habsburg-Salvator, Persenbeug.
26. Festetics, October 15, 1875.
27. Ibid., July 15, 1872.
28. Corti Papers, March 5, 1876.
29. Festetics, October 8, 1876.
30. Corti Papers, to Ida Ferenczy, March 16, 1876.

31. Ibid., from Easton Neston, March 20, 1876.

32. John Welcome, *Die Kaiserin hinter der Meute* (Vienna, 1975), p. 99.

33. Festetics, March 5, 1876.

34. Scharding, p. 162.

35. Wallersee, *Vergangenheit*, pp. 47f.

36. Corti, *Elisabeth*, p. 299.

37. Rudolf, box 16, to Latour, December 3, 1877.

38. Reprinted in Brigitte Hamann, ed., *Kronprinz Rudolf, Majestät ich warne Sie* (Vienna, 1979), pp. 19–52; quotation from p. 33.

39. Festetics, February 1878.

40. Ibid., January 4, 1878.

41. Ibid., February 1878.

42. Corti, *Elisabeth*, p. 300.

43. Sexau Papers, from Cottesbrook, February 3 [1878].

44. Corti Papers, July 26, 1869.

45. DStB, Collection of the Preussischer Kulturbesitz, collection Darmstaedter Lc 18. July 7, 1878.

46. Fürstenberg, from Bad Ischl, August 13 [1877].

47. Festetics, July 1, 1880.

48. Corti Papers, from Schönbrunn, May 26, 1878.

49. Corti, *Elisabeth*, p. 301.

50. Festetics, September 18, 1878.

51. Ibid., September 20, 1878.

52. Hübner, January 8, 1879.

53. Ibid., July 24, 1878.

54. Coronini to Crenneville, April 26, 1876.

55. Ibid., November 25, 1878, and January 22, 1879.

56. Festetics, February 14, 1880.

57. Corti, *Elisabeth*, pp. 290f. May 29, 1876.

58. Corti Papers, from Summerhill, February 11 [1880].

59. Welcome, p. 190, from Summerhill, February 22, 1879.

60. Festetics, March 20, 1879.

61. Corti Papers, from Summerhill, March 16, 1879.

62. Festetics, March 22, 1879.

63. Corti, *Elisabeth*, p. 307.

64. *Wiener Zeitung*, April 24 and 25, 1879.

65. Wallersee, *Elisabeth*, p. 170.

66. *Die Grosse Politik der europäischen Kabinette 1871–1914*, vol. III (Berlin, 1927), p. 42 (September 5, 1879).

67. Festetics, December 28, 1880.

68. Corti, *Elisabeth*, p. 312.

69. Wallersee, *Elisabeth*, p. 64. The quotation that follows is from the same source.

70. Festetics, July 21, 1880.

71. Corti Papers, from Summerhill, February 29, 1880.

72. Corti, *Elisabeth*, p. 316.

73. Festetics, March 13, 1880.

74. Welcome, p. 285.

75. Corti Papers, to Ida Ferenczy, 1881.

76. Festetics, April 19, 1882.

77. Ibid., January 6, 1874.

78. Elisabeth, *Winterlieder*, p. 20.

79. Ibid., pp. 1f.

80. Valerie, September 15, 1882.

81. Festetics, September 18, 1882.

82. Valerie, September 20, 1882.

83. Hübner, January 1, 1882.

84. Festetics, April 24, 1882.

85. Valerie, August 9, 1885.

86. Festetics, September 20, 1882.

87. Freiherr Robert Lucius von Ballhausen, *Bismarck-Erinnerungen* (Stuttgart, 1920), p. 398, October 24, 1887.

88. Wallersee, *Elisabeth*, p. 210.

89. Corti Papers, to Ida Ferenczy from Amsterdam, June 6, 1884.

CHAPTER 9

1. Festetics, October 15, 1872.

2. Ibid., February 6, 1872.

3. Ibid., June 21, 1878.

4. Ibid., January 21, 1875.

5. Ibid., February 6, 1874.

6. Corti Papers, from Budapest, April 14, 1869.

7. Ibid., from Gödöllö, April 30, 1869.

8. Ibid., January 31, 1867.

9. Ibid., December 18, 1868.

10. Ibid., September 6, 1868.

11. Ibid., January 1870.

12. Ibid., July 8, 1868, and June 22, 1867.

13. StBW, manuscript collection, Friedjung Papers, Interview with Marie Festetics, March 6, 1913.

14. To her niece Amélie, Valerie, September 3, 1908.

15. Wallersee, *Vergangenheit*, pp. 93f.

16. Quoted here from Pacher's reports, contained in Corti Papers. A slightly different version appears in Corti, *Elisabeth*, pp. 254ff.

17. Elisabeth, *Nordseelieder*, p. 96.

18. Corti, *Elisabeth*, pp. 350f.

19. Elisabeth, *Nordseelieder*, p. 61.

20. Elisabeth, manuscript. Already in Corti, *Elisabeth*, pp. 384ff.

21. Festetics, January 9, 1874.

22. Marie Louise von Wallersee, *Kaiserin Elisabeth und ich* (Leipzig, 1935), pp. 60ff.

23. Ibid., p. 59. A longer and weaker version of this poem in Elisabeth, *Winterlieder*, pp. 206–9.

24. Hübner, May 23, 1876.

25. Wallersee, *Elisabeth*, p. 202.

26. Konstantin Christomanos, *Tagebuchblätter* (Vienna, 1899), pp. 98–9.

27. Elisabeth, *Nordseelieder*, p. 59.

28. Valerie, September 4, 1891.

29. These lines and the compilation "Titania und Alfred" are in the unpaginated manuscript section of the literary bequest in Bern.

30. Corti Papers, from Barcelona, February 6, 1893.

CHAPTER 10

1. Richard Sexau, *Fürst und Arzt* (Graz, 1963), p. 131.

2. Philipp Fürst zu Eulenberg-Hertefeld, *Aus fünfzig Jahren: Erinnerungen des Fürsten Philipp zu Eulenburg-Hertefeld* (Berlin, 1925), p. 130.

3. Luise von Kobell, *Unter den ersten vier Königen Bayerns* (Munich, 1894), p. 241.

4. Scharding, p. 191, Ludwig to Count Dürckheim, January 8, 1877.

5. Marie Louise von Wallersee, *Kaiserin Elisabeth und ich* (Leipzig, 1935), pp. 74f.

6. Philipp Fürst zu Eulenberg-Hertefeld, *Das Ende Ludwigs II. und andere Erlebnisse*, Vol. I (Leipzig, 1934), p. 96.

7. Oskar Freiherr von Mitis, *Das Leben des Kronprinzen Rudolf*, revised by Adam Wandruszka (Vienna, 1971), p. 225, March 9, 1878.

8. Sexau Papers, Ludwig to Sophie, from Munich, April 28, 1867.

9. Ibid., Ludwig to von der Pfordten, July 19, 1865.

10. GHA, from Schönbrunn, December 11 (no year).

11. Rudolf, box 18, March 31, 1865.

12. Sexau, p. 174.

13. Gottfried von Böhm, *Ludwig II, König von Bayern*, Vol. II (Berlin, 1924), p. 402.

14. Festetics, September 21, 1872.

15. Otto Gerold, *Die letzten Tage Ludwigs II* (Zurich, 1903).

16. Corti Papers, from Steephill Castle, September 26, 1874.

17. Festetics, January 18, 1874.

18. Elisabeth, manuscript, for both poem and letter.

19. Festetics, January 18, 1874.

20. Valerie, June 4, 1885.

21. Konstantin Christomanos, *Tagebuchblätter* (Vienna, 1899), pp. 92f.

22. Valerie, December 13, 1902, Interview with Count Dürckheim. This

source must be given credence over a letter from Prince Philipp Eulenburg to Herbert Count Bismarck of August 5, 1886, which is based on Munich gossip and describes Elisabeth's alleged plan to flee with Ludwig II. "She intended driving to Gudden and begging him to be allowed to walk alone with the King for 1/4 hour—which he would undoubtedly have permitted. Thereupon she planned to flee with the King.— That would have made a fine mess!" Elisabeth's low emotional state after Ludwig's death was well known in Munich. According to Eulenburg, "the Empress fell into a despair that bordered on madness." John C. G. Röhl, ed., *Philipp Eulenburgs Politische Korrespondenz*, Vol. I (Boppard, 1976), p. 191.

23. Valerie, June 16, 1886.

24. *Berliner Tageblatt,* April 21, 1889.

25. Corti Papers, from Feldafing, June 10, 1886.

26. Amélie, June 14, 1886, and May 23, 1887.

27. Valerie, June 20, 1886.

28. Ibid., June 10, 1886.

29. Ibid., June 19, 1886.

30. Amélie, August 23, 1888.

31. Valerie, August 19, 1888.

32. Amélie, March 21, 1889.

33. Elisabeth, manuscript, 1888, "Dem todten Aar."

34. Valerie, May 18, 1887.

35. Ibid., June 18, 1887.

36. AA, Österreich 86, No. 1, Vol. II, from Munich, May 2, 1888.

37. Valerie, June 21, 1884.

38. Wallersee, *Elisabeth,* p. 252.

39. Maria Freiin von Wallersee, *Meine Vergangenheit* (Berlin, 1913), p. 82.

40. Wallersee, *Elisabeth,* p. 164.

41. Wallersee, *Vergangenheit,* pp. 123ff.

42. Valerie, December 20, 1885.

CHAPTER 11

1. Karl Hasenauer, in *Neues Wiener Tageblatt,* April 6, 1930.

2. Valerie, May 25, 1887.

3. Ibid., May 24, 1886.

4. Elisabeth, *Nordseelieder,* p. 141.

5. Wallersee, *Elisabeth,* pp. 5f. See also Valerie, December 10, 1887.

6. Elisabeth, enclosure with the poems.

7. Ibid.

8. Valerie, April 4, 1887.

9. Ibid., August 23, 1887.

10. Ibid., July 3, 1884.

11. Festetics, August 19, 1882.

12. Wertheimer, Vol. III, p. 338, July 7, 1889.

13. Valerie, August 23, 1887.

14. Amélie D., June 27, 1887.

15. "Maximilian in Bayern," *Allgemeine Deutsche Biographie.*

16. Corti Papers, from Gödöllö, November 11, 1886.

17. Valerie, August 26, 1889 (with the note, "three years ago").

18. *Vossische Zeitung,* June 5, 1907.

19. *Wiener Tageblatt,* September 15, 1898.

20. Corti Papers, to Valerie, from Corfu, October 29, 1888.

21. Marie Freiin von Redwitz, *Hofchronik 1888–1921* (Munich, 1924), p. 69.

22. Dr. M. C. Marinaky, *Ein Lebensbild der Kaiserin Elisabeth,* ed. by Carlo Scharding (n.p., n.d.), p. 69.

23. Redwitz, pp. 108f.

24. Braun Papers, from Corfu, November 4 [1885].

25. Corti Papers, December 1, 1888.

26. Braun Papers, from Corfu, October 22 (no year).

27. Ibid., from Corfu, October 22 [1888].

28. Corti Papers, to Ida Ferenczy, from Corfu, October 18, 1888.

29. Ibid., October 30, 1887.

30. Nostitz, Vol. I, p. 190 (November 1, 1887), pp. 192 (November 6, 1887), and 194 (November 9, 1887).

31. Valerie, December 3, 1888.

32. Ibid., November 11, 1884.

33. Elisabeth, *Winterlieder*, p. 83.

34. Eugen Wolbe, *Carmen Sylva* (Leipzig, 1933), p. 137.

35. Carmen Sylva, "Die Kaiserin Elisabeth in Sinaia," *NFP*, December 25, 1908.

36. Corti Papers, from Mehadia, May 2, 1887.

37. Elisabeth, *Winterlieder*, p. 84.

38. Bourgoing, p. 354, from Budapest, October 1, 1897.

39. Hugo Graf Lerchenfeld-Koefering, *Erinnerungen und Denkwürdigkeiten 1843–1925* (Berlin, 1935), pp. 134f.

40. Nostitz, Vol. I, p. 267, from Vienna, January 6, 1893.

41. Elisabeth, *Winterlieder*, pp. 23ff.

42. Wallersee, *Elisabeth*, p. 253.

43. Valerie, November 27, 1888.

44. Elisabeth, *Nordseelieder*, pp. 142ff.

45. *Winterlieder*, p. 173.

46. Marinaky, p. 55.

47. Christomanos, pp. 71f.

48. Ibid., p. 134.

49. Valerie, September 6, 1885.

50. Christomanos, pp. 157f.

51. Ibid., p. 154.

52. *NFP*, April 29, 1934.

53. Irma Gräfin Sztaray, *Aus den letzten Jahren der Kaiserin Elisabeth* (Vienna, 1909), p. 83.

54. Eduard Leisching, *Ein Leben für Kunst und Volksbildung*, ed. by Robert A. Kann and Peter Leisching (Vienna, 1978), pp. 130ff.

55. Valerie, March 18, 1891.

56. Christomanos, pp. 221f.

57. Marinaky, p. 38.

58. Index of names to Elisabeth's expenses in the reserved files of the sovereign Family Fund, HHStA.

59. Brigitte Hamann, *Rudolf Kronprinz und Rebell* (Vienna, 1978), p. 406.

60. Volume VI, No. 9, p. 115.

61. Ibid., No. 4, p. 44.

62. Édouard Drumont, *La Fin d'un monde* (Paris, 1889), p. xii.

63. Christomanos, p. 238.

64. "Kaiser Wilhelm und Heine," *Deutsches Volksblatt*, August 2, 1907.

65. Gerhard Söhn, *Heinrich Heine in seiner Vaterstadt Düsseldorf* (Düsseldorf, 1966), p. 53.

66. Corti Papers, to Ida Ferenczy from Corfu, October 11, 1891.

67. Julius Kornried, "Kaiserin Elisabeth und Heinrich Heine," *NWT*, May 9, 1926.

68. *Deutsches Volksblatt*, August 2, 1907.

CHAPTER 12

1. Heinrich Benedikt, *Damals im alten Österreich* (Vienna, 1979), pp. 70f.

2. Bourgoing, p. 43.

3. Princess Stephanie of Belgium, Princess von Lonyay, *Ich sollte Kaiserin werden* (Leipzig, 1935), p. 152.

4. Bourgoing, p. 44.

5. Ibid., p. 45, May 23, 1886.

6. Ibid., p. 60, from Vienna, April 21, 1887.

7. Valerie, July 14, 1886.

8. Franz von Matsch, "Als Maler bei Kaiserin Elisabeth," *NFP*, April 29, 1934.

9. Valerie, March 1, 1887.

10. Bourgoing, p. 56, February 17, 1887.

11. Ibid., from Vienna, February 7, 1887.

12. Ibid., p. 121, from Vienna, December 6, 1888.

13. Ibid., p. 75, from Gödöllö, November 29, 1887.

14. Ibid., p. 85, from Budapest, February 14, 1888.

15. Ibid., p. 101, from "Villa bei Lainz," June 1, 1888.
16. Ibid., p. 225, from Vienna, December 30, 1890.
17. Ibid., p. 250, from Vienna, February 13, 1892.
18. Ibid., p. 273, March 4, 1893.
19. Ibid., p. 274, March 5, 1893.
20. Sexau Papers, Conversation with Prince Taxis of July 27, 1938.
21. Valerie, August 4, 1888.
22. Ibid., June 9, 1889.
23. Sexau Papers, Conversation with Duchess Marie José of Bavaria, August 27, 1938.
24. Bourgoing, p. 143, from Budapest, February 16, 1889.
25. Valerie, June 1889.
26. Ibid., May 7, 1890.
27. Corti Papers, from Vienna, December 6, 1890.
28. Corti Papers, from Vienna, December 17, 1890.
29. Bourgoing, p. 218, from Mürzsteg, October 4, 1890.
30. Ibid., p. 215, from Teschen, September 5, 1890.
31. Prince Philipp zu Eulenburg-Hertefeld, *Erlebnisse an deutschen und fremden Höfen* (Leipzig, 1934), Vol. II, p. 205.
32. Bourgoing, p. 263.
33. Hübner, October 28, 1889.
34. Eulenburg, Vol. II, p. 200.
35. Valerie, June 2, 1889.
36. Ibid., July 21, 1889.
37. Ibid., November 4, 1889.
38. Ibid., December 26, 1889.
39. Ibid., November 18, 1889.
40. Ibid., December 5, 1889.
41. Ibid., May 28, 1890.
42. Bourgoing, p. 289, from Cap Martin, March 2, 1894.
43. Ibid., p. 345, from Cap Martin, March 10, 1897.
44. Eulenburg, Vol. II, p. 213.
45. Ibid., p. 199.
46. Valerie, July 11, 1899.
47. Ibid., August 28, 1890.
48. Eulenburg, Vol. II, p. 226.
49. Bourgoing, p. 426, June 1901.
50. Valerie, July 6, 1899.

CHAPTER 13

1. Festetics, May 13, 1874.
2. Richard Sexau, *Fürst und Arzt* (Graz, 1963), p. 346.
3. Valerie, May 4, 1886.
4. Princess Stephanie of Belgium, Princess von Lonyay, *Ich sollte Kaiserin werden* (Leipzig, 1935), pp. 95f.
5. Elisabeth, *Winterlieder,* p. 169.
6. Valerie, May 29, 1884.
7. Index to Crown Prince Rudolf's writings, in Brigitte Hamann, *Rudolf Kronprinz und Rebell* (Vienna, 1978), pp. 523–26.
8. Brigitte Hamann, *Das Leben des Kronprinzen Rudolf nach neuen Quellen* (PH.D. diss., Vienna, 1978), pp. 224–64.
9. The pamphlet is reprinted in its entirety in Brigitte Hamann, ed., *Rudolf. Majestät ich warne Sie. Geheime und private Schriften* (Vienna, 1979), pp. 19–52.
10. Hamann, *Rudolf,* p. 103.
11. Ibid.
12. Festetics, October 21, 1877.
13. Reprinted in Hamann, *Majestät,* pp. 55–78.
14. Hübner, June 12, 1879.
15. Ibid., June 18 and 19, 1879.
16. Ibid., September 24 and 25, 1879.
17. Rudolf, box 16, Prague, October 28, 1879.
18. Hamann, *Rudolf,* pp. 13f., from Prague, January 16, 1881.
19. Festetics, January 3, 1882.
20. Hamann, *Rudolf,* p. 303.

21. Elisabeth, manuscript.
22. Elisabeth, *Nordseelieder,* pp. 4f.
23. Stephanie, *Ich sollte Kaiserin werden,* p. 152, from Kremsier, August 25, 1885.
24. Hamann, *Rudolf,* p. 295, July 23, 1885.
25. Oskar Freiherr von Mitis, *Das Leben des Kronprinzen Rudolf,* revised by Adam Wandruszka (Vienna, 1971), from Prague, December 2, 1881.
26. Hamann, *Rudolf,* pp. 173f.
27. AA, Österreich 86, No. 1, Vol. I, secret, March 8, 1883.
28. Valerie, June 3, 1884.
29. Valerie, December 24, 1887.
30. StBW, manuscript collection, Friedjung Papers, Interview with Countess Marie Festetics, March 23, 1909.
31. Fritz Judtmann, *Mayerling ohne Mythos* (Vienna, 1968), pp. 18ff.
32. Valerie, August 18, 1883, and others.
33. Corti Papers, Valerie, November 17, 1883.
34. Valerie, November 11, 1884.
35. Ibid., August 17, 1884.
36. Ibid., May 30, 1884.
37. Ibid., June 13, 1884.
38. Ibid., June 24, 1886.
39. Ibid., December 6, 1886.
40. Ibid., May 25, 1887.
41. Hamann, *Rudolf,* pp. 408ff.
42. Corti, *Elisabeth,* p. 401.
43. Valerie, May 23, 1887.
44. Ibid., February 6 and 7, 1887.
45. Ibid., May 22, 1887.
46. Ibid., May 13, 1888.
47. Ibid., March 4, 1889.
48. Ibid., August 6 and September 6, 1888.
49. Ibid., September 16, 1887.
50. Ibid., December 16, 1888.
51. Friedjung Papers, Interview with M. Festetics, March 23, 1909.
52. Ibid.
53. All quotations by Valerie concerning Mayerling, February 8, 1889.

54. Stephanie, p. 203.
55. Hamann, *Rudolf,* pp. 109f.
56. Corti, *Elisabeth,* pp. 419f.
57. Corti Papers, Copied from Valerie's diary.
58. Valerie, February 8, 1889.
59. Friedjung Papers, Interview with Marie Festetics, March 23, 1909.
60. Sexau, *Fürst und Arzt,* p. 352.
61. Valerie, quoted from Corti Papers.
62. Valerie, June 29, 1890.
63. Ibid., February 18, 1889.
64. Valerie, February 8, 1889.
65. Sexau, *Fürst und Arzt,* p. 351.
66. Valerie, August 21, 1889.
67. Maria Freiin von Wallersee, *Meine Vergangenheit* (Berlin, 1913), pp. 234ff.
68. AA, Österreich 86, secret, March 6, 1889.
69. Corti Papers, Valerie, February 18, 1889.
70. Scharding, p. 301, June 23, 1890.
71. Hübner, February 3, 1889.
72. *Wiener Zeitung,* February 6, 1889.
73. Bourgoing, p. 133, from Vienna, February 5, 1889.
74. Valerie, February 10, 1889.
75. Bertha von Suttner, *Lebenserinnerungen* (Berlin, 1979), p. 376.
76. Valerie, May 24, 1889.
77. Ibid., June 17, 1890.
78. Ibid., December 8, 1889.
79. Ibid., February 15, 1889.
80. Amélie, July 30, 1890.
81. Ibid., December 4, 1890.
82. Valerie, February 24, 1889.
83. Scharding, p. 301, February 24, 1889.
84. Amélie, December 4, 1889.
85. Valerie, October 25, 1889.
86. Ibid., February 1, 1890.
87. Ibid., February 4, 1890.
88. Ibid., February 21, 1890.
89. Ibid., May 19, 1890.
90. Ibid., April 30, 1889.
91. Ibid., May 24, 1889.
92. Ibid., December 9, 1889.

93. Amélie, February 4, 1891.
94. AA, Österreich 86, January 28, 1890.
95. Valerie, July 23, 1890.
96. Ibid., May 28, 1890.
97. Ibid., July 31, 1890.
98. Valerie, January 26, 1891.

CHAPTER 14

1. Wallersee, *Elisabeth*, p. 46.
2. Ibid., pp. 45f.
3. Konstantin Christomanos, *Tagebuchblätter* (Vienna, 1899), pp. 104f.
4. Nostitz, Vol. I, p. 188, from Vienna, October 29, 1887.
5. Valerie, August 4, 1894.
6. Cissy von Klastersky, *Der alte Kaiser, wie nur einer ihn sah* (Vienna, 1929), p. 41.
7. Corti Papers, from Corfu, November 11, 1888.
8. Nostitz, Vol. I, p. 391, April 10, 1894.
9. Valerie, March 23, 1891.
10. Article by F. Pagin, *NWJ,* July 3, 1932.
11. Valerie, April 23, 1892.
12. Harold Kurtz, *Eugénie* (Tübingen, 1964), p. 423.
13. Corti Papers, from Genoa, March 29, 1893.
14. HHStA, P. A. from Cairo, November 23, 1891.
15. Valerie, January 14, 1891.
16. Eduard Suess, *Erinnerungen* (Leipzig, 1916), p. 411.
17. Corti Papers, from Corfu, October 18, 1888.
18. HHStA, Braun Papers, from Corfu, October 22 (no year).
19. Corti Papers, from Corfu, November 20 [1888].
20. Corti Papers, from Genoa, March 29, 1893.
21. Christomanos, p. 129.

22. Ibid., pp. 65ff.
23. Corti Papers, to Ida Ferenczy from Corfu, October 11, 1891.
24. Christomanos, p. 165.
25. Nostitz, Vol. I, pp. 307f., from Vienna, April 6, 1893.
26. Corti Papers, September 13, 1892.
27. Ibid., to Ida Ferenczy from Messina, December 4, 1892.
28. HHStA, Adm. Reg. F1/57, from Vienna, October 24, 1890.
29. AA, Österreich 86, No. 1, Reuss to Wilhelm II, October 29, 1890.
30. Ibid., Vol. VI, from Vienna, January 2, 1893.
31. Irma Countess Sztaray, *Aus den letzten Jahren der Kaiserin Elisabeth* (Vienna, 1909), p. 203.
32. Corti Papers, Newspaper clipping: Fritz Seemann, "Der Mann, der Könige überwachte."
33. Alfons Clary-Aldringen, *Geschichten eines alten Österreichers* (n.d.), p. 114.
34. Rosa Albach-Retty, *So kurz sind hundert Jahre* (Munich, 1979), pp. 123f.
35. Suttner, *Erinnerungen,* p. 343.
36. *Berliner Tageblatt,* April 21, 1889. Similarly, *Le Matin,* April 12 and 17, and *Gaulois,* April 13, 1889.
37. *Wiener Tagblatt,* April 26, 1889.
38. Translated and denied in *Magyar Hirlap,* March 11, 1893.
39. Corti Papers, to Ida Ferenczy, March 14, 1893.
40. *Der Bund,* March 22, 1893.
41. Sexau Papers, to Marie José of Bavaria, from Territet, March 2, 1893.
42. Valerie, February 21, 1893.
43. Corti Papers, to Ida Ferenczy, April 14, 1893.
44. Redwitz, pp. 68f.
45. Valerie, February 25, 1897.
46. Ibid., August 15, 1891.
47. Edmund von Glaise-Horstenau, *Franz Josephs Weggefährte* (Vienna, 1930), p. 400.

48. Viktor Eisenmenger, *Erzherzog Franz Ferdinand* (Zurich, n.d.), p. 77.

49. Corti Papers, from Biarritz, December 22, 1896.

50. Bourgoing, p. 304, from Budapest, December 29, 1894.

51. Nostitz, Vol. II, p. 307, from Schönbrunn, September 8, 1897.

52. Bourgoing, p. 344, from Cap Martin, March 3, 1897.

53. Corti Papers, Sztaray to Ida Ferenczy, from Corfu, April 7, 1896.

54. *Magyar Hirlap,* May 3, 1896.

55. Valerie, December 16, 1897.

56. AA, Österreich 86, No. 1, Vol. IX, from Vienna, March 26, 1897.

57. Bourgoing, p. 359, from Budapest, February 28, 1898.

58. Valerie, May 8, 1898.

59. Ibid., July 2, 1898.

60. Ibid., July 22, 1898.

61. Ibid., August 25, 1898.

62. Corti Papers, from Bad Nauheim, July 25, 1898.

63. Valerie, September 7, 1898.

64. Christomanos, pp. 209f.

65. BAB, Polit. Department 2001/801, from Zurich, May 4, 1898.

66. Sztaray, p. 245.

67. More detailed versions of the assassination in Brigitte Hamann, "Der Mord an Kaiserin Elisabeth," in Leopold Spira, ed., *Attentate, die Österreich erschütterten* (Vienna, 1981), pp. 21–33, and Maria Matray and Answald Krüger, *Der Tod der Kaiserin Elisabeth von Österreich* (Munich, 1970).

68. Valerie, September 7, 1898.

69. Carmen Sylva, "Die Kaiserin Elisabeth in Sinaia," *NFP,* December 25, 1908.

70. Valerie, September 10 and 13, 1898.

71. Glaise-Horstenau, p. 400.

72. Erich Graf Kielmannsegg, *Kaiserhaus, Staatsmänner und Politiker* (Vienna, 1966), p. 106.

73. Kielmannsegg, p. 105.

74. Valerie, September 20, 1898.

75. HHStA, Reserve Files of the directors of the Family Fund, 1898.

76. Ibid.

77. Valerie, October 3, 1898.

78. Ibid., September 20, 1898.

79. Ibid., September 17, 1898.

80. Kielmannsegg, p. 93.

81. Valerie, April 9, 1899.

82. Ibid., July 25, 1900.

83. Ibid., December 2, 1898.

84. Ibid., January 18, 1900.

INDEX

ILLUSTRATION CREDITS

Brigitte Hamann was born in Essen, Germany, in 1940. She studied history and German literature in Münster and Vienna, having both a teaching diploma and a doctorate. She has worked as an editor on a daily newspaper and currently lives in Vienna as a freelance historian. Internationally she is known for her biographies, *Rudolf, Crown Prince and Rebel, Elisabeth, The Reluctant Empress, Bertha von Suttner: A Life for Peace* (Syracuse University Press 1996) and *Hitler's Vienna* (Oxford University Press 1999).

Dr. Hamann was the first to obtain permission to examine and study thoroughly Elisabeth's literary heritage in Bern, Switzerland.

These and other previously unknown sources enabled Dr. Hamann to create a scholarly and fascinatingly written biography; portraying most vividly this highly intelligent, talented, clear-sighted woman, to whom justice can only be given now, when we are able to appraise her with the standards of our time.

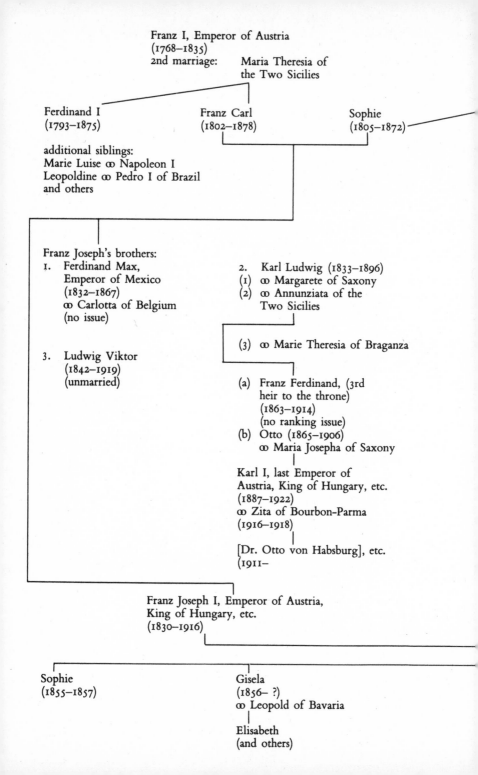

Franz I, Emperor of Austria
(1768–1835)
2nd marriage: Maria Theresia of
the Two Sicilies

Ferdinand I
(1793–1875)

Franz Carl
(1802–1878)

Sophie
(1805–1872)

additional siblings:
Marie Luise ∞ Napoleon I
Leopoldine ∞ Pedro I of Brazil
and others

Franz Joseph's brothers:
1. Ferdinand Max,
   Emperor of Mexico
   (1832–1867)
   ∞ Carlotta of Belgium
   (no issue)

2. Karl Ludwig (1833–1896)
(1) ∞ Margarete of Saxony
(2) ∞ Annunziata of the
        Two Sicilies

(3) ∞ Marie Theresia of Braganza

3. Ludwig Viktor
   (1842–1919)
   (unmarried)

(a) Franz Ferdinand, (3rd
    heir to the throne)
    (1863–1914)
    (no ranking issue)
(b) Otto (1865–1906)
    ∞ Maria Josepha of Saxony

Karl I, last Emperor of
Austria, King of Hungary, etc.
(1887–1922)
∞ Zita of Bourbon-Parma
(1916–1918)

[Dr. Otto von Habsburg], etc.
(1911–

Franz Joseph I, Emperor of Austria,
King of Hungary, etc.
(1830–1916)

Sophie
(1855–1857)

Gisela
(1856– ?)
∞ Leopold of Bavaria

Elisabeth
(and others)

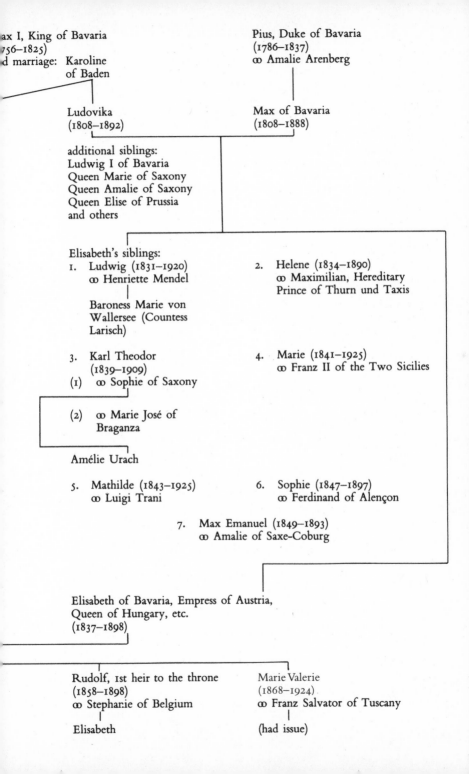

ax I, King of Bavaria
756–1825)
d marriage: Karoline
of Baden

Pius, Duke of Bavaria
(1786–1837)
∞ Amalie Arenberg

Ludovika
(1808–1892)

Max of Bavaria
(1808–1888)

additional siblings:
Ludwig I of Bavaria
Queen Marie of Saxony
Queen Amalie of Saxony
Queen Elise of Prussia
and others

Elisabeth's siblings:
1. Ludwig (1831–1920)
   ∞ Henriette Mendel

   Baroness Marie von
   Wallersee (Countess
   Larisch)

2. Helene (1834–1890)
   ∞ Maximilian, Hereditary
   Prince of Thurn und Taxis

3. Karl Theodor
   (1839–1909)
   (1) ∞ Sophie of Saxony

   (2) ∞ Marie José of
        Braganza

4. Marie (1841–1925)
   ∞ Franz II of the Two Sicilies

Amélie Urach

5. Mathilde (1843–1925)
   ∞ Luigi Trani

6. Sophie (1847–1897)
   ∞ Ferdinand of Alençon

7. Max Emanuel (1849–1893)
   ∞ Amalie of Saxe-Coburg

Elisabeth of Bavaria, Empress of Austria,
Queen of Hungary, etc.
(1837–1898)

Rudolf, 1st heir to the throne
(1858–1898)
∞ Stephanie of Belgium

Elisabeth

Marie Valerie
(1868–1924)
∞ Franz Salvator of Tuscany

(had issue)

A NOTE ON THE TYPE

The text of this book was set in a digitized version of Bembo, a well-known Monotype face. Named for Pietro Bembo, the celebrated Renaissance writer and humanist scholar who was made a cardinal and served as secretary to Pope Leo X, the original cutting of Bembo was made by Francesco Griffo of Bologna only a few years after Columbus discovered America.

Sturdy, well-balanced, and finely proportioned, Bembo is a face of rare beauty, extremely legible in all of its sizes.

Composed by The Haddon Craftsmen, Inc., Scranton, Pennsylvania

Designed by Iris Weinstein

Werner Sikorski
Rainer Laabs

CHECKPOINT CHARLIE
AND THE WALL

A DIVIDED
PEOPLE REBEL

Why was the Wall built and where did it stand?
This documentation takes the reader through
five momentous centuries of German history.

Ullstein paperback
Distributed in Germany
by Ullstein ip and
in Austria by Mohr Morawa

ULLSTEIN TASCHENBUCH